Tibet in Agony

TIBET IN AGONY

Lhasa 1959

Jianglin Li

Translated by Susan Wilf

Harvard University Press
CAMBRIDGE, MASSACHUSETTS
LONDON, ENGLAND
2016

An earlier version of this book was originally published as *1959 Lasa!* in Traditional Chinese by Linking Publishing Company, Taipei City, Taiwan and in Simplified Chinese by New Century Press, Hong Kong.
Printed in the United States of America

First printing

Design by Dean Bornstein

Library of Congress Cataloging-in-Publication Data

Names: 880-01 Li, Jianglin, 1956– author. | Wilf, Susan, translator.
Title: Tibet in agony : Lhasa 1959 / Jianglin Li ; translated by Susan Wilf.
Other titles: 880-02 1959 Lasa!. English
Description: Cambridge, Massachusetts : Harvard University Press, 2016. | Includes bibliographical references and index.
Identifiers: LCCN 2016014170 | ISBN 9780674088894 (hardcover : alk. paper)
Subjects: LCSH: Tibet Autonomous Region (China)—History—Uprising of 1959. | China—Relations—China—Tibet Autonomous Region. | Tibet Autonomous Region (China)—Relations—China. | Tibet Autonomous Region (China)—Politics and government—1951– | Bstan-'dzin-rgya-mtsho, Dalai Lama XIV, 1935–
Classification: LCC DS786 .L4619213 2016 | DDC 951 / .5055—dc23
LC record available at https://lccn.loc.gov/2016014170

CONTENTS

Preface to the English Edition

LATE ONE OCTOBER NIGHT in 2008, I finally arrived at Gangtok, the capital of Sikkim, after a bumpy fourteen-hour ride. This was one of my yearly trips from New York to South Asia to explore the origins of the Tibetan diaspora, one of the most highly polarized issues in the world today.

As a Han Chinese from mainland China, daughter of two lifetime Communist Party members, I grew up with the Party line that Tibet is a legitimate part of China and that the Dalai Lama is a "wolf in sheep's clothing"—a treasonous "splittist" who has spent his life conspiring to detach Tibet from the motherland. I must confess that I accepted this view unquestioningly in my youth, for our media was heavily censored and our educational system did not train people to think critically.

When I first came to the United States for graduate study at Brandeis University in the late 1980s, I became aware of the widespread respect—in the world outside of China—for the Dalai Lama as a Nobel Peace Prize laureate, and of the popularity of the Tibetan cause that he represents. My horizons were further broadened by my training at Brandeis, where my professors, unlike those in China, insisted that we weigh all sources—even "authoritative" ones—objectively.

I eventually became a librarian and program coordinator at the International Resource Center of Queens Library, New York, which serves one of the most ethnically diverse communities in the world. There I met some members of the local Tibetan refugee community and discovered how their views differed from what I had been taught in China. Intrigued by this huge disparity, I resolved to seek the truth about Tibet. How and why had it been annexed to China in the 1950s? I had found my life's work as an independent Chinese historian.

I began to take yearly research trips across South Asia—from New Delhi to Kathmandu, and from Dharamsala to Gangtok—seeking out enclaves of Tibetan refugees to record their life stories. My visit to Gangtok in October 2008 provided the focus of this book.

It was barley harvest season on the southern slopes of the Himalayas. I sat down in the sunshine on the balcony of the local Tibetan community center to listen to Lobsang, an elderly former monk and veteran of the lost guerrilla war against the Chinese. The defining event of his life had been his escape from Tibet in March 1959; the contradictions between his story and what I had learned in China piqued my curiosity as a researcher.

Lobsang's harrowing exodus, like that of the Dalai Lama and thousands of other Tibetans, came in the wake of the pivotal moment in modern Tibetan history: the crisis that erupted in Lhasa on March 10, 1959, later downplayed by the Chinese as the "Lhasa Incident" while commemorated by the Tibetans as "Tibetan Uprising Day." On that fateful day, thousands of Tibetans surrounded the Dalai Lama's summer palace, the Norbulingka, anxious to prevent him from attending a theatrical performance at People's Liberation Army (PLA) headquarters in Lhasa. The gathering escalated into a demonstration, with the crowd shouting slogans demanding Tibetan independence and the withdrawal of the PLA from Tibet. On March 17, in the midst of the furor, the Fourteenth Dalai Lama, twenty-three-year-old Tenzin Gyatso, along with his family and key members of his cabinet (*kashag*), fled the palace in the middle of the night and trekked across the Himalayas for two weeks to gain political asylum in India.

Forty-eight hours after the Dalai Lama's departure, heavy Chinese artillery fire began pummeling Lhasa, inflicting thousands of casualties and damaging irreplaceable heritage sites. By March 22, 1959, the Chinese Communists were able to claim that they had "pacified" a "treasonous rebellion," but most Tibetans thought otherwise.

The lingering questions about this confrontation, which came to be known as the "Battle of Lhasa," have never been fully addressed, especially in Chinese publications. Why were the people of Lhasa so agitated on March 10, 1959? Was there any truth to Chinese allegations that the Dalai Lama and his cabinet plotted the demonstrations or that the Tibetans initiated the battle? If so, why had the Tibetans been so poorly organized, while the Chinese were ready to unleash enormous firepower on short notice and with clockwork precision? How did the suppression of this rebellion fit into Mao's overall plan for Tibet? What was the real story behind the Dalai Lama's fabled escape?

With these questions bubbling in my mind, I returned to New York and plunged into my research, but the issues turned out to be much more complicated than I imagined at the outset. At first I thought I would find all of the answers by studying the crisis of March 1959 itself, but the evidence indicated otherwise: that crisis stemmed from Mao's little-known but brutally repressive campaigns during the preceding three years in the four Chinese provinces with significant Tibetan populations. Moreover, while honing his policies on the Tibetans already under his control during this earlier period, Mao was laying intricate groundwork for his ultimate takeover of Tibet itself.

The strife in this story, which still echoes today, is rooted in an old and sensitive geographical question: What is Tibet? Today's Tibet Autonomous Region (TAR), commonly referred to in both China and the West as "Tibet," covers less than half of the traditional Tibetan area, corresponding roughly to only one of the three original Tibetan provinces, a region known as Ü-Tsang (central and western Tibet). The other two traditional Tibetan provinces, Kham (eastern Tibet) and Amdo (northeastern Tibet), have been largely subsumed into the four neighboring Chinese provinces of Sichuan, Gansu, Yunnan, and Qinghai, although the portion of western Kham known as Chamdo is part of today's TAR. This book will generally refer to the TAR area as "Tibet" (although some of the primary-source documents quoted herein will use the term "Central Tibet"), and to the areas under the jurisdiction of the four neighboring Chinese provinces to its east as "Tibetan regions."

Tibetologists have devised various models to describe this situation. One that has gained fairly widespread acceptance is the use of the term "ethnographic Tibet" for the broader geographic area inhabited by Tibetans, and "political Tibet" for the narrower political or administrative region that corresponds roughly to today's TAR. Originally proposed by British scholar-diplomat Charles Alfred Bell in 1920, the general concept was adopted by later scholars such as Hugh Richardson and further refined by Tsering Shakya of the University of British Columbia (who prefers the term "ethnic Tibet" for the larger traditional area).

During China's Republican period (1912–1949), the area corresponding to today's TAR enjoyed de facto independence under the Thirteenth Dalai Lama and his sophisticated administration in Lhasa. Meanwhile, Amdo and eastern Kham were divided among the Chinese provinces of Qinghai, Yunnan, Gansu, and Xikang.[1] The Chinese provincial administrative control over these Tibetan regions tended to be merely nominal during this period, however, and many regions, especially pastoral ones, remained beyond its reach. Moreover, the Tibetan government in Lhasa refused to relinquish the Chinese-occupied regions of Kham and Amdo, and tried repeatedly—with varying degrees of success—to retake them by force.

Power politics aside, under the Republic of China, the Tibetan tribespeople in Kham and Amdo were ruled day-to-day by their monasteries or their hereditary tribal headmen. In Kham, each tribe had its unique, customary set of practices and laws, some of them quite ancient, and unlike those of the Chinese. This system of headmen also had an administrative component, especially in some of the larger areas such as Derge, Palyul, and Mili,[2] which in fact resembled small principalities. Most of Amdo functioned under a simpler tribal system, although there were some notable headmen in Amdo as well: in Jonê,[3] for example, an area that straddles today's Qinghai and Gansu, headmen ruled for more than six hundred years before the arrival of the Chinese Communists.

In October 1950, the Chinese Communist People's Liberation Army invaded Chamdo, forcing the Lhasa government to sign the "Seventeen-Point Agreement for the Peaceful Liberation of Tibet," which ceded Tibetan sovereignty to China. The Agreement proclaimed that Tibet "shall return to the family of the Motherland, the People's Republic of China," and that the "local government of Tibet" would henceforth be subordinate to the "Central People's Government" in Beijing. It also promised, among other things, to allow Tibet to preserve its existing political system;[4] nonetheless, between 1951 and 1959, as the first stage in building their apparatus for ultimately taking complete charge of the region, the Chinese Communists proceeded to superimpose their own layer of control over the existing Tibetan structures. During this interim period, Tibet was divided into three jurisdictions: Chamdo, which was administered by the Chinese-run Chamdo Liberation Committee, and Lhasa and Shigatse, still nominally under the governance of the Dalai Lama and the Panchen Lama respectively.

PLA troops marched into Lhasa by the thousands in the fall and winter of 1951, and three main arms of Chinese rule were soon established.

For Chinese Communist Party affairs, there was the CCP Tibet Work Committee in Lhasa, which—although initially kept secret from the Tibetans—reported directly to the Central Committee in Beijing and spread to more than fifty subsidiary Tibetan locations.[5] The Chinese military also had a nerve center in Lhasa, the PLA Tibet Military Command, created in early 1952 as an addition to the existing PLA system of military regions. The Chinese also founded a preliminary governmental administration in Lhasa in 1956, called the Preparatory Committee for the Autonomous Region of Tibet (PCART).

This book will document and show that Mao had active plans from very early on to impose his policies throughout Tibet despite the promises of the "Seventeen-Point Agreement," even though he was aware that this would entail bloodshed. By the mid-1950s, he had directed his subordinates in Tibet to begin laying the groundwork for this goal, and by mid-1958, he was signaling his clear readiness to get started in earnest. His explicitly stated view was that he welcomed Tibetan unrest and rebellion—and even hoped it would increase in scale—as it would provide him with an opportunity to "pacify" the region with his armies. When turmoil began in Lhasa in March 1959, he seized the moment to put his war plans into action. After their triumph in Lhasa, the Chinese Communists extended their control over all of Tibet, and by 1965, they had divided the entire Tibetan ethnocultural region into eleven administrative entities: the Tibet Autonomous Region and ten autonomous prefectures in the neighboring Chinese provinces.

During the 1950s, the Chinese Communists—who had the upper hand after the signing of the Seventeen-Point Agreement—maintained that the Tibetan regions within Yunnan, Qinghai, Sichuan, and Gansu were beyond Lhasa's jurisdiction, and as such, were fair game for the early imposition of the set of socialist policies that they called the "Democratic Reforms."[6] Socialist land reform, antireligious campaigns, and early collectivization were introduced on varying timetables throughout these regions from 1956 to 1958, somewhat ahead of their implementation in Tibet itself, and they aroused waves of opposition and ill-fated local rebellions. These regions are still highly troubled today: the overwhelming majority of the Tibetan protest self-immolations since 2009 (143 as of August 2015) have occurred in Sichuan and Qinghai, in areas that were once the traditional Tibetan provinces of Kham and Amdo.

Divided as they were administratively, and despite regional variations in dialect and custom, Tibetans were largely bonded by language, culture, and religion. Thus, when the Chinese Communists suppressed the Tibetans in Qinghai, Yunnan, Gansu, and Sichuan, thousands of Tibetan refugees chose to flee across the border to Lhasa.[7] Their presence, and the reports of Chinese excesses that they brought with them, were a root cause of the general mood of fear and suspicion of the Chinese in Lhasa that led to the fateful demonstrations of March 10, 1959. Therefore, the initial chapters of this book will be devoted to uncovering the little-known history of the early Chinese Communist social engineering program in the Tibetan regions of the four Chinese provinces neighboring Tibet, and the resistance that it engendered.[8]

: : :

For decades, historical accounts of the March 1959 crisis in Lhasa have been based on two principal sources. Studies written outside of China have relied mainly on the Dalai Lama's two autobiographies, whereas those within China hark back to a short memoir first published in Beijing in 1988 by Ngabo Ngawang Jigme, who held concurrent posts in the Tibetan and Chinese administrations in Lhasa in 1959.[9] However, neither the Dalai Lama nor Ngabo provides the full picture. Fortunately, plenty of other materials are now available to the historian wishing to reconstruct this missing chapter in history. This book is the first—in Chinese, and now in English—to present an independent examination of the extensive Chinese record. The Chinese, who had occupied Tibet for eight years before March 1959, are principal actors in this story, and their own paper trail, when weighed judiciously, is highly telling.

Finding the histories published in China in latter decades to be unsatisfactory, I have turned to primary sources, in particular to Chinese Communist civil and military policy documents from the time period under study. Thanks to the Chinese love of bureaucracy, these are surprisingly abundant. Chinese officials at the grassroots level are required to submit reports of all occurrences in their jurisdictions upward through a strict hierarchy, sometimes reaching all the way to the Central Committee; directives from on high similarly make their way down through each tier of the bureaucracy. Moreover, because the Chinese Communist bureaucracy includes the military, administrative, and Party systems under its umbrella, documents are often circulated in duplicate, or even in triplicate, to parallel officials in each system. Party documents are strictly categorized as public, semiclassified, classified, or top secret, but their sheer number has made it impossible for the Chinese government to keep them all under wraps. Many documents at all levels of classification have slipped out of China and ended up in libraries and archives in the United States, Hong Kong, Taiwan, and India, where I have been able to examine them.

The recollections of eyewitnesses and participants constitute another key set of primary sources, although the extreme political sensitivity of the material makes it difficult to conduct personal interviews with such individuals in China today. Luckily, a wealth of highly revealing memoirs by Chinese eyewitnesses has been appearing in China since the 1980s. These include the recollections of Communist Party cadres, and of officers and rank-and-file veterans of the PLA and the Chinese-run militia in Lhasa at the time. I have been able to collect and consult more than one hundred such memoirs, as well as a number of informative, recently published biographies of Chinese decision makers of the day.

The full picture does not take shape until the Chinese materials are cross-checked with other sources, especially Tibetan ones, and many Tibetan primary sources are available. Some Tibetan documents have been preserved, and I have conducted personal interviews with hundreds of Tibetan exiles in India and elsewhere, most notably the Dalai Lama and his youngest brother, Ngari Rinpoché.[10] There are also the published memoirs of Tibetan eyewitnesses who stayed in the TAR, of those who served as cadres for the Chinese Communists, and of exiles. In 2012, I was able to arrange a valuable, rare series of interviews in China with a prominent Tibetan political figure who remained in Qinghai until his recent death.[11] In addition, recorded oral histories of some instrumental

Tibetans, including those who planned the Dalai Lama's escape, have been published in Dharamsala.

The juxtaposition of this variety of sources from both sides has brought the facts of the little-known Battle of Lhasa, among other things, into much clearer focus than ever before. Seventeen locations in the city were subjected to heavy Chinese artillery bombardment, including five major heritage sites—Chakpori Hill, the Jokhang Temple, Ramoche Temple, the Norbulingka Palace, and the Potala Palace. Each of these major confrontations has been examined in detail herein, and new findings are introduced regarding the battle's causes, its outbreak, and its aftermath, as well as the intriguing question of Central Intelligence Agency (CIA) involvement.

I had long wondered why the outside world had lacked awareness of the Chinese Communist crackdown on Tibetan resistance within China from 1956 to 1958, even though it had amounted to a military action of considerable scope, involving infantry, heavy artillery, cavalry, and air force. New light was finally shed on this question with the release in India of the *Selected Works of Jawaharlal Nehru: Second Series,* which contains declassified documents revealing the contents of private talks between Zhou Enlai, Nehru, and the Dalai Lama in India in late 1956 and early 1957. The dynamics of these talks, and the secret pact between Zhou and Nehru in particular, gave China a relatively free hand in its suppression of the Tibetans. As these talks fill in some important gaps, they are discussed at some length in Chapter 2.

:::

In certain portions of this book, I have chosen to present my conclusions in a narrative style, and to include the reminiscences of a number of ordinary individuals, which I have gathered from personal interviews and memoirs that I have cross-checked with other sources. This approach seemed particularly appropriate at times, not only because ordinary people are key to the story, as is the case at so many turning points in history, but also because their impressions add a vivid human element to the historical mosaic and stand as essential commentary on the period. Narrative style notwithstanding, my conclusions are based on an unprecedented number and variety of sources, all of which are thoroughly documented in the Notes and Bibliography for the benefit of readers who may wish to investigate further.

A wealth of new sources has appeared since the original publication of this book in Chinese by Linking Publishing in Taiwan and by New Century Press in Hong Kong in 2010. This new English edition includes updates, expansions, corrections, and additional source references, as well as some minor abridgments. In several cases, the availability of new sources has made it possible to substitute primary source references for secondary ones, delving more deeply and precisely into the historical facts.

This English edition also contains a newly created set of maps and additional illustrations, as well as many new explanatory notes. Tibetan names are transcribed phonetically in the text, and a Glossary of Names has been provided as a quick reference for the reader wishing to identify the principal characters in the story. A Wylie transliteration of Tibetan names is also supplied as a supplement to the Glossary.

The geographical nomenclature used herein presents a set of extraordinarily complex problems. Most important, it is politically fraught, like much of the dialogue surrounding Tibetan issues, and the majority of the places mentioned have different names in Chinese and Tibetan. In general, since this is a study of Tibetan history, the Tibetan place names have been adopted for primary usage, with their Chinese alternatives supplied for reference. For the sake of readability, place names have even been translated into Tibetan in many instances where Chinese speakers and documents are cited, even though the original terms were in Chinese.[12] A second, unrelated problem is that in some places the regional names demarcate a general area, but the precise administrative lines were drawn after the events described in this book took place, or the divisions and their appellations have continued to shift over time, or both.[13] A third complicating factor is the ethnic diversity of a number of the regions, such that places may have names in major languages other than Tibetan and Chinese. And to confuse matters even further, the phonetic transcription of Tibetan place names is not completely standardized and can vary between reputable sources.[14] For example, the spellings "Vindo," "Bimdo," and "Beudo" all appear for the same place name, and "Dowi" can appear as "Dobei" or "Dobi."

: : :

Another Lhasa Incident, one of a series of disturbances in Tibet since 1959, broke out in March 2008, while I was doing the original research for this book. During the riots, one young Tibetan cried out: "We are the same people you massacred forty-nine years ago. We have returned!" His cry shook my soul. Until we uncover the facts about Lhasa in 1959, we will never understand the Tibetan people's agony—expressed in the violence that continues to erupt cyclically in their land, their ongoing wave of self-immolations, and their continuing loyalty to the Dalai Lama.

Since 1949, the Chinese Communist government has used large-scale military might to crush popular uprisings in capital cities on two occasions: Lhasa in 1959, and Beijing in 1989. The two incidents have much in common, but thanks to the advent of instantaneous global media coverage by 1989, the Chinese Communists were unable to stop the flow of information about their suppression of the protest in Beijing. In contrast, Tibet's isolation in the 1950s allowed the Chinese to manipulate the story for decades, and they have continued to deny the painful truth. In a meeting with the Dalai Lama's elder brother Gyalo Dondrup in July 1981, then Chinese Communist Party Chairman Hu Yaobang proposed a list of five premises for the Dalai Lama's return to China, the second of which was, "We should all let bygones be bygones and simply forget about what happened in 1959."[15]

To this date, the Chinese have not advanced beyond Hu's position, but the wounds of history cannot be healed by "forgetting," nor will they simply vanish with time. My hope is to remove the wraps from these events, taking a step toward setting the historical record straight. I invite my readers to contribute their opinions, and hope that even more eyewitnesses will come forward with their testimony.

Map 1. The three traditional Tibetan provinces of Kham, Ü-Tsang, and Amdo, overlaid on a contemporary map of the People's Republic of China (PRC).

Map 2. The Tibetan ethnocultural region covered by Kham, Ü-Tsang, and Amdo, shown with 2013 administrative divisions. The divisions within the Tibet Autonomous Region (TAR) are at the prefectural level. Those in Yunnan, Sichuan, Gansu, and Qinghai are Tibetan Autonomous Prefectures (TAPs), except for Pari and Mili, which are Tibetan Autonomous Counties, Ngaba, which is a Tibetan and Qiang Autonomous Prefecture (TQAP), and Tsonub (Chinese: Haixi), which is a Mongolian and Tibetan Autonomous Prefecture (MTAP). The Drichu (Chinese: Jinsha) River is the upper course of the Yangtze. Kham is divided among the TAR and Sichuan, Yunnan, and Qinghai, while Amdo is divided among Qinghai, Sichuan, and Gansu.

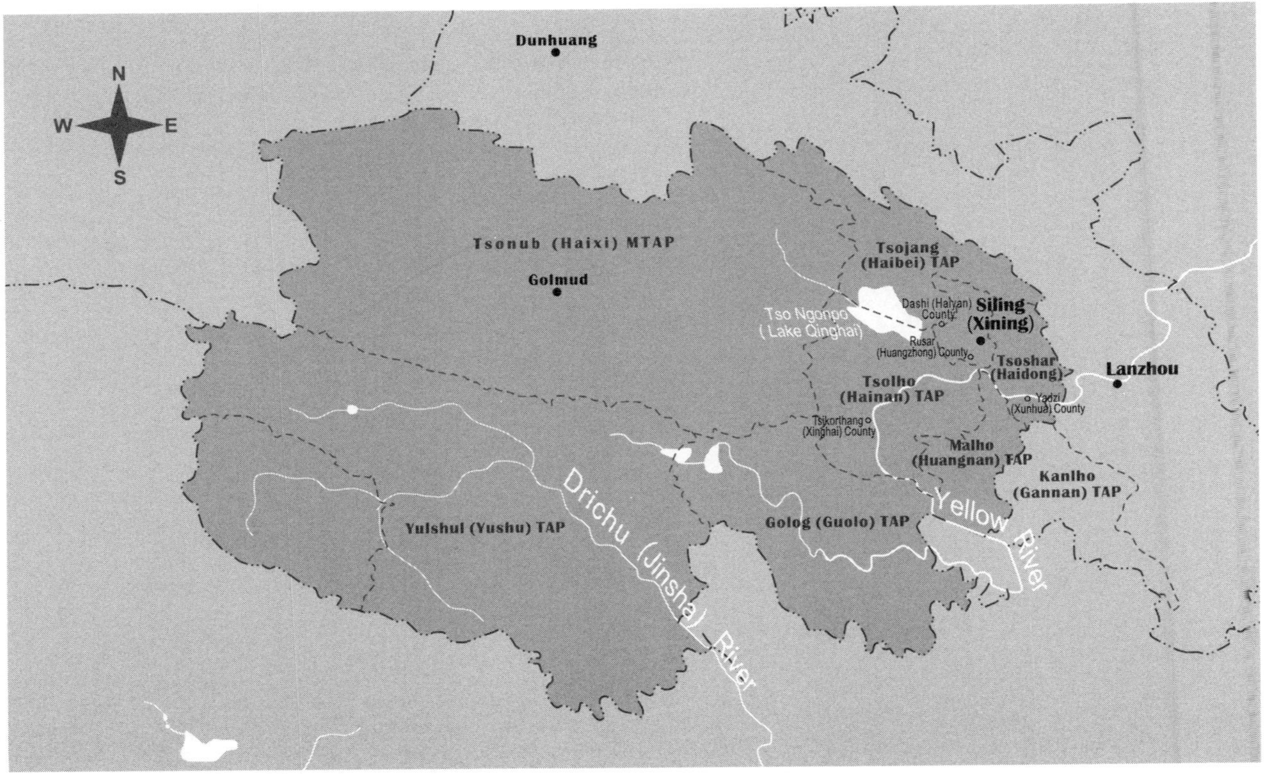

Map 3. The Tibetan regions of Qinghai and Gansu, shown with modern administrative divisions. The abbreviation "TAP" stands for Tibetan Autonomous Prefecture, and "MTAP" stands for Mongolian and Tibetan Autonomous Prefecture. Tsoshar (Haidong) was designated a prefecture in 1978, and upgraded to a prefecture-level city in 2013. Golmud became a county-level city after the events of this book.

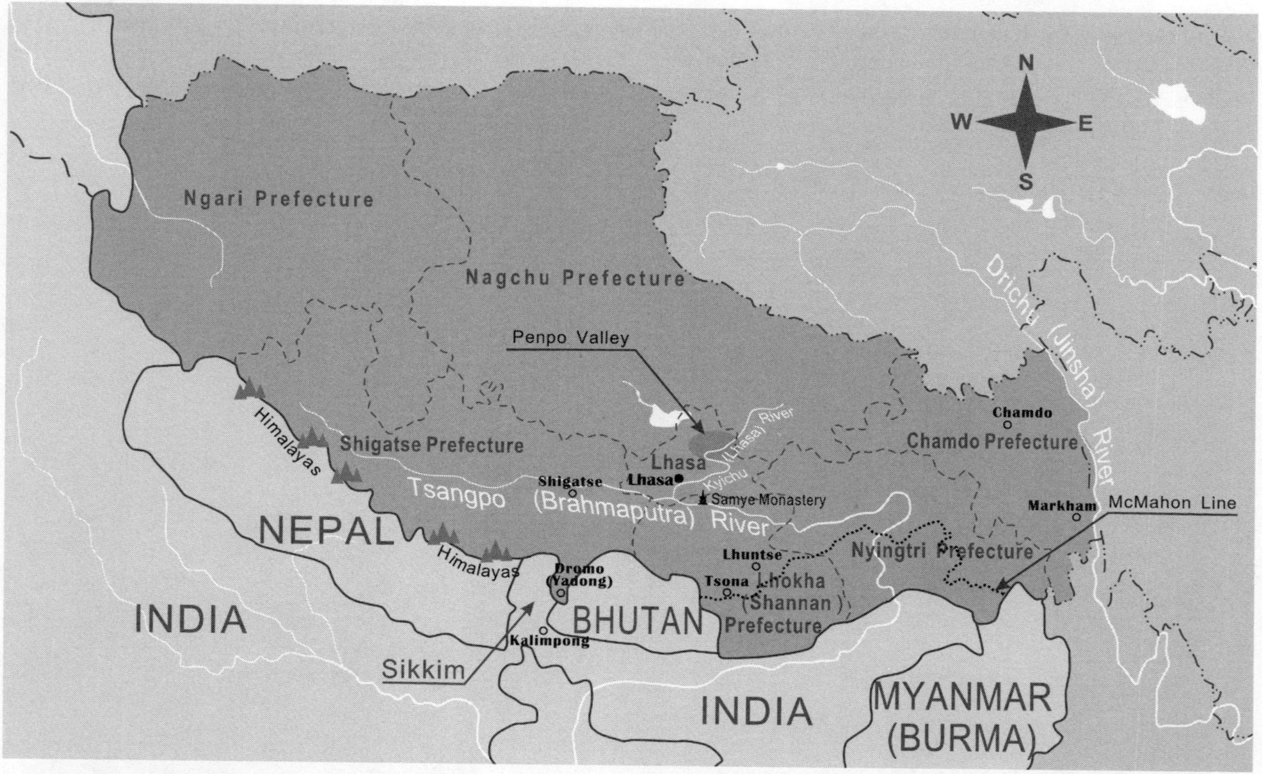

Map 4. The Tibet Autonomous Region shown with administrative divisions as of 2013. Tsakhalho (Chinese: Yanjing), which is not shown on this map, was in the general area of today's Markham County.

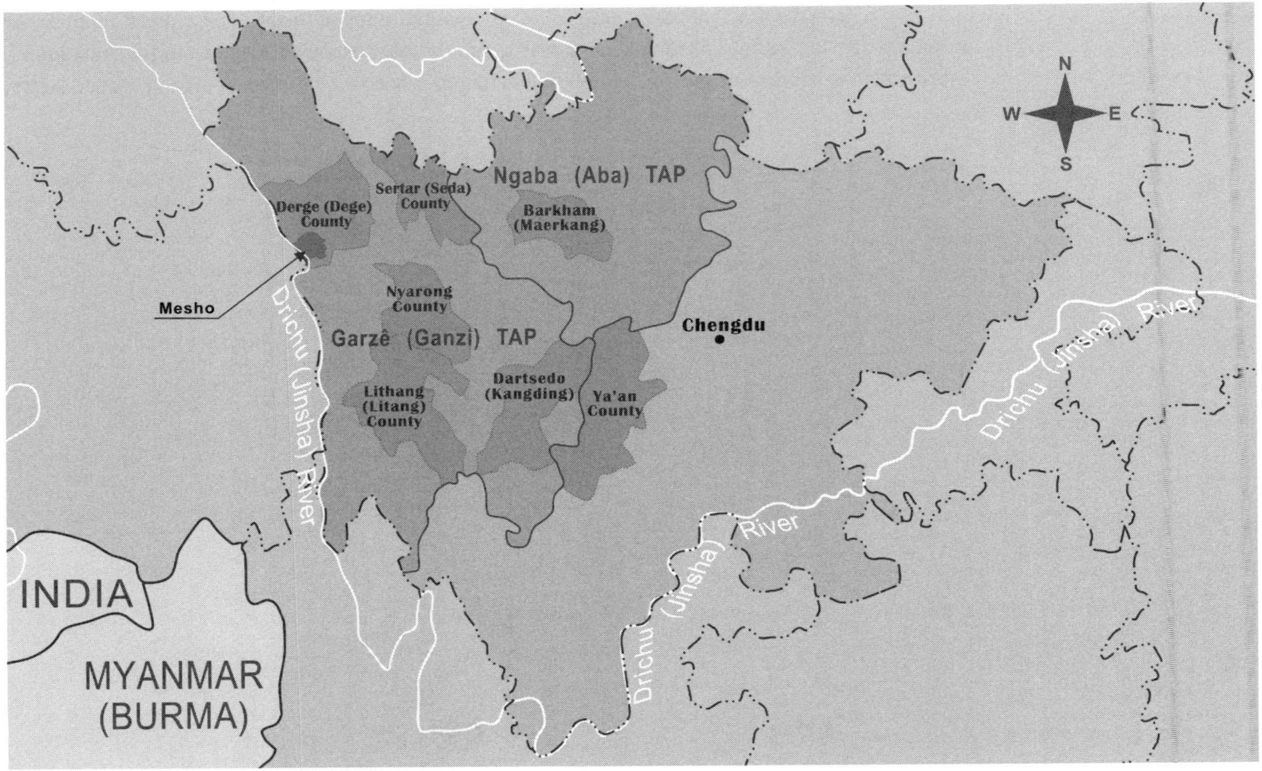

Map 5. The Tibetan regions of Sichuan, shown with modern administrative divisions. The abbreviation "TAP" stands for Tibetan Autonomous Prefecture. Ngaba was a TAP in 1959, but is now the Ngaba Tibetan and Qiang Autonomous Prefecture. Mesho was a vaguely delineated area in 1959, and its location on this map is approximate.

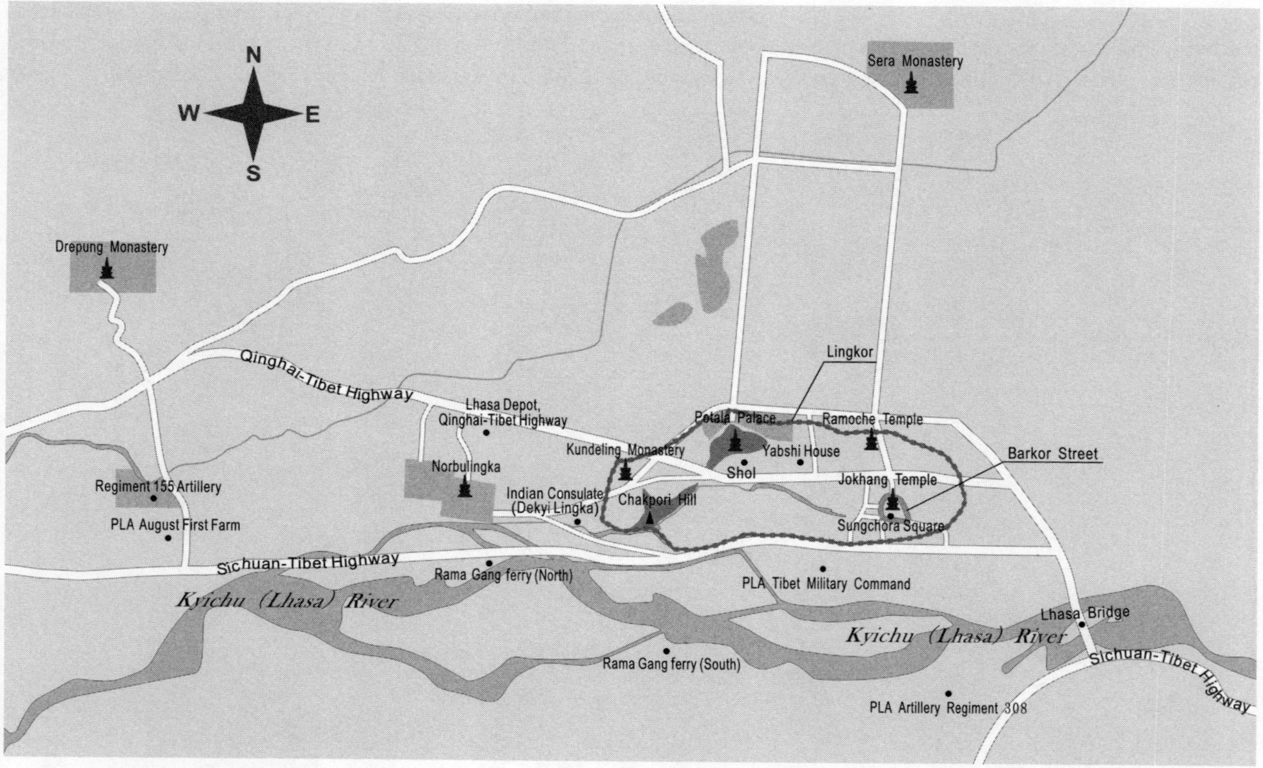

Map 6. Lhasa in 1959. The Lhasa cityscape has changed almost beyond recognition in the intervening decades; many sites, including much of the ancient pilgrimage circle known as the Lingkor, have vanished or been replaced. The course of the river also seems to have shifted. Locations are approximate for some sites no longer extant today.

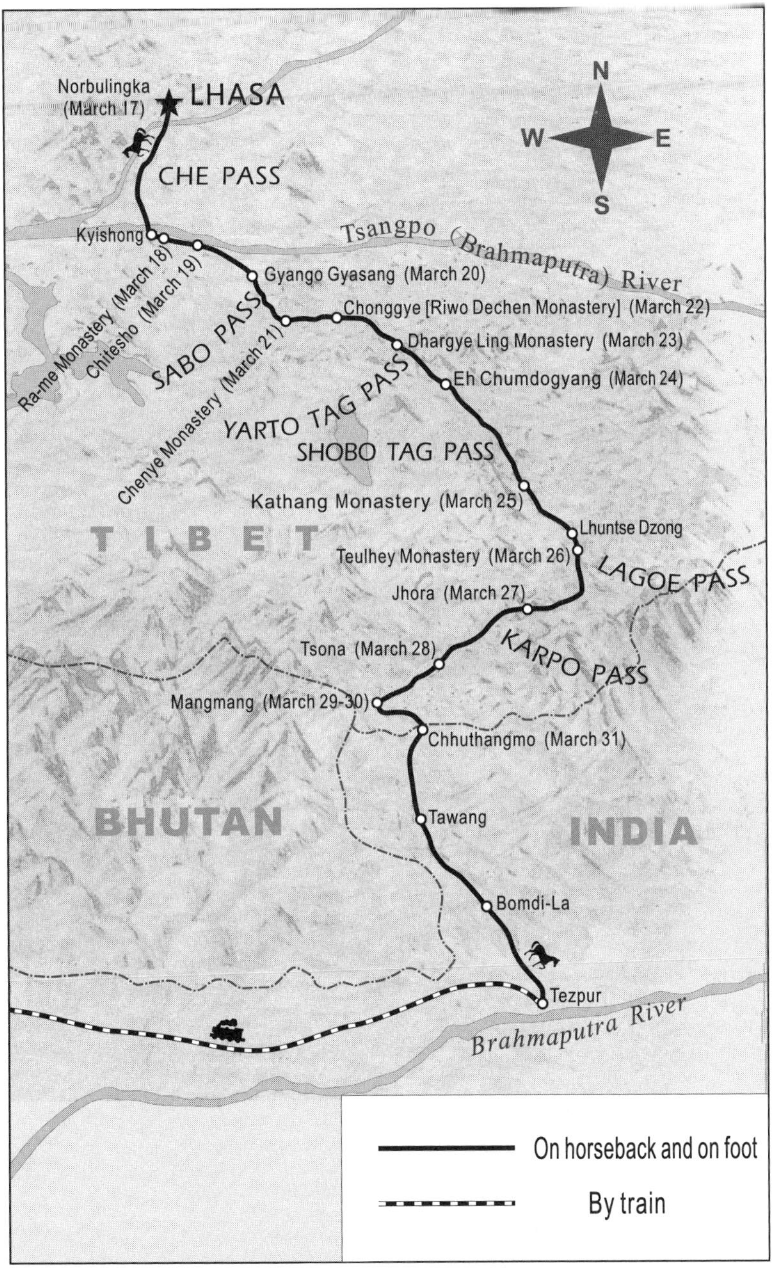

Map 7. The escape route of the Dalai Lama and his entourage in March 1959.

Prologue

"THE PLA HAD SURROUNDED Lithang Monastery,[1] and the Great Hall was jammed with refugees—monks, nuns, and local villagers. There were thousands of people. . . ."

I put down my pen. "Thousands? Is that possible?"

"That's the story I heard," stated Geshe Lobsang,[2] a middle-aged monk from Lithang. Sipping milk tea, he continued: "PLA legions were posted outside the building, and their commanding officer had ordered them to douse it with gasoline, intending to burn the 'rebel bandits'[3] alive unless they capitulated."

We were on the southern slopes of the Himalayas, in an Indian teahouse that jutted out from a steep mountainside like a flying buttress. The scorching early afternoon sun spilled across our rustic wooden table. Geshe Lobsang pulled his crimson robe over his head as a shield from the glare. I picked up my glass and found that my lemon tea had gone cold.

"Right at that moment, Yorupon suddenly returned."

"Yorupon!" I grabbed my pen. "You mean Yorupon, the Bumyak headman?"[4]

"Yes. He and about a dozen others had slipped out of the back of the monastery and disappeared into the hills."

Geshe Lobsang put down his glass of tea and made an arc-shaped gesture to indicate their roundabout getaway route. I pictured Lithang Monastery, which I had seen in photographs, a cluster of classic Tibetan temple buildings nestled against splendid jade-green mountains.

"Some people had found him and warned him that the PLA was about to torch the Great Hall. He hurried back to the monastery with his men and declared his surrender, asking the Chinese officer to let the people go. Oh, I forgot to mention that this officer was a bit strange." Geshe Lobsang stuck out his hand and spread his fingers. "His fingers were webbed, like a bird's feet." I stared at Geshe Lobsang's hand, imagining a web between his fingers—history had taken on aspects of legend.

"Yorupon had three guns: a rifle and two pistols. He surrendered the rifle first." Geshe Lobsang reenacted Yorupon's respectful submission of the rifle. "Then he took one of his pistols out of his breast pocket and handed it over to the Chinese officer, who ordered his men to take Yorupon into custody. But then Yorupon swiftly fished his other pistol out of his boot and shot the officer—a PLA colonel."

Geshe Lobsang's variant of this tale was somewhat different from the ones I'd heard before, but the conclusion was the same: at that point, the PLA had opened fire, and Yorupon had collapsed in front of the Great Hall, dead at the age of twenty-five.[5]

"Geshe-la,"[6] I asked, "when did you hear this story?"

"In 1996, when I went home to visit my family."

Tibetan and Chinese historical records both lend credence to the story of Yorupon's death. A Tibetan source contains a relatively straightforward account,[7] whereas a Chinese chronicle provides the Communist slant: "On March 30 [1956], the PLA wiped out the armed insurgents entrenched at Lithang Monastery and executed their bandit chieftain, [Yorupon], breaking the siege in Lithang County."[8]

Forty years later, the young headman's tale was still circulating in his hometown. As the story went, he had taken off his protective talisman and laid it before the Buddha, pledging to share the monastery's fate. In his people's collective memory, he lives on as a lone hero.

: 1 .

The Seeds of War

IT WAS EARLY 1956 in Mesho, Derge County, Sichuan Garzê Tibetan Autonomous Prefecture. Juchen Tubten crept toward the doorway of the temple. Just as he reached the threshold, he sensed someone blocking his way.[1]

"What's wrong?" a voice demanded, "Hasn't your clay bodhisattva given you anything to eat these few days?"

Juchen Tubten looked up. The speaker was a Chinese task force cadre with a gun at his belt. Beside him were several "local activists."

"Admit it! All your food comes from the working people! Doesn't it?" The cadre glared at him.

Juchen Tubten silently locked gazes with the cadre until his head began to spin. He took a deep breath, composed himself, and forced a nod. The cadre stepped aside and let him leave the building, still firing questions from behind. The task force had detained Juchen Tubten and more than sixty other prominent members of the local monastic and lay community inside the temple for almost three days without food, in retaliation for their refusal to close their monastery. No one, not even their families, had been allowed to bring them any sustenance, but now they were finally being released.

Huddled in his fur gown, Juchen Tubten stood in the icy sunlight on the hilltop, gazing at the desolate valley below. The barley fields were thickly blanketed with snow, and the river that flowed past the village was frozen into a silver thread. There were no humans in sight, only a sprinkling of isolated houses that seemed to shiver in the cold wind. Like heaps of white silk prayer scarves, the snowcapped mountain peaks jutted into the stark blue sky. Juchen Tubten focused on a red temple complex perched on a snowy mountainside in the distance: Dzongsar Monastery.

Dzongsar, founded in 1275, was one of the oldest and largest monasteries in Derge. Believers—Han and Tibetan, monastic and lay—came from afar to study there, and it had several hundred resident monks.

"That place won't last long," thought Juchen Tubten as he staggered down the hill.

Mesho, at an elevation of approximately thirteen thousand feet above sea level, was nestled in the southern foothills of Mount Trola, in the ancient kingdom of Derge. It was more than sixty miles from the county seat, and almost four hundred miles from the nearest city of Dartsedo,[2] the seat of the Sichuan Garzê Tibetan Autonomous Prefecture. Many of its inhabitants, traditional herdsmen and barley farmers, had never left their mountain valley. The monastery was their spiritual mainstay, especially during life's major passages, and it offered food and shelter in times of trouble.

In late 1955, an armed Chinese task force had arrived in Mesho and moved into a manor house known as Sokmo Potrang. As the local people watched in bewilderment, the task force cadres embarked on a campaign called the Democratic Reforms. Like the Land Reform campaign in the Han Chinese areas, the program focused mainly on redistribution of land and property according to Marxist principles. Confiscation of firearms was also essential. In minority ethnic regions such as the Tibetan ones, there was an added emphasis on curtailing the power of religion.[3]

First, the task force cadres called a meeting of beggars and other outcasts, informing them that they were poor because of the "exploitation" of the headmen, "landlords," "rich peasants," and the monasteries, and inciting them to appropriate the property of their exploiters. Next, they called on people to relinquish their weapons. Guns were unnecessary now, they claimed, since the Party leadership had "liberated" the area, destroyed all the bandits and Guomindang[4] reactionaries, and eliminated the need for violent feuds. In fact, however, this call was a move to forestall armed opposition to the Communist program. Under the slogan of "transferring firearms from the shoulders of the rich to the shoulders of the poor," weapons were confiscated from the "exploiters" and used to establish local Communist-controlled militias known as "the people's armed forces." Only those whom the task force designated "members of the laboring classes" were allowed to keep their weapons, and only on the condition that they join these militias.[5]

The task force used words the local people had never heard before, such as "revolution," "social class," "reactionary," and "struggle." Although these terms were puzzling at first, the meaning of "struggle" soon became apparent—it signified dragging in the headmen and high lamas so that the task force and the "local activists" it had enlisted to its cause could browbeat them into confessing their alleged crimes. Next came the confiscation of property—fields, pastures, livestock, and houses—of those classified as "wealthy," even though few of the sixty households in Juchen Tubten's community were actually rich.

The task force had its eye on Dzongsar Monastery, which had grown by the 1950s to encompass hundreds of buildings, including twenty-three subtemples. It also boasted a vast library of antique books, comprising Buddhist scriptures, medicine, literature, astronomy, calendar calculation, crafts, fine arts, and writings of the masters. Most valuable of all was its collection of gold and silver Buddhist statuary.

Declaring lamas, monks, and nuns the "exploiting class," the task force organized people to surround the monastery, evict most of its inhabitants, inventory its property, and confiscate everything of value. Next it rounded up the high lamas and head monks, along with all of the local headmen, conducted "struggle" sessions against them, and then locked them in jail. Only a few elderly, displaced monks remained in the ancient monastery.[6]

By this time, Land Reform had already swept rapidly across the Han Chinese areas of the People's Republic of China. Within the space of a few short years, almost 43 percent of the nation's land had been redistributed, and landlords and rich peasants had been "eliminated as a class."[7] Houses, livestock, and private property had been confiscated, all with minimal resistance. Now the task forces were trying to repeat the process in the Tibetan regions. But they met with fierce opposition from the Khampas—the "Men of Kham." These men, renowned for their unusual blend of fighting prowess and religious devotion, were deeply attached to their steeds, swords, and firearms. From an early age they learned equestrian skills and marksmanship, acquiring their first rifles as a rite of manhood. The Tibetan aristocrats of Lhasa regarded them as boors, while the traditional Chinese histories scorned them as "barbarous ruffians." Indeed, at times they seemed like brigands with their red cloth headbands, hard-bitten faces, robust physiques, and freewheeling manner. Nonetheless, they were pious Buddhists, and they bristled at any affront to their religion. In their eyes, the task force that had humiliated their lamas was an "enemy of the Dharma," the Buddhist law.

Juchen Tubten and some other young Khampa stalwarts got together to vent their outrage. Now that the sacred Dzongsar Monastery was imperiled, and even the high lamas had been taken prisoner, who would be next? Grabbing their swords, the young men vowed to fight to the death.

Their insurrection began in the early spring of 1956. Wielding knives, swords, hatchets, and a few guns, the Khampa rebels surrounded the Sokmo Potrang manor, cut off its water supply, and demanded the withdrawal of the task force from Mesho. After a few days, the Khampas allowed the task force an exchange: one bucket of water for every rifle that the task force surrendered. Bucket by bucket, rifle by rifle, this went on for seven days, until the task force agreed to leave Mesho. The Khampas sheathed their weapons and let the task force emerge, but at this point, a skirmish broke out in which six members of the task force were killed. A few days later a large, disciplined PLA contingent rolled in. Overwhelmed, the Khampas took to the hills.

The Khampas of Mesho lacked decent weapons and ammunition, a unified command, or even a clear objective. They had simply banded together, declaring themselves a brotherhood. Their numbers rose and fell, at times topping one hundred, and at others dwindling to mere handfuls. In this unruly group, each decided independently whether to stand and fight or to run away. They had no concept of modern warfare or "guerrilla war," nor did they have any idea that they were now known as "rebel bandits" and "reactionary elements." All they knew was that they should snipe at the "Han Chinese army men" if they were not too numerous, but they had better flee if reinforcements came.

: : :

Derge County, in the eastern portion of the traditional Tibetan province of Kham, is located in today's Sichuan Garzê Tibetan Autonomous Prefecture, just east of the Drichu River.[8] The river here divides eastern and western Kham, and also constitutes the border between Sichuan and Tibet. Thus, Jomda County of western Kham, directly across the river from Derge, falls within the region known as Chamdo, which is in Tibet.

The geopolitical nomenclature for the portion of Kham where Derge is located changed during the 1950s, reflecting increasing Communist control of the region. As in the other remote Tibetan regions in the four Chinese provinces neighboring Tibet, Chinese control over eastern Kham had been virtually nominal under the Qing dynasty and the Guomindang; for centuries, the Tibetans had retained their traditional systems of social organization along with a high degree of autonomy. When the Communists first established their government in Beijing in 1949, this region of eastern Kham was technically part of Xikang Province, which had been established by the Guomindang. The Communists' first steps were to delineate the "Tibetan Autonomous Region" within Xikang, which they did in 1950, and to begin to set up their administration. After a few years, they were ready for their unprecedented assumption of control over the area, all the way down to the grass roots. This process began in earnest in November 1955, shortly after they dissolved the old province of Xikang and subsumed it into Sichuan, and the Tibetan Autonomous Region of Xikang was renamed Garzê.

Derge boasted a long, proud history as an ancient Tibetan kingdom. Ruled continuously for thirteen hundred years by a hereditary lineage of kings (known as *gyalpo* in Tibetan) until it was partitioned by the Chinese in the late Qing dynasty, it was much larger than today's Derge County, even extending as far as Jomda (in today's TAR). Located in an area long contested between Tibet and China, Derge suffered two border wars between these great powers in the early twentieth century, leaving a legacy of mistrust toward both sides among its inhabitants and spawning a strong Kham autonomy movement.

The first Khampas in Derge to cast their lot with the Communists were not "the masses," but members of the hereditary ruling class, and that it was Communist policy to woo this elite actively. During the Chinese Communist struggle for ascendancy in the 1930s, an influential Derge headman named Jago Topden, sent by his king to fight the Chinese Red Army, was wounded and captured in battle; Red Army general Zhu De, recognizing the opportunity, treated him well and convinced him to support the Communists, after which Jago Topden became a reliable supplier of grain for the Red Army. In the early days of the People's Republic, a number of Derge leaders, including a wealthy merchant named Dorje Pandatsang and the last queen of Derge, Jangyang Palmo, also embraced Communism enthusiastically. Jangyang Palmo worked with the Chinese Communists dispatched to administer the area, and Jago Topden even dispatched a delegation to Beijing to pledge his loyalty.[9]

Such support was very useful to the Communists. In the early days of their administration of the minority ethnic regions, linguistic and cultural barriers prevented them from interacting directly with the local people, necessitating a transitional policy known as the "United Front." This doctrine called for reliance on headmen, high lamas, and other native leaders as intermediaries; these assorted figures were appointed to positions of prominence, although they often held little real power. Thus, when the Chinese Communists formally established the Tibetan Autonomous Region of Xikang in November 1950, they installed Jago Topden (who was already vice-chairman of Xikang) as the new region's vice-chairman, and Jangyang Palmo was also given high office. Jago Topden was also vice-chairman of the Kangding Military Committee, in charge of the rear supply lines of food and fuel for the Chinese invasion of Chamdo, Tibet, in the fall of 1950. His loyalty to the Communists was unquestioned, and they did not expect to encounter problems when they introduced their policies in his region of Derge.[10]

With the ruling class in the Communist camp, why did the Communist program spark Tibetan rebellion?

: : :

Mao set the Chinese Communist policy for the socialist transformation of ethnic minorities in a June 1950 speech, several months before Communist administration was established in the Tibetan regions of Xikang: "Social reforms in [minority] areas are a matter of great importance and must be handled cautiously. On no account must we be impetuous, for impatience will lead to trouble. No reform is to be instituted unless the conditions are ripe. . . . Of course, this is not to say that no reform at all is to be carried out."[11]

The key portion of Mao's statement is its last sentence. By June 1954, the Chinese State Ethnic Affairs Commission had completed its initial investigation of the Tibetan regions of Xikang as a prelude to the Party's program of Democratic Reforms.[12] In September of that year, Liao Zhigao, party secretary of Xikang, casually let it slip during a conversation with Sichuan representatives at a major congress in Beijing that the Democratic Reforms were soon to begin in Xikang. Even though he was vice-chairman of Xikang and a Communist supporter, Jago Topden had no inkling that the program was to begin so precipitously, and he "blanched" when he heard the news. Tibetan Communists and their backers among the local leadership were acutely aware that their people would protest unless adequate groundwork was laid for socialist reform, and that undue haste would lead to bloodshed.[13]

Nonetheless, Communist plans proceeded apace. A proposal was soon made for "reforms" in the Tibetan Autonomous Region of Xikang (soon to become Garzê), and approved by the Central Committee in September 1955.[14] The province of Xikang was dissolved and subsumed into Sichuan soon thereafter, and the reform policy was officially set in motion in January 1956.[15]

With all plans now fully in place from the top down, it was time for the Chinese Communists to seek rubber stamping from the local Tibetan leadership. To achieve this, in late January 1956, the Party convened a three-month meeting of sixty-nine of the most important minority leaders in Garzê, upon whom it relied to help administer the region under its United Front policy. The ostensible purpose of this meeting was "broad democratic consultation," but the Party's own description of the methodology used reveals this terminology to be a euphemism for arm-twisting: "[The goal is] to mobilize the majority of the minority leaders present to admit publicly that they have exploited and oppressed the masses, and to conduct self-criticism for this behavior; [we shall] bring in the local activists who are being trained in instituting the Democratic Reforms to take part in small-group sessions to persuade and struggle with these minority leaders." In addition to these formal sessions, the "consultations" were also to be continued daily on an informal basis. The same process was repeated on the local level, until approximately one thousand minority leaders had gone on record as "in favor of the resolution to begin Democratic Reforms."[16]

These meetings had the added advantage of keeping the local Tibetan leadership out of the way while the Party sent task forces to take charge of the entire region and begin Land Reform. The Party Committee sent task forces totaling seven hundred members into Dirge to conduct Land Reform in February 1956,[17] while the meetings with local leaders were still in session, even though the final authorization for this process was not formally approved at the prefectural level until July. Meanwhile, the entire county had erupted in rebellion by March.[18]

At approximately the same time, Li Weihan, head of the United Front Bureau for the entire nation, announced boldly—but unrealistically—that the Party would "create a showcase of peaceful transformation in Qinghai, Gansu, and Sichuan, and invite the masses and the leadership of Tibet to come see it." This, he claimed, would "energize the Tibetans for reform and expedite the peaceful transformation of Tibet."[19]

However, the process in the Tibetan areas of Sichuan was anything but peaceful. The intense Tibetan opposition to the rapid reforms, and some of its causes, are described in a rare, semiclassified memoir by Zhang Xiangming, vice-chairman of the CCP's United Front Bureau. He writes that in April 1956 he led a group of twenty cadres from Tibet to Sichuan to study the model of Land Reform in Garzê, but discovered upon arrival in Derge that task force members had been killed by "thugs" when they tried to start their campaign. The problem was, as the Tibetan cadres explained to him, that there had been no discussion at all with the local Tibetan leaders. Instead, they had been called to a meeting in Chengdu and presented with the summary decision to launch the reforms as a fait accompli.[20]

The validity of Tibetan complaints is strongly borne out by Li Weihan's wording, despite his claim that the campaigns were "peaceful and democratic." As Li put it, the target was "the exploiting ruling class, including slave owners, feudal lords, capitalists, aristocrats, headmen, chieftains, Thousand and Hundred Household[21] leaders, Living Buddhas,[22] imams, monks, nuns, lamas, rangeland owners, and others."[23] In other words, during the process of Land Reform, the "minority leaders" whom the Communists had courted with their United Front policy were now to be eliminated.

The Communist Land Reform campaigns in the Han areas of China were premised on the doctrine of class struggle, and the treatment of those designated as class enemies was avowedly ruthless.[24] A great deal of ink has been spilled on this subject by both Communist theorists and their critics, and while Mao's supporters prefer to emphasize the social and economic injustices that were supposed to have been corrected in the campaigns, the egregious excesses are well documented.[25] The same was true in the minority regions, where the campaigns often turned arbitrary. "Class lines" were not always drawn according to strictly economic criteria and the label "serf owner" was slapped onto some people simply because they were prominent in the community, or to meet quotas set from above.[26] The Sichuan Party Committee had determined that 7 to 8 percent of the population of the Tibetan regions—more than forty-nine thousand people[27]—should be branded "landlords" or "rich peasants," although Mao ordered this quota lowered to 3 to 5 percent. There was no substantive basis for Mao's quotas, however; he had merely concocted them on the spot after listening to reports from United Front head Li Weihan and Third Secretary of the Sichuan Party Committee Liao Zhigao in Beijing.[28]

The widespread, desperate opposition that the Communist Land Reform program engendered in the Tibetan regions of China stands as eloquent testimony to its excesses. Moreover, as pointed out above, the overwhelming majority of the rebels were members of "the masses" rather than the ruling classes, while most of the latter either cooperated with the Communists or maintained a position of neutrality. The first shots were fired in Sertar,[29] an area of Garzê, a few days before Li Weihan's February 1956 speech. On the day of his speech, the Tibetans of Palyul[30] County attacked their county seat. On the same day, at Lower Chakdu in Nyarong County[31]—the site of a famous Qing dynasty battle with the native Tibetans—the local people attacked the Land Reform task force and engaged them in fierce combat, killing twelve task force members. The Tibetan casualty toll is not known.[32] By the end of March 1956, one month after the Communist program had begun, rebellions had broken out in eighteen of the twenty-one Tibetan counties and forty-five of the seventy-seven Tibetan districts in Garzê, involving sixteen thousand poorly armed Tibetan rebels,[33] including Juchen Tubten and the Khampas of Mesho.

Another noteworthy rebellion took place in February 1956 elsewhere in Garzê, in the Upper Chakdu region of Nyarong County. Here, a young woman named Dorje Yudon disguised herself as a man, mounted her horse, and led a few hundred people to besiege the local stronghold, Drukmo Castle, which had been taken over by a Land Reform task force.

As in other Tibetan regions, the United Front policy had prevailed here in the early days of Communist control, and Dorje Yudon's husband, the local headman Gyari Nyima, was county commissioner of Nyarong. However, when the Land Reform task force arrived in January 1956, it brought class struggle, which entailed drawing "class lines" and conducting "struggle sessions," abolishing the system of tribal headmen, confiscating firearms, seizing property, and redistributing grain and land.

The immediate cause of the rebellion was a clash that broke out while the Land Reform task force was confiscating firearms, implementing a policy designed to prevent armed rebellion and to appropriate weapons for the use of newly formed local militias under Chinese control. All guns had to be given up, and the task force was instructed to use military force if necessary.

One day, the task force came to collect firearms at the house of a headman named Gyurme, but he had gone on a trip to the city of Dartsedo, leaving his mother, wife, children, and old housekeeper at home. They told the task force that Gyurme had taken their only gun with him, and denied that there were any weapons in the house, but the task force killed them all. Shocked, the local tribes cast aside their traditional enmities to join in revolt.[34]

The uprising, which lasted for a couple of weeks, was widespread, with 3,972 participants from 2,787 households, drawing on 70 percent of the households in the county and including almost 17 percent of its population. Although forty-one headmen and thirty-nine religious leaders were involved,[35] the rest of the rebels were ordinary individuals. In other words, most of the "rebel bandits" were actually people the Communists had officially designated "emancipated serfs," supposedly the core of the revolution.

Dorje Yudon's band, a few hundred strong, besieged the Land Reform task force in Drukmo Castle and cut off its water supply. They lacked the heavy weaponry to breach the ancient walled castle, however, and a month-long standoff ensued. Finally, the Chinese sent in a PLA regiment. The few surviving rebels who did not end up as prisoners either took to the hills or fled to Lhasa. The Communists then cast a wide dragnet across the area and jailed large numbers of Tibetans, including some women charged with transmitting messages for their "rebel bandit" relatives or secretly supplying their mountain hideouts with food and clothing.[36]

Many Tibetan regions were similarly troubled during this early period. The available, incomplete statistics indicate that three thousand people had joined uprisings in seventeen townships in the Ngaba[37] Tibetan Autonomous Prefecture of Sichuan by late March 1956,[38] and that the number of rebels there had quadrupled by mid-May.[39] In June, uprisings broke out among Tibetans in Gansu and Yunnan as well.[40]

: : :

The CCP Central Committee and the Chinese Central Military Commission immediately deployed PLA troops from the Chengdu Military Command to suppress these local rebellions,[41] and by mid-March, special headquarters had been set up at both the Chengdu and the Kunming Military Commands to coordinate the "pacification" campaigns in Sichuan and Yunnan.

In early 1956, the PLA rolled out brand-new secret weaponry to crush rebellion in Sichuan: Tupolev TU-4 long-range heavy bombers. Three years earlier, in January 1953, Stalin had presented Mao with ten of these planes, nicknamed "bulls," and the Chinese Air Force had organized them into a special regiment—Independent Long-Range Heavy Bomber Regiment No. 4—which was trained by Soviet instructors. Between the end of March and the middle of April 1956, the Chinese Air Force used the new planes to bomb three historic monasteries in restive areas of Sichuan: Jamchen Chokhor Ling (in Lithang), Samphel Ling (in Chatreng), and Gaden Phendeling (in Bathang).[42] The choice of these monasteries as targets for the powerful new weapons represented more than an attack on "rebels"—it was an attack on Tibetan heritage itself. The bombings greatly alarmed the Tibetans who experienced the attacks, but perhaps more importantly, they raised the public fear level among the Tibetan multitudes who eventually heard the news elsewhere, especially in Lhasa.

In fact, the Central Committee had issued specific instructions in January 1956 to proceed cautiously with the "reforms" of the monasteries, to avoid stirring up Tibetan opposition: "Although the Buddhist monasteries occupy arable land in the Tibetan regions, we had best leave them alone for now, in order to avoid provoking an unfavorable reaction among the Tibetans or finding ourselves on the defensive with regard to the problem of religion."[43] Evidently, the policy outlined in this directive had been superseded by a harder line, but its words proved prophetic. The appalling destruction had the opposite of its intended effect: it galvanized the Tibetan resistance.

: : :

At this moment, a Chinese Communist delegation led by Marshal Chen Yi was ready to set off for Lhasa to establish the Preparatory Committee for the Autonomous Region of Tibet (PCART),[44] which was to be the preliminary administration of the Chinese Communist Party in Tibet.

Before 1956, relations between the Communists and the Tibetan government in Lhasa were not as strained as later propaganda might lead us to believe. The Communists did not move quickly to incite the masses to overthrow "feudal rule," as they had in Kham. Rather, they cultivated their "patriotic United Front" for years, while founding local Party branches with a corps of grassroots members, and recruiting promising Tibetan youths for training in Beijing as future cadres. At the highest echelons, the Tibetans and the Communists had a relatively amicable working relationship. Each Communist official in Lhasa had a confidential assignment to woo certain Tibetan "United Front Targets." General Li Jue, vice-commander at the PLA Tibet Military Command, was assigned to Tibetan Chief Cabinet Minister Surkhang and the Dalai Lama's Junior Tutor, Trijang Rinpoché. Whenever Li Jue "happened to pass by" the Rinpoché's official residence, he would "drop in" for a cup of tea and ask the Rinpoché to teach him some Tibetan, probably hoping to use the Rinpoché as a pipeline to the ear of the young Dalai Lama.[45]

The Tibetan government demonstrated a measure of goodwill toward the Chinese Communist highway-building projects in Lhasa, Lhokha, and Kongpo in 1953 by contributing more than ten thousand Tibetan corvée laborers[46] from forty-eight local districts[47] and manors. Despite their official disapproval of the Tibetan corvée system as "feudal," the Chinese accepted this aid. A memorandum from the Tibetan government in Lhasa to one of the districts that provided laborers illustrates its upbeat mood at the time:

> In the spirit of the [Seventeen-Point Agreement], interethnic fraternal bonds are growing. The Chinese government has been building a highway between Kham and Lhasa. Our local governments and our entire populace, monastic and lay, recognize the benefits of this project and have been providing appropriate local support. Soon there will be a thoroughfare where there had always been a natural barrier, which will promote local development and strengthen the unity between peoples. His Holiness [the Dalai Lama] strongly supports solidarity with our brothers of all nationalities of the motherland. All Tibetans, with Kham as their center, are developing bonds of absolute trust with every nationality in China. This is in accord with the wishes of Chairman Mao and the central government of the People's Republic of China.[48]

Under the surface, however, the harmony between the Communists and the Tibetans of Lhasa was far from perfect. The Communist ideal that the army and the people should be "as close as fish and water" was problematic in Lhasa because the rapid influx of PLA troops had caused soaring inflation, antagonizing the populace. Even the upper classes, who were relatively unaffected by the economic pinch, remained dubious about "returning to the extended family of the motherland." This is reflected in a diary entry by Le Yuhong, a prominent Chinese official in Lhasa at the time:

> Most Tibetans don't understand [the Seventeen-Point Agreement]. Poisoned by imperialist culture, they emphasize that both the Tibetan script and the Buddhist religion originated in India, a longtime conduit for foreign culture into Tibet. Even now, they point out . . . India is the

> most convenient place for Tibetan aristocrats to send their children for schooling. "Why can't Tibetans be counted as an Indian ethnic group?" is the question they ask.[49]

Le concluded his entry with the admission that "some of our cadres would be unable to provide convincing answers to such questions."

The Chinese had already had a major clash with the Tibetan government as far back as 1952: the "People's Assembly" (Mimang Tsongdu) episode, in which the Dalai Lama and his government had bowed to Chinese pressure to accept the resignations of the anti-Chinese acting prime ministers Lukhangwa and Lobsang Tashi.[50] For decades afterward, the Chinese trumpeted the outcome as a victory, but it had rankled ordinary Tibetans, including the middle- and low-level bureaucrats.[51] These sectors of society accused the aristocrats of "betraying Tibet" and "helping the Chinese to turn the Dalai Lama into a puppet," and their disaffection contributed later to the aristocratic Tibetan government's powerlessness to stem the tide of the Lhasa Incident in 1959.

These tensions failed to detract from the veneer of harmony between the two sides at the top echelons of leadership. The Chinese, in their effort to gather Tibetan officialdom into the United Front, had even established a theatrical troupe[52] especially for the Dalai Lama, which gave exclusive performances for him and the Tibetan aristocrats at the Potala and Norbulingka palaces, sometimes appearing jointly with its counterparts from the PLA. On holidays, the Tibetans and the Chinese would exchange invitations, and the monks of the Potala's Namgyal Monastery—the personal monastery of all successive *dalai lamas*—are known to have performed Tibetan ritual dances for audiences that included beribboned PLA officers.

High-ranking Tibetan and Chinese Communist officials also entertained each other socially and exchanged gifts. Le Yuhong recorded a number of such interchanges with elite Tibetans and their families in his *Tibet Diary:*

> The Dalai Lama's[53] band and our troupe rehearsed together for a joint performance of "The East is Red". . . . In the evening, the Tibetan government hosted a celebratory banquet. The spirit of unity was in the air, and most of the Tibetan officials got drunk. The Tibetan colonels and

> lieutenant colonels and the PLA cadres drank plenty of toasts to each other. (May 23, 1952, the first anniversary of the Seventeen-Point Agreement)
>
> Our Tibetan garrison hosted a banquet at Yuthok House as a send-off party for the Panchen Lama's Administrative Council. I left early, and on my way home, I ran into [Cabinet Minister] Ngabo, who invited me to stop by his house and then return to the party at Yuthok House with the rest of the family. There I visited with Representative Zhang [Jingwu], General Zhang [Guohua], and Deputy Secretary Fan [Ming], after which I strolled home in the moonlight. (June 7, 1952)
>
> Ngabo and his family invited us to the Sampo Garden. We spent a wonderful day there, joking and laughing together to our heart's content. At our evening banquet, we poured drinks for each other, clowned around, and sang at the top of our voices until late at night. I felt as if I were celebrating a holiday with my own family. (July 2, 1952)[54]

By April 1956, however, this honeymoon was beginning to lose its luster. The upheaval in Kham had created thousands of refugees, who crossed the icy Drichu River into Tibet to flee toward Lhasa, their religious center and home of the young Dalai Lama. Many of them moved into a tent camp that sprang up on the barren fields outside the city. They brought with them appalling news of the troubles in Kham, arousing suspicion and hostility in Lhasa toward the arriving Chinese delegation. Zhang Jingwu, the Chinese government representative in Tibet, hastily tried to stabilize the situation by offering explanations to the higher-ups in Lhasa and donating alms to the leading Tibetan monasteries.

It was at this juncture that Chen Yi's delegation reached Lhasa; they arrived on April 17, 1956, and the PCART was established on April 22. An editorial appeared in *People's Daily* that day, hailing the birth of the PCART and dubbing it "a triumph for our nation's ethnic policy," but it avoided mentioning the unrest that Chinese "reforms" had caused in the Tibetan regions of neighboring Sichuan.

There is strong evidence that Mao was aware of the nature of Tibetan grievances in Sichuan. On April 29, he received a report from Chen Yi's delegation in Lhasa, informing him that people in Lhasa were wary of the situation in Sichuan, where "rebellion had been provoked by attacks on the elite, confiscation of weapons, tax collection, and destruction of religion."[55] Mao responded by asking the Sichuan Party Committee to perform a "fact check," the results of which were never published, although Mao presumably saw them.

Mao received similar feedback from the prominent Tibetan Communist Phuntsok Wangyal,[56] who led an investigative Tibetan delegation to Sichuan in June 1956, where he found that Han cadres had rushed the local people into the Democratic Reforms without adequate preparation or consultation with the local leadership. At the end of the month, he submitted his findings in Beijing, and Mao and Zhou Enlai later received his written report in brief.[57]

Nonetheless, Mao pressed ahead with his policies. At a Politburo meeting on July 22, he issued his well-known "July directive," which stated in no uncertain terms that the crackdown in Sichuan was "class war" and a "war of liberation." Therefore, all was justified: "pacifying the rebellion" and "implementing reform" must proceed hand in hand.[58] This directive continued to serve as the doctrinal underpinning for ongoing PLA "pacification" campaigns.

Still, the Party seemed aware of a need to present a more cautious face in public. At a meeting of prominent United Front representatives of minority religions on July 24, not long after the bombing of the three Tibetan monasteries, Zhou Enlai delivered a report, later published as "Steadily Implement the Democratic Reforms in the Minority Ethnic Areas," in which he announced to his audience: "We should adopt a more prudent attitude regarding the monasteries in the Tibetan areas."[59] Meanwhile, Tibetan rebellion continued to spread, reaching Jomda, on the Tibetan side of the Drichu River in Chamdo, which was under the administration of the Chinese-controlled Chamdo Liberation Committee.[60]

By the end of 1956, the minority uprisings in Sichuan in 1956 had involved more than 100,000 rebels armed with approximately 8,000 guns, and reached 43 counties and more than 450 townships.[61] Sichuan had set a terrifying example for Tibet.

The Dalai Lama was appalled when he heard the news that summer. Especially grieved by the destruction of Lithang Monastery, he decided to write to Mao to protest the Communists' use of force. Translation and transmission of the Dalai Lama's letter were problematic, however.

Phuntsok Wangyal, the Tibetan Communist whom he most trusted, had been transferred to Beijing, and Phuntsok's younger brother, Thuwang, who had been the Dalai Lama's Chinese tutor, was also not available. The Dalai Lama wrote two letters to Mao in Tibetan and asked Zhang Jingwu to submit them for him, but he never received a reply.[62] In late 1955, Zhang had been promoted to director of the Chairman's Office of the People's Republic of China. This positioned him to communicate directly with the top leadership—even with Mao—so the lack of a response was highly telling.

Two years later came the bloody suppression of Tibetans in Qinghai by Party Secretary Gao Feng. The people of Tibet could see the handwriting on the wall.

: : :

Meanwhile, in Mesho, Juchen Tubten and his men had been hiding in the woods for months. Over the summer, they had absorbed a number of men from neighboring tribes, gradually forming a loose guerrilla band, and two local men—Azom Phuntsok and Atsezom—had taken command. The group harassed the Chinese in a number of small-scale raids.

With the onset of winter came a large PLA contingent, which surrounded the guerrillas' forest hideout and gradually closed in on them. The outcome of this battle was clear from the start: the rebels were outnumbered and their weapons were no match for those of the PLA. Azom Phuntsok ran out of bullets in the heat of battle, whereupon he tossed aside his rifle, drew his sword, and charged down the mountainside, his two sons bringing up the rear with their swords also drawn. All three, along with Atsezom and his son, perished in a hail of PLA bullets, as Juchen Tubten watched in horror. Now leaderless, the guerrillas broke ranks: some surrendered and others fought to the death, while others still were taken prisoner or managed to slip away. This battle effectively snuffed out the spontaneous resistance in Derge.

After nightfall, when the gunfire had died out, the surviving guerrillas collected themselves and took a head count by moonlight: by some miracle, they were almost one hundred strong. What should they do? All eyes turned to Juchen Tubten.

Juchen Tubten did not know where to turn. He had no idea that a group of émigré Lithang merchants in Lhasa was organizing the spontaneous resistance fighters into an army, to be known as the Chushi Gangdruk Defenders of the Faith. Nor could he possibly have imagined the epochal events that he would witness in the future. All he knew was that he had no choice but to abandon his homeland, wife, and children, and flee into exile. The rest of his band realized they had to follow him.

Juchen Tubten, the twenty-five-year-old "Man of Kham," shouldered his old rifle with its few remaining bullets and led his men toward Lhasa.

Meanwhile, the twenty-one-year-old Dalai Lama, the eighteen-year-old Panchen Lama, and their retinues were on their way to India to take part in the Buddha Jayanti celebrations in honor of the 2500th anniversary of the Buddha's birth.

: 2 :

Summit in Delhi

ON NOVEMBER 20, 1956, the Dalai Lama and his entourage started eagerly on their road trip to India via Dromo. The group included his mother Diki Tsering, his eldest sister Tsering Dolma, his elder brother Lobsang Samten, his youngest brother Ngari Rinpoché, his Senior Tutor Ling Rinpoché, his Junior Tutor Trijang Rinpoché, then Tibetan Army Commander-in-chief Khemey Sonam Wangdu, Cabinet Ministers Surkhang and Ngabo, and the State Oracle of Tibet, known as the Nechung Oracle.[1]

The Dalai Lama had traveled to Dromo before, in December 1950, after the Chinese victory at Chamdo in October of that year. Fearful that the PLA might press on toward Lhasa, the Tibetan government had hastily invested the fifteen-year-old Dalai Lama with his temporal powers and advised him to evacuate to Dromo, near the Indian border, so that he could withdraw to India if necessary. He and his family, tutors, and cabinet had slipped out of Lhasa in panic and disarray, under cover of night.

This trip was completely different. This was an official visit to India, and Dromo was merely a stop on the way to New Delhi via Sikkim. The Chinese had been quick to build highways into Tibet. The Sichuan-Tibet Highway and the Qinghai-Tibet Highway now linked Tibet with China, and a new smaller highway within Tibet had reduced travel time between Lhasa and Dromo from almost two weeks to two days. Nevertheless, it had been no simple matter for the Dalai Lama to arrange this departure. He was devastated by the news that had been pouring in from Kham all summer: senior monks and local headmen arrested, battles raging, temples and monasteries laid to waste. Even the occasional report that Tibetans had won some skirmish could not cheer him up. He knew that resistance was futile against the Chinese, given their sheer military superiority. On a deeper level, he was convinced that there was no genuine victor in war: in the end, both sides were losers. Moreover, the bloodshed was unnecessary, as he was not opposed to reform. But why did the Communists have to impose theirs through violence?[2]

Indeed, the Dalai Lama had taken steps toward reform. As a boy in his cloistered palace, surrounded by aristocrats, servants, and high lamas, he had been shielded from firsthand understanding of the poverty of his people. Before his trip to Dromo in his teens, he had encountered only a few poor laborers, and heard their tales of woe. On his way to Dromo, however, he had seen shocking destitution up close, and it had saddened him and reminded him of his own humble farming origins. Upon his return to Lhasa, he charged his cabinet and chief of staff with the task of addressing the problems. In 1952, his government established a Reform Bureau, which began an overhaul of the corvée labor and taxation systems. Although the changes had met with some opposition, they had shown that peaceful transformation was not impossible.

Now, with the troubles in Kham, the Dalai Lama had nowhere to turn. He knew that his secluded land had drifted beyond the ken of world politics. Instead of raising protest from the worldwide religious community, the bombs that had thundered down onto Lithang Monastery seemed to have gone as unnoticed as tiny grains of sand slipping silently into an ocean. Time and again the Dalai Lama implored Zhang Jingwu and other Chinese officials in Lhasa to halt the destruction of monasteries and the slaughter of innocent people, but his appeals fell upon deaf ears. Kham was beyond his jurisdiction, he was told. To the atheistic Communists, monasteries were "feudal strongholds" that had to be destroyed. Resistance against enforced land reform was deemed "counter-revolutionary insurrection," which must be put down with an iron fist.

As the Dalai Lama faced this impasse, the Crown Prince of Sikkim, Palden Dondrup Namgyal, turned up in Lhasa with an invitation from the Mahabodhi Society of India to attend the Buddha Jayanti celebrations in New Delhi. To the Dalai Lama as spiritual leader, the proposition was irresistible: India was holy, the wellspring of Buddhism. As temporal leader, he viewed India as Tibet's sole salvation in its time of unprecedented crisis. India had a deep cultural bond with Tibet, and it was a model of nonviolent struggle for independence. What was more, India seemed to have some leverage with China. The Dalai Lama eagerly accepted the invitation, but there were hurdles to cross before he could go.

At the time, the Dalai Lama was theoretically the highest leader of Tibet. Moreover, as chairman of the PCART, Mao's engine for completing his control over Tibet, and a deputy chairman of the Standing Committee of the National People's Congress, his rank was ostensibly higher than that of the leading Chinese power brokers in Lhasa: Generals Zhang Jingwu, Zhang Guohua, and Fan Ming. In fact, however, Party membership trumped sheer administrative rank,[3] meaning the Dalai Lama was actually a mere figurehead, and he had to ask his so-called subordinate, Fan Ming—deputy secretary of the CCP Tibet Work Committee and acting vice-chairman of the PCART in Zhang Guohua's absence—to submit his request to Beijing for travel permission.

Fan Ming was not well liked by his peers in the upper echelons of Chinese and Tibetan leadership in Lhasa. As a veteran of the Northwest Military Region, he did not mix easily with Zhang Jingwu and his cohorts from the Southwest, and the Tibetans knew him as a swaggerer.[4] He rebuffed the Dalai Lama's request on the spot, but he knew better than to take sole responsibility for such a weighty matter, and he transmitted it to Beijing. It landed on Mao's desk.

Mao is on record as having stated his intent to take over Tibet even before he had actually established the People's Republic of China. As he said to Soviet statesman Anastas Mikoyan at a secret meeting in Xibaipo, Hebei Province, in February 1949: "Actually, the problem of Tibet is not hard to solve, but we must allow some time and not rush things. There are a couple of reasons for this. First, transportation is poor in the region, making it difficult to move large numbers of troops and keep them supplied. Second, it takes longer to solve the ethnic question in regions where religion holds sway, so our pace will need to be steady but not precipitous."[5] This statement illustrates that Mao's concern about sending troops to take over Tibet was primarily logistical, but he had set aside his misgivings by November 1949, shortly after the founding of the People's Republic, when he sent a telegram to Marshal Peng Dehuai stating, "sending in the military is the only way to solve the Tibet question."[6] In January 1950, he expounded his ideas further in a cable to the Central Committee: "Although Tibet is not heavily populated, its location is strategic, and we must occupy it and then transform it into a people's democracy."[7] Mao envisioned the takeover as a two-stage process; military conquest was only the prelude to the imposition of his social engineering program.

What follows is history. The Chinese PLA invaded Tibet at Chamdo on October 6, 1950, and concluded its victory over the Tibetans there on October 24. The Seventeen-Point Agreement, granting China sovereignty over Tibet, was signed in Beijing in May 1951. The PLA vanguard entered Lhasa on September 9 of that year, followed by forces led by Generals Zhang Guohua and Tan Guansan on October 26.

With this, the Chinese Communists had formally occupied Tibet, although the task of consolidating their control still remained, and it presented one headache after another for Mao. In disregard of the promises of the Seventeen-Point Agreement not to alter Tibet's existing system, as early as November 1955 Mao had secretly ordered the CCP Tibet Work Committee to prepare Tibet for his intended reforms.[8] Fan Ming, to whom Zhang Guohua relayed these instructions by telephone, attests to Mao's emphasis on military backup for his policies, and his willingness to accept the consequences. As Fan recalls, Mao's words were: "If the aristocrats oppose the reforms, we'll subjugate some of them and others will run away. It won't matter if there are a few more people denigrating us from Hong Kong or Kalimpong."[9]

With Central Committee approval, the CCP Tibet Work Committee had launched its experimental land reform program in Chamdo[10] in late June 1956.[11] By July, armed Tibetan protests had erupted in Jomda County, which was just across the border from Sichuan.[12] Jigme Gonpo, a Jomda headman and ex-member of the Chinese-run administration for the region, the Chamdo Liberation Committee, protested the imposition of "Kham-style" Land Reform and formed a guerrilla band in the hills. The uprisings spread in August and September, when bands of Tibetans raided Chinese maintenance crews and troops on the Sichuan-Tibet Highway, precipitating a full-scale PLA military operation to clear the way for the transportation of supplies. The Tibetan unrest continued, however, reaching southern Chamdo by November. The Communists in Lhasa and Beijing understood clearly that the uprisings were a protest against their policies, as can be inferred from the following message from the CCP Tibet Work Committee to the Central Committee on December 6, 1956:

> The uprisings in southern Chamdo (i.e., the Markham, Dzogang, and Tsakhalho areas) are a protest against our reforms, instigated by some members of the ruling classes along the Jinsha [Drichu] River (including Dorje Pandatsang). These ruling class leaders have coerced many of the Tibetan masses to follow them. These rebellions should be defined as mass ethnic uprisings, fomented by the counterrevolutionary ruling classes, using issues of ethnicity and religion as a lever.[13]

The Chinese Communists put their own slant on the story here by placing the blame on "counterrevolutionary ruling class" instigators, but the passage reveals how they had missed their opportunity with this group of influential Tibetans. As mentioned above, Dorje Pandatsang had backed the Communists at first. Although there is no explicit historical record on his change of heart, it seems reasonable to infer that his disillusionment—like that of Jago Topden and other local leaders—was a response to the abuses of the Communist program in practice.[14]

On August 18, Mao sent the Dalai Lama a conciliatory letter. He acknowledged that there had been "a little trouble in Sichuan," although he blamed it on "proimperialist elements and leftover Guomindang elements." Nonetheless, he admitted, "there were also flaws in our work there." Instead of suggesting remedies for these "flaws," however, he merely remarked that he hoped "Tibet would do its best to prevent trouble." He also tried to soothe the Dalai Lama with the concession that Tibet was not yet ripe for Land Reform and an expression of confidence: "We understand you, and we believe that you can handle the work that needs to be done in Tibet."[15]

In the fall of 1956, the eyes of the world turned to the Hungarian uprising, in which Soviet forces ultimately crushed a popular revolution, killing thousands, and reasserting Soviet control over Hungary.

Concerned at the lack of a reply from the Dalai Lama, India decided to raise the ante. The first invitation had come from the Mahabodhi Society, a nongovernmental organization; this time, the Indian government sent a second, official invitation for the Dalai Lama directly to the Chinese government. The Dalai Lama's absence would be a gaping hole in the birthday celebration; he was the leader of Vajrayana Buddhism,[16] which was paramount in the Himalayan region.

On November 6, 1956, two days after the Soviet invasion of Hungary, Zhang Jingwu made a special trip back to Lhasa from Beijing with the news that Zhou Enlai had granted permission for the Dalai Lama's India trip, and that the Panchen Lama[17] would be going too. Zhang urged the Dalai Lama to travel by plane so as to avoid the land route through Kalimpong, where he might be beset by "a motley bunch of people." He followed this with a political lecture about the Hungarian uprising, but with his limited understanding of world politics, the young Dalai Lama failed to get the hint about what the events in Hungary had to do with him. The "motley bunch of people" in Kalimpong included Gyalo Dondrup (the Dalai Lama's elder brother), and numerous Khampa refugees.

: : :

Tibet, with Lhasa as its hub, had a complicated historical relationship with the eastern Tibetan region of Kham. Historically, both Lhasa and the Chinese tended to draw the boundary line between their two governmental jurisdictions along the Drichu River within Kham, which both regarded as a remote frontier region. Although the Khampas living east of the Drichu were under Chinese jurisdiction, and those to the west were in Tibet, all were Khampas. They were followers of Tibetan Buddhism, but they did not answer to the Lhasa government politically, and they had their own distinctive customs and dialect of the Tibetan language.

Chinese rulers throughout history regarded the Khampas as a problem, but they were also a headache for Lhasa. Age-old frictions persisted between Lhasa and the Khampas, which had even clashed militarily as recently as the 1930s, when Khampa autonomy advocates had rebelled against both Lhasa and Nanjing.[18] The Thirteenth Dalai Lama, Tubten Gyatso, had toyed with the idea of establishing a local military force in Kham instead of stationing troops from Lhasa there, but had decided not to, lest it exacerbate tensions.[19]

Intraethnic strife notwithstanding, whenever the peoples combined under the term "Tibetan" are juxtaposed as a whole against the outside world, the bond between them is likely to outweigh any antagonism. The people of Kham shared the piety of Lhasa, and their religious leaders had been trained in its famous monasteries. Even though most of Kham was in the Chinese domain, the Khampas were more loyal to Lhasa than to faraway Nanjing or Beijing, which, across an enormous linguistic, cultural, and religious divide, might as well have been in a foreign land. In times of crisis, the inhabitants of Kham would bury the hatchet with Lhasa—or among themselves—and unite against a common enemy.

Lhasa was where the Khampas had to turn for help with their resistance against the Chinese Communists. However, Lhasa and the Khampas had conflicting concerns. While Kham was embroiled in conflict, Lhasa was still relatively peaceful even though the PLA had established a foothold there, and the cabinet in Lhasa believed that the city was protected by the Seventeen-Point Agreement signed with the Chinese after their October 1950 invasion of Chamdo. Aware of its powerlessness against further PLA encroachment, the cabinet in Lhasa clung to the fragile Agreement, and shrank from actions that might provoke the use of PLA force. As the strife-ridden areas were part of Sichuan, any substantive assistance to the Khampas would be an invitation to trouble, and the cabinet had trouble enough already.

Things looked different to the Khampas. Although they fervently identified themselves as Tibetans, they were neither bound nor protected by the Seventeen-Point Agreement. Instead, they were under the control of Sichuan, with its full-throttle collectivization program, and they knew that appeals to the upper echelons of the Chinese government would be futile. They had no choice but to turn westward to Lhasa for help, or to flee there in desperation.

Fortunately for the Khampas, who had a flair for business in addition to their famed righteous ethos, they had an established ancient trade route to the west. There were already enough Khampa-owned businesses in Lhasa to constitute a Khampa interest group whose affiliates became spokesmen for the Khampa cause. In 1956, one eminent member of this circle was a merchant from Lithang named Gonpo Tashi. When trouble broke out in Kham, he drafted a letter to Indian prime minister Nehru and the World Buddhist Society to protest Chinese destruction of Tibetan monasteries, and asked the "great three" monastic universities—Drepung, Sera, and Ganden—to endorse it with their seals. They refused, however, lest foreign intervention aggravate the Chinese.[20] He also sought military support from the Dalai Lama's Lord Chamberlain Phala, but

Phala turned him down, fearing that Lhasa's involvement with the Khampa cause might provoke Chinese reprisals against his city.[21] Frustrated, Gonpo Tashi realized that he would have to try something different.

The Khampas had an alternative avenue of assistance, also to their west: the small but significant Tibetan community in the northern Indian hill station of Kalimpong, a historic crossroads between Tibet and India. Tibetan refugees had been fleeing to northern India—especially Darjeeling and Kalimpong—in waves since 1951. Before 1959, the only news of the events in Kham that reached the outside world was the trickle of eyewitness reports brought to Kalimpong by merchants and refugees. These reports often appeared in a local Tibetan-language newspaper called the *Tibet Mirror,* run by a man named Gegen Dorje Tharchin, an émigré from the Khunu region of the western Himalayas who had converted to Christianity.[22] News of the strafing of Lithang Monastery eventually surfaced in this newspaper, which gave its source as "an eyewitness report from a recent arrival from Kham." The Tibetans of Kalimpong came from various regions and lacked a united vision of Tibet as a whole, but they agreed on the main problem: the clashes between the people of Kham and Amdo and the Chinese Communist army.

In 1956, the Dalai Lama's elder brother, Gyalo Dondrup, was living unobtrusively in Kalimpong, but when he heard the bad news from Kham that summer, he suddenly decided that the quiet life of a businessman was no longer appropriate for him. The eldest of the Dalai Lama's brothers, Taktser Rinpoché, had moved to the United States. Wondering if America might be willing to aid the Tibetan cause, Gyalo Dondrup began to develop contacts with the US government, and with the CIA in particular.

A new wave of Tibetan refugees surfaced in Kalimpong in 1956. On September 13, three brothers arrived from Lithang: Wangdu, Burgang, and Kelsang Gyadotsang. Their uncle was the merchant Gonpo Tashi, who had tried in vain to get backing for the Khampas in Lhasa.[23]

A few months later, Wangdu Gyadotsang would become one of the first CIA-trained agents in the Tibetan resistance, while his brother Kelsang began transmitting intelligence to their uncle in Lhasa, and buying weapons and radio communications equipment. Wangdu also brought in an acquaintance named Athar Norbu, a penniless former monk from Lithang Monastery who was to make his mark on history.

: : :

Tibetans thronged out joyously for the Dalai Lama's send-off from Lhasa on November 20. The festive mood contrasted sharply with that of his trip to China to meet with Chinese leaders in 1954, when wailing crowds, fearful that they might never see him again, had lined the banks of the Kyichu River[24] to bid him farewell. The Dalai Lama sensed that this pilgrimage to India was the last shred of hope not only for him but also for his people. He and Zhang Jingwu each delivered a speech, and then he set out with his fifty-member delegation. Little did he know that this trip would mark the end of his "honeymoon" with the Chinese Communists.

The first stop was Shigatse on November 21 to join up with the Panchen Lama. It was the third time that the twenty-one-year-old Dalai Lama had met the eighteen-year-old Panchen Lama, and the two were greeted by a queue of forty thousand worshipers with offerings of white silk prayer scarves, flowers, and incense.

The next day, they left Shigatse together for the Sikkim border, escorted by General Chen Mingyi, vice-commander of the PLA Tibet Military Command. The long Himalayan mountain chain, which forms natural borders for India, Sikkim,[25] Nepal, and Tibet, is intersected by various natural passes and ancient trade routes, which have served as conduits of merchandise and ideas across the Himalayas throughout the ages. Over time, the peoples straddling the Himalayas developed deep cultural links. Sikkim and Tibet, connected by Nathu Pass, were closely entwined: the royal family of Sikkim had intermarried with the Tibetan aristocracy for generations, and in 1956, the consort of its current crown prince was a daughter of the Tibetan Sampo family.

Now three hundred miles from Lhasa, the Dalai Lama's party arrived at Nathu Pass, thirty-two miles from Dromo. There was no road to the top, so they got out of their cars at the foot of the pass, where they said good-bye to General Chen Mingyi and mounted horses for the climb to more than fourteen thousand feet above sea level. In November, the pass was cloaked in snow and mist. The Dalai Lama, in his gold satin hat, padded gown, and russet scarf, sat on a white horse in the middle of the entourage, flanked by his officials, with rifle-bearing foot soldiers on either side. As it snaked its way slowly up the age-old pass, the procession seemed dwarfed by the vast backdrop of blue sky and endless Himalayan peaks.

At the top, they paused at a huge cairn, or *mani,* decorated with gaily colored prayer flags flapping in the breeze. In accordance with tradition, each traveler added a stone to it and shouted "Victory to the Gods!" Then they crossed the pass and descended into Sikkim. In the mist ahead they saw a line of people, a small honor guard and band sent by the Sikkimese government, which greeted them with the Tibetan and Indian national anthems. The welcome party included the Crown Prince of Sikkim, the Indian political officer in Sikkim, Apa B. Pant, and a translator for the Dalai Lama. A pleasant surprise awaited the Dalai Lama in a village at the bottom of the hill: his two émigré brothers, Taktser Rinpoché and Gyalo Dondrup. With Lobsang Samten and Ngari Rinpoché already in the group, it was the first reunion of all five brothers in years.

On November 24, the delegation traveled by car thirty-four miles to Gangtok, the capital of Sikkim, where they stopped for a brief overnight rest. The next day, they boarded two planes for New Delhi. There they had a red-carpet greeting, a gesture of Indian support for Tibet. Prime Minister Jawaharlal Nehru and Vice-President Sarvepalli Radhakrishnan exchanged white silk prayer scarves with them; the Buddhist dignitary Geshe Sherab Gyatso[26] was also present. Two rows of Indian children strewed the guests' path with flower petals as a Sikh officer draped a garland around the Panchen Lama's neck. The two young Tibetan leaders, accompanied by the prime minister of India, reviewed the Indian military honor guard. In the crowd of onlookers, Tibetan men in their black fedoras craned their necks to get a better view.

The delegation plunged immediately into a whirlwind of activity. The first stop was the president's palace, the Rashtrapati Bhavan, to pay a call on President Rajendra Prasad. The mood was celebratory: the Tibetan officials in their colorful finery and the Indian attendants in elegant maroon uniforms circulated around the room to a background of festive music. The simple gray jackets of the Indian dignitaries and the red monastic robes of the Panchen Lama and the Dalai Lama seemed austere amid such splendor. Attendants bearing small dishes rubbed fragrant ointment into the backs of their hands, and Prime Minister Nehru led the Dalai Lama into a magnificent reception room, where his daughter Indira was sitting. The Dalai Lama presented Nehru with the gifts he had brought: a *thangka,* a statue of the Buddha, a set of sutras, and an exquisite large silver pot. Then they began their meeting. Nehru was a seasoned, world-famous diplomat more than forty years the Dalai Lama's senior. He smiled cordially at the Dalai Lama, who looked at him expectantly, hoping for guidance.

Nehru jotted down the following notes during his talks with the Dalai Lama on the following day, November 26:

> Three areas of Tibet: (1) Eastern area liberated by force; (2) Central Tibet under Dalai Lama; (3) Tsang Tibet[27] under Panchen Lama. Originally all these under Dalai Lama, thus limiting Dalai Lama's authority—at present preparation for local self-government in Tibet—creating three parts as autonomous regions.
>
> [All three regions] to carry out orders of the Chinese Government.
>
> Chinese say that Tibet very backward and wanted help to advance.
>
> No present intention but future idea to take lands from monasteries—schools—new educational institutions—equal distribution of land—postpone because of people's opposition.
>
> State authority must be based on people having faith; otherwise religion suffers.
>
> Hope lies in India.
>
> Some fighting still going on in Eastern areas. In other areas, preparation going on, including Lhasa.
>
> No definite idea among Tibetans. They have grown desperate, prepared to die.
>
> Foreign sympathy and aid—majority do not think they can fight out Chinese.
>
> Chinese troops about 120,000.
>
> Talks with Chairman Mao In Peking—attempts to convert Dalai Lama to communism.
>
> Dalai Lama did not commit himself to communist ideology but expressed objections.
>
> Jawaharlal Nehru: Panchen Lama's views?
>
> Dalai Lama: Panchen Lama's party gaining power because of friendship with Chinese authorities.

> Russians playing a part in Tibet . . . no representatives in Lhasa . . . only Indian, Nepal and, in a way, Bhutan.[28]

Afterward, Nehru asked his foreign secretary, Subimal Dutt, to add the following record of the conversation:

> PM [prime minister] told me [Dutt] that he had advised Dalai Lama to accept Chinese suzerainty[29] and try to secure the maximum internal autonomy. If he contested Chinese suzerainty, then the Chinese would try to take over Tibet entirely, thereby eliminating any idea of autonomy. Dalai Lama appealed to India for help. PM's reply was that, apart from other considerations, India was not in a position to give any effective help to Tibet; nor were other countries in a position to do so. Dalai Lama should not resist land reforms. The Chinese Government have not yet started such reforms, but in India and other underdeveloped countries, land reform has been the main plank in the political platform of progressive parties. Dalai Lama himself should take the lead in such reforms. He should be the leader of the people. It is not possible for Tibet to remain isolated from the rest of the world. PM's feeling was that Dalai Lama was still thinking in terms of Tibetan independence and looked to India for guidance.

The day after this conversation with Nehru, the Dalai Lama and the Panchen Lama made a pilgrimage to Rajghat, the site of Mahatma Gandhi's cremation. The Dalai Lama laid a wreath of fresh flowers on Gandhi's black marble memorial slab and spread a white silk prayer scarf beside it. Then he bowed his head and prayed softly. "Could freedom be achieved through nonviolence?" he wondered solemnly. As the leader of the Tibetan people, what should he do?

As the state visit continued, the Dalai Lama attracted crowds of onlookers wherever he went. Everyone seemed to want a glimpse of the youthful leader of India's enigmatic neighbor to the north.

At a garden party at Nehru's residence, Teen Murti House, he mingled with foreign dignitaries and the upper crust of Indian society. Among the guests were some Tibetans, mostly young aristocrats attending modern colleges in India, who approached to pay their respects. Dressed fashionably—the men in formal Indian suits, and the women with short jackets over their Tibetan gowns—they greeted Nehru with handshakes and white silk prayer scarves, and presented his daughter Indira with finely wrapped gifts. Then they knelt before the Dalai Lama so that he could touch the crowns of their heads in traditional blessing. The Tibetan officials flanked him, gazing into an uncertain future in their old-fashioned regalia: each with a long formal robe, an elaborately braided coiffure, a black felt hat, and the single, dangling earring that was the hallmark of their officialdom. With his tutors Ling Rinpoché and Trijang Rinpoché behind him, and a smiling Nehru before him, the Dalai Lama was keenly aware that Tibet faced a crossroads in its history. Still eager to absorb the novelty of his surroundings, however, he even enjoyed a couple of turns around the garden atop an elephant. Then he turned to the long line of people who had come for his blessing. Farmers, peddlers, and herdsmen of all ages with stoical weathered faces and traditional Tibetan robes and jewelry bowed as they filed quickly and reverentially past him to receive his ritual touch to the crowns of their heads. They left the ground before him strewn with offerings: heaps of white silk prayer scarves, gold and silver jewelry, and cash.

: : :

At the front of the crowd on the tarmac of Palam Airport in New Delhi stood a girl with a big red bow on the top of her head and a boy with a stylish haircut, each holding a lavish bouquet of roses and watching the approach of a plane.

Applause burst out as a familiar figure emerged from the cabin door: Chinese premier Zhou Enlai. He waved, beamed at the welcoming crowd, and stepped onto the gangway. In his crisp uniform, Marshal He Long, China's vice-premier, followed him with a salute, and the Indian brass band, dressed smartly in red, struck up a tune. Bedecked in garlands, the visitors walked with Prime Minister Nehru between them and the Chinese ambassador to India and his retinue behind. Two crimson-clad figures followed them. Then Nehru gave an enthusiastic welcome speech, to which Zhou Enlai replied with equally warm words of thanks. Those were the days of the Sino-Indian "honeymoon"; wherever the Chinese premier went, he was greeted with Hindi cheers of Nehru's slogan: "Indians and Chinese are brothers!"

The date was November 28, 1956, and this was a historic summit. Gathered here, in the homeland of the Buddha and Mahatma Gandhi, were the premier and vice-premier of China, both of the young leaders of Tibet, and the first prime minister of an independent India.

Zhou Enlai had a mission: to make sure the Dalai Lama did not try to seek political asylum in India and to discover to what extent India might be willing to support him.[30] It would mar China's image in the eyes of the world if the Dalai Lama stayed in India. China was seeking entry into the United Nations; it had the support of India and the Soviet Union, but it needed more. The Chinese Communists did not want to appear as bullies, or as having violated their own anti-imperialist, anticolonial precepts. Also, the timing was particularly inopportune in terms of the Cold War propaganda contest: if the Dalai Lama fled at this point, it would add to the international furor over the crushing of the uprising in Hungary and create a further blot on the name of international communism.

Zhou was also concerned about the unrest that might erupt without the Dalai Lama's presence. The Tibetan areas of Sichuan were rife with rebellion, and Tibet was highly unstable. The PCART was too new to have taken firm root. Without the Dalai Lama, Tibet would probably degenerate into chaos, impeding its socialist transformation.

Zhou was welcomed with great fanfare at the India Gate in Delhi, where he addressed a crowd with the Dalai Lama at his side. Next he was whisked off to a performance of Indian folk dance and acrobatics. The festivities were just a prelude to the real agenda of the visit, however, which he addressed promptly in a meeting with the Dalai Lama the next day. Urging the Dalai Lama to return to Lhasa as soon as he had finished his religious activities, Zhou offered a concession from Mao as enticement: "Chairman Mao has asked me to assure you that none of our reforms in Tibet will be implemented without the consent of your government. Chairman Mao doesn't even want to talk about reforms in Tibet yet, not until everyone is ready for them."[31]

The Dalai Lama agreed to return to Lhasa, but had two pointed questions for Zhou: What had happened during Land Reform in Kham and Amdo that had driven so many thousands of refugees into Tibet? And given that the Communists' Common Program,[32] their Constitution, and the Seventeen Point Agreement all guaranteed the preservation of temples and monasteries and respect for religious faith, why had they brutally persecuted so many lamas in Kham and shelled a monastery?[33]

Zhou's reply was equivocal: "There were some flaws in our Land Reform work in Kham. Some matters were handled imperfectly. . . . One of our units was encircled and facing extermination, so we had to send reinforcements to the rescue."[34]

Zhou hosted a banquet for the Dalai Lama and his entourage at the Chinese embassy on November 30, and on December 7, he sent a guardedly optimistic report of his visit to Mao and the Central Committee.

On December 22, Zhou and He Long left India[35] and continued on to Pakistan. Meanwhile, the Dalai Lama and the Panchen Lama set out on a brief diversion, a first-in-a-lifetime pilgrimage to the Four Holy Places, the sites of the Buddha's birth, enlightenment, first sermon, and death. On December 27, they reached the second of these sites, Bodh Gaya. But on December 30, the worries of the outside world intruded once more: a message came for the Dalai Lama that Zhou Enlai had returned to India from Pakistan, and wished to meet with him as soon as possible. He boarded a train for Delhi right away. As soon as he arrived at the station, the Chinese ambassador to India, Pan Zili, bundled him directly into a car to the embassy. The Dalai Lama's attendants jumped into a separate car to follow him there, but the Dalai Lama was already sequestered in his interview with Zhou by the time they arrived. In a personal interview more than fifty years later, the Dalai Lama recalled, laughing uproariously as he told the story: "They were milling around outside the door, wondering if I was inside. They were afraid I'd been abducted. Then they thought up a ruse: they asked an embassy guard to take me an extra robe for warmth. I couldn't figure out why they would be sending me clothes while I was having my interview with Zhou."[36]

But there was nothing lighthearted about the meeting with Zhou. The youthful Dalai Lama was alone during the interview, his advisers all barred from the room. The trio of men he faced—Premier Zhou Enlai, Marshal He Long, and Ambassador Pan Zili—had the advantage of age and experience, and seemed to represent China's political, military, and diplomatic domination of Tibet. Mustering his nerve, the Dalai Lama voiced his fear that the Communist Party would force unacceptable reforms on the Tibetans. In response, Zhou offered him a new concession from Mao: an offer to shelve the Democratic Reforms in Tibet for six years, at which point it would be up to the Dalai Lama whether or not to implement them. The Dalai Lama thought it best to reserve judgment on this offer, however.

Zhou continued to evade the Dalai Lama's questions about the troubles in Kham, focusing instead on the refugee problem. Beijing and Lhasa should work together, he suggested, to persuade the refugees to go back where they came from.

But then he turned to a thinly veiled threat: "We will not tolerate the outbreak of armed insurrection [in Tibet]. . . . Our best course of action right now is to dissuade people from rash action. The last thing we want is to provoke any untoward events there." He pressed the Dalai Lama again to return directly to Lhasa as soon as possible, and to travel by air instead of taking the land route through Kalimpong. India would not support him or allow Tibetans to create trouble in India, he warned, and he had cautioned Prime Minister Nehru to be on the lookout for any "provocative, destructive activities of the imperialists in India." Moreover, the Panchen Lama had already canceled his plans to visit Kalimpong, and it would create an impression of disunity if the Dalai Lama went there alone. He also reminded the Dalai Lama in no uncertain terms that the Communists stood ready to use military force to pacify any uprisings that might break out in Tibet. The Dalai Lama replied by injecting a note of praise for the stature of religiosity in India.[37]

The Dalai Lama had not completely decided whether to visit Kalimpong. In addition to the "imperialist elements" and "separatist elements" that Zhou was warning him about, there were also thousands of ordinary people in Kalimpong who were eagerly anticipating his sermon.

Tensions within China, and within the Communist Party, had driven Zhou to revisit India for a second meeting with the Dalai Lama. For two years, change had been sweeping across China: large-scale "socialist transformation of the city and the countryside," the "high tide" of the agricultural cooperative campaign, and the general rise of leftism in the Party. But the resistance to Land Reform in the minority ethnic regions, especially among Tibetans within China's borders—and now even within Tibet—was getting out of hand. That was why Mao and the top echelons of Chinese Communist leadership had decided to moderate their original plans for Tibet. Still, their long-range goal had not changed. The Democratic Reforms would be imposed eventually, by military force if necessary, but the process could wait until Mao and the Central Committee felt the time was ripe.

In November 1956, five days before the Dalai Lama's trip, Mao had touched on "the dear Dalai Lama" in a speech to the Central Committee. Warning that the CCP Tibet Work Committee and the PLA Tibet Military Command needed to make a plan in case the Dalai Lama didn't return, he ordered them to "strengthen fortifications and stock up on grain and water" in preparation for war. He went on to sneer: "If one Dalai runs away, I won't miss him. And if nine more come along and ten of them run away, I won't miss them either."[38] Mao's tone had toughened markedly since the letter he had sent the Dalai Lama in August acknowledging "flaws" in the Party's work. Fan Ming believed that this shift was Mao's response to the intelligence reports Fan had been sending him about the Dalai Lama's opposition to the Democratic Reforms in Kham.[39]

Fan failed to see through Mao's bluster, however. The very fact that Mao felt it necessary to make this statement belies the insouciance of his speech, as does Zhou's return to India to try to lure the Dalai Lama with Mao's new offer to postpone Land Reform in Tibet.

Marshal He Long also called on the Dalai Lama in Delhi to pressure him to return to Lhasa. In a personal interview fifty years after these events, the Dalai Lama recalled the proverb that He Long quoted him: "The snow lion looks dignified if he stays in his mountain abode, but if he comes down to the valleys, he is treated like a dog."[40]

At this point in the interview, the Dalai Lama recalled with a chuckle, "So sometimes I reflect that fifty years have passed, and I not only have not turned into a dog, but have even become a more prestigious snow lion than I was in Tibet."[41]

After his second meeting with the Dalai Lama, Zhou paid a visit to Nehru. He had the trump card up his sleeve: he was ready to offer Nehru a significant concession on the long-disputed Indo-Chinese border if Nehru would refuse the Dalai Lama safe haven. Nehru was unable to resist.

: : :

Bhakra Dam, in the northern Indian state of Himachal Pradesh, sits at the entry to Bhakra Gorge, in the upper reaches of the Sutlej River, an eastern tributary of the Indus. Seven hundred and forty feet high, the colossal dam was the hub of India's water conservation program in the area. It was one of Nehru's pet projects, and he inspected the site more than ten times during its construction. An added attraction of the dam for Nehru was his villa in the secluded Sutlej Sadan garden nearby. The villa opened onto a stone path leading to the Glass House, a small pavilion overlooking the river, where he would relax in the breeze, or entertain visiting dignitaries. In 1954, several days of pleasant conversation with Zhou Enlai there had produced the "Five Principles of Peaceful Coexistence" between India and China.[42]

Two years later, on December 31, 1956, Nehru and Zhou met again in this picturesque spot, this time to begin a round of private talks that they concluded on their train ride back to Delhi late that night. The conversation began with Nehru's account of his recent visit to the United States, where he had met with Eisenhower at his Gettysburg farm. Among other things, he told Zhou, he and Eisenhower had discussed the Hungarian uprising, and Eisenhower had said that America did not intend to support Hungary militarily.

The mention of Hungary launched Nehru and Zhou into a gentlemen's debate, which reveals a split in their attitudes that had far-reaching implications for their policies in Asia, and for the fate of Tibet in particular. Zhou saw the events in Hungary as a product of the struggle between socialism and capitalism. While conceding that socialist countries did not necessarily "do everything well in making progress," he blamed the uprising on defeated "landlords and capitalists . . . supported by subversive activities of Western countries." Nehru, on the other hand, viewed nationalism as paramount. As he put it, "socialism has to be based on nationalism or otherwise it is weakened." He saw the Hungarian uprising as "mainly a national uprising of the workers, students, and youth . . . to get rid of foreign domination, namely, that of Soviet Union." The forceful imposition of a socialist system on Hungary deprived its people of national freedom. This was the crux of the matter for Nehru: "A great majority of Hungarians do not oppose socialism, but they want their own people to run the Government and the feelings are very strong on this point."[43]

Nehru deplored the use of violence in the name of socialism:

> Shooting down is not any solution . . . can socialism succeed by military force, without freedom? Is it compulsory socialism? These problems arise. The Hungarian uprising may have been suppressed, but the Hungarian people cannot be won over that way . . . [the Soviet use of force has] harmed the cause of socialism . . . and many of us who are friends of USSR [Union of Soviet Socialist Republics] are very much distressed and find it difficult to justify what has happened there.

Zhou strongly disagreed. While acknowledging that nonviolent persuasion was preferable, he maintained that military force was often justified:

> Yes, to win over the people one must use persuasion and socialism will win, if only people accepted it. This is one thing. But to put down internal or external forces of reaction which are originally oppressing people, it is necessary to have military strength. Counter-revolutionaries can also be a part of the people or sent from outside and hidden among the people. . . . After the success of the revolution, again military strength is necessary to defend socialism from foreign aggression and internal subversion. So, these are two different matters.

With regard to Tibet in particular, he warned that "our [enemies] are trying to carry out subversive activities, but they will not be successful."

A little later in the conversation, Zhou pointedly addressed the problems he saw surrounding the Dalai Lama's proposed visit to Kalimpong. There were more than ten thousand Tibetans in Kalimpong, he told Nehru. If the Dalai Lama went there, he was sure they would cause trouble and try to keep him there. Nehru seemed somewhat skeptical that there were so many Tibetans in Kalimpong, suggesting that some of them might be Tibetan-speaking Sikkimese or Nepalese. Still, he acknowledged that Kalimpong was a "nest of spies," and that they might even outnumber the original inhabitants. Nehru must have been aware that there were also Chinese Communist spies, sent by the CCP Tibet Work Committee, in Kalimpong.

Nehru assured Zhou that if the Tibetans of Kalimpong caused any trouble, the Indian government would take action. He asked Zhou to spell out his concerns so that India could try to address them with preventive measures. Zhou hedged:

> The situation is really very complicated and it is difficult for me to say as to what specifically might happen. . . . There are two possibilities: (1) . . . We have already raised this matter seriously with the Dalai Lama. Now the Dalai Lama will naturally go back and talk to his officials and maybe perhaps nothing would happen except some small quarrels or verbal exchanges and he returns to Lhasa safely. Alternatively, (2) a possibility is that attempts might be made at Kalimpong to detain [the] Dalai Lama. In fact, that is exactly the slogan raised there: "Won't let Dalai Lama go back."

Zhou added that if any such incidents occurred, the Indian government should "intervene and check them."[44]

Equipped with Nehru's assurance, Zhou scheduled a third session with the Dalai Lama on January 1, 1957. This time, he finally delivered his reply to the Dalai Lama's questions about the troubles in Kham: "Xikang can be divided into two regions: one embraced the reforms without rebellion; the other is the Lithang area, which was more recalcitrant. Some troublemakers there got the wrong idea and besieged our troops. They starved our officers and men for several days, so we mobilized the Air Force to drop in some food. Another battle broke out at that point. We've sent a team in to take care of the aftermath."[45] But Zhou simply neglected to mention that the Air Force had dropped bombs in Kham in addition to food.

Zhou had another meeting with Nehru right after this conversation with the Dalai Lama. Later that day, Nehru distributed a summary of his talks with Zhou to the Indian ambassador to China, the Indian political officer in Sikkim, and the Indian foreign secretary, concluding his document with an injunction that it be kept top secret.[46]

On January 2, Nehru saw Zhou off at the airport. A photograph of the occasion shows the two men facing the camera in a cheek-to-cheek embrace. Strictly speaking, Nehru is embracing Zhou. Nehru looks genuinely happy, while Zhou has a cryptic smile. He had succeeded in depriving Tibet of its only possible ally, and in choking off the possibility that it would receive military aid. In the shadow behind them stood the eighteen-year-old Panchen Lama, eyes cast downward, his face impassive. The Dalai Lama was not in the picture, as if Tibet had become a secret bargaining chip between the two great powers.

His mission accomplished, Zhou returned to Beijing.

: : :

On January 2, 1957, the same day he saw Zhou off at the airport, Nehru met with the Dalai Lama, who did not know about Zhou and Nehru's secret talks at Sutlej Sadan and on the train back to Delhi. At those meetings, Zhou had unveiled his tantalizing offer to Nehru: to abide by the controversial "McMahon Line"[47] as the border between China and India. Here are his words:

> People like me never knew about [the McMahon Line] till recently. Perhaps [Prime Minister of Burma] U Nu might have told Your Excellency that we studied this question and although this Line was never recognized by us, still apparently there was a secret pact between Britain and Tibet and it was announced at the time of the Simla Conference. And now that it is an accomplished fact, we should accept it. But we have not consulted Tibet so far. In the last agreement which we signed about Tibet,[48] the Tibetans wanted us to reject this Line; but we told them that the question should be temporarily put aside. . . . But now we think that we should try to persuade and convince Tibetans to accept it. . . . The question will be decided after the Dalai Lama's return to Lhasa. So, although the question is still undecided and it is unfair to us, still we feel that there is no better way than to recognize this Line.[49]

Zhou had linked the Dalai Lama's return to Lhasa with a Chinese territorial "concession" to India. The McMahon Line was key to settling the long-standing Indo-Chinese border dispute. The 1914 Simla Convention, signed by Tibet and British India—but rejected by China (under the Guomindang) on grounds that Tibet was part of China—had determined a Tibet-Indian border at this line, which had served as the boundary and preserved the peace between the two during the period of Tibet's de facto independence from 1914 to 1951.[50] But the Chinese invasion of Tibet had thrown the boundary into question again, raising the specter of

Chinese claims to the disputed territory and placing India in a worrisome face-to-face with China's military juggernaut. Zhou was keenly aware of Nehru's hope that China would accept the McMahon Line, which would provide India with a generous Tibetan buffer zone.

Nehru, seasoned politician that he was, got the hint. Realizing immediately that it was in India's interests to acquiesce to Zhou, even if Tibet had to pay the price, he shot back: "Our policy has been to deal with the Chinese Government about Tibet and the treaty on Tibet was also signed with the Chinese Government. We are naturally interested in what happens in Tibet as one of our near neighbours but we don't want to interfere."[51]

The Dalai Lama had no say in the matter. By this time, the PCART had been operating in Lhasa for six months. The Dalai Lama had told Nehru in November that his government had been effectively stripped of all authority in foreign affairs, as Tibet's Foreign Ministry had been subsumed under the CCP Tibet Work Committee before the establishment of the PCART, and the Lhasa government, the Panchen Lama's Administrative Council in Shigatse, and the Chamdo Liberation Committee all now answered to the PCART.

The outside world remained oblivious to the Tibetans' troubles. Nehru placed a ban on "anti-Chinese propaganda" in the Indian media, restricting reports on the Tibetan uprisings.[52] The United States, which was clandestinely aiding the Khampa rebels, had to keep quiet. And as China's ally, the Soviet Union also maintained silence, even though Soviet experts helping the Chinese build Damshung Airport, the first airport in Tibet, had been attacked during raids on the PLA by the Tibetan Chushi Gangdruk guerrilla forces.

On January 22, 1957, the Dalai Lama went to Kalimpong, while the Panchen Lama flew directly back to Shigatse on January 28.

: : :

In Kalimpong, the Dalai Lama stayed in Bhutan House, where his predecessor, the Thirteenth Dalai Lama, had also stayed, in refuge from a Chinese invasion decades earlier. He and his cabinet ministers huddled with Tibetan exiles there, including his two elder brothers, Gyalo Dondrup and Taktser Rinpoché, and W. D. Shakabpa, former finance minister of Tibet, to discuss his choices.

Shakabpa presented him with a petition decrying the Communists' destruction of monasteries and expropriation of property in Kham and Amdo, and begging him to stay in India to mobilize international backing for Tibetan independence. Gyalo Dondrup reported that the United States had agreed to support their cause. Sensing that the promised American support might be insubstantial, Cabinet Minister Ngabo left for Lhasa on his own. The historical record bears him out: United States aid turned out to be limited.

Unable to make up his mind, the Dalai Lama consulted the Nechung Oracle, who told him: "Return." On his way back through Sikkim, he had to wait for a month in Gangtok until Nathu Pass was clear of snow. Chinese embassy officials kept up steady pressure on him all the while to go back to Tibet.

On February 11, 1957, Pan Zili, the Chinese ambassador to India, reported to the Central Committee that the Dalai Lama was going to leave Gangtok on February 14, cross the Tibetan border the following day, and arrive in Lhasa in mid-March after making some stops along the way for religious activities.[53] His report is a catalogue of the serious problems at hand:

> The Dalai Lama keeps repeating that he has concerns about our work in Tibet and about the problems in Xikang. He is sympathetic to the Tibetan exile community in India, and sets great store in the opinions of Lukhangwa,[54] whom he may try to restore to his former post.
>
> The Dalai Lama says that he is going to try to learn more about his people's grievances as he performs his religious duties on his way back to Tibet, because he says Tibetans have no suitable channel for redress, and no one pays any attention to their complaints. He plans to raise these grievances once he gets back to Lhasa, even if Zhang [Jingwu] curses him and beats him, and to send a delegation to console the people of Xikang. In fact, he wants to go there personally to see if the people there might be willing to listen to him, and whether they are amenable to the possibility of uniting with Central Tibet into a "Unified Greater Tibetan Autonomous Region." . . .
>
> He says that Tibet must depend on China for construction for the time being, as Tibet has no ability to complete the task on its own, but that once construction is complete, Tibet should have nation status,

> with a relationship toward China like that of the Eastern Bloc nations toward the Soviet Union.
>
> He maintains that although we Chinese make an outward display of respect for Tibetan religion by donating to temples and presenting white silk prayer scarves, our confirmed atheism leads us to downgrade the importance of religion when we should be appreciating and promoting it.[55]

Ambassador Pan's report intimates that despite the Dalai Lama's ostensible high position, he had to approach Zhang Jingwu as a supplicant, and that Zhang was highly unreceptive. It also indicates that even though the Dalai Lama's government had refrained from taking action on behalf of the rebels in Kham, he was willing to plead their case to the Chinese.

In mid-February, the Dalai Lama set out sadly for Lhasa. His entourage had dwindled. The Panchen Lama had already flown back to Shigatse. Lobsang Samten, the Dalai Lama's beloved elder brother, had decided to stay in India, as had his minister Yuthok, who had been sent from Lhasa according to ancient protocol, to ask him to return. Instead of fulfilling his ritual task, Yuthok had warned the Dalai Lama that the situation in Lhasa was dire, urged him to seek refuge in India, and stayed there himself. Despite these desertions, the Dalai Lama was locked into his plans. On February 25, 1957, he reached Dromo.

Meanwhile, Gyalo Dondrup's efforts were coming to fruition. The Far Eastern Division of the CIA had established a Tibet task force and sent a representative to ask him to recruit Tibetans for training as agents. There were plenty of willing Khampa youths in Kalimpong. Gyalo Dondrup had chosen six of them—including twenty-six-year-old Wangdu Gyadotsang and twenty-five-year-old Athar Norbu—and they were on their way to the training camp.

In Tolung Dechen County of Tibet, on the outskirts of Lhasa, the political commissar of the PLA Tibet Military Command, General Tan Guansan, and the Tibetan Communist Phuntsok Wangyal, were waiting for the Dalai Lama with a message: the unrest was spreading in Chamdo. Tan Guansan asked the Dalai Lama to send a group of eminent lamas, including the Sixteenth Gyalwa Karmapa,[56] to urge the people to lay down their arms.[57]

: 3 :

Tragedy at Lake Qinghai

TSO NGONPO—"TEAL SEA" in Tibetan—is a vast blue lake set among snowcapped peaks at ten thousand feet above sea level in the northeastern corner of the Qinghai-Tibetan Plateau. In Mongolian, "teal sea" is Kokonor, and in Chinese, it is Qinghai, the eponymous lake of Qinghai Province.

Qinghai, which lies outside the Great Wall, remained for thousands of years beyond the fold of Han Chinese culture. Tibetans comprised between 80 and 90 percent of the population of Qinghai before the seventeenth century. Mostly as a result of Han Chinese immigration, this had diminished to approximately 29 percent by 1950, around the time of the founding of the People's Republic of China.[1] In geographic terms, however, regions classed administratively as Tibetan still account for more than 97 percent of the total area of Qinghai today. These include the Tsolho, Malho, Tsojang, Golog, and Yulshul[2] Tibetan Autonomous Prefectures, and the Haixi[3] Mongolian and Tibetan Autonomous Prefecture. Most of Qinghai was once the northeastern Tibetan province of Amdo (the remainder was Kham), and the majority of the Tibetan inhabitants are nomadic herdsmen who speak the Amdo dialect of Tibetan. Under their traditional social system, which lasted until 1958, there were a few hundred tribes of varying sizes, controlled by hereditary headmen. Each tribe had its own army, temples, and laws, and there were periodic clashes over conflicting claims to pasture, which resulted in shifting alliances and rifts over the ages.

The rapid flux in mid-twentieth-century China did not leave these remote peoples untouched. Soon after 1949, the Chinese Communists began to use Qinghai as their gulag, sending thousands of political prisoners there for "reform through labor." Meanwhile, for the indigenous Tibetans, the region was transformed into a land of carnage and famine. According to official Chinese data published in 2000, the total Tibetan population of Qinghai grew from 434,535 in 1950 to 513,415 in 1957, but dropped sharply to 408,132 by 1963.[4] In other words, between 1957 and 1963, the population had shrunk by 20.5 percent, at an average rate of 17,547 people per year, ending up with 26,403 fewer people than it had started with in 1950. These figures belie the rosy claims of the Chinese Communists that they had "liberated the downtrodden Tibetan people." What had gone wrong?

In oral interviews, Tibetans from Qinghai inevitably mention the year 1958. That was the year of the Great Leap Forward, but even more traumatic for Tibetans was the cruel "pacification of rebellion" ordered by Qinghai Party Secretary Gao Feng. Gao was later scapegoated, but he was doing Mao's bidding.

: : :

In April 1958, the Chinese Communist crackdown on an uprising of Tibetans and Salars in the Xunhua[5] Salar Autonomous County in eastern Qinghai, a predominantly agricultural region, ushered in an ominous shift in CCP ethnic policy. Although it was only one among many localized uprisings that the Chinese Communists deemed "counterrevolutionary armed rebellions" in this period, its brutal suppression became a model for handling minority resistance in general. As such, the "Xunhua Incident" of 1958 merits study as a precursor to the "Lhasa Incident" of 1959. The following account of the uprising is based entirely on official Chinese Communist sources, some of which have not yet been declassified.

Xunhua was an ethnically diverse area, with Salars, who were Muslims, comprising the largest group, but there were also Tibetans, Mongolians, and Han Chinese, as well as other groups such as the Hui, Bonan, and Dongxiang. The Communists had established a relatively quick foothold in Xunhua. By 1952, only its four predominantly Tibetan townships were still untouched by Land Reform; the other seven townships had already completed the process. The Xunhua Salar Autonomous County administration was installed in 1954.

In the summer of 1955, Mao delivered a landmark speech at Zhongnanhai, the CCP headquarters in Beijing, signaling a major shift to the left and calling for faster collectivization of agriculture; this was the speech in which he famously rebuked "some comrades" for "tottering along like a woman with bound feet" right on the verge of the "high tide of social transformation in the countryside."[6] Qinghai Party Secretary Gao Feng, who was in Mao's audience, hurried home from Beijing to initiate the leap into socialism, and quickly churned out a series of urgent directives for rapid collectivization. Practically overnight, Xunhua County rushed more than 90 percent of its farmers into collectives. Haste notwithstanding, the process did not trigger an uprising.

At this point, Beijing started to push for more. In early October 1955, the Central Committee approved its "Decisions on Agricultural Cooperation,"[7] which stipulated that by the spring of 1958, most of the country should have instituted first-stage Agricultural Producers' Cooperatives, a step on the way toward complete socialist collectivization.

Some regional United Front leaders, alarmed by the violence in Sichuan, decided to speak out. For example, the Buddhist master Geshe Sherab Gyatso, vice-governor of Qinghai, spoke at the First National People's Congress in June 1956 to urge the Party to "pay attention to the unique features of ethnic minorities during the high tide of collectivization." In July 1957, he repeated his hope that the Party would "respect the unique features of Tibetan culture and proceed cautiously with social reforms." He also proposed that "pilot programs for the collectivization of Tibetan nomads err on the side of leniency rather than severity," and that "taxes paid by monasteries . . . be reduced."[8] His suggestions fell on deaf ears, however; the nation was engulfed in a whirlwind of collectivization.

Spurred by the twin tempests of the Great Leap Forward and the Anti-Rightist Campaign, the leadership of Qinghai resolved to "complete the democratic revolution and the socialist revolution simultaneously."[9] There was no need to be finicky about the process; it was fine to "use any means necessary to accomplish the revolution."[10]

In November 1957, the Qinghai Party Committee divided the pastoral regions of the province into three types, and a staggered plan was devised for collectivization, taking into account the differing conditions in each of the three. This plan was scrapped a few months later, however. In March 1958, Qinghai Party Committee Vice-Secretary Zhu Xiafu lambasted the "rightist" former Qinghai governor, Sun Zuobin, at a provincial Party plenum, while calling for "actively spreading the high tide in animal husbandry" and completing the "socialist transformation" of all nomads within five years. The system of Agricultural Producers' Cooperatives was to be imposed province-wide, with specific targets for each area. Aware that the collectivization process had already ignited rebellions among Tibetans in Sichuan, Yunnan, and Gansu, the Qinghai Party Committee—following a Central Committee directive—instructed all autonomous prefectures and counties in the spring of 1958 to "use meetings and study classes to rein in the minority religious leaders" so as to "prevent revolt."[11]

Accordingly, Jnana Pal Rinpoché of Bimdo Monastery in Xunhua was bundled off to the county seat for what the Communists called "study classes," along with some other religious leaders. He was vice-commissioner of the county, but his status as a venerated senior monk and former tutor to the Panchen Lama—a native of Xunhua—mattered much more to the pious Tibetans, and the attempt to muzzle him provoked their outrage.

By 1956, three of the four Tibetan townships in Xunhua County (the farming townships of Karing, Bimdo, and Dobei) had instituted higher-level cooperatives, leaving the pastoral county of Kangtsa, with its intact tribal system and its own hundred-man army, as the principal remaining target for collectivization. On April 17, 1958, a popular revolt broke out there, led by livestock owner Nori Ponpo, demanding the halt of collectivization and the release of Jnana Pal Rinpoché. The rebels took the township Party branch secretary captive and chopped down electric poles. The next day, their protest escalated into an armed clash in which the head of the Communist Party's task force was killed, and there was some opportunistic looting of local government buildings and stores.

At this point, the Salars joined the revolt. Led by a Salar headman and an imam, on April 24 four thousand rebels of various ethnicities surrounded the county seat, where they assaulted cadres and looted stores. At dawn on April 25, two PLA regiments crossed the Yellow River and marched in to "neutralize the rebel bandits." The Salar leaders had gotten wind of the PLA mobilization and fled during the night with their men, however, leaving behind all the civilians, many of whom were still demanding the release of their *rinpoché*. The PLA opened fire immediately upon arrival, no questions asked. Despite the lack of resistance, the "battle" raged for hours. When the soldiers finally realized how powerless the "rebel bandits" were, they held their fire and found that the dead and wounded were all virtually unarmed. A "counterrevolutionary armed rebellion" had been victoriously "pacified" within the short space of four hours. There were 719 civilian casualties, including 435 dead. After the battle, the PLA conducted a manhunt, and in a single afternoon took 2,499 prisoners, including 1,581 Salars, 537 Tibetans, 38 Han Chinese, and 343 Hui people.[12]

When Jnana Pal Rinpoché heard the news, he took his own life, right at his "study class." Afterward, the official verdict was that he had been the organizer of the incident and that he had committed suicide "to evade punishment,"[13] but the details of how he was supposed to have masterminded this uprising from his confinement have never been made public.

The government side sustained seventeen casualties, along with property losses totaling nine hundred thousand yuan, including grain, oil, cash, and varying degrees of damage to a couple of hundred buildings.

This episode, which has gone down in Chinese history as the "Xunhua Counterrevolutionary Uprising," lasted a full week and spread from Kangsta to a total of seven townships (four Tibetan and three non-Tibetan) distributed widely across the county. All but one township (Kangtsa) had been collectivized in some way or other prior to the revolt: two of them directly, skipping the Land Reform stage, and the remaining four through the two-stage process of Land Reform and collectivization.

Allowing for a Communist slant, we can deduce the extent of the antagonism toward collectivization from official sources, which complain, "numerous landlords, rich peasants, and upper-middle peasants took advantage of the turmoil to extract livestock and farm equipment and try to break up the Agricultural Producers' Cooperatives." Official sources also reveal that a surprising number of Communists in the affected areas joined the resistance: 68.4 percent of the Party members and 69.5 percent of the Communist Youth League. Almost half of them—156 Party members and 262 Communist Youth League members—took part in the attack on the county seat. Some of these people were later charged with being "core elements," or with "opportunistically looting state property."

On May 2, Xue Keming, vice-governor of Qinghai, delivered a detailed report to the Provincial Party Committee on what he called the "Xunhua Bandit Uprising," in which he listed the numbers killed, captured, and wounded, and outlined the punishments for the rebels. He pronounced the incident "a planned, organized, armed counterrevolutionary rebellion led by at-large counterrevolutionary elements, in collusion with puppet army officers and administrators, landlords, and rich peasants." He also presented eleven guidelines for dealing with the aftermath. The second of these guidelines, "Policies and Regulations for the Treatment of Captives," listed twenty-one different gradations of punishment, depending on the social status of the captive. Targeted for the heaviest punishments were "monastery religious personnel," who were, without exception, to be sentenced to long prison terms and "paraded before the masses as living teaching materials or caricatured in cartoons." In a section on "quelling future counterrevolution," Xue warned: "Our policy toward counterrevolutionaries should be severe rather than lenient. We need to crack down hard." He added: "There are no quotas for this task. We must show no mercy."[14]

: : :

Soon afterward, in the summer of 1958, another armed revolt broke out in Qinghai. This time it was Tsikorthang[15] County of Tsolho Prefecture, a predominantly pastoral region, in which 61 percent of the total population of 16,572 were nomads. There were 10,840 participants in the rebellion, of whom 1,020 were monks and nuns from ten different monasteries.[16] So many of the inhabitants of the county were involved that the government officially designated it a "rebel area," attributing the uprising to "opposition to the leadership of the Chinese Communist Party, opposition to socialism, and opposition to collectivization."[17] But why hadn't this happened earlier?

In early February 1958, the National People's Congress in Beijing had issued a hard-line call for the suppression of ethnic minorities. Wang Feng, vice-chairman of the State Ethnic Affairs Commission, delivered a speech in which he pushed for "the struggle to rectify and criticize local nationalism." This message was interpreted in Tsikorthang County as license for a campaign, conducted in tandem with the rapid collectivization drive, to arrest and hold formal "struggle sessions" against local ethnic religious leaders. In April came the "Speak Bitterness Struggle," and official sources boasted: "More than 130 'Speak Bitterness' gatherings were held . . . at which more than 20,000 tales of bitterness were told, and all of the local livestock owners, headmen, and religious leaders were struggled against. . . . 217 monastery personnel were also locked up for 'training.' "[18] What were these mysterious "training" sessions? In fact, they were secret prisons, or distribution hubs for the prison system. They are little known, even today, but there is conclusive evidence that many people died in them. Among other sources, a Communist Party document published in a classified compendium in the 1980s mentions them as a significant sector of an overall toll of 23,260 deaths caused in Qinghai in 1958 by "wrongful arrest, wrongful verdicts, and collective training."[19]

On May 29, 1958, the nation was plunged into "Three Red Banners"[20] hysteria by a *People's Daily* editorial titled "Plant the Red Banner of the General Line [of Socialist Construction] throughout China." That same month, Tsolho Prefecture announced that it had collectivized approximately 86 percent of its herdsmen, which it hailed as the completion of the process. Nonetheless, slightly more than a month later, Tibetans in three counties in Tsolho Prefecture, including Tsikorthang County, rose up in arms against collectivization. Although the public record does not delve explicitly into the rebels' grievances, they can be deduced from a series of Qinghai Party Committee directives issued in late May 1959. Here, for example, is a revealing inside view of the troubles caused by overly zealous Communist procedures in the drive to collectivize livestock:

> When the communes were first established, our inexperience . . . led us to some inappropriate methods. We collectivized all livestock without compensation, regardless of the wealth or social class of the owner. We also neglected key principles such as brigade ownership of the means of production and "to each according to his work." Our problems were compounded by the fact that most of these pastoral regions had only instituted lower-level Agricultural Producers' Cooperatives a few months earlier, or, at best, had only recently progressed to the higher-level Agricultural Producers' Cooperatives. Consequently [once the

> communes were formed], many of the masses, mistakenly believing that "all livestock belonged to the state," and that the masses had become mere "hired hands," stopped taking care of the livestock: [they were] not looking for lost animals, treating sick ones, or even skinning the carcasses of the dead.[21]

Later propaganda described the nomads of Qinghai as utterly destitute and living the lives of "medieval slaves," but an official 1955 census indicates the falsity of this claim—at least in Tsikorthang County. In fact, the nomads there were largely categorized as middle-level, and the economic circumstances of all classes were improving before the setbacks caused by collectivization. The case of the Upper Amchok tribe in Tsikorthang County is illustrative. In 1949, it had 133 households, 5 of which were "wealthy nomads" and 53 were "poor," while most households (75) were "middle-level." In 1955, the tribe had grown to 157 households, with 12 "wealthy" nomads and only 50 "poor" ones, while the number of "middle-level" households had increased to 95. And even the "poor" and "middle-level" nomads owned more animals than they had in 1949.[22]

Again, official documents reveal indirectly that some higher-ups at the provincial level tried to take a stand against the injustices of forced collectivization. This can be seen in a published attack on a Party Committee secretary named Zhang Guosheng, who was accused of leading an "anti-Party clique" and "slandering the People's Communes." His alleged crime was having blamed the communes for "ruining family fortunes and wrenching families apart," and having "slandered the Party for 'stabbing the people repeatedly and leaving them no alternative but to revolt.' "[23]

The devastation caused by the misguided social leveling of the period was compounded by ill-informed, high-handed management of labor and resources. An official report[24] of the debacle in one production brigade of herdsmen acknowledges that 5,324 adult animals died after the livestock was taken over by the commune, and that only 38 percent of the young survived to maturity. The cause of the problem can be inferred from the report: 57 percent of the herdsmen had been forced to switch to farming, a poor economic decision for the terrain. Their livelihood imperiled, some herdsmen even turned to "banditry" in desperation and tried to run off with livestock that had originally been theirs, but they were brutally punished for "looting state property."

On July 29, 1958, PLA Infantry Regiment 402 marched into Tsikorthang County and engaged the local nomads in combat for the next five months. By the end of the year, it had "neutralized 6,898 rebel bandits and liberated 6,630 members of the masses." That winter, after the PLA had withdrawn, these "liberated masses" took to the hills again. A local chronicle admits: "The herdsmen in the brigades on the edge of the county fled in droves. From the Wulong and Namthang areas alone, more than 1,900 people left between December 1958 and May 1959."[25]

What caused this mass exodus? Evidently, even Mao knew the answer. He scrawled his approval on the following unusually candid classified report submitted in late May 1959 by the Hainan[26] Counter-Insurgency Command, which held military responsibility for "pacifying" the area:

> Between the PLA withdrawal from Tsikorthang County last year (1958) and February of this year, 235 runaways were retrieved, but because Party policy was not correctly implemented, there were indiscriminate killings, with disastrous results for our work. In Namthang Township, ten who surrendered were arrested and sentenced, but four of the arrests were entirely mistaken, and five people were wrongly executed. When the Melang tribal headman Lhatse surrendered in response to a letter from Secretary Dalo of the County Party Committee, he brought back with him more than fifty followers, but they were all arrested and dealt with summarily. A Kharku tribal headman who surrendered was killed while under transport toward Tahupa. At present we have insufficient information to confirm the precise number of people mistakenly arrested and killed county-wide. Sometimes we can find the killer but don't know who issued the orders. Although these events took place half a year ago, local witnesses of the killings have exhumed the victims' corpses, and this has damaged our credibility. The rebel bandits refuse to surrender, insisting, "the Communists can't be trusted." . . . Therefore, we haven't managed to convince anyone to come back since February. Instead, a thousand more people have run away to join the bandits.[27]

Popular support for the rebels was endemic in the Tibetan community. The Hainan Command's report reveals:

> Most production brigades in the county are harboring evildoers with connections to the rebel bandits. Whenever our cavalry in Namthang

leaves town on a mission, the bandits hear about it and swoop in for some quick looting, always managing their getaway by the time the cavalry returns. This has happened six times, with no arrests made. The masses are confused and have not ostracized the enemy. Four hundred forty-one people ran away to join the bandits between January and May 15 of this year. . . . When the people of Ngama Valley were moving their yurts on March 16, they deliberately put their old and weak yaks at the front of their procession and their 660 dairy-producing *dri*[28] at the rear so that the bandits could seize them all from behind. . . . Countywide, more than a thousand people have fled to join the bandits since the PLA withdrew last year. Some of the masses even house the bandits without reporting them to the authorities.[29]

The strife in Tsikorthang County was compounded by the acute food shortages caused by the state monopoly, as collectivization provided a convenient avenue for the imposition of rapacious levies. In 1957, the state took 57.31 percent of the grain and 88.6 percent of the vegetable oil in the county, leaving 26.4 kilograms of grain and virtually no vegetable oil as an entire year's per capita ration. In 1958, the levy was eased somewhat, but the rations were still inadequate: the state took 35.94 percent of the grain and 83.5 percent of the vegetable oil, leaving only 78 kilograms of grain and 0.06 kilograms of vegetable oil per capita.[30] Theoretically, meat and dairy were staple foods for the herdsmen, but they were no longer permitted to slaughter their animals, which were now collective property. Famines ensued. According to the Hainan Command's report:

Severe grain shortages are occurring in the pastoral regions, compounded by poor management. . . . The masses in Namthang Township have resorted to eating the spoiled flesh of yaks and goats that died last winter, which has caused widespread illness and death. Lhamode, a woman from Shuanglonggou, encountered six runaway rebels while gathering firewood. They asked her: "Will they kill us if we surrender?" She replied, "There's nothing to eat, so you'll die either way." In Namthang Township, 319 people—comprising 24.7 percent of the population—have died of illness since last November. The masses report that these people died of starvation (although the actual causes vary), and they are blaming us. One hundred sixty-five people ran away to join the bandits between last December and this May 10. The grain shortage has had far-reaching effects and is hurting our efforts to win over the enemy. The Provincial Party Committee has reportedly set standard rations for these regions of approximately 250 grams per person per day, but some districts have had to cut that amount by about one-third. Another factor in the scarcity has been poor management that has failed to actively seek out substitute sources of nutrition.[31]

One-quarter of the inhabitants of Namthang died of starvation at this time, but even so, the PLA was vying with the local people for food. Instead of returning the escaped animals "retrieved" during its "pacification" campaign, it had appropriated them to create three ranches for its own use.

With a very few notable exceptions, Party officialdom generally tended to cover up the famine, submitting overblown reports of success instead. Here is a typical example, from a report delivered on January 9, 1959, by Qinghai Party Secretary Gao Feng:

> In 1958, we took a great leap forward in all aspects of socialist construction, and socialist revolution was victorious in the pastoral areas of our province. . . . Total grain production reached eleven hundred million kilograms, a 71.96 percent increase over the year 1957, the actual increase in grain production for this single year already being almost double that called for in the entire First Five-Year Plan (2.69 hundred million kilograms). We've crossed the Yellow River in a single leap! . . . If we calculate based on the current population, it comes to an average of almost five hundred kilograms per person.[32]

The actual figures indicate that this report was false, at least in the case of Tsikorthang County, where the yearly grain yield was in fact less than one hundred kilograms per capita, before the state levy.[33]

In September 1958, the herdsmen of Tsikorthang County were desperately hunting for game and scavenging for silverweed and other edible plants. Incredibly, at this moment of crisis, they were deprived of precious pastureland to accommodate six thousand Han Chinese "pioneer" immigrants from Henan. The herdsmen were cowed into giving up their land by Vice-Chairman Wang Feng of the State Ethnic Affairs Commission, who warned that questioning the desirability of Han Chinese immigration into minority regions was tantamount to doubting the desirability of "socialism and prosperity for our ethnic minorities."[34]

The Han Chinese pioneers did not bring "prosperity," however, and untold numbers of them perished of hunger and disease. Their farms were disbanded within a few years, and most of the survivors returned home, leaving behind a wake of environmental devastation. To make matters worse, that was the year everyone in Qinghai had to jump on the Party bandwagon to forge "backyard steel."[35]

By December 1958, almost one-third of the nomads of Namthang Township had died in the famine. Many of those who had managed to flee were tracked down and "neutralized" by the PLA. There is evidence that internal directives were circulated to the PLA permitting indiscriminate shooting throughout officially designated "rebel areas," of which Tsikorthang County was one. By the time Mao scribbled his approval on the Hainan Counter-Insurgency Command's eye-opening report in the spring of 1959, 7,217 of the Tsikorthang County Tibetans had either starved to death or been "neutralized."[36] This figure constitutes 43.5 percent of the original total population of 16,572; it does not even include those who were soon to be rounded up in the upcoming Four-Antis Campaign.[37]

On June 29, 1958, the Qinghai Party Committee reported to Mao that there had been "counterrevolutionary armed insurrections" all across Qinghai. Uprisings had raged across 6 autonomous prefectures and 24 autonomous counties, involving 307 monasteries, and more than 100,000 people of 240 tribes. The number of known rebels constituted one-fifth of the Tibetan population of Qinghai.

Mao inscribed his approval on the Qinghai Party Committee's report: "It is extremely good that the counterrevolutionaries of Qinghai are rebelling. This will create an opportunity for the laboring masses to be liberated. The policy of the Qinghai Party Committee is absolutely correct."[38] In reality, it was precisely the "laboring masses" who were the rebels. Nevertheless, the Qinghai Party Committee had received Mao's blessing.

On July 5, the Qinghai Party Committee submitted a second report to the Central Committee, which, while purporting to "sum up the lessons" of the Xunhua uprising, provided a dogmatic justification for Chinese Communist abuses in ethnic minority regions. It started from the dangerous premise that the contradiction at the center of ethnic strife was actually "class struggle," and that it was "bourgeois" and "utterly mistaken" to "harp on contradictions between ethnicities" instead. In other words, since "class enemies" rather than any ethnic differences in culture, religion, history, and customs were at the root of the conflicts in Qinghai, the correct response of the Party should be to crack down.

This was the theoretical underpinning for the ensuing religious persecution of ethnic minorities. The Xunhua uprising, the report claimed, had demonstrated that "the religious question" was "the main ideological obstacle to the Party's taking root in the ethnic minority regions." The problem, it maintained, was that religion was obstructing the process of "making Communists out of minority Party and Youth League members." This, it continued, was because "78 percent of the Party and Youth League members who joined the rebels had extremely confused ideas about religion"; they wanted "to 'protect religion,' preferring to forsake the Party rather than forsake their religion, or even preferring death to forsaking their religion."

As a remedy, the report urged that the Party "do penetrating work in the monasteries, completely transform the thinking of religious personnel, plant the 'red banner,' and uproot the 'white banner.'" It would be necessary to "fully discredit the reactionary religious leadership, singling out the rightists and publishing exposés of the worst of them . . . and to take over the battleground of the monasteries, placing the banner of religion firmly in the hands of the progressive elements of the religious community." The report concluded grandly that it was essential to "continue to strengthen the dictatorship of the proletariat and thoroughly suppress counterrevolutionary elements."[39]

After approving this report from Qinghai on August 27, the Central Committee forwarded it to all relevant local Party committees, including the CCP Tibet Work Committee, along with a reiteration and endorsement of its main points. "In a class society," it reminded its readers, "the ethnic problem is essentially a class problem, and thus the ethnic problem can never be solved until the class problem is under control." Moreover, ethnic minority Party members who still clung to religion needed to be educated about "atheism, and about drawing a clear line between Communism and nationalism, and between theism and atheism, in order to firmly establish a Communist worldview and become bona fide Communists."[40] This Central Committee seal of approval essentially gave local Party branches the green light to ride roughshod over the cultures of minority peoples and to destroy their religious institutions.

In the case of the Xunhua uprising, the Qinghai Party Committee was guilty of a massacre. But cover-ups were endemic to Communist Party practice; in fact, they were necessary to survival in officialdom at all levels in the hierarchy. In instances such as the Xunhua uprising, it probably seemed safest to the culpable officials to label the victims of the massacre "counterrevolutionaries" and to pronounce the matter "a life-and-death class struggle."[41]

The circulation of the three documents discussed above illustrates a dangerous flaw in the Chinese Communist Party's policy-making process. The upper echelons of Party leadership in the cities were dependent on the information they received from their subordinates in remote regions, but these subordinates often chose to report only good news to protect themselves. This Catch-22 in the information flow heightened the risk of local incidents ballooning into national catastrophes. This is one of the principal lessons of the Xunhua uprising.

:::

In the second half of 1958, the Campaign to Reform Religion roiled the Tibetan regions of Qinghai, Sichuan, Gansu, and Yunnan. Ostensibly targeting what the Communists termed "feudalism," this campaign laid temples to waste and persecuted believers far and wide. The extent of the destruction is openly vaunted in the official sources. The Qinghai representative to the National United Front Bureau reported in Beijing in late 1958, "since August . . . 731 of the 859 Tibetan Buddhist monasteries in Qinghai have been disbanded, and 24,613 of their original 54,287 religious personnel have been returned to the laity to take part in production."[42] The Ngaba Tibetan Autonomous Prefecture in Sichuan reported laconically that of its 320 Tibetan Buddhist monasteries, "seven were designated for preservation as national cultural heritage sites by the government."[43] It did not mention the fate of the rest.

The crackdown on religion was particularly intense in the Kanlho[44] Tibetan Autonomous Prefecture in Gansu, the province's main Tibetan region. According to a later official Chinese source, at the start of the campaign there were 196 Tibetan monasteries with 17,096 monks, including many *tulku*, abbots, and other religious officials. By the end of 1958, all but four of the monasteries[45] had been dismantled or repurposed. Four thousand one hundred monks had been killed or captured in battle, and thousands more were arrested, leaving a total of 11,431. Of these, only 249 of the frail or elderly were allowed to stay in the four remaining monasteries. The rest were sent back home to be "reformed," or to makeshift prisons for "training," where untold numbers died in the harsh conditions.[46]

Mosques and churches were also ravaged in this campaign. Drotsang[47] County of Qinghai reported the following:

> In our religious reform campaign between September and December [1958], we confiscated the property of 18 Buddhist monasteries and 5 mosques, which we auctioned, donating the proceeds to the county. We arrested 43 top religious leaders and repatriated the remaining 320 religious personnel to their original homes to take part in agricultural production. . . .[48]
>
> Two of the 18 monasteries are being used as commune offices, 10 are serving as feedlots for production brigades, and one has become a potato processing plant. One of the 5 mosques has been converted into a county museum, another is now a commune granary, and two have been torn down. Two of the 4 Catholic churches are being used as commune granaries and one has been turned into a people's hospital. . . . We have arrested 3 caretakers, 7 monastic officials, 11 ordinary lamas, one imam, 2 *mawlas,*[49] 13 Islamic school directors and local elders, 5 ordinary believers, and one Catholic nun. We have sent 12 young believers to study classes and put 18 people to work. Six people have committed suicide.[50]

As the passage above suggests, the Campaign to Reform Religion was not purely ideological; it also cloaked considerable expropriation of property. Along with the abolition of all the privileges held by the monasteries, the campaign also annulled their real estate property rights and seized their fields, forests, livestock, and business capital. At Kumbum, the leading monastery in Qinghai, the Communists reported confiscating "twenty different kinds of items, including gold, silver, cash, jewels, jade artifacts, fine clothing, and daily use articles, worth a total of almost 1.6 million yuan (in 1959, 535,000 yuan was returned as mistakenly confiscated)."[51]

In October 1958, Vice-Chairman Wang Feng of the State Ethnic Affairs Commission justified all this in the name of "class struggle," directing Party cadres to "mobilize the masses" to "oppose the exploitation of religious privilege," but to avoid any public mention of "reforming the religious system."[52] The Qinghai Party Committee spelled this disingenuous strategy out even more explicitly:

> Religious reform is actually class struggle, pitting the poor against the rich, the common people against the aristocracy, and the lower classes against the upper classes. The socialist revolution will not be victorious unless we . . . obliterate the large livestock owners as a class. . . . But . . . if we want the masses to accept our slogans, we should keep quiet about our aim to reform the religious system. Instead, we should speak of purging the religious institutions of counterrevolutionary elements and eliminating their feudal exploitative privileges. This strategy will take us to our goals of reforming the religious system and expediting socialist revolution.[53]

The Chinese Constitution guaranteed religious freedom, but the Party apparently saw this promise mainly as a cover for its atheistic program. To quote Wang Feng: "Why do we speak of protecting freedom of religion? We must not discard this clause of our constitution. As long as we keep it on the books, counterrevolutionary elements won't be able to accuse us of destroying religion."[54] This strategy is spelled out more explicitly by Ji Chunguang, head of the United Front Bureau of the Qinghai Party Committee, in his instructions concerning the Party's propaganda work: "The only reason we play up our policy of 'religious freedom' and 'strengthening our religious work' is to win the trust of the religious masses so that we can gradually increase restrictions on religion until we have eradicated it completely."[55]

The effect of this rhetoric was painfully apparent to the victims of this modern Inquisition. Religious activities were banned as reactionary, becoming grounds for arrest, public humiliation, and imprisonment. Believers risked their lives to hide heirloom Buddhist statues, sutras, and altar supplies underground, in caves, or on river bottoms. Votive lamps, prayer wheels, incense, and scriptures were all proscribed. To elude the fierce scrutiny of the cadres, the "local activists," and the armed militia, the faithful held clandestine prayer sessions in their yurts. Someone was posted to stand watch outside, and the worshipers would quickly try to look busy with chores if cadres or militia members were spotted in the distance. Repatriated monks and nuns who were seen to be moving their lips were arrested for praying silently and subjected to "struggle sessions."[56]

The situation degenerated to the point where even the armed forces charged with crushing the resistance felt compelled to advocate mercy for the persecuted believers. The Hainan Counter-Insurgency Command recommended that local governments "show respect for Tibetan customs and allow the masses to conduct reasonable religious activities in the open." It also urged that "monks who had been returned to lay life be permitted to continue to say their prayers," and that Tibetan women be allowed to "wear their traditional small plaits and hair ornaments instead of Chinese-style pigtails."[57] Since Mao initialed this document, we can assume that he and his government in Beijing were aware of the causes of Tibetan unrest.

Oppression catalyzed more uprisings across the province, and the official policy for their suppression was avowedly brutal. Xue Keming, vice-governor of Qinghai, is on record as having made the following grim statement at an important meeting on September 14, 1958: "We must arrest all of the religious authorities and reactionary headmen. None must escape our net. If they die, we must make sure that they die in prison. This is preferable to having them die [outside of jail] in their social milieux."[58] Yang Shufang, the chief of Public Security for the province, echoed him: "Within the next three years we must wipe out every last one of the religious authorities, running dogs, and henchmen of the feudal class, as well as all die-hard counterrevolutionaries."[59]

Once the PLA had quelled each uprising, it would cast its dragnet far and wide: all the able-bodied men of a given tribe might be sent to a reform-through-labor farm, or locked up for "training." Their families were branded "counterrevolutionary relatives" and strictly monitored. The extent of the devastation is clear from the official reports of "success."

In 1958, the Tsolho Tibetan Autonomous Prefecture claimed to have "handled a total of 16,727 assorted criminals," including "10,276 sent for 'training,' and 6,451 arrestees."[60] In Gepa Sumdo[61] County of the prefecture, 36 percent of the total population was blacklisted as "rebel family members, returned monks and nuns, released criminals, and captives."[62]

In Chentsa[63] County of Malho Tibetan Autonomous Prefecture, where only certain regions saw rebel action,[64] the official tally was 618 acknowledged rebels, including 25 CCP members, 24 Communist Youth League members, one township-level cadre, 398 ordinary people, and 2 lamas. This group comprised almost 17 percent of the total population (3,646 people) in the "rebel areas" and about 3 percent of the total county population of 21,310. The Communists were able to "win over most of the rebels politically," which meant that 596 of them were induced to surrender. However, 2,074 more people were arrested in the ensuing mop-up campaign, equaling more than half the population of the "rebel areas," and almost 10 percent of the total county population. Of those arrested, 561, that is, 27 percent of the arrestees, died in reform-through-labor camps. The arrestees included a number of people associated with the United Front: "40 currently in office, 9 who had been dismissed, and 117 in 'training.'" During the process, 38,500 yuan of savings was confiscated, and five people committed suicide.[65]

Here is what happened in Chikdril[66] County in the Golog Tibetan Autonomous Prefecture:

> We arrested and imprisoned 1,050 people—802 in 1958, 116 in 1959, and 132 in 1960—comprising 9.57 percent of the total population of the county. In 1962, in response to the new policy set during the Central Committee's Northwest Bureau Ethnic Minority Work Conference, we reexamined the cases of all arrestees, and 862 were determined suitable for release. As of July 15, 1963, we had released 258 of them and ascertained that 346 of them had died in reform-through-labor camps. Two hundred fifty-eight more who had been sent to the camps were unaccounted for. No further action was taken.[67]

In other words, almost 10 percent of the county population was arrested, more than 80 percent of the arrests were wrongful, and well over half of the arrestees perished or disappeared in the process.

Rusar[68] County of Qinghai, the Dalai Lama's birthplace,[69] reported, "in 1958, 1,479 people were arrested and sentenced, of whom 414 died and 75 were crippled." Later, 1,207 of these people were exonerated.[70] In other words, 81.6 percent of the arrests were ultimately deemed wrongful, 28 percent of those arrested lost their lives, and 5 percent were crippled.

In Yulshul Tibetan Autonomous Prefecture, the slaughter created ghost towns and "widows' villages." Young men escaped death by donning their sheepskin jackets inside out as camouflage and hiding among their flocks of sheep.[71]

Prominent citizens mysteriously disappeared forever, including numerous ethnic minority religious leaders who had—under the United Front policy—been entrusted with government posts and helped the Communists establish power. Following a Central Committee directive, the authorities in Qinghai lured such people—some of them *tulku* and Thousand and Hundred Household leaders—to political study classes or meetings that turned out to be the deadly, secret prisons known as "training." One person jailed under this policy was the Seventh Rongpo Drubchen, Lobsang Thinley Lungtok Gyatso, formerly an "eminent patriotic personage," governor of Malho Tibetan Autonomous Prefecture, and member of both the National People's Political Consultative Conference and the State Ethnic Affairs Commission.[72]

Two decades later, after Mao's death, the Tibetans of Qinghai finally began—with great difficulty—to obtain some measure of redress for their grievances. On June 2, 1979, the Supreme People's Court of Qinghai Province announced the release of 122 prisoners who had been held as "rebels" since 1958,[73] and in 1981, the provincial government finally began to rehabilitate many people who had been unjustly accused.

Arjia Rinpoché, abbot of Kumbum Monastery in Qinghai—one of the paramount monasteries of Tibetan Buddhism[74]—reveals how difficult it was to make this happen. As he recalls, the man who started the ball rolling was Tashi Wangchuk, secretary of the Qinghai Party Committee at the time, and one of the first ethnic Tibetans to attain a leadership position in Qinghai.[75] He encountered stubborn resistance to the idea at all tiers of the Communist bureaucracy. The local cadres who had actively participated in the "pacification" campaign presented the biggest obstacle, because they had risen to their posts in reward for suppressing the "insurrection," and were at most willing to concede grudgingly that some excesses might have occurred. But Tashi Wangchuk took his quest to Beijing, where he repeatedly sought out Central Committee members and finally gained the support of Deng Xiaoping in early March 1981.

A man who helped him reach this goal was Li Wei, chief of the Qinghai bureau of the newspaper *Guangming Daily*. In January 1980, he composed an internal document titled "Excesses in the Qinghai Pacification Struggle," pointing out that there were injustices still awaiting correction. With Tashi Wangchuk's permission, he submitted the document to Beijing, where it landed on the desk of Hu Yaobang, then director of the CCP Organizational Department. Hu transmitted the document to the three most powerful men in the nation: Deng Xiaoping, Hua Guofeng, and Li Xiannian.[76] Thus, when Tashi Wangchuk sent his personal petition to the Central Committee, Deng expressed approval.

With Deng's recommendation, the Central Committee authorized the official request from the Qinghai Party Committee for redress of 1958 grievances later in March.[77] Equipped with this backing from on high, Tashi Wangchuk and the Qinghai Party Committee bypassed the obstinate local cadres and unsealed classified local archives under heavy security at a closed-door session. In those archives, which were quickly locked up again, they discovered shocking evidence of the crimes against the minorities of Qinghai, which finally served as the basis for political rehabilitation and minimal financial restitution for many deceased "counterrevolutionaries," and for their families.[78]

In 2003, the Chinese Communist Party officially acknowledged—albeit in an obscure collection of documents—that atrocities had been widespread in 1958, and placed the blame on Qinghai Party Secretary Gao Feng:

> In pacifying the rebellion, Gao Feng disregarded the dual nature of Party policy: "in military matters, strike back with force; in political matters, use persuasion and mobilize the masses." He made undue use of military force, emphasizing that "use of the military is the way to unmask feudalism in the pastoral areas." He issued orders to shoot to kill whenever possible in battle, and advocated the "summary execution of any captured reactionary headmen by firing squad." Some army units

> and regional personnel shot captives and prisoners at will, and horrific, unforgivable crimes were committed.[79]

This assessment accords with the historical facts, although it refrains from mentioning that Gao Feng's actions were encouraged, and sanctioned, by Mao himself.

By early 1959, the Tibetans of Qinghai had been brought into the Chinese Communist fold in the name of "democratic reform," but at immense human cost. The provincial authorities boasted that they had "neutralized" more than eighty thousand "rebel bandits" and arrested more than thirty-nine thousand "reactionaries and bad elements"[80] in the "high tide of socialist revolution."[81] In some areas of the province, more than 20 percent of the population had been arrested. Countless people died in the "pacification" campaigns or in the Great Famine[82] of the ensuing years.

All but a few Tibetan monasteries had been demolished, occupied, or closed, and religious activities had been forced underground. The monks had been evicted from Kumbum Monastery; instead, the premises now housed a Class Struggle Exhibition. At this monastery alone there were 427 cases of arrest and sentencing, later officially overturned as "mistaken."[83] Land Reform was complete, and, as in the Han areas, people had been pushed into communes, where many had to smelt "backyard steel," eat in canteens, or donate their valuables to "aid national construction." There was an extra twist for the Tibetans: in the name of "transforming their customs," many were required to adopt Han ways such as arranging their yurts into permanent "streets" and switching to Chinese styles of dress, to say nothing of giving up their pastoral economy and lifestyle in favor of farming ill-suited to the terrain.[84]

Nonetheless, the plight of these remote borderland peoples was little known among the Chinese public. The nomads of Qinghai were even more isolated than the Khampas, and the outside world was unaware of their ordeal. With regard to Tibet proper, the Party's stated policy was to "postpone the reforms for six years."[85] Although this sounded lenient, everyone knew that it was only a matter of time before "reform" came to these regions.

Meanwhile, a highly classified project that would further impact the Tibetans of Qinghai was underway: "Nuclear City," where China's first atomic bomb and hydrogen bomb would be developed, was under construction at a place called Jinyin Tan, on the steppes of Dashi[86] County in the Tsojang Tibetan Autonomous Prefecture. As Mao elbowed his way into the nuclear club, he shifted away from his United Front policy and clamped down on the indigenous minority peoples of Qinghai.

Almost ten thousand Mongolian and Tibetan nomads were forcibly relocated to realize Mao's dream.[87] On October 20, 1958, with a mere day's notice, the nomads were hustled out of their homes and onto the road by a group of cadres and land reclamation militia. Ordered to leave their yaks, dogs, and yurts behind, they were able to take only the simplest of household items. Hundreds froze or starved to death in the bitter cold of their early winter march on the high plateau.[88]

With Qinghai as a model, Mao was ready to turn his attention to Tibet. On June 24, 1958, he inscribed a postrebellion report from the Qinghai Party Committee with the following: "We must prepare for the possibility of large-scale rebellion in Tibet. The bigger the rebellion, the better."[89] In July 1958, PLA General Staff Headquarters sent twenty-eight armored vehicles into Tibet, thirteen to Damshung Airport, and the remaining fifteen to the PLA Tibet Military Command in Lhasa.[90] Soon thereafter, on August 18, Deng Xiaoping, general secretary of the Central Committee Secretariat, instructed Commander Zhang Guohua and Vice-Commander Deng Shaodong of the PLA Tibet Military Command to consolidate their positions and increase vigilance, while allowing the "rebellion" to build up a head of steam. The idea was that the bigger the uprising, the harder the Party could crack down, and the more "thorough" the "reforms" could be.[91]

The full story of Communist social engineering and the crushing of opposition among the Tibetans of Yunnan, Gansu, Sichuan, and Qinghai in the 1950s is rightly the subject of another book; it has been touched upon in these chapters only as necessary background to the crisis in Lhasa in 1959. While the suppression had been relatively complete in Qinghai, war persisted in both the Ngaba and Garzê regions of Sichuan, prompting the Communists to impose their program at gunpoint under a policy known as "simultaneous fighting and reform." Analogous patterns were repeated in Yunnan and Gansu, which, for reasons of space, shall be mentioned here only in passing. In Yunnan's main Tibetan region, the

Dechen Tibetan Autonomous Prefecture, the cycle of Land Reform, rebellion, and suppression lasted from late 1956 through 1958.[92] Gansu's Kanlho Tibetan Autonomous Prefecture, home of most of the province's Tibetans, was particularly hard hit. The devastation of its monasteries has been discussed above; moreover, as the Chinese Communists themselves later admitted, their campaigns destroyed tens of thousands of lives.[93]

By the end of 1958, the Chinese had largely won their battle in all four provinces—at a staggering cost to the Tibetans. Now they were ready to attempt the same in Tibet.

: 4 :

Uneasy Spring in Lhasa

IF A CITY could be said to have a heart, then the heart of Lhasa is the magnificent temple known as the Jokhang. It is the Tibetan holy of holies, for centuries the destination of endless streams of pilgrims who pour in from afar, performing grueling full-body-length prostrations after every third step of their journey. Established in the seventh century by Songtsen Gampo, the first king of the Tibetan empire, the temple has been renovated and expanded over the ages. The main hall boasts one of the oldest Buddha statues in Tibet, a golden figure of the twelve-year-old Sakyamuni brought by Princess Wencheng from China,[1] and worshiped by Tibetans as "Jowo Rinpoché." The 380 prayer wheels around the main hall have been spun by millions of devout hands over the centuries. The turning of the prayer wheels ushered Lhasa into the year 1959, an Earth-Hog year in the traditional Tibetan calendar.[2]

: : :

The year 1959 was special for Tenzin Gyatso, the Fourteenth Dalai Lama. He was going to turn twenty-four, making it a portentous "critical year" for him in the Tibetan calendar.[3] For many of his people, this was a potent symbol: they believed that he, and therefore the Tibetan people as a whole, were at risk. But the Dalai Lama himself had other things to think about: he was studying for his *Geshe Lharampa*[4] final examinations at the Jokhang Temple during the upcoming Monlam Prayer Festival.

He had begun his rigorous education shortly after being recognized as the reincarnation of the Thirteenth Dalai Lama and brought to Lhasa as a child. After he assumed temporal powers at the age of fifteen, his two tutors—Ling Rinpoché and Trijang Rinpoché—accompanied him wherever he went, even on his travels to China and India, so that his training would continue uninterrupted. He never let his studies lapse, no matter how overwhelming affairs of state became. His lofty position as the head of Tibetan Buddhism did not exempt him from the traditional requirement for all monks seeking the doctorate: to win the degree on his own merit by debating the sutras with a committee of eminent Buddhist scholars, in the presence of the hallowed Sakyamuni statue and a distinguished audience. His preparation was as intensive as that of a doctoral candidate in a Western university getting ready for his or her thesis defense.

But the Dalai Lama's people were in crisis. The flames of war were licking his land, although the cities of Lhasa and Shigatse had so far been spared. And unbeknownst to him, Mao had already issued instructions to his men in Lhasa to prepare for war in Tibet.

: : :

It was June 16, 1958, in the brief summer on the Tibetan plateau. A ragtag band of a few hundred men from thirty-seven different tribes, headed by former Lhasa merchant Gonpo Tashi, had gathered in a valley in Triguthang, Lhokha,[5] a couple of hundred miles from Lhasa. They were farmers, nomads, peddlers, and monks. They carried their own rifles, flintlocks, hunting guns, and swords, and wore their everyday clothes: leather or felt boots, assorted caps, and the traditional Tibetan robes known as *chupas,* with the sleeves tied around their waists. At the head of their scraggly formation was a tall wooden flagpole grounded in a pile of stones, flying a yellow flag that rippled against the ultramarine sky.

The wind from the high plateau swept down the valley, unfurling the flag and revealing a pair of gleaming holy swords crossed on its field of yellow, the symbolic color of Tibetan Buddhism. One had a sharp, fiery blade, representing the wisdom of the Bodhisattva Manjushri. The other was blunt, and stood for valor and strength.

The Chushi Gangdruk Defenders of the Faith Army was born.[6]

"Gonpo Tashi never expected to win," his eighty-year-old nephew, Kelsang Gyadotsang, commented in an interview at his New Jersey apartment more than fifty years later, gazing across the Hudson River at the view of Manhattan. In one corner of his living room hung the Chushi Gangdruk flag, originally designed by an anonymous *thangka* artist. A few yellowed photographs on the table showed men in bulky Tibetan robes facing the camera with bashful smiles: ordinary, unsoldierly men robbed of their homeland, ready to fight to the death in desperation.[7]

In addition to its significance as a self-defense force, the Chushi Gangdruk also marks a major milestone in modern Tibetan history. Having appealed to the aristocrats in Lhasa and found them wanting, the ordinary Tibetan people had chosen to take matters into their own hands. The founding of the Chushi Gangdruk also signifies a rift between the Khampas and the Chinese. The Khampas, who made up most of the Chushi Gangdruk, had been considered the most pro-Chinese Tibetan subgroup, and much of Kham had been under Chinese rule since the late Qing dynasty. Historically, they had not aligned themselves with Lhasa, and had even tended toward separatism, but now they cast their lot in with Tibet as a whole.

:::

In Lhasa, the CCP Tibet Work Committee needed the cooperation of the Tibetan cabinet to get things done. In the first place, the Seventeen-Point Agreement allowed the Tibetan government to retain authority over certain parts of Tibet, including Lhasa. In addition, the committee knew that the people of Lhasa would listen only to their cabinet. The committee did not trust the cabinet, and it tried to turn the historical animosity between Lhasa and the Khampas to its own advantage.

Accusing the cabinet of surreptitiously backing the Khampa "bandits," the CCP Tibet Work Committee asked it to send Tibetan troops to Lhokha to quell the activities of the Chushi Gangdruk, and to issue an ordinance forbidding the people of Lhasa from communicating with or aiding the rebels. But even though the flocks of Khampa refugees in Lhasa were also a headache for the cabinet, it could not bring itself to send its army to Lhokha. Hastily concocting an excuse of "military weakness," it refused to deploy its troops, and complied only with the request to issue the ordinance.[8] Faced with the cabinet's insubordination, Generals Zhang Guohua and Tan Guansan each called on the Dalai Lama to pressure him into giving the desired order.

Caught between the insistent Chinese and his duties to his suffering people, the Dalai Lama was distraught. The situation was beyond his control. He knew that even if he did send Tibetan troops to fight against other Tibetans in Lhokha, they might never come back; they would probably join the rebels instead, bolstering the resistance. As a compromise, the cabinet resolved to send a peace delegation to convince the Chushi Gangdruk leader Gonpo Tashi to lay down his arms. Given the Khampas' lack of faith in the cabinet, this plan was a setup for failure. The Khampas had founded their volunteer army out of sheer exasperation with the cabinet's appeasement of China.

Nonetheless, after extensive deliberations, the cabinet chose a five-man peace delegation, headed by Tsi-pon Namseling,[9] who was known for his good relations with the Khampas. The delegation never returned, however—its members joined the resistance instead.

Their choice seemed reasonable from the Tibetan point of view, and it demonstrated widespread sympathy for the Khampa rebels in Tibetan society at all levels, even among government officials. But it fueled Chinese suspicions that the Tibetan government was collaborating with the rebels and might cast its lot with them at any time.

Whether one called the Khampas' actions a "rebellion" or "resistance" depended on what one regarded as legitimacy. For the CCP Tibet Work Committee and the PLA, the central Party leadership in Beijing represented unquestioned authority, and resistance against it—whether in intention or in action—was heresy. But such reasoning went against the grain for Tibetans, for whom heresy meant opposition to the Dalai Lama and his government.

In early November 1958, the cabinet called a large group of monk and lay officials, including representatives from Lhasa's "great three" monastic universities to a special plenary meeting of the National Assembly, held over a number of days at the Norbulingka Palace. It was the Tibetan tradition for such meetings to be relatively open exchanges of opinion, intended to arrive at consensus through lengthy discussion. Consensus, however, could be elusive when knotty topics arose. To complicate matters, the Tibetan government was split into two mutually distrustful factions. The Communists had managed to win some Tibetan support through their United Front policy, which had been in effect since 1951. Cabinet Minister Ngabo was considered pro-Chinese, and if he was present, the other cabinet ministers kept their true feelings to themselves. The middle- and lower-level bureaucrats were divided, and many of them were reluctant to speak up against their superiors. Cabinet members tended to censor themselves even in closed sessions, and were far more wary of speaking their minds at such large gatherings, lest someone report them to the Communists.

After the initial large-group session, the participants divided into small discussion groups. Kelsang Dramdul, the Tibetan Army delegate, delivered a fiery oration to his group: "The government has been providing for and promoting our Tibetan Army up to now for a reason, and if this milk-fed baby conch is of no use when hurled into the jaws of the threatening sea monster, then it serves no purpose at all. We soldiers are ready to fight whenever the government gives the order, and we will give our lives in defense of the Buddhist polity."[10] A cabinet secretary suggested that the Dalai Lama be temporarily evacuated from Lhasa for safety's sake, possibly even to Europe, "while we recruit every able-bodied Tibetan to fight for our freedom."[11] Later, the Communists cited these individual opinions, which never became formal resolutions, as evidence for their spurious claims that there had been a conspiracy or that the Dalai Lama had been abducted.

Nothing substantive emerged from the plenary meeting, despite days of talk. The small groups submitted suggestions to the cabinet, but there was no follow-up. The gathering brought the divisions within the Tibetan government into sharp relief, however. Those at the bottom of the hierarchy tended to support the resistance, while those at the top advocated compromise and forbearance,[12] and these divisions became more marked with time. There were a couple of uncontroversial decisions. One was to send a delegation to Beijing to "dispel the central Party leadership's misconceptions about our local government."[13] Such a plan suggests that the leadership in Lhasa may have been unaware of the Chinese preparations for war. The other decision was to step up security around the Dalai Lama, adding more gate guards and round-the-clock patrols at the Norbulingka, recalling guards from vacation, and transferring guards back from Shigatse to Lhasa.[14]

The status quo returned after the meeting was done. The cabinet continued its watchful waiting and the Dalai Lama kept studying for his examinations. But bands of Tibetans slipped out of Lhasa to join the resistance in Lhokha, among them hundreds of Tibetan Army men. The ranks of the Chushi Gangdruk Defenders of the Faith swelled quickly.

: : :

Tenpa Soepa filed into the Jokhang Temple amid a stream of worshipers and stood before the golden statue of Sakyamuni to say his morning prayers before starting the day's work.

The Tibetan New Year was approaching, and crowds of worshipers were flocking into the city. People left their homes well in advance every year to arrive in Lhasa in time for the yearly Monlam Prayer Festival. This year had the added attraction of the Dalai Lama's oral examinations, and monks were pouring in from all over Tibet to watch.

Tenpa Soepa stood before the statue, his palms pressed together. After performing three prostrations, he left the temple and went up to the second floor of the building. The Jokhang complex also housed government offices, and the Ministry of Finance had been on the premises ever since the days of the Seventh Dalai Lama in the mid-eighteenth century. The Reform Bureau, where Tenpa Soepa worked, was also here.

The Reform Bureau was new. The Dalai Lama had established it in 1952, in response to his glimpse of his people's poverty during his evacuation to Dromo as a teenager. Under the leadership of cabinet ministers Ngabo and Surkhang, the new bureau had drawn up seven proposals to address such problems as corvée labor, district administration, rents, and taxation. All officials, monastic and lay, were to be placed on government payroll, and the bureau was to review district tax ledgers. There was also discussion of appropriating land from the manors and redistributing it to the peasants, but the aristocracy protested. "If you take away the pastures, you lose the flowers too," they warned, meaning that once they were deprived of their land, they would no longer be liable for paying back their government loans. Although the Reform Bureau was stymied by this impasse,[15] action plans to address the remaining issues were officially promulgated in 1954.[16]

Tenpa Soepa was in charge of payroll at the Reform Bureau. He sat down at his desk and sipped a cup of tea brought by an attendant while he caught up on the morning's gossip. "I hear that Gyalwa Rinpoché[17] is going to Beijing for the Second National People's Congress," said one of his young colleagues, "and so 'Yuthok House' has made a special trip back here."[18]

News travels fast, Tenpa Soepa thought to himself. In the Lhasa parlance of the day, "Yuthok House" was an epithet for Zhang Jingwu, who lived on the estate of former cabinet minister Yuthok[19] when he was in Lhasa, or for the CCP Tibet Work Committee, which had its headquarters there in earlier years.

The CCP Tibet Work Committee had undergone some recent personnel changes. Zhang, who held the position of director of the Chairman's Office in Beijing in addition to his post as secretary of the CCP Tibet Work Committee, had been absenting himself from Lhasa during winters.[20] And when the Anti-Rightist Campaign had reached faraway Tibet in April 1958, old enmities within the CCP Tibet Work Committee had surfaced, and its deputy secretary, Fan Ming, had been disgraced as an "ultra-rightist" and expelled from the Party.[21] From then on, whenever Zhang Jingwu and Zhang Guohua were out of town, General Tan Guansan, Fan Ming's replacement, took charge.

It was impossible to keep a secret in Lhasa, with its tight-knit community and whirring gossip mill. The Reform Bureau offices in the Jokhang Temple, located in the center of town, had become a convenient gathering place and news hub for the local elite.

"Has Gyalwa Rinpoché agreed to go?" asked one of Tenpa Soepa's colleagues.

"I heard that he has, but the cabinet is worried about it," someone interjected. "And the great three monastic universities don't like the idea either, so nobody knows if he's going."

"When is the Congress?" someone asked.

"I heard the date isn't settled yet," was the reply.

"I don't think this is a good time for Gyalwa Rinpoché to go to Beijing," said Tenpa Soepa, picturing the sandbag fortifications on top of the "Chinese people's" houses in the Barkor neighborhood.[22]

A prayer bell clanged outside the window, and Tenpa Soepa went to look outside. In the yard was a group of Khampas prostrating themselves in the direction of the main temple. Tenpa Soepa watched them with mixed feelings. Lhasans like himself tended to dismiss the Khampas as hicks, but now, with the aristocratic leadership paralyzed, these crude men seemed to have an answer, and Lhasans were regarding them with new respect.[23]

: : :

The palpable antagonism in Lhasa was setting Chinese nerves on edge. Quietly, the PLA Tibet Military Command ramped up its capabilities with the establishment of a Lhasa militia on November 8, 1958, while the Tibetan government was holding its special National Assembly meeting at the Norbulingka. Militia members, some of them PLA veterans, were recruited at Chinese-run shops, post offices, banks, and newspaper offices, and organized into companies and platoons, which were merged into battalions. At the battalion level, there were machine guns and mortars, and each militia member was equipped with a rifle or a submachine gun and four hand grenades. They began their military training immediately and posted round-the-clock sentries.[24]

On November 16, the CCP Tibet Work Committee warned the Central Committee that the Tibetans planned to send a delegation to Beijing with what it saw as deceptive intent. It said: "[They intend] to cajole the high echelons of leadership into overriding us, and to shirk responsibility for pacifying the rebellion and maintaining order. They're trying to lead us astray." As a response, the committee recommended the following: "Our general policy should be to try to keep them divided. The more they strive for unity, the more we should try to divide them, and the more they try to avoid responsibility for maintaining the peace, the more we should force it on them."[25] The CCP Tibet Work Committee's shrewd maneuvering stands in stark contrast to the disarray and vacillation of the Tibetan leadership.

The reply from Beijing arrived a month later. While it saw no need for a Tibetan delegation to visit Beijing, it wished to invite the Dalai Lama to the Second National People's Congress in the spring. Such a reply demonstrated that the Central Committee was more concerned with obtaining the cooperation of the Dalai Lama and the Tibetan elite than it was with soothing the discontent of ordinary Tibetans. This bias contributed greatly to the later troubles in Lhasa. The Dalai Lama readily accepted the invitation,[26] but neither side anticipated the ramifications of his decision in the turbulent atmosphere of the time.

In December, some middle- and lower-level Tibetan bureaucrats and Tibetan Army lieutenant colonels and captains[27] met in the Reform Bureau office to discuss the Dalai Lama's proposed trip. They resolved to oppose it, and came up with a plan to petition the CCP Tibet Work Committee. Because the meeting had not been sanctioned by their superiors, they took an oath of secrecy, each man touching a photograph of the Dalai Lama respectfully to his forehead as a gesture of conviction.[28] Nonetheless, news of the meeting spread quickly through the grapevine, and it was later cited as evidence of a "conspiracy for rebellion."

Meanwhile, military conflict outside of Lhasa was escalating. From the summer of 1958 through January 1959, there had been a number of battles between the Chushi Gangdruk and the PLA; about 250 Chinese soldiers and cadres were killed, and at least 146 wounded.[29] Between September and December alone, the PLA was ambushed three times, with 109 soldiers killed, 35 soldiers wounded, 10 vehicles destroyed, and 8 machine guns taken.[30]

Although Lhasans were alarmed by the reports of turmoil in other regions, the trouble was still a certain distance away. But things had also started happening closer to home. First was the incident of Kunsang the stable boy. It was Tibetan tradition to add a new palace to the Norbulingka for each new incumbent Dalai Lama, and construction was underway. One day, a stable boy named Kunsang had an altercation with some PLA sentries while driving his horse cart across the Lhasa Bridge to bring back stones for the new building. He brandished his whip at the sentries, and they shot and killed him. Afterward, Zhang Guohua made a special visit to the Norbulingka to apologize to the Dalai Lama.[31] The Tibetans and the Chinese had always been uneasy bedfellows in Lhasa, but now tension was building to the point that even the tiniest spark could set off a conflagration.

Relations between the PLA and the Tibetan Army in Lhasa were highly volatile. The Seventeen-Point Agreement stipulated that the Tibetan Army be gradually subsumed into the PLA, and certain steps were taken in this direction. The PLA allocated some funding for a new Tibetan security guard barracks, and all Tibetan colonels were commissioned as PLA officers in April 1956. Even the Dalai Lama's brother-in-law, Security Chief Phuntsok Tashi,[32] was a PLA colonel. These goodwill gestures notwithstanding, the Tibetan Army resisted complete absorption into the PLA, and a number of skirmishes broke out between PLA and Tibetan soldiers in 1957. One of the more serious of these occurred in October, when three Tibetan soldiers from Regiment 2, on a mission to transport lumber, got into a brawl with a Chinese soldier. He called for reinforcements, who opened fire and killed two of the Tibetan soldiers. Another time, a PLA soldier who came to the Potala Palace, ostensibly to sightsee, was apprehended by the Tibetan security guards on charges of carrying a concealed weapon.[33] These incidents brought the Lhasans' trust in the Chinese Communists to its nadir. Both sides sensed that a larger confrontation was in the offing.

: : :

In January 1959, Juchen Tubten, along with a dozen other Khampa survivors of the Mesho uprising, arrived at the Kyichu River in Lhasa. The winter air was dry and cold, and the mountains along the river valley were a drab olive-brown. Despite the brilliant sun, the men and their horses were exhaling clouds of steam.

Reining in his horse, Juchen Tubten looked up at the Potala Palace on the summit of Marpori Hill, and took a deep breath while he waited for the ferryman to pole over his only wooden boat—instead of one of the usual yak-hide coracles—to transport all the horses. Juchen Tubten dismounted and signaled his men to lead their horses onto the ferry, and they slowly made their way across the river. On the water's clear surface, reflections of the men's weary faces were superimposed on the images of the bleak mountains.

As they went, the ferryman pointed out the landmarks. First they saw the Norbulingka, nestled among a grove of trees on the riverbank. To its east was the Tsedrung Lingka,[34] now housing the PLA Tibet Military Command. Other sacred gardens to the west of the Norbulingka had also been converted to Chinese encampments, and there was an artillery camp on the south side of the river. In the shadow of the Potala, near the Shol neighborhood, they saw the Shuktri Lingka,[35] now the site of Chinese offices. Facing the Potala was Chakpori Hill, topped with the famed Chakpori Tibetan Medical Institute.

With one hand on the reins, Juchen Tubten took in the sights. His heart sank: the strategically arranged PLA encampments had Lhasa by the throat. The Chinese controlled all possible exit routes, and the

Norbulingka and Potala palaces and Chakpori Hill were squarely within PLA artillery range. The ominous new encampment on the south bank of the river boasted cannons big enough to reach any building in the city. If war broke out, the PLA could easily blockade the entire valley, trapping everyone within it.

It was a logistic challenge for the Chinese to maintain this presence in Lhasa at the time. Fighting in Chamdo had cut off both the Sichuan-Tibet and the Qinghai-Tibet Highways, and Chinese cadres had to travel in and out of Tibet under substantial military escort. Highly placed Chinese personnel made the journey by special plane, transferring from the airport to Lhasa under cover of night, the military officers in plain clothes. By this time, fighting between the PLA and the Tibetan resistance had spread from Jomda, near the Chinese border, southward and westward through Tramok, Tengchen, and even to Tsethang, the site of a big PLA garrison in Lhokha, not far from Lhasa. By now there had been hundreds of PLA casualties, and all Chinese organizations in Tibet were operating in a state of high alert.[36]

The ferry reached the north bank of the river. Juchen Tubten and his men disembarked, remounted their horses, and ambled toward town.

Lhasa displayed an outward calm. The refugee tent camp had disappeared during the Cleanup Campaign conducted by the Chinese in April 1958, which had begun with the deportation of all the Han Chinese refugees who had fled to Lhasa from the brutal Land Reform in Sichuan and other nearby areas of China. Next had come the arrest of more than four hundred more such refugees in Shigatse, Gyantse, and Dromo. Then, inspectors had returned to the tent camp in Lhasa to "register" the Tibetan refugees from Kham and Amdo, but they had been quick to flee, and their settlement vanished without a trace in a matter of days. The refugees slipped across the Tsangpo River[37] into Lhokha, where many of them joined the Chushi Gangdruk resistance forces.

Juchen Tubten, now in his late twenties, had been on the road to Lhasa for more than two years. To avoid war zones along both sides of the Drichu River, his group had taken a detour to the north through Sershul, and then zigzagged through adjoining border regions of Sichuan, Qinghai, and Tibet.[38] But this route took him through areas where the Chinese were conducting air raids and ground attacks on the Tibetans, who were fleeing the strife in their homeland in droves.

In March 1958, the Chinese Central Military Commission had ordered the Air Force to begin aerial strikes in the Tibetan regions of Qinghai, and in September of that year it established a foothold closer to its target, at Yulshul Airport in southern Qinghai.[39] From 1958 to 1961 overall, the Chinese conducted 2,731 missions over Qinghai, including hundreds of combat flights.[40] Most of the missions took place in 1958, and approximately one hundred of the combat missions occurred during the first half of that year, while Juchen Tubten was on the road.[41]

In addition to their main purposes of aerial resupply and combat, these missions also provided inexperienced pilots with much-needed practice over the high plateau. As one pilot recalls: "Through this practical tempering, the Air Force pilots learned the basics of maneuvering and maintaining their aircraft on the high plateau . . . and also grasped the principles of the rebel bandits' movements. This experience proved invaluable when it came to successfully pacifying the rebellion in 1959."[42] In officially designated "rebel areas," the PLA men were authorized to kill anyone they regarded as suspicious,[43] and the Chinese pilots were taught that all groups of nomads with livestock and black tents, even if they looked like civilians from the air, were actually the "rebel bandits" whom they should be bombarding. The reminiscences of another Chinese pilot shed light on how Chinese policy led to many civilian deaths:

> To foster unflinching determination in pilots who had never experienced combat, Vice-Commander Sun took them up on scouting missions, providing on-the-spot instruction as they flew over the war zones. On one such mission . . . he asked [pilot-in-training] Min Chaoyu to report what he saw about the enemy, and then he offered his critique and advice.
>
> "The enemy's clothes and yurts are mostly black," he said. "They do not travel in orderly ranks, and they have yaks and horses with them. They look very different from our organized ground troops."[44]

Careful scrutiny of the passage above strongly suggests that the targeted nomads were traveling with their families and livestock; they were probably tribes trying to flee the Communist "reforms." Pilots were taught that the nomads' portable yurt-temples were "rebel bandit command posts," and that their women and children were "abducted members of the masses."[45] Tibetan nomads, who customarily carried rifles to protect their herds and families, probably fired back in self-defense at Chinese fighter planes strafing them from above, but this does not justify Chinese claims that they were "rebel bandits." This misperception emerges even more clearly in the recollections of another Chinese pilot: "To tell the truth, there was not much difference in appearance between the rebel bandits and ordinary Tibetan farmers and herdsmen, especially because the herdsmen all carried rifles on horseback. We chose our targets based on military intelligence, or sometimes we just dropped our bombs on people we saw with guns who were running away from us or shooting at us."[46] To further bolster the pilots' morale, they were heavily indoctrinated with the official Party line, which is still commonplace in China today, on the need for Communist Chinese intervention in Tibet. According to a popular magazine from Qinghai in 1958, Tibetan religious leaders, who spoke of compassion, were actually "callous murderers," who "regularly tortured and killed any who committed even the slightest errors." They had "slaughtered countless members of the laboring masses and used their skulls for rice bowls and their skins for drums; they also killed young women and used their femurs for horns."[47] With this kind of indoctrination, the PLA soldiers' enthusiasm for their task[48] should come as little surprise.

Juchen Tubten witnessed widespread carnage on his travels toward Lhasa. In one spot he discovered a pile of approximately two hundred Tibetan corpses, including women and children. It was explained to him that the deadly Chinese attack on these fleeing civilians—from the air and on the ground—had been a reprisal for a failed attempt by the tribe's men to ambush some Chinese troops. He also encountered ravaged Tibetan encampments all along the way, with corpses of slain Tibetan civilians lying in yurts while their yaks and sheep continued to graze quietly nearby. By turns Juchen Tubten and his men hid, fought, or fled, never sure whether they would make it to their holy capital—and in fact, most of the members of the band had perished by the time he finally reached Lhasa.

Sitting in his little yard half a century later in Dharamsala, Juchen Tubten, more than eighty years old, reflected, "I killed some people when I was young. Those men, those Chinese soldiers, they had parents and brothers too. . . ." The Himalayan sky was blue and cloudless, his hair snowy white in the brilliant autumn sun. "Sometimes I wonder what it was all for," he asked, and then lapsed into silence, staring at the entrance to his house.[49]

: : :

Now that Juchen Tubten and his bedraggled band had arrived in Lhasa, they found a place to stay with a Khampa acquaintance on the outskirts of the city. Leaving their horses and rifles at the house, they went to pray at the Jokhang Temple. After kneeling before the golden statue of Sakyamuni and lighting votive candles, they spun the prayer wheels and then went out for a stroll on Barkor Street.

Lhasa seemed like another world to these young men freshly arrived from the strife-ridden grasslands. Barkor Street was bustling as always: peddlers hawking their wares; customers browsing in Nepalese, Indian, and Kashmiri shops crammed with imported goods; monks strolling in their russet robes; beggars sitting beside the road; old pilgrims circumambulating the Jokhang Temple with their handheld prayer wheels and prayer beads. Still, Juchen Tubten was aware of an almost imperceptible tension in people's faces. All was strangely tranquil, as in the brief calm before a storm.

On January 22, 1959, about the time that Juchen Tubten arrived in Lhasa, Mao directed the CCP Tibet Work Committee as follows:

> During the next few years in Tibet, we will be vying with the enemy for mass support as we both build up our military capability. The final showdown will come within the next few years, maybe three or four, maybe five or six, maybe seven or eight. The Tibetan rulers did not have much military power before, but now they have been reinforced by ten thousand determined, armed rebels—an enemy to be reckoned with. But there's nothing bad about this. It's actually a good thing, because it will probably give us a chance to settle the Tibet question through war. We need to (1) get the masses aligned with us and isolate the reactionaries, and (2) get our troops into good fighting condition. These two tasks will be accomplished during our struggle with the rebels.[50]

In other words, Mao welcomed war in Tibet as a training and proving ground for his armed forces, and as a lead-in to a "final showdown" to "settle the Tibet question."

Juchen Tubten saw no uniformed PLA soldiers on the streets, but unbeknownst to him, they were being indoctrinated inside their encampments, building fortifications by day and conducting drills at night. The artillerymen were poised for action, and PLA trenches had been dug all the way to the banks of the Kyichu River on the edge of the city. PLA Transport Regiment 16 had trucked in massive piles of lumber, and all units were furiously constructing pillboxes and bunkers.

Meanwhile, the Dalai Lama was cramming for his examinations, and the cabinet was embroiled in endless debate. Regiment 4 of the Tibetan Army, which was stationed right next door to the PLA Tibet Military Command's guard regiment, had no inkling of its neighbor's preparations for war.

When Juchen Tubten and his men reached Sungchora Square, just south of the Jokhang Temple, they stopped in their tracks: there were sandbags and brick fortifications on top of a mansion by the street, and in a small bunker over its window, they saw black gun muzzles aimed right at the temple.[51]

1. Portrait of the Dalai Lama with his family at Yabshi House in the early 1950s. *First row, left to right:* The Dalai Lama's eldest sister, Tsering Dolma; his mother, Diki Tsering; the Dalai Lama (seated in the center); his youngest brother, Ngari Rinpoché; Security Chief Phuntsok (Tsering Dolma's husband).

2. The Chinese People's Liberation Army (PLA) entering Lhasa in 1951.

3. Tibetan officials of the 1950s. *Left to right:* Lukhangwa, Shakabpa, Ngabo, Namseling.

4. Tibetan and Chinese officials in Lhasa, 1951. *Left to right:* Ngawang Namgyal (chief of the Ecclesiastic Office), General Li Jue (appointed PLA Tibet Military Command chief of staff in 1952), General Wang Qimei, General Zhang Guohua, the Dalai Lama, General Zhang Jingwu, General Tan Guansan, General Liu Zhengguo, and Phuntsok Wangyal (founder of the Tibetan Communist Party). All of the Chinese officials in the picture, and Phuntsok Wangyal, were members of the CCP (Chinese Communist Party) Tibet Work Committee, although its existence was not revealed publicly until 1955.

5. Founding ceremony of the Patriotic Tibetan Women's League, March 8, 1954. *First row, left to right:* Li Guangming (Tan Guansan's wife), Dekyi Lhatse (Surkhang's wife), Tsetan Dolkar (Ngabo's wife), Yang Gang (Zhang Jingwu's wife), and Tsering Dolma (the Dalai Lama's eldest sister). *Second row, third from the left:* Sonam Dekyi (Lhalu's wife). *Third row, far right:* Rinchen Dolma (Jigme Taring's wife).

6. The Dalai Lama (*center*), with his Senior Tutor, Ling Rinpoché (*left*), and his Junior Tutor, Trijang Rinpoché (*right*), during their 1956–1957 visit to India.

7. The Dalai Lama and Jawaharlal Nehru in New Delhi, 1957.

8. Security Chief Phuntsok, the Dalai Lama's brother-in-law. The single dangling earring is a mark of his official status.

9. Coracle boats crossing the Kyichu River near Lhasa, mid-twentieth century. Boats of this type were used in the Rama Gang ferry, and can still be found in some places in Tibet today.

10. The Potala Palace, showing the Shol neighborhood just beneath it, early twentieth century.

11. Drawing of the bombardment of Lithang Monastery (Jamchen Chokhor Ling), published in Kalimpong in the October 5, 1956, edition of the Tibetan émigré newspaper the *Tibet Mirror*. The original English caption reads: "They are killing several thousand of our freedom loving, brave, ill-armed Khampas, with modern weapons; and distroying monasterees [*sic*]. The world is protesting the aggressor in Europe and W. Asia, but alas! There is no voice for Tibet."

12. Gonpo Tashi, founder and commander-in-chief of the Chushi Gangdruk Defenders of the Faith.

13. Chushi Gangdruk founding ceremony, June 1958.

14. The *vajra* (Tibetan: *dorje*), a Buddhist ritual weapon symbolizing power and enlightenment.

: 5 :

The Exorcists' Dance at the Potala Palace

TIME RACED BY in the charged atmosphere of Lhasa, and soon it was time for Losar, the Tibetan New Year. The Earth-Dog year was on its way out, and the Earth-Hog year was about to begin. On the twenty-ninth day of the twelfth month of the traditional calendar, the day before the Tibetan New Year's Eve, came the holiday of Gutor, the day for exorcisms. Tibetans everywhere observed Gutor with rituals to drive away evil spirits and their attendant illness, disaster, and misfortune, so that people could usher in the New Year with a clean slate and prayers for good luck.

The highlight of the Gutor ritual at the Potala Palace was the ancient masked *Cham* dance. This was performed in all Tibetan Buddhist regions, but had added meaning at the Potala, symbol of the entire nation: the exorcism here was not only for the personal welfare of the Dalai Lama but also for that of Tibet as a whole. Rooted in Tantric tradition, the *Cham* performance transcended mere entertainment. Every detail of form, character, costume, music, movement, and pacing had powerful religious connotations. It was a mystery play, the depth of which could be expressed only by skilled monk-performers, steeped in Buddhist study and practice.[1]

The *Cham* dancers at the Potala were monks from Namgyal, the elite monastery within the palace. Founded in the sixteenth century by the Third Dalai Lama, Sonam Gyatso, Namgyal was headed by the *dalai lamas* thereafter, who also counted as members of its monastic order. In 1959, in addition to the Fourteenth Dalai Lama, Namgyal had 174 monks, who trained there to become officials or to conduct state ceremonies such as the Potala's *Cham* performance.

The Chinese Communist leaders in Lhasa had been invited to the *Cham* performance every year since 1951. Although they were confirmed atheists, they could appreciate the spectacle as folk art, and they found it a rather pleasant exercise in public relations. They were invited as usual in 1959, despite the storm clouds over Lhasa that year.

In 1959, Gutor fell on February 7. That afternoon, crowds of people from the city and its environs streamed toward the Potala. Trudging up the long steep flights of steps into the palace, they gathered in the yellow-painted porticos on either side of its internal courtyard, known as Deyangshar, to view the performance. The underside of each portico was draped with an exquisite brocade canopy, dozens of yards long, with colorful images of protector deities floating among stylized blue clouds, and multicolored fringes that fluttered in the wind. The monks from Namgyal Monastery sat under the canopies, ready to play their musical instruments and chant the sutras when the auspicious moment arrived.

The Potala was divided into the Red Palace—with its halls of worship and holy stupas enshrining the remains of past *dalai lamas*—and the seven-story White Palace, location of the living chambers and political offices of successive generations of *dalai lamas*, their regents, and their tutors in Buddhism. The Dalai Lama's chambers were in Sunlight Hall, on the top floor. On the east side of the White Palace, at approximately the height of a fifteen-story building, was the 1,900 square-yard Deyangshar courtyard. The main door to the White Palace, which was perched above the courtyard, had three sets of narrow wooden stairs: a central one reserved for the *dalai lamas,* and two on either side for everyone else. Above the door were three long rectangular windows, vertically stacked. The Dalai Lama, his cabinet, and various aristocrats viewed the spectacle from these windows, while the ordinary people watched from the covered porticos.

The monk-musicians sounded their five-yard-long copper horns, which were propped on finely carved wooden stands. The loud droning of the horns was joined by dozens of sheepskin drums, punctuated by the clashing of huge copper cymbals. A group of performers in traditional warrior costumes, guardians known in Tibetan as *yushungpas,* burst onto the courtyard. Bedecked in towering feather headdresses and metal armor, and wielding shields, lances, swords, and flintlocks, they whirled in mime of the thrusts and parries of ancient battle, firing earsplitting shots into the air to inspire awe. Then a parade of otherworldly Buddhist creatures pranced in, transporting the crowd to the spirit realm.

Juchen Tubten was in the crowd under the porticos. He glanced up at Sunlight Hall on the top of the White Palace, its golden awning fluttering in the breeze, envisioning the Dalai Lama watching from inside. Little did he know that the Dalai Lama was hosting two Chinese dignitaries at that moment: Deng Shaodong, vice-commander of the PLA Tibet Military Command, and Guo Xilan, administrative director of the CCP Tibet Work Committee.

With a clang of the cymbals, the dancers exited. The horns wailed and the drumbeats pattered like rain. All eyes turned to the door of the White Palace.

Led by Namgyal's "disciplinarian,"[2] a procession of gods, demons, and humans in dazzling masks and brocade costumes, including Black Hats, protector deities, children, Lord of the Cemeteries, gate guardians, Indian pilgrims, King Yama of Hell, stag and yak spirits, and skeletons, danced out the door and down the right-hand staircase.

No one present had any idea that this was the last Gutor *Cham* performance that Tenzin Gyatso, the Fourteenth Dalai Lama, would attend at the Potala.

: : :

The two high Chinese leaders—one military and one civilian—gazed down at the show from the top floor of the White Palace. Vice-Commander Deng Shaodong, who had joined the Red Army at the age of nineteen and the Communist Party at the age of twenty, may not have been very interested in the performance. By then he had received Mao's instructions about the "final showdown" in Tibet, and his PLA Tibet Military Command had been gearing up for war since 1956. PLA Artillery Regiment 308 had established a fully functional encampment on the south bank of the Kyichu River, with trenches extending to the river, and completing PLA control of all motorable passages from the Norbulingka in and out of the Kyichu River Valley.[3] The professed policy of the Chinese Communists was still the United Front, however, and Vice-Commander Deng had to be polite in the name of diplomacy.

A group of children in gaily colored costumes surrounding a character with a big doll's-head mask entered and frolicked around the courtyard. The doll's-head figure was called a *hashang,* a transliteration of the Chinese word for "monk," and was supposed to be a legendary Chinese monk who had donated alms to the first Tibetan Buddhist temple. Gesticulating comically, he circled the performance space to relax the crowd after the fierce war dance. Then he swaggered over to the staircase of the White Palace and plopped down onto a chair that had been placed there for his use. From that point on, he became a spectator.

Next came six Buddhist pilgrims in elaborate robes, and masks with big noses and deep-set eyes to represent the Indian monks who had brought Buddhism to Tibet. Upon their exit, a contingent of rowdy demon soldiers leaped in, followed by four screeching skeletons with grotesquely grinning masks, who cavorted wildly to the banging of the cymbals.

For the two high-ranking Communists, the sepulchral dance of the skeletons represented a culture they deemed barbaric and backward, which they were supposed to reform. In addition, although the Chinese dignitaries may not have grasped the intricate symbolism of this section of the dance, the four skeletons represented the four boundless states of mind in Buddhism, chief among which was compassion.[4] As this Buddhist concept was to be applied universally to people of all social classes, it stood in stark contrast to the Communist doctrine of class struggle.

Next to enter was the Lord of the Cemeteries, sovereign of sky burial, water burial, and cremation. His mask was a wrathful red, with bulging eyes and bared teeth. His eyebrows flamed, his beard bristled, and his prickly hair was crowned with five small skulls. He performed a majestic, bloodcurdling dance to the clang of the cymbals and the wail of the horns.

That year, the *Cham* dance was performed solely in the areas of ethnocultural Tibet still under the jurisdiction of the Dalai Lama and the Panchen Lama. The regions controlled by the Chamdo Liberation Committee were seething with unrest, and the monasteries in Sichuan, Gansu, Yunnan, and Qinghai had almost all been closed or demolished. The Tibetan people were facing a catastrophe far worse than the notorious persecution of Buddhists by King Langdarma in the ninth century. Back then, some Tibetan monks had managed to flee deep into Kham, where the Khampas had protected their religion, but there was no escaping the Chinese Communists in the mid-twentieth century.

: : :

High above the courtyard in Sunlight Hall, the Dalai Lama chatted with his guests as they watched the spectacle. Their conversation ranged from Tibetan dance to the subject of the PLA theatrical troupe. Vice-Commander Deng casually remarked that it had just returned from a study trip to China, bringing a fresh repertoire.

What happened next became a pivotal controversy regarding the Lhasa Incident of 1959. The Chinese and the Tibetans have disagreed ever since about the details of the conversation between the three men that day. Somehow it emerged from their conversation that the Dalai Lama would attend a show at the PLA Tibet Military Command, but the sources conflict regarding a key point: Did the Chinese invite him, or did he invite himself?

With historical hindsight, this seemingly trivial question took on enormous importance. From the Tibetan point of view, reports that the Chinese had invited the Dalai Lama to see a show at the PLA Tibet Military Command stoked popular suspicions that there was a Chinese plot against him, suspicions that have persisted to this day. The Chinese, on the other hand, needed to base the legitimacy of their subsequent "pacification" of Lhasa on the premise that it was not planned or plotted beforehand. The story that the Dalai Lama invited himself to the PLA Tibet Military Command absolves the Communists of the charge of scheming. It also supports their claim that the Dalai Lama's self-invitation was a deliberate Tibetan ploy to provoke public anxiety and foment rebellion.

Considering what came afterward, this conversation spawned many later retellings in China, mostly aimed at presenting the story that the Dalai Lama invited himself. Given the highly charged nature of the material, it is no surprise that the sources seem contradictory, flawed, or partisan, leaving the origin of the invitation forever murky.

Key among later retellings was the short memoir published in 1988 by former Tibetan cabinet minister Ngabo, who stayed in Tibet and cooperated with the Chinese after 1959. He suggests that it was the Dalai Lama's idea to attend a PLA performance:

> At the time of the Gutor dance performance in 1959 (the Earth-Hog year), only Political Commissar Tan Guansan and Vice-Commander Deng Shaodong of the PLA Tibet Military Command were in Lhasa, so

> they accepted the invitation to the Potala. While the Dalai Lama was entertaining them in his chambers, he volunteered the following: "I hear that your theatrical troupe brought back a great new repertoire from their study trip to China. I'd like to see one of the shows. Can you arrange this for me?" Commissar Tan and Vice-Commander Deng gladly agreed, and told the Dalai Lama it was a simple matter. All he had to do was name a time, and the PLA would send the troupe over to the Norbulingka for an exclusive performance. The Dalai Lama replied that the Norbulingka lacked a stage and proper facilities, so he would attend a show at the auditorium at the PLA Tibet Military Command. Thus, the matter was settled.[5]

In this account, the Chinese officials who attended the performance at the Potala were Tan Guansan (rather than Guo Xilan) and Deng Shaodong. Ngabo makes no mention of how the Dalai Lama knew about the PLA troupe's new repertoire. When an expanded version of Ngabo's original memoir appeared in 2003, corrections had been attempted, although the new version introduced a glaring error:

> At the time of the Gutor dance performance in 1959, only Political Commissar Tan Guansan and Vice-Commander Deng Shaodong of the PLA Tibet Military Command were in Lhasa. Deng Shaodong and Guo Xilan, administrative director of the CCP Tibet Work Committee, accepted the invitation to the Potala. While the Dalai Lama was entertaining them in his chambers, he volunteered the following: "My chief of staff, Lobsang Samten, tells me that your theatrical troupe brought back a great new repertoire from their study trip to China. I'd like to see one of the shows. Can you arrange this for me?" Vice-Commander Deng gladly agreed, assuring the Dalai Lama that it was a simple matter. All he had to do was name a time, and the PLA would send the troupe over to the Norbulingka for an exclusive performance. The Dalai Lama replied that the Norbulingka lacked a [modern] stage with footlights, and so forth, so he would attend a show at the auditorium at the PLA Tibet Military Command.[6]

The Dalai Lama's chief of staff[7] was named Gadrang Lobsang Rigzin. Lobsang Samten was the Dalai Lama's elder brother, who had stayed in India at the conclusion of his trip there with the Dalai Lama in 1956–1957, and later emigrated to the United States. He was not in Lhasa at the time.

The powerful chief of staff, the highest-ranking monastic official in the Dalai Lama's inner circle, was the Dalai Lama's right-hand man and his event coordinator. Even a high cabinet minister such as Ngabo had to apply to the chief of staff, or Lord Chamberlain Phala, when he wanted to see the Dalai Lama. It seems inconceivable that Ngabo could have confused the chief of staff with the Dalai Lama's brother.

One might wonder how and why Ngabo, a former Tibetan cabinet minister who was not even present at the disputed conversation, came to publish these error-ridden 1988 and 2003 memoirs, which espouse the official Chinese Communist Party line that the Dalai Lama initiated the invitation.

In 2008, the Chinese Communist Party compiled its official *History of the Liberation of Tibet,* with a preface by Chi Haotian, former minister of defense and deputy chairman of the Chinese Central Military Commission. The preface reveals that the book "was six years in the making, with an editorial board of more than eighty people, mostly eminent comrades in their eighties who are veterans of many battles, more than sixty of whom have been military leaders at the provincial level or higher."[8] This description, along with Chi Haotian's imprimatur, identifies the book squarely as the officially sanctioned version of history.

The editors of this book must have noticed the mistakes in Ngabo's accounts. Correctly giving Deng and Guo as the Chinese in attendance at the Potala that day (as in Ngabo's second account), it basically follows his report of their conversation, but it omits the problematic mention of Lobsang Samten (which is also absent from Ngabo's first account).[9]

There are puzzling variations of this contested story. According to a description published in February 1993 by Ji Youquan, resident writer in the Propaganda Department of the PLA Tibet Military Command: "The Dalai Lama received Deng Shaodong, Guo Xilan, and the others at the Potala with hospitality and friendly conversation. Deng Shaodong told the Dalai Lama that the PLA theatrical troupe had just brought back the latest repertoire from a study trip to China. His intent, of course, was to find out whether the Dalai Lama wanted to attend a performance. The young Dalai Lama told Deng that he wanted to go." Deng Shaodong invited him, and told the troupe to prepare a performance for him.[10] This vague passage suggests that Deng enticed the Dalai Lama into inviting himself, in a seeming contradiction of Party line.

However, in another retelling of the same story, published less than a year after the first one, Ji Youquan unambiguously puts forth the official Chinese Communist position that the Dalai Lama initiated the invitation:

> Deng Shaodong happened to mention to the Dalai Lama that the PLA theatrical troupe had just brought back the latest repertoire from a study trip to China. The Dalai Lama was eager to see one of the new shows. He had seen the troupe many times before and found it very attractive.
>
> "Vice-Commander Deng, are they ready to perform the new shows?" the Dalai Lama asked, after a thoughtful pause.
>
> "Yes," replied Deng, sensing the Dalai Lama's drift. "They've been rehearsing, and they're all ready."
>
> "I'd like to go see one of the new shows," said the Dalai Lama.
>
> "Fine," replied Deng. "They will perform at your convenience. Your visit, and your feedback, would be most welcome anytime."[11]

To cloud the issue further, there is also a 2008 account by Tibetan historian Jampel Gyatso, which comes close to the Chinese position:

> Deng Shaodong and Guo Xilan went to the Potala, where they enjoyed the Dalai Lama's hospitality. While they watched the *Cham* performance, they chatted cordially with the Dalai Lama, and their conversation carried them from the subject of Tibetan ritual dance to the performances of the PLA theatrical troupe. Deng Shaodong mentioned in passing that the troupe had just come back with a new repertoire from China.
>
> "How are the new shows?" asked the Dalai Lama. "I'd like to go see one."
>
> "Mr. Deputy Chairman,"[12] Deng replied, "we will perform at your convenience."[13]

Oddly, there are even accounts from within China that seem to resonate with the Tibetan view. According to Luo Liangxing, a member of the PLA troupe at the time, the leaders of the CCP Tibet Work Committee and the PLA Tibet Military Command brought the theatrical troupe to the Potala on Tibetan New Year's Eve—February 8, 1959—to wish the Dalai Lama a happy New Year, and they performed on Deyangshar courtyard. Luo recalls an article about the occasion from that day's Chinese-language newspaper, the *Tibet Daily,* which said:

> Vice-Director Hong Liu happily introduced the Dalai Lama to the troupe, which had just returned from a performance tour of places such as the Democratic People's Republic of Korea, our motherland's capital city of Beijing, Northeast China, and Sichuan. He told the Dalai Lama that the troupe had learned some excellent new programs from our fraternal nationalities all around China, and asked whether the Dalai Lama would like to see them. The Dalai Lama said that he would. Vice-Director Hong replied that the programs required footlights and stage sets.
>
> "In that case," replied the Dalai Lama, "I'll go to the auditorium at your headquarters."[14]

Luo's memoirs were published in 1989; if his memory is reliable, the invitation came from the Chinese.

The Dalai Lama has personally confirmed in an interview that the idea of going to a show at the PLA Tibet Military Command came up in casual conversation during the *Cham* dance performance, and that he did not formally request an invitation, nor did the Chinese issue one. No Tibetan cabinet ministers, including Ngabo, were present during the conversation.[15] Thus, it seems suspect that Ngabo rather than Deng Shaodong and Guo Xilan (or their Tibetan interpreters) should be the source of our information, especially since Deng and Guo were both still alive in 1988, the year Ngabo first penned his memoir.

There was only a week between New Year's and the Monlam Prayer Festival, when the Dalai Lama's examinations were scheduled. Although he agreed to go to a show at the newly constructed PLA auditorium, he did not name a date, simply saying that he would go after his examinations. The Dalai Lama is the only actual participant to have shared his version of the story, but he dismisses the controversy over who initiated the invitation as mere trivia.

No matter how these three men arrived at the idea of the Dalai Lama's attending a show at the PLA Tibet Military Command, none of them imagined at the time that it would develop into the fuse that set off the Lhasa Incident, and even the Battle of Lhasa. To this day, there has been no proof that either side was plotting in that conversation. It seems far more likely that both sides were casting about for an opportunity to alleviate the nerve-racking tension in the city.

: : :

The crowds in the porticos at Deyangshar courtyard were savoring an interlude of mime, guffawing at the histrionics of a white-haired old man and a tiger entangled in mock battle. This was an act that the Thirteenth Dalai Lama had introduced, probably inspired by a trip to Mount Wutai.[16]

The climax of the *Cham* performance was the dance of the Black Hats. Led by monks with smoldering incense, sixteen of them filed onstage, wearing black wizards' hats and magnificent long robes, and wielding an array of Buddhist ritual weapons. They formed a ring and began their stately swirling and stomping in time with the clanging cymbals, slowly building up to a crescendo. Exactly sixteen in number, they embodied the divine Sixteen Voids and the magic power of the *Cham* over evil. Finally, they closed in on their symbolic target, a *lingga,*[17] and locked it in iron fetters. Then they brandished their *vajras,*[18] cutlasses, swords, and axes, and hacked it to bits.

On their way downstairs and out of the Potala, the Chinese guests ran into the Tibetan cabinet ministers, whom they informed that they were going to make arrangements with the Dalai Lama's chief of staff for the Dalai Lama to attend a show at the PLA Tibet Military Command after his examinations. According to Security Chief Phuntsok Tashi, the Dalai Lama's brother-in-law, the Tibetan cabinet ministers expressed no opposition or misgivings.[19]

The Chinese historian Ji Youquan describes the Tibetan cabinet ministers' response rather differently, however:

> The entire cabinet was present. When the ministers heard about the Dalai Lama's proposed visit to the PLA Tibet Military Command, they seemed flustered, and they replied that the matter required further consideration. . . . Afterward, they agreed among themselves that the invitation should be reported to the two acting prime ministers, along with a request that the Dalai Lama be prevented from accepting. They feared that the Communist Party would lure the young Dalai Lama astray

with the troupe's enticing female entertainers, with whose performances he had been smitten before.

When consulted for his advice, however, Acting Prime Minister Lukhangwa disagreed with the cabinet. Stroking his grizzled beard and nodding, the wily old man ruled on the spot that the Dalai Lama should accept the PLA invitation. Seizing the opportunity to foment revolt, he sent someone to the PLA Tibet Military Command to make the arrangements for the Dalai Lama's visit, while he surreptitiously plotted an uprising.[20]

Ji Youquan's descriptions of the Tibetans sometimes tend toward the fanciful, and the passage above shows poor command of the historical facts. Lukhangwa was one of the two acting prime ministers forced to resign after the "People's Assembly" episode in April 1952,[21] and he had been in exile in India since January 1957. He could not possibly have been present at this alleged cabinet meeting. In fact, the Dalai Lama had never replaced the two ministers;[22] there were no acting prime ministers in the Tibetan government in February 1959, and hence none were consulted about the invitation. Furthermore, no other sources corroborate Ji's suggestion about fears of a Chinese plot to tempt the Dalai Lama with female entertainers.

After sunset, the monks carried a five-foot-tall *torma*[23] down the long Potala staircases and outside, where they hurled it into a bonfire of barley hay. Fed by the melting butter-sculpture decorations, the flames blazed skyward, while the monks shouted at the top of their lungs to drive away the evil spirits.

The groundwork had been laid for the Dalai Lama to attend a show at the PLA Tibet Military Command. No one guessed at the time that this would push the people of Lhasa over the edge.

: 6 :

Peril at the Prayer Festival

AT 5:00 IN THE MORNING on Saturday, February 14, 1959, a light flicked on in a top-floor window of the White Palace in the Potala. A chamberlain delivered a washbasin of water from the sacred spring on the north face of Chakpori Hill for the Dalai Lama's use. His Master of the Table brought in his breakfast. After he had eaten, he went into his prayer room, made an offering at the altar, and sat down to meditate and chant the sutras.

Then he entered the Great Hall, where Lord Chamberlain Phala, Senior Tutor Ling Rinpoché, Junior Tutor Trijang Rinpoché, and an array of monk and lay officials awaited him, lined up according to rank. Four *tsi-pons* had wrapped his jade and gold seals in yellow satin and strapped them onto their backs, ready to set out when the propitious moment came. Monks from Namgyal Monastery were chanting the *Verses of the Eight Noble Auspicious Ones* to pray for his success. Once the Dalai Lama had ascended his throne, the Assistant Master of the Table entered, gingerly bearing a heavy silver teapot inlaid with pearls and jade. Supporting the teapot from underneath with his left hand, he steadied it with his right while he veiled his mouth by clenching a corner of his robe in his teeth, head cocked to one side. When he reached the Dalai Lama's throne, he handed the teapot to the Master of the Table and pulled some teacups out of the folds in his robe. The Master of the Table filled a cup with tea, which the Assistant Master drained quickly, presenting a second cup to the Dalai Lama with a respectful bow. Then a chamberlain served tea to the tutors, cabinet ministers, and assembled officials. The Dalai Lama drank his tea and stepped down from his throne.[1] A chamberlain brought white silk prayer scarves, which Lord Chamberlain Phala draped on the pillars and on the Dalai Lama's throne.

Long Tibetan horns blared from the golden roof of the Potala, and ritual music wafted out over the city, announcing that the time had come for the Dalai Lama to move from the palace to the Jokhang Temple to lead the yearly Monlam Prayer Festival. People flocked out of their houses and lined the roadsides, hands pressed together in prayer and chanting sutras, waiting for the Dalai Lama's procession to pass by.

The Monlam Prayer Festival was introduced in 1409 by Tsongkhapa, founder of the Gelug school of Tibetan Buddhism, and was eventually added into the two weeks of New Year's festivities at the Jokhang Temple. According to tradition, the Dalai Lama moved from his winter palace, the Potala, to the Jokhang to conduct the prescribed yearly rituals during the festival. At this time of year, the population of Lhasa ballooned with throngs of believers from the provinces eager to catch a glimpse of him. Ordinarily, he did not move to the Jokhang until the middle of the first month of the new year, but he was moving early this year to take his final examinations for the *Geshe Lharampa* degree on February 21.

The Dalai Lama descended from the Potala into a sea of people. His retinue was ready and waiting: monk-bodyguards, Potala gate guards, Norbulingka cavalry guards, eight palanquin-bearers, thirty-two army officers to escort the palanquin, and a phalanx of official procession managers. On his back, Lord Chamberlain Phala carried a cushion for the Dalai Lama to kneel on before the Buddha at the Jokhang. The Master of the Robes bore a bundle of the Dalai Lama's clothes on his head, while his chamberlains had his meditation cushions. Escorted by his chief of staff and key cabinet members, the Dalai Lama stepped across his gold satin carpet and into his matching palanquin. With three notes from the band as a signal, the palanquin-bearers hoisted their load.

Clouds of fragrant juniper[2] smoke enveloped the city. To the strains of ritual music, the procession left the Potala. The monks from Namgyal Monastery, in rows at the gate area, bowed farewell to the Dalai Lama as they lifted their censers respectfully overhead.

Juchen Tubten waited in the crowd lining the road, his gaze fixed on the long slope down from Marpori Hill, the perch of the Potala. The grand procession snaked toward him, its brightly colored prayer flags offset by the white walls flanking the road. As the music drew nearer, all the bystanders pressed their hands together and bowed in unison.

The road was decorated with a huge red, yellow, and white Eight Auspicious Signs diagram[3] painted in clay. A team of majestic snow-white horses carrying men with lances wrapped in tiger pelts led the way, followed by a mounted shaman with a bow and arrow. Forty standard-bearing monks spurred their horses on by. Then came a group of monk-officials leading horses laden with incense. The music grew louder as the twenty-member courtly music ensemble, also on horseback, rode by. Next came a team of horses with the Dalai Lama's luggage, led by a group of officials, followed by contingents of monk and lay officials and military officers, some on horseback and others on foot, all in sumptuous regalia. Then came the Dalai Lama's inner circle, including his Master of the Table, Master of the Robes, Master of Religious Ceremonies, Lord Chamberlain, and Chief of Staff. After them came two rows of men holding lead-ropes to the palanquin and clad in green silk gowns with blue satin sashes and white silk cuffs, broad-brimmed red hats, and high boots.

The bystanders drew back slightly from the roadside, prostrating themselves. Juchen Tubten caught a glimpse of a large peacock-feather parasol, followed by the palanquin-bearers in yellow robes, red belts, and red hats, along with the great golden palanquin and an oversize matching parasol with a silk curtain that fluttered in the wind. He watched as these hurried past him, followed by a white horse with clacking hooves, carrying a red-robed monk with the reins in his right hand and a sacred parasol in his left.

Next came the four cabinet ministers, the four *tsi-pons,* the four secretaries of the Ecclesiastic Office,[4] the Dalai Lama's tutors, the Holder of the Ganden Throne,[5] and the high reincarnate lamas. They marched in hierarchical order, with those of the highest rank closest to the Dalai Lama's palanquin: monks in the lead and on the left; lay behind and on the right.[6]

The Dalai Lama worried as he rode past the reverent crowds. The Monlam Prayer Festival had been a concern for both Chinese and Tibetans ever since the PLA's original entry into Lhasa in 1951. The population of the city always spiked during the festival, and the Drepung Monastery disciplinarians, a formidable monastic police force equipped with fifteen-foot poles, assumed responsibility for the maintenance of public order. People were alarmed by reports from the refugees who had been streaming in from Kham and Amdo, and the outbreak of fighting in Lhokha had exacerbated the tension: the Chinese had sent more troops to Lhasa and built fortifications atop their office complexes facing the Jokhang Temple. Nerves were frayed on both sides.

An anomalous dual administrative structure had been forced on Tibet during the 1950s. Three regions, each independent of the other, remained nominally under Tibetan control: Lhasa, with its cabinet; Shigatse, seat of the Panchen Lama's Administrative Council; and Chamdo, with its Chinese-run Chamdo Liberation Committee. Although each of these administrations had a certain amount of say over local affairs, all three were merely interim structures that answered to the PCART. Meanwhile, the Communists were engaged in full-scale party building, which they kept underground at first because the Seventeen-Point Agreement did not explicitly authorize the establishment of a Communist Party presence in Tibet. The agreement did, however, stipulate that the PLA would enter Tibet to "consolidate the national defense," enabling the Communist Party to cloak its entry into the region in the guise of a purely military phenomenon.

In fact, the CCP Tibet Work Committee had been founded in Sichuan on January 18, 1950, even before Chinese forces entered Tibet at the Battle of Chamdo,[7] and the large "PLA Vanguard Detachment" that entered Lhasa on September 9, 1951, was not truly a military force, as it included only one company of armed soldiers. It consisted mostly of CCP cadres and staff, the underground nucleus of the CCP Tibet Work Committee.[8] Additional troops, led by Generals Zhang Guohua and Tan Guansan, arrived on October 26, but this group also concealed a "southwest" contingent of the CCP Tibet Work Committee. A further installment, the "18th Army Independent Detachment"—actually the disguised "northwest" CCP Tibet Work Committee—arrived under General Fan Ming on December 1.

These groups were formally merged in early 1952 to become the CCP Tibet Work Committee, but neither its existence nor the Communist Party's presence in Tibet was publicly revealed until July 1, 1955, with the completion of the Sichuan-Tibet and the Qinghai-Tibet Highways.[9] The Tibetans interacting with the Chinese in Lhasa before July 1955 did not fully understand whom they were dealing with, as the CCP Tibet Work Committee had been known to Communist Party outsiders only by the mysterious quasi-military title of "Independent Detachment."[10]

Starting with zero presence in Tibet in 1951, by the end of 1958 the Party had enrolled 4,186 members, 484 of whom were non-Han, and established sixteen Party general branch offices and 236 local branches, with 8,967 cadres, including 2,767 who were non-Han.[11] By the beginning of 1959, the Communist Party apparatus was completely in place in Tibet, ready to replace the existing government at the drop of a hat.

Under the complex dual system of the day, Lhasa had two mutually distrustful administrative structures, a pair of antagonistic armies, two separate currencies, and even two modes of telling time. Chinese personnel stationed in Lhasa still set their watches to Beijing time, which was two hours later than the local Lhasa time.[12] The snow-lion flag, which had not yet been banned, still flew over the Tibetan army barracks. Following Mao's April 1952 instructions to "let them [the Tibetans] do all the dirty work,"[13] the CCP Tibet Work Committee preferred to leave the knotty problem of Lhasa's public security mostly to the Tibetan government. Regiment 6 of the Tibetan Army had been transferred from Shigatse to Lhasa to reinforce the municipal police and create police booths at major intersections around town, although the PLA retained control over key thoroughfares such as the Lhasa Bridge.[14]

The Drepung Monastery disciplinarians were traditionally in charge of crowd control during the Monlam Prayer Festival. At one such festival in 1938, they had even burst into the Nepalese Consulate, apprehended a Nepalese robber, and clubbed him to death.[15] But Beijing had instructed the CCP Tibet Work Committee in January 1959 to start "monopolizing power" and "centralizing leadership."[16] This policy shift threw into question the disciplinarians' prerogative to apprehend Han Chinese troublemakers during the festival. The Tibetans asked the CCP Tibet Work Committee to grant and publicize the necessary authorization, but the committee dismissed the request as a challenge to its mandate and even as a sign of conspiracy.

The cabinet and the Dalai Lama had disagreed about whether he should travel by palanquin from the Potala to the Jokhang Temple that year. He had proposed going by car as more in keeping with the times, but the cabinet had ruled in favor of preserving hallowed tradition. Meanwhile, to counter the dangers this posed, the Tibetan Army had requested permission to post sentries on the fortified Chinese buildings along Barkor Street. The Chinese had refused outright, however, which had unnerved the Tibetans still further.

There was an incident involving the Dalai Lama's safety during the procession. Tibetan soldiers arrested two members of the Chinese militia, both night watchmen from the Qinghai-Tibet Highway Bureau, who stood among the onlookers, armed with submachine guns and hand grenades.[17] The Tibetans suspected the two of "attempted assassination" of the Dalai Lama, but the Chinese, not unexpectedly, denounced the arrest as a "deliberate provocation," and "a ploy to create tension and disrupt unity between ethnicities."[18] The Dalai Lama, in his great golden palanquin, was unaware of the trouble at the time.

The Dalai Lama's grand procession marched onward, crossing the Yuthok Samba Bridge and entering Barkor Street. The disciplinarians guarding the main gate of the Jokhang Temple herded the crowds to the sides of the street with their poles.

Tubten Khetsun, the seventeen-year-old incense-bearer for that year's festival and a new hire at the Norbulingka, was waiting at the gate with a smoking censer. A monk spread a carpet on the spot where the Dalai Lama would descend from his palanquin. The crowds in their holiday finery were chanting sutras and holding up incense, white silk prayer scarves, and images of the Buddha.

The Dalai Lama stepped out of his palanquin. A group of monks doubled over at the waist and preceded him, walking backward and unrolling a golden carpet for him all the way up the stairs to his living chambers on the top floor.

: : :

On February 21, 1959, the thirteenth of the first month of the Earth-Hog year, before an audience of thousands, the Dalai Lama passed his qualifying examinations for the *Geshe Lharampa* degree. There was a graduation celebration for him at the Jokhang the next day, attended by monks from the "great three" monastic universities of Lhasa, representatives of various religious sects, and government officials.

On the fifteenth of the month in the Tibetan calendar, which fell on February 23 in 1959, it was customary for the Dalai Lama to preach from his dais in Sungchora Square on the south side of the Jokhang Temple. Security Chief Phuntsok Tashi arrived in the square that morning and found it already mobbed. Standing at the Dalai Lama's dais, he anxiously surveyed the scene. People were stoking the giant censer with dried juniper boughs, and an attendant was setting up a loudspeaker at one corner of the dais. Crowds were pouring in from Barkor Street: women with colorful aprons over their long robes; Khampa men, hair braided with red thread and coiled atop their heads; weather-beaten nomads; frisky children; and monks in russet robes.

The Dalai Lama was scheduled for two major activities that day: in the morning he would deliver his sermon in the square on the *Previous Life Stories of Sakyamuni Buddha*.[19] After dark, he and his monk officials would view the Chö-nga Chöpa Festival[20] butter sculptures along Barkor Street.

Security Chief Phuntsok squinted across the square at the historic Sampo and Kyitö mansions. The former, only a dozen yards from the square, had belonged to the descendants of the Seventh Dalai Lama until the Chinese bought it in 1951 and converted it into offices. In 1958, they fortified the roof with sandbags, creating an eyesore in the temple neighborhood. Armed men patrolled the roof, and guns poked ominously through the sandbags, aimed straight at the Jokhang Temple. The holiday crowds in the square did their best to avoid looking at the sandbags and to pretend that nothing was amiss, but people looked nervous, and some of the men were scowling.

Security Chief Phuntsok noted that the Dalai Lama's dais was an easy target, and that some windows along the street had also been sandbagged. People might be lurking behind them with guns, he figured, and they too had clear aim at the dais. The Dalai Lama was completely exposed. The city was teeming with visitors from the provinces, all packed into this one neighborhood. If the crowd got unruly, the Chinese might shoot. It was a formula for disaster.

Security Chief Phuntsok returned to the Jokhang Temple to report his findings. He and the cabinet, the chief of staff, and the lord chamberlain had already debated canceling the day's activities. The Dalai Lama and the cabinet wanted to proceed according to schedule to avoid creating general panic, whereas the others had been inclined to cancel. The security chief's report convinced everyone that the events should be called off, however. If anything untoward were to occur, no matter whose fault it was, the Dalai Lama would be imperiled.[21]

An announcement was made in the square that the Dalai Lama was feeling slightly indisposed after the stress of the last two days, necessitating cancellation of his morning lecture and evening viewing of the butter sculptures. The crowd began to buzz, fearing that the Dalai Lama was in danger.

The early, tenuous Chinese-Tibetan bonds of goodwill in Lhasa had frayed to the snapping point by this time; each side inevitably assumed the worst of the other. The Chinese were doubtless aware that the Dalai Lama's cancellations had aroused suspicions among the populace. Two days after the canceled festivities, the former head of the CCP Tibet Work Committee's United Front Bureau, Chen Jingbo, went to the Jokhang Temple to confront the Dalai Lama about his canceled appearances, the disciplinarians' request to apprehend Han Chinese offenders, and the arrest of the two Chinese workers. Tan Guansan and his colleagues at the CCP Tibet Work Committee cabled the results of this conversation to Beijing, using wording strongly indicative that they were oblivious to public opinion in Lhasa and strangely indifferent to the anti-Chinese sentiments of the lower classes. Clinging to their dogma of class struggle, they blamed all the trouble on the "reactionary Tibetan elite." Faced with Chen Jingbo's accusations, the Dalai Lama awkwardly tried to be as conciliatory as possible. Nonetheless, the CCP Tibet Work Committee's cable concluded: "The Dalai Lama and his cabinet know perfectly well what is happening. They discuss everything at every point along the way. This proves they are hatching a plot."[22]

: : :

It was Thursday, March 5, 1959, the twenty-fifth of the first month in the Earth-Hog year. The Monlam Prayer Festival was finished, and it was time for the Dalai Lama to move from the Jokhang Temple to the Norbulingka, his summer palace. At the auspicious moment chosen by the Nechung Oracle, the horns blared on the gilded monastery roof, and the Dalai Lama's grand ceremonial procession set out to the strains of ritual music. The entire populace of Lhasa turned out to watch, lining the two-and-a-half-mile route to the Norbulingka. Little did they know that they were witnessing the last such procession in the history of Tibet.[23]

The Dalai Lama's advisers had agonized again over the question of whether he should ride in his palanquin or in a car. This time, they had suggested that he travel by car for safety, but the Dalai Lama had objected, lest any sudden change of plans set off a panic reaction. He thought it best to follow the tradition and ride in his palanquin. The procession left the Jokhang Temple and followed Barkor Street toward Yuthok Samba Bridge. As it passed Sungchora Square, the Tibetan soldiers along the route nervously pointed their loaded rifles at the PLA perches atop the buildings. The Dalai Lama watched anxiously from within his palanquin.

Once they had left the heart of the city, the danger seemed to ebb. Still, the Tibetan sentries kept their guns trained on the Chinese posts—even the faraway ones—as the Dalai Lama proceeded, until he arrived safely at the Norbulingka.

Now that the long holiday was over, the Dalai Lama's thoughts returned to the insistent affairs of state. One problem was whether he should attend the Second National People's Congress in Beijing. The Dalai Lama had heard that Mao intended to step down as chairman of the People's Republic of China[24] at the Congress, and he wondered what this meant for Tibet.[25] He also hoped to find an opportunity to voice his concerns to Mao in person. But an actual date had not been set for the Congress, and given the volatility in Lhasa, he did not know whether his cabinet and his people would let him go.

There was also the question of the show at the PLA Tibet Military Command. At the *Cham* dance performance, he had told Vice-Commander Deng that he would go after his *Geshe Lharampa* examinations. Four days prior, United Front Bureau Vice-Chairman He Zuyin and Section Chief Li Zuomin had come to the monastery to congratulate him on the attainment of his degree and to set a date for his attendance at the PLA performance. He had suggested sometime between March 10 and 12, and asked them to make arrangements with his chief of staff, Gadrang Lobsang Rigzin.[26]

The air along the Dalai Lama's procession route was redolent with incense. Through the smoky haze, the palatial gate of his summer palace, the Norbulingka, with its sentries and stone snow lions, loomed like a mirage. The procession marched into the gate to the stirring strains of ritual music. The Dalai Lama's escort dismounted and stood in rows, bowing while his palanquin, heralded by the golden silk parasol, proceeded into the yellow-walled inner courtyard.

: 7 :

The Dalai Lama May Not Bring Bodyguards!

ON THE AFTERNOON OF SATURDAY, March 7, 1959,[1] Chief of Staff Gadrang Lobsang Rigzin hurried to the Dalai Lama's New Palace[2] to report that the PLA Tibet Military Command had telephoned again to press for a date for the Dalai Lama's visit.

"They're very persistent," added Gadrang. The PLA had also sent men to the Norbulingka to prod him.

The PLA invitation had slipped to the bottom of the Dalai Lama's to-do list. He had only had two days to catch up on his duties at the Norbulingka since the end of the prayer festival, and he was expected to perform a set of rituals, such as donating to the Panchen Lama's Tashilhunpo Monastery in Shigatse, and making a pilgrimage to the Ngari *dra-tsang,*[3] Dakpo *dra-tsang,* and Chokorgyel Monastery.[4] Besides, it was no simple matter for him to go on an excursion. The Nechung Oracle had to designate an auspicious time, Lord Chamberlain Phala and Chief of Staff Gadrang had to choose his retinue, and Security Chief Phuntsok and the cabinet had to make plans for his safety.

In this case, since the Chinese were so insistent, and attending the show seemed like a minor jaunt, the Dalai Lama told Gadrang to give them the date of March 10, which was three days hence, and to work with Phuntsok to make the customary arrangements for his retinue and security. The next morning, March 8, Gadrang phoned the PLA with the Dalai Lama's reply, and set the time for 1:00 in the afternoon on March 10, Lhasa time (3:00 Beijing time).

According to two official Chinese sources, United Front section chief Li Zuomin went to the Norbulingka the next day, March 9, to get Gadrang's approval of the draft protocol for the event.[5] These official sources neglect to mention that the draft included no invitation for the Dalai Lama's customary retinue, which would normally have been chosen by

Phala and Gadrang. Instead, the PLA bypassed the Dalai Lama's handlers and issued its own invitations—decrees, in fact—also on March 9, to high-ranking Tibetan officials, the Dalai Lama's family, and eminent lamas. Possibly through oversight, Lord Chamberlain Phala was omitted from the list. For its own reasons, the PLA had chosen to handle protocol rather differently from the PCART, a civilian organization.

Three or four years earlier, the Dalai Lama's acceptance of such an invitation might not have aroused unusual alarm among the general public. By March 1959, however, word had spread in Lhasa that local Communist governments in Kham and Amdo had abducted a number of headmen and distinguished lamas by luring them to "meetings," "study classes," or "banquets." Moreover, Tibetan fears had been further inflamed by the behavior of General Tan Guansan, who was left in charge of the CCP Tibet Work Committee in the absence of both Zhang Jingwu and Zhang Guohua. General Tan was de facto the most powerful man in Tibet, which was unfortunate because his behavior grated on the Tibetans. They remember him as a boorish, foul-tempered man.

First came General Tan's thinly veiled threats at a recent meeting of the Patriotic Tibetan Women's League.[6] "There's a piece of rotten meat here in Lhasa, and flies have been swarming in," he had railed. "We'll have to dispose of the rotten meat to get rid of the flies." As his words made the rounds of Lhasa's rumor mill, people interpreted the "flies" as the refugees from Kham and Amdo, and the "rotten meat" as the Dalai Lama. There was no need to spell out what "dispose of" meant.[7]

General Tan's insensitivity created further discord on March 8, International Women's Day. The Lhasa Youth and Women's Council[8] held a party to celebrate the occasion, chaired by General Tan in his capacity as secretary of the council. In those days, most of the high-ranking Chinese Communists in Tibet held several concomitant posts, in order to concentrate power. But Tan, a military man and peasant organizer, was poorly suited to lead the aristocratic ladies of Lhasa, and the gathering ended, unsurprisingly, in a debacle. He stood at the podium waving his fist and barking that unless the Khampas surrendered, the PLA would make short work of smashing all their monasteries to smithereens. Appalled, the ladies in the audience surged at him, shouting at the top of their lungs, and mayhem ensued. Since the ladies had no language in common with Tan, they hurled abuse at him in their own language, and he responded in kind. The interpreters were completely at a loss, not knowing whether to translate or not.[9] Jigme Taring's[10] wife, Rinchen Dolma, a leader of the Patriotic Tibetan Women's League, eventually managed to calm the ladies down. Several days after this incident, thousands of women took to the streets of Lhasa in protest.

: : :

At 6:00 A.M. on March 9, a car pulled up to the Dalai Lama's security guard station. Two PLA cadres got out and asked to see Security Chief Phuntsok.[11]

Phuntsok, who had just rolled out of bed, assumed there was an emergency and invited them in immediately. They said they had orders to bring him to the PLA Tibet Military Command to discuss the arrangements for the Dalai Lama's visit the next day. This was the first time Phuntsok heard that the occasion had been scheduled for March 10. He asked to be allowed a moment for a quick breakfast, but the answer was no: he must not keep their commanding officer waiting. Phuntsok told them to start back, promising to follow right away. Just as he began to gulp down a cup of tea, they returned for him, so he put down his tea and went. He had no need of an interpreter because he spoke fluent Chinese.[12] When he arrived at the PLA Tibet Military Command, Vice-Commander Deng Shaodong and a Brigadier Fu were waiting impatiently.

The Tibetan government and the PLA still preserved a veneer of cordiality at this point, but this interaction between Phuntsok and the PLA typifies the chafing between the two sides. The PLA men, especially the lower-ranking officers, who were stationed in Lhasa without their families, were rough-and-ready types, prepared for duty at any hour of the day, and accustomed to militaristic efficiency and punctuality. The Tibetan officials, on the other hand, tended to be sticklers for etiquette and had a rather different concept of time. Innumerable small frictions resulted, compounding the mutual ill will.

"We won't be following all your rigmarole during tomorrow's event," Brigadier Fu announced as soon as Phuntsok sat down. "This is a visit to the PLA, not the PCART office, so the Dalai Lama won't be able to bring his usual retinue."[13] He went on to say that the PLA had already made plans for the Dalai Lama's safety during the visit. He would be allowed to bring a few chamberlains, but no bodyguards, as the PLA would provide them. Moreover, the Tibetans should not post sentries along his travel route. The PLA would deploy them if necessary.

Phuntsok was stunned. From the Tibetan point of view, it was out of the question for the Dalai Lama to venture on such an outing without his bodyguards. Even leaving aside matters of tradition, the festering discord in Lhasa made the PLA proposition inconceivable. A heated negotiation ensued.

Phuntsok clung to precedent. Tibetan sentries should guard the Dalai Lama's travel route, ostensibly "to prevent counterrevolutionary sabotage," and the Dalai Lama would need at least ten or twenty of his own bodyguards while he was inside the PLA Tibet Military Command.

Brigadier Fu countered that if Tibetan sentries were posted, they could go only as far as the stone bridge that led into the PLA Tibet Military Command. No outsiders were allowed past the PLA sentries at the bridge. If the Dalai Lama insisted on bringing bodyguards, he could bring no more than two or three, and they had to be unarmed.

Phuntsok pointed out that the people of Lhasa would object to such an arrangement. Pleading that "reactionaries might cause trouble" without Tibetan guards along the Dalai Lama's route, he added that ten or twenty of the Dalai Lama's personal bodyguards should present no problem for his hosts inside the PLA Tibet Military Command. His implication was that twenty bodyguards would be outnumbered in the event of a conflict.

In fact, the Dalai Lama's security force—created by the Thirteenth Dalai Lama in 1917—was only an honor guard, a purely ceremonial unit that had never had to fire a single shot.[14] Although Tibet had its share of run-of-the-mill crime, a public attack on the Dalai Lama was unimaginable. His outings were occasions of grand pageantry, attended by throngs of faithful believers, none of whom had ever tried to harm him. As Tibetans saw it, the prohibition of his bodyguards while on Chinese turf was not only dangerous: it was an affront to their sense of tradition. The Dalai Lama's guard unit was emblematic of his authority and dignity; this was not the PLA officers' concern, however.

Deng Shaodong ultimately dictated the terms. Reminding Phuntsok that the PLA Tibet Military Command was a strategic location, generally off-limits to outsiders, he went on to assure him that the PLA would guarantee the Dalai Lama's safety. The general public would not be unhappy with the arrangement, he continued, and the most that could go wrong would be "isolated provocation by counterrevolutionary elements." He also told Phuntsok that the PLA had invited the cabinet members, and that each of them was allowed to bring one attendant, but all must be unarmed. Considering the matter settled, Deng stood up and invited Phuntsok to inspect the lounge that would be provided for the Dalai Lama's use.

A cadre escorted Phuntsok to the lounge and opened the door. Phuntsok noted with dismay that the room was crammed with junk, an environment hardly befitting the Dalai Lama.

The PLA had laid out two options. One was for the Dalai Lama to travel in a PLA-chauffeured car, along a PLA-guarded route. The other was for the Tibetans to guard the route as far as the stone bridge into the PLA compound, and then to send the Dalai Lama inside with only a few unarmed guards or attendants. Painfully aware of how Tibetans would react to both proposals, Phuntsok returned to the Norbulingka in a quandary.

In their later recollections of the incident, the leading Tibetan policymakers of the day cite the universal shock over the PLA prohibition of the Dalai Lama's bodyguards as a principal trigger of the Lhasa Incident. Therefore, it is important to determine the facts about the PLA restrictions. Not surprisingly, Tibetan sources tend to stress the prohibition, whereas Chinese Communist sources tend to play it down.

Several major Tibetan primary sources underscore the impact of the PLA injunction. One is the memoir of Lord Chamberlain Phala, a key figure in the events in question; a second is that of Khenchung Tara,[15] personal secretary to the Dalai Lama. Both memoirs appeared in the comprehensive Oral History Series published by the Library of Tibetan Works and Archives in Dharamsala. Another invaluable Tibetan source is Security Chief Phuntsok's extensive memoir, *A Life,* also published in Dharamsala, which includes his detailed recollections of the causes of the

1959 Lhasa Incident, the reasons for the Dalai Lama's decision to flee, and the circumstances of his escape.

In 1995, a memoir by a Tibetan security guard lieutenant colonel, Sesing Lobsang Dondrup, appeared in an official Chinese Communist compilation published in the Tibet Autonomous Region.[16] Seshing corroborates Phuntsok's account, recalling that on March 9, Phuntsok told him that the PLA had forbidden the Dalai Lama's customary bodyguard unit from entering the PLA Tibet Military Command, with the exception of a few unarmed men. He also states that Phuntsok ordered him to station one hundred armed sentries the next day "in the customary locations on both sides of the avenue outside the main gate of the Norbulingka."[17]

However, other official Chinese publications, both public[18] and semi-classified,[19] tend to skirt this controversial issue and mention the March 9 planning meeting between Deng Shaodong and Phuntsok only in passing, although not bothering to disprove that it took place. A notable exception is the key memoir by former Tibetan cabinet minister Ngabo, who cooperated with the Chinese after 1959, which aims to refute the Tibetan contention:

> Some Tibetans now in exile have alleged that the reason the Dalai Lama did not go to the PLA Tibet Military Command to see a show was that the PLA had specified that he would only be allowed to bring a few personal attendants and bodyguards, and that his usual retinue would not be invited. This is patently false. According to convention, how could it be possible for the Dalai Lama, the leader of Tibet and chairman of the PCART, to go out without his retinue and bodyguards?[20]

Such rhetoric has the earmarks of sophistry. The matter in question is not whether it was theoretically possible for the Dalai Lama to go out "without his retinue and bodyguards." What needs to be determined is whether the PLA in fact unilaterally determined the guest list and forbade the Dalai Lama's armed bodyguard unit to step onto PLA turf. In 1959, Ngabo was concurrently a member of the Dalai Lama's cabinet and first vice-commander of the PLA Tibet Military Command, with the rank of lieutenant general. As such, he must have been well aware of the subtleties of protocol.

Most official Chinese sources simply gloss over the security guard controversy, accusing the Tibetans of a mutinous plot instead. Here is a typical example:

> On March 9, the day that Gadrang agreed to let us [Chinese] take care of all the arrangements for the Dalai Lama's visit, Ngabo learned that Phala, Cabinet Minister Liushar, and Kundeling Dzasa[21] were conspiring to kidnap the Dalai Lama. The plan was to try to scare him into fleeing, based on rumors that the Chinese were planning to stamp out religion and kill high lamas. If that didn't work, the next step of their plot was to start an uprising in Lhasa and to use our efforts to defend ourselves as a pretext to force him to flee.[22]

This inflated, erroneous charge was copied into another major official history[23] and quoted in abridged form in yet another,[24] but no source is ever given for the information. No Tibetan-language sources, including Phala's memoirs, mention any such skullduggery. Even Ngabo does not mention it—an omission that the historian Jampel Gyatso finds highly telling.[25]

Chinese silence about the unusual arrangements for the Dalai Lama's security is deepened by the absence of any record on the subject by the principal PLA figures in the episode, Deng Shaodong and Tan Guansan. Instead, Chinese sources rely entirely on Ngabo, who was not involved in the policy making on either side. Nonetheless, it is possible to infer a reason that the PLA may have wished to bar the Dalai Lama's bodyguard unit.[26]

The CCP Tibet Work Committee believed that the Tibetan government was planning an uprising. Accurate or not, this judgment call clearly influenced the Central Committee's decisions. Unbeknownst to the Tibetans, PLA preparations for war in Tibet had begun in 1956 and reached full swing by the start of 1959. However, Mao's instructions to the CCP Tibet Work Committee in January 1959 indicate that he was not quite ready to launch his "final showdown." He had only about three thousand PLA troops in Lhasa at that point, and it would take time for reinforcements to arrive. Meanwhile, the Chushi Gangdruk guerrilla army's morale was high. It had defeated the PLA several times, occupied a large area of Lhokha, and stationed some squads by the Tsangpo River, only a two days' march from Lhasa. Feeling that he was surrounded by hostile

Tibetans, Tan Guansan did not want to reveal his hand prematurely in Lhasa. The PLA was busily fortifying its headquarters with bunkers, trenches, and tunnels at that moment, and a phalanx of Tibetan soldiers snooping around the premises would have been highly undesirable.

Given the possible need for secrecy at the PLA Tibet Military Command, why did Deng Shaodong invite the Dalai Lama? Judging from all available sources, the invitation occurred spontaneously, and did not represent an official policy decision. But once the Dalai Lama had accepted, there was no turning back. Both sides probably hoped that a pleasant social interaction would defuse the explosive situation, and realized that a cancellation by either side would aggravate the suspicions of the other. Neither side guessed that the invitation might as well have been a match dropped into a tinderbox.

: : :

Security Chief Phuntsok returned to the Norbulingka and informed Lord Chamberlain Phala of the security guard dilemma. Phala was alarmed, and they went together to talk to Chief of Staff Gadrang, who decided that the problem merited consultation with the Dalai Lama. The three men went to the Dalai Lama's New Palace.

After hearing them out, the Dalai Lama lowered his head pensively.

"Maybe this isn't as serious as it sounds," he muttered, as if to himself. "Everything's set for tomorrow, and it seems like a bad idea to cancel."

His three officers informed him of their grave concerns.

"It'll be all right," the Dalai Lama countered, after another thoughtful pause. "Don't worry about it."[27]

Gadrang decided to proceed with the plans for the visit and to do his best to ensure the Dalai Lama's safety.

Phala, Phuntsok, and Gadrang left the New Palace and set to work on the arrangements for the outing. Phuntsok called an emergency meeting at security guard headquarters to brief the lieutenant colonels and captains, and ask for their advice. They recommended that all colonels should be notified. Phuntsok agreed, and sent an officer around with orders for them to report to security guard headquarters the next morning. He also assigned a hundred of his soldiers to mingle with the crowds in plainclothes the next day.[28]

Phala sent someone to the cabinet office to choose two *tsedrungs* to accompany the Dalai Lama to the performance. Khenchung Tara, who was passing by on his way to perform his Sojong rites,[29] happened to overhear. Stunned, he found himself too worried about the Dalai Lama being locked up in Beijing to concentrate on his prayers. He went to ask Phuntsok if the story was true; just then two *tsedrungs* also arrived, Yeshi Lhundup and Barshi Ngawang Tenkyong.

When Barshi heard the story, he was badly shaken. Six days before, he had gone to consult the Nechung Oracle. "In these dire times," he had asked, "what is the best way to protect the Dalai Lama and the religion and polity of Tibet?" The oracle solemnly pronounced, "It is time to tell the all-knowing Guru not to venture outside." The oracle's words were recorded and the official seal affixed. Barshi took the document directly to Phala, asking him to transmit it to the Dalai Lama.[30] It is not known whether Phala did so. Barshi, however, firmly believed that the oracle's words pertained to the Dalai Lama's visit to the PLA Tibet Military Command; he also feared that the timing of these events in the Earth-Hog year, the Dalai Lama's critical year in the zodiac, could augur ill.

Tara, Yeshi, and Barshi all agreed that the Dalai Lama should be dissuaded from such a perilous excursion. At that moment, an administrator called Khenchung Gyaltsen walked in and joined in the chorus of alarm. The men reminded Phuntsok that the Chinese had been using deceptive invitations to lure away and abduct headmen and high lamas in Amdo, and that Lhasa was swirling with rumors about the risks of the Dalai Lama's proposed trip to the National People's Congress in Beijing. They warned him that trouble might break out in the city if the Dalai Lama accepted the Chinese invitation as it stood, and proposed asking Lord Chamberlain Phala to cancel.

Phuntsok felt the burden of his responsibility for the Dalai Lama's safety. The arrangements had worried him from the start, and now he was convinced something was seriously amiss. The men went together to Phala to urge him to cancel the outing. Hesitant to make the decision on his own, he sent them to see Chief of Staff Gadrang.

Bearing white silk prayer scarves, the four men presented their request to Gadrang.

"It's all decided," he replied brusquely. "We can't change anything at this point."[31]

The men begged him, insisting that the Dalai Lama's safety was a life-and-death matter for the Tibetan people as a whole, and imploring him to transmit their opinion to the Dalai Lama. Gadrang agreed to ask the Dalai Lama again, and Tara, Barshi, and Yeshi left to wait for news.

Gadrang, Phala, and Phuntsok brought the men's entreaty to the Dalai Lama.

"It's too late to back out now," he replied. "There's no real danger. Tell them to simmer down and keep a lid on the panic. I think I should go."

The Dalai Lama had spoken, and his decision was announced. That afternoon, Tara, Barshi, and Yeshi heard that the Dalai Lama intended to go as planned. Tibetan sentries would be posted along his route until he reached the stone bridge, where he would cross into the PLA Tibet Military Command with a handful of unarmed bodyguards. Onlookers would be barred from the area.

Ngabo states in his memoirs that United Front section chief Li Zuomin came to his house at three o'clock that afternoon claiming to have instructions from the Dalai Lama for all of his cabinet ministers regarding the following day: instead of assembling at the Norbulingka first to accompany him en route, they were to meet him at the PLA Tibet Military Command. Ngabo advised Li against this breach of tradition, warning him that ill-considered Chinese arrangements could be risky in the current volatile situation. Li Zuomin, however, was unwilling to budge.

Neither of the Dalai Lama's two autobiographies mentions his having entrusted Li Zuomin with any such message for Ngabo, and Ngabo is the only cabinet member to claim having received one. The claim seems suspect. If the Dalai Lama had a message for Ngabo, he would probably have sent it through the usual channels. But Ngabo's memoir goes on to say that Acting Cabinet Minister Liushar phoned him a few hours later with contradictory instructions: the cabinet ministers were supposed to meet at nine in the morning at the Norbulingka to discuss the Dalai Lama's plans, after which they were to escort him en route. Ngabo also relates that Liushar told him to take the message to Chief Cabinet Minister Surkhang at his house.[32]

Chinese chronicler Ji Youquan constructs the following backdrop for the assembly of the cabinet on the morning of March 10:

> Once the reactionary clique of leading cabinet ministers had decided to start their revolt on March 10, the plan was to call a "meeting" of the entire cabinet at the Norbulingka that morning, at which they would assassinate Ngabo, a die-hard Communist sympathizer, and then kick off their rebellion. Once Lukhangwa and Lobsang Tashi had decided on this action plan, they sent a messenger to Ngabo on the afternoon of March 9 with instructions to go to the Norbulingka for a meeting the following morning. Meanwhile, they continued to plot his assassination.[33]

Ji Youquan gives no source for this story, which appears nowhere else. Ngabo himself never mentions a cabinet scheme to assassinate him. As for Lukhangwa and Lobsang Tashi, they had been removed from their posts years earlier, during the People's Assembly incident of 1952. Lukhangwa had emigrated to India in early 1957; he was in Kalimpong at the time of the events in question and entirely out of the picture.

News of the Dalai Lama's visit to the PLA Tibet Military Command had not filtered down to the general public by the afternoon of March 9. Determined to prevent the excursion, Yeshi and Barshi decided to arouse the populace. First they notified the lower-rung civil servants who had taken part in the secret meeting to keep the Dalai Lama from traveling to Beijing.[34] Then Barshi rode his bicycle from the Norbulingka to the Potala to spread the word among the soldiers stationed in the Shol neighborhood below the palace, while Yeshi galloped around town on horseback to mobilize the citizenry to assemble at the Norbulingka the next morning. Barshi even appropriated an official government seal on a letter he composed to the leadership of Drepung and Sera monasteries, warning of the threat the Dalai Lama faced and requesting that they send all their monks to the Norbulingka.[35] Yeshi and Barshi may not have realized how incendiary their actions were.

The news of the Dalai Lama's outing spread like wildfire.

When Tara returned home from work on the evening of March 9, he sent a messenger with a letter to his friend Khenchung Tubten Sangpo to apprise him of the situation and ask him to go to the Norbulingka first thing in the morning to beg the Dalai Lama to stay home.[36]

Meanwhile, the PLA was busily inviting the elite of Lhasa to the performance.

Juchen Tubten, who was living in the Banak Shol neighborhood on the east side of town, was awakened by a commotion outside before dawn on March 10. With a vigilance bred of his fugitive years, he bolted out of bed and ran to his door. People were surging into the streets and yelling.

"Don't let Gyalwa Rinpoché go to the PLA camp!"

"It's dangerous!"

"He'll never come back!"

The Chinese had invited the Dalai Lama to the PLA camp? Stunned, Juchen Tubten threw on some clothes, grabbed his rifle, and charged outside into the predawn chill.[37]

: 8 :

The Most Momentous Day in Tibetan History

ON MARCH 10, 1959, the Dalai Lama awoke from a restless sleep at 5:00 A.M. He washed his face, drank the butter tea his chamberlain had brought, and went into his prayer room. Fragrant incense was swirling in the air. Reflections of the butter lamps in front of the Buddha glimmered in the seven little gold and silver bowls of saffron-tinged holy water along the altar. After performing three prostrations to the Buddha, he settled into lotus position on the floor for his morning meditation. Then he stood up, stretched, and quietly left the prayer room.

He could not dispel a gnawing sense of foreboding about the unorthodox plans for that afternoon. He was to attend the PLA theatrical performance without his usual guards and retinue. Tibetan sentries would be posted along his route from the Norbulingka, but he would have to cross the stone bridge into the PLA compound on his own. Gadrang and Phuntsok's warnings echoed in his ears. Although he had no fear for his own personal safety, there was no telling what the general public might do.

He went uneasily downstairs to his garden, which was bursting with new life on that breezy March morning. Gilt roofs sparkled in the sun, and his green prayer flags fluttered in the wind like comforting tidings from heaven. Green was his lucky color, according to the reckonings his astrologists had made almost ten years before, when, with the Chinese at the doorstep, the Nechung Oracle had pronounced that he should assume his temporal powers ahead of schedule. Forgetting his cares for the moment, he took a bucket and ladle from one of the gardeners and started watering the plants. Gardening was one of his hobbies, along with repairing clocks and watches.

A sudden commotion outside the palace wall shattered his moment of peace, and he stopped and stood up from his watering. He could hear people shouting, but he could not make out what they were saying. Putting his bucket down, he darted back inside to ask one of his chamberlains to go take a look.[1]

Meanwhile, at Drepung Monastery, the twelve-year-old Ngari Rinpoché, Tenzin Choegyal, had just finished his breakfast and started to pore over his scriptures when the head monk opened the door curtain and came in to say that a PLA car had arrived to pick him up. It was waiting outside the main gate, the head monk said, and the driver wanted him to come right away. Ngari Rinpoché dropped his book and went to the gate, where he found several parked cars. A soldier from one of the cars told him that the Dalai Lama was scheduled to arrive at the PLA Tibet Military Command at noon to see a show, and that they had come to drive Ngari Rinpoché to the show too. The boy was puzzled. This was the first he had heard of the matter. As the Dalai Lama's little brother, he often received invitations to events of this sort, but the usual procedure was for Chief of Staff Gadrang or Lord Chamberlain Phala to send a courier to invite him to join the Dalai Lama's entourage first at the Norbulingka and proceed from there. It seemed peculiar for the PLA to be sending a car to pick him up. The soldier told him his mother and eldest sister were also invited, but Ngari Rinpoché knew that neither was likely to be interested.

Ngari Rinpoché, the youngest child in the family, had an ebullient personality and an inquisitive mind, and he was fascinated with guns and airplanes, like many other boys his age. However, at the age of four he had been recognized as the fifteenth reincarnation of the Ngari Rinpoché and sent to Drepung Monastery to take the tonsure and embark on a life of study and meditation. He found it terribly dreary, as he detested memorizing scriptures, and was far more interested in the guns left behind by his previous incarnation. A trip to the PLA Tibet Military Command sounded like great fun to him.

Glad to be free of a day of study, Ngari Rinpoché gave the matter no further thought and stood chatting with the soldiers while they waited for some high lamas who had also been invited. After a while, the lamas finally meandered into view, greeted the soldiers ceremoniously, and seated themselves in the cars. The young Rinpoché hopped in with them, noting that the sun was just peeking out over the mountains.[2]

For seventeen-year-old Tubten Khetsun, incense-bearer at the recently concluded prayer festival, March 10 started out like any other normal workday. He got up, washed his face, ate breakfast, and got ready to go to his job at the Norbulingka, where both his uncle and his elder brother also worked.[3] He was thrilled to have been chosen to accompany the Dalai Lama on his upcoming pilgrimage to Lhakha, and was eager to get started on the trip. As usual, he and his elder brother started out the door with their bicycles. But just then a relative—a monk-official named Ngawang Chopei—appeared and intercepted them breathlessly.

"Be careful today," he warned them. "And bring your guns."

Tubten asked him what was wrong.

"You'll see!" Ngawang replied, entering the house.[4]

As the brothers rode past the Jokhang Temple, they encountered an old government supervisor leading a crowd in the direction of the Norbulingka and noticed that some of the elderly people were weeping. Then the brothers passed another overwrought throng near the Potala, headed by a man from the Norbulingka storeroom. When they reached the Norbulingka, all seemed normal. The security guards were at their usual posts, and some locals were milling around near the stone snow lions. The brothers dismounted and walked their bicycles into the palace grounds.

That same morning, a young lama named Jampa Tenzin set out toward the PCART for his routine political study class. He was barely twenty-three, and had just started working as an accounting trainee in the PCART business office. He also had a job at the Norbulingka, on the stage crew for Tibetan dramas performed for the Dalai Lama during festivals.

The night before, a close colleague had hinted mysteriously that he should go to the Norbulingka instead of the PCART the next morning. Jampa asked him to explain, but the colleague only repeated his cryptic insistence that Jampa go to the palace. Jampa had set out as usual for the PCART in the morning when he suddenly remembered his colleague's tip and stopped in his tracks in front of the Potala to decide where to go. Just then, another colleague from the PCART happened to walk by. Possessed by a sudden, irresistible urge to go to the Norbulingka, Jampa stopped the colleague and asked him to tell the people at the office that he would be missing work that day. Seemingly aware that trouble was afoot, the colleague cautioned him to stay away from the palace, but Jampa decided to ignore the advice. He was astounded to find himself in a sea of people all surging in the same direction. "What's going on?" he wondered. Then he ran into another acquaintance, who answered his question.

"Terrible news—the Chinese are trying to lure Gyalwa Rinpoché to their military headquarters. He's in great danger!"

Jampa paled and broke into a trot, all the way to the Norbulingka.[5]

Captain Sethar Phuntsok was in charge at the main entrance to the Norbulingka. At around 8:00 A.M., he was shocked to see hordes of screaming people suddenly converging on the palace from the direction of town. He promptly alerted his subordinates to secure the main gate and phoned Security Chief Phuntsok at home to ask for instructions.

After tossing and turning all night, Security Chief Phuntsok had finally dozed off at dawn, only to be awakened by the telephone. He directed Sethar to bolt the gate to the Dalai Lama's New Palace and to summon all guard officers immediately to headquarters, after which he hung up and made his way there as quickly as he could. As soon as his men had assembled, he ordered them to secure the palace gates, putting Lieutenant Colonel Seshing in charge of the front gate. Then he ran to the New Palace to brief Chief of Staff Gadrang and Lord Chamberlain Phala. By that time, a number of civil servants had arrived for work, but they were milling around in confusion.[6]

Meanwhile, people were pouring in from downtown and the Shol neighborhood, gathering in front of the palace. Some wielded clubs, swords, or guns, while others prostrated themselves in the direction of the main gate or circumambulated the palace walls.

Some people were simply standing and wailing at the gate.

"Please don't go, Gyalwa Rinpoché!"

"Noblemen, don't sell out our Supreme Jewel to the Chinese!"[7]

The Chinese militia in Lhasa was put on alert and all members sprang to their posts. Grabbing their guns, they scrambled into their rooftop bunkers.[8]

Some young clerks who had reported to the Norbulingka for work as usual that day were ordered to help guard the main gate. Tubten Khetsun was one of them, and this was when he finally found out what was wrong.

After hearing the gossip from his servant that the Chinese were going to abduct the Dalai Lama and take him to Beijing, Tenpa Soepa, who worked at the Reform Bureau, set out for the Norbulingka instead of his office in the Jokhang Temple. All along the way, people were barging past him toward the Norbulingka. At the Dekyi Lingka,[9] he spotted Khenchung Sonam Gyatso whizzing by on a scarlet motorcycle, wearing a monk's habit and evidently on his way to the morning tea service at the Norbulingka. Sonam was suspect for his links to the Chinese. He served on the Chamdo Liberation Committee and was nicknamed the "Chamdo Khenchung."[10] When Tenpa Soepa finally reached the main palace gate, he found it sealed off; the area was packed with clamoring people.[11]

At 9:00, twenty-five-year-old Thinley Phuntsok started walking toward the Norbulingka from an estate on the southern outskirts of town, carrying a confidential missive in the folds of his *chupa*.

The estate belonged to the eminent Ling Rinpoché, the Dalai Lama's tutor. Thinley, a boy from an ordinary Lhasa craftsman's family, had started working there as a servant at the age of eighteen. Since he had some education, having attended both the private academy attached to Gyuto Upper Tantric College and a British school in Lhasa, he had risen above mere courtyard sweeping to become Ling Rinpoché's clerk.

Out on the streets that morning, he was puzzled to see people—mostly ordinary citizens, and a few civil servants—rushing toward the Norbulingka. He asked a passerby what was happening and was told of the Chinese scheme to kidnap the Dalai Lama and take him away to China.

Thinley shuddered, and stepped up his pace. He could not resist the urge to check on the letter in his robe, a folded square of paper tightly bound with thread and affixed with sealing wax. He knew it contained a divination that the cabinet wanted the Dalai Lama to perform. The Dalai Lama was the diviner in name only, however; Ling Rinpoché was the one who usually did the job. Two days prior, the cabinet had delivered this inquiry to him at his estate, but he was still living at the Norbulingka because of the recent New Year's holiday. Thinley's job was to forward the message to him there.

"I wonder what they're worried about," he mused, as he slid it back into the folds of his *chupa*.[12]

: : :

When Barshi, Yeshi, and their colleagues decided to spread their news around Lhasa, they might not have realized how seriously it would be blown out of proportion as it passed along the grapevine. Some people heard that the Dalai Lama had already been abducted, others that the Chinese had invaded the Norbulingka and were trying to make off with him. Such rumors seemed entirely plausible in the highly charged atmosphere, and people feared that the removal of the Dalai Lama from Lhasa would seal their doom. Vendors shuttered their shops and stalls, while panicky citizens converged in droves on horseback, on foot, or on bicycles at the Norbulingka. By 10:00 in the morning a crowd of thousands had gathered at the palace gates.[13]

Despite the commotion in the streets, all was quiet in Yabshi House, the residence of the Dalai Lama's family. The Dalai Lama's mother, Diki Tsering, had her breakfast and picked up her embroidery to while away the time. Her servants were dying cloth and her steward was going over the accounts. She lived alone with her eighty-seven-year-old mother: three sons and one daughter were abroad; her eldest daughter, Tsering Dolma, lived nearby in the officers' barracks with her husband, Security Chief Phuntsok; and her youngest son, Ngari Rinpoché, was at Drepung Monastery.

Before long, her tranquil morning was interrupted by a friend with news of the demonstration at the Norbulingka. Fearing for Ngari Rinpoché's safety, she quickly sent a servant to Drepung Monastery to fetch him.[14]

The crowd in front of the Norbulingka was in an uproar. Some people said that the Dalai Lama was going to Beijing for a meeting and that the Chinese had an airplane at Damshung Airport waiting to whisk him away. Others added that the Chinese were going to hold him hostage in Beijing to force the Chushi Gangdruk guerrillas to surrender. Speakers from Kham and Amdo[15] were whipping up their listeners with wrenching tales of distinguished headmen, abbots, and high lamas who had been lured to meetings, study classes, banquets, or theater performances and then abducted by the Chinese, never to return.[16] One example was the Seventh Rongpo Drubchen, Lobsang Thinley Lungtok Gyatso of Rongpo

Monastery, and another was the widely venerated, seventy-year-old Third Arotsang Rinpoché of Treldzong Monastery in Qinghai.[17] It was said that such people had been swept away into prisons, and some had even been killed. Tears rolled down the speakers' faces as they told of these events, and the crowd reacted with fury.

Just after 9:00, the cabinet members began to arrive at the Norbulingka for their prearranged meeting to discuss the Dalai Lama's excursion that afternoon. Ministers Shasur and Liushar, who came first, were taken aback at the sight of the crowd, but they managed to enter the gates unimpeded.

At around 10:00, a PLA jeep approached the palace carrying Cabinet Minister Sampo Tsewang Rigzin, Tibetan Army commander-in-chief, who had just been commissioned to major general in the PLA and had his own PLA jeep, driver, and armed bodyguard.[18] Seeing the crowd, he got out of the jeep to walk, but the arrival of the PLA jeep and the uniformed bodyguard sent the demonstrators into a furor. Assuming that the PLA had come to cart the Dalai Lama away, people pelted the jeep with stones. One hit Sampo in the head, knocking him unconscious.

Juchen Tubten had been milling around the Norbulingka gates for several hours by that time, watching the crowd grow. As he happened to be nearby when Sampo's jeep approached, he witnessed the entire disturbing episode. A close friend of Sampo's family, he believed that Sampo was a good man, and that the crowd was mistaken.

Tenpa Soepa and some other young civil servants who had been assigned to guard the gates rushed over and loaded the wounded cabinet minister back into his jeep, and the driver rushed him to the clinic at the Indian Consulate.

By then, the Tibetan government had been reduced to mere figurehead status. The area under its jurisdiction had shrunk to a third of its original size, its diplomatic and defense functions had been abrogated, and it had no say in substantive affairs of state. The only realm in which it preserved a modicum of authority was the maintenance of public order in Lhasa. The cabinet's sole agenda for the day was to review the arrangements for the Dalai Lama's visit to the PLA Tibet Military Command, and then to accompany him there. Cabinet Minister Ngabo would normally have been with them that morning, but he had gone to the PCART office to conduct a political study session.[19]

Soon after Sampo's jeep sped off, Chief Cabinet Minister Surkhang arrived by car. Spotting the crowd from afar, he got out to cross the bridge to the palace on foot. Jampa Tenzin and some *tsedrungs* who were guarding the gate saw Surkhang approach and hurried over to help him, attracting the rage of the mob.

"Don't let the Dalai Lama go to the PLA camp!" people shouted, charging at them.

"You traitors!" came the veiled threat. "You'd better not let Gyalwa Rinpoché go to that meeting in China!"

"Don't sell our Gyalwa Rinpoché for Chinese silver!"

Some women were sobbing. "Please, please, don't let our Supreme Jewel go to the Chinese camp!"[20]

There were grounds for the people's suspicions that their upper-crust government had privileged connections to the Chinese. By that time, many elite Tibetans had (whether they knew it or not) been purposefully courted by the Communists under their United Front policy, from Chief Cabinet Minister Surkhang and the Dalai Lama's Junior Tutor, Trijang Rinpoché, to members of the Dalai Lama's family. His eldest sister, Tsering Dolma, was designated chairwoman of the Patriotic Tibetan Women's League; she was also the United Front Target of Su Zhuqing, wife of Guo Xilan, administrative director of the CCP Tibet Work Committee.[21] Diki Tsering, the Dalai Lama's mother, was another noteworthy "target."[22] On a broader scale, by 1957, the committee had sent more than a thousand prominent Tibetans on study tours to China, where they received red carpet treatment. General Zhang Jingwu had also paid his respects and donated alms at the "great three" monastic universities upon his arrival in Lhasa.

By and large, the approach had worked. By 1959, most of the top aristocrats in Lhasa had ties with the Communist-run trading outfits in Tibet: more than twenty such Tibetan families had business contracts with Chinese enterprises, with a trade volume of more than nine million yuan.[23] Approximately one-third of the six thousand middle- and upper-middle-class Tibetans were employed in Chinese-run enterprises.[24] Aware of the aristocracy's vested interest in China, ordinary Tibetans tended to mistrust their leaders and accuse them of selling out to the Chinese.

As Surkhang approached the Norbulingka, he knew better than to provoke the angry demonstrators. Turning a deaf ear to their jeers, he smiled ingratiatingly and, shielded by Jampa Tenzin and his cohorts, wended his way into the palace.

The gate clanged shut behind him.

At around 11:00 A.M., Tenpa Soepa, who was still guarding the gate, saw a man in a Tibetan robe and a white surgical face mask[25] approach on a bicycle. Someone jumped to the conclusion that he was a Chinese cadre posing as a Tibetan, and snatched off his mask. Tenpa Soepa saw that he was the "Chamdo Khenchung," Sonam Gyatso, whom he had spotted earlier in different attire. Some demonstrators also recognized him.

"He's a Chinese spy!" came the shout.[26]

The crowd went berserk and swarmed toward Sonam, who turned and pedaled southward as fast as he could. People started clubbing him and pelting him with stones. An old monk tried to stop them but they brushed him aside. Juchen Tubten, who was about a dozen yards away, watched as Sonam was engulfed by the crowd like a rock sinking into the sea.

By this time, a number of Tibetan guests had arrived at the PLA Tibet Military Command, and were chatting idly or playing mahjong. Bored with the wait, Ngari Rinpoché explored the building. He sensed tension in the air as the Chinese officers bustled around, speaking in hushed tones. Having learned some Chinese on his 1954 trip to China with the Dalai Lama, he asked some officers what was wrong.

"You little imp!" they replied playfully. But they told him nothing.[27]

At around this time, Thinley Phuntsok arrived at the Norbulingka. The gate area was seething. Some demonstrators dragged a corpse into his view, and a bystander told him it was Sonam Gyatso, who had worked for the Chinese at the PCART. Unable to make his way through the crowd, Thinley stayed outside.

From within the white palace walls, Security Chief Phuntsok heard two gunshots. He phoned the main gate guard post to ask what had happened and was told that the crowd had assaulted Sonam. Phuntsok hurried to the gate, but he did not get there in time. Sonam's corpse was lying next to one of the stone snow lions. As he gazed dismally at the young monk-official's body, Phuntsok realized with alarm that the crowd was out of control.[28]

He turned and went back into the palace to report the situation to the Dalai Lama, whom he found in a prayer room built by the Seventh Dalai Lama, worshiping at the altar statue of Mahakala.[29] When he heard Phuntsok's report, he led him solemnly outside onto the roof and gazed up at the cloudless blue sky. The sun was beaming down on his rugged land.

"Everything's going to be all right, isn't it?" the Dalai Lama suddenly blurted out.

Phuntsok was at a loss for words.[30]

: : :

As events snowballed that morning, the top leaders on both sides called emergency meetings. PLA officers were mobilized to ready their units for battle.

On the Tibetan side, the commanders of Regiments 2, 4, and 6 hurried to the Norbulingka and reported to Security Chief Phuntsok that they had posted security and army forces in the streets. However, they were wondering what they should do if people prostrated themselves in the streets to block the Dalai Lama's excursion.

Chief of Staff Gadrang went with cabinet ministers Shasur, Surkhang, and Liushar to the Dalai Lama's New Palace, and implored him again to cancel the afternoon's plans.

Ngabo was still conducting a political study session at the PCART office. Hearing of Sonam's death, he decided to bypass the Norbulingka and meet the Dalai Lama at the PLA Tibet Military Command instead. Lhalu Tsewang Dorje, former governor of Kham,[31] was on his way to the Norbulingka with a servant, but he turned around and went straight home as soon as he learned of Sonam's fate.

Su Zhuqing went to invite her United Front Target, the Dalai Lama's eldest sister, Tsering Dolma, to the PLA show, but a servant turned her away at the door. A PLA courier arrived at the Dalai Lama's mother's house with her invitation, but her steward declined on the pretext that she was not feeling well. Word of these unconventional invitations leaked out among the people, confirming their suspicions that the PLA was plotting a dragnet. When the Tibetan staff of the Youth and Women's Council heard the news, some rushed to the Norbulingka, while others ran home.

Tibetan dignitaries kept filtering into the PLA camp, where they waited for the Dalai Lama, and the PLA theatrical troupe was in full costume, ready to go on stage as soon as he arrived. Diki Tsering's servant returned from Drepung Monastery and reported to the steward that Ngari Rinpoché had been taken to the PLA Tibet Military Command. Diki Tsering told the steward to send someone there to check on him at once. The Dalai Lama's photographer, Jigme Taring, rode his motorcycle from his house to the Norbulingka but could hardly get through the crowd.

General Tan Guansan called an emergency meeting to discuss the developments at the Norbulingka and how they should be reported to the Central Committee.

Security Chief Phuntsok, following Phala's instructions, ordered armed soldiers to guard the palace gates while he sent a car to pick up the Dalai Lama's mother. The demonstrators were still swarming in front of the palace, demanding an audience with the Dalai Lama to beg him to cancel the trip. The cabinet asked them to choose some representatives. Monks from the "great three" monastic universities and people from nearby towns kept pouring in. As soon as the car for the Dalai Lama's mother pulled out of the palace gates, the demonstrators—suspicious that the Dalai Lama was hidden inside—mobbed it, forcing it to turn around and go back. The demonstrators chose thirty people—representing each of the three traditional Tibetan provinces—who were allowed into the palace.

A group of ten demonstrators went to the Indian Consulate with a petition asking the Indian government to come to the aid of Tibet on the grounds that the Chinese were violating the Seventeen-Point Agreement. A mob of several hundred people tied Sonam Gyatso's corpse behind a horse and dragged it toward town, parading it through Barkor Street.

The cabinet made three emergency decisions: (1) the Dalai Lama would cancel his outing to soothe public unrest, (2) Chief Cabinet Minister Surkhang would personally announce this news to the crowd, and (3) Ministers Surkhang, Liushar, and Shasur would go to the PLA Tibet

Military Command to explain the change of plans to General Tan Guansan.

At noon, the appointed hour for the Dalai Lama's arrival at the PLA Tibet Military Command, Surkhang appeared with a megaphone atop the watchtower over the main gate of the Norbulingka. He called to the crowd to calm down, announcing that the Dalai Lama had canceled his plan to go to the PLA Tibet Military Command, and adding that he, Liushar, and Shasur were on their way there to inform the Chinese of the reasons for the Dalai Lama's decision. Unappeased, the demonstrators continued to call out further demands: the Dalai Lama must do more than simply cancel that day's outing; he had to promise never to attend any Chinese functions at all. Surkhang gave his consent and urged the crowd repeatedly to disperse, but to no avail.[32] It is worth noting that all Chinese narratives intended for general consumption omit any mention of Surkhang's efforts to keep the peace.

The demonstrators had achieved their objective of forestalling the Dalai Lama's excursion, but the trouble was just beginning. Once the people's passions were inflamed, events continued to hurtle out of control.

: : :

After Surkhang's announcement, a car with the three cabinet ministers exited the Norbulingka gate, where the mob halted it to search for the Dalai Lama before allowing it to speed on its way to the PLA Tibet Military Command.

The crowd continued to mill around. People were not ready to leave just yet.

"What if the noblemen send the Dalai Lama to the PLA Tibet Military Command as soon as we're gone? Let's stay here!" came the shouts.[33]

Some people, including Juchen Tubten and his compatriots, went home for tents to set up camp at the Norbulingka gates, to make sure no one smuggled the Dalai Lama out. Others went back for weapons.

At the PLA Tibet Military Command, Ngari Rinpoché, bored stiff, saw the cabinet ministers arrive and go into a meeting with the Chinese. This was the last time the two sides ever talked face-to-face. None of the main participants—the three cabinet ministers, Ngabo, Tan Guansan, or Deng Shaodong—ever provided a written record of the encounter. The best available extant sources are the cable the CCP Tibet Work Committee sent to Beijing later that day, and Security Chief Phuntsok's memoirs. Phuntsok may have been present at the meeting as interpreter; if not, he probably based his account on the three ministers' report to the Dalai Lama after their return from the PLA Tibet Military Command.

According to the CCP Tibet Work Committee's cable, the three ministers arrived at the PLA Tibet Military Command at approximately 2:30 P.M. Beijing time, half an hour before the performance was to begin. Here is the committee's carefully worded summary of the events that led to the meeting:

> Yesterday (March 9) afternoon, five members of the Dalai Lama's staff told him of their opposition to his visit to our headquarters, but the Dalai Lama told Phala to notify them that it was too late to cancel his plans. Today, the masses surrounded the Norbulingka to petition the Dalai Lama to cancel his visit, and (some) abbots from the "great three" monasteries along with a group of civil servants asked the cabinet ministers to submit their request to the Dalai Lama. Deciding that the outing was no longer feasible, the Dalai Lama sent three cabinet ministers to discuss this with us.[34]

According to Phuntsok's memoirs, Tan Guansan, Deng Shaodong, Brigadier Fu, and Ngabo were at the PLA Tibet Military Command when the cabinet ministers arrived. Tan Guansan invited them to sit down, and they sat facing their hosts. Ngabo, who had been sitting with the Chinese officers, remained in his seat. Surkhang's message raised Tan Guansan's hackles. His face beet red, he shouted expletives at the Tibetan ministers and waved his finger in their faces until they began to fear that he was going to take them into custody.

Tan asserted that the protest demonstration at the Norbulingka was "a deliberate plot," "executed by counterrevolutionary elements in the local government." The ministers apparently countered that the Tibetans had not had enough advance notice of the PLA invitation to plot any such thing. Tan replied, "The Dalai Lama decided on his own to come here more than a month ago, and Comrade Deng Shaodong told the cabinet about it at the time. It is highly suspect for the cabinet to claim no prior knowledge of the invitation, and especially to deny awareness of the counterrevolutionary plot behind today's events."[35]

Tan Guansan had omitted one crucial fact: when Deng Shaodong had told the cabinet about the invitation at the Potala a month earlier, no date had been set for the Dalai Lama's visit. Ngabo states in his memoir that the first he heard of the March 10 date was at 3:00 P.M. on March 9, although it was not until three or four hours later that he received formal notification from the cabinet to transmit the information to Chief Cabinet Minister Surkhang.

In fact, the PLA arrangements for the occasion were high-handed and clumsy, and this, to a great degree, was what led the Tibetan general public to believe there was a Chinese plot.

When Tan Guansan had finished venting his temper, Shasur tried to placate him.

"The Party has helped us a great deal," he said soothingly, "but the masses are poorly educated, so they have acted inappropriately. Thanks to the kind indulgence of the Party, the Dalai Lama's religious rites were completed smoothly, and this is a great achievement. We will continue to strive for Chinese–Tibetan unity, and have never done anything to disrupt it. Minister Ngabo, who is present today, is best qualified to comment, so I think we should hear what he has to suggest."[36]

This request notwithstanding, Ngabo appears to have remained silent throughout the meeting.

"You're making a big mistake if you pin all your hopes on that band of Khampa rebels in Shannan [Lhokha]," Vice-Commander Deng chimed in icily. "They've only got a few thousand men, ten thousand at most. We're not a bit scared of them, and we're going to trounce them before long. Don't forget that we beat the Guomindang, who had an army eight million strong. The Party is showing forbearance for now. Think it over carefully!"[37]

Tan Guansan made some demands: the cabinet was to keep the Dalai Lama safe, track down the conspirators, compensate Sonam Gyatso's family, and bring the murderers to justice. The cabinet ministers assured him that they were duty bound to protect the Dalai Lama. Before they returned to the Norbulingka, they went to see Sampo—now transferred to the hospital at the PLA Tibet Military Command—but found him asleep.[38]

While the ministers were in the meeting, United Front section chief Li Zuomin presented Gyatsoling Rinpoché,[39] one of the guests at the

PLA Tibet Military Command that day, with a letter from General Tan Guansan, asking him to transmit it to the Dalai Lama in the Norbulingka. A PLA car took Gyatsoling home so that he could avoid suspicion by setting out from there, instead of from the PLA camp, to deliver the letter.

The curtain rose on time at the PLA auditorium. Despite the absence of the guest of honor, the theatrical troupe was right on cue, "radiating political enthusiasm" for the benefit of the assembled visitors. It was a bizarre scene: the Tibetan dignitaries, the very breed of men whom the Chinese Communists later accused of "deliberately plotting and setting off an armed uprising,"[40] exchanging pleasantries with their hosts at the PLA Tibet Military Command, while the ordinary people had taken to the streets to vent their rage at both sides in attendance at the performance.

Ngari Rinpoché enjoyed the show. In an interview several decades later, he chuckled that he still remembered it very clearly, particularly one choral number, and he categorically denied the rumor that the PLA had held him hostage that day.[41] He had been unaware of the arrival of the servant whom his distraught mother had sent to look for him, and the servant never found him. The servant did, however, happen to peek into a room where he saw the three cabinet ministers sitting, with a "Chinese officer" haranguing them. When he reported back to Diki Tsering, she was beside herself, and sent people to scour the city for her little boy.

Once the three ministers had left, the CCP Tibet Work Committee cabled its summary of the situation to the Central Committee, which concluded:

> We plan to step up our military preparedness in response to the events outlined above, and to adopt the following measures:
>
> 1. We will continue to seek the Dalai Lama's cooperation and to support progressive forces, while exposing the plots of instigators. This means that we shall—in response to the events Comrade [Tan] Guansan has outlined above—expose (exclusively by word of mouth) the reactionary plots to the officials, the masses, and the cadres.
> 2. We will hold a memorial meeting for the progressive personage who was martyred, and arrange for compensation for his family.[42]

Meanwhile, Gyatsoling Rinpoché, bearing the letter from General Tan Guansan, rode his horse from his house to the Norbulingka, but could not make his way through the gate, and had to wait outside.

: : :

A seminal assembly took place in the Ceremonial Hall at the Norbulingka that afternoon. Since controversy has swirled around this assembly ever since, the tangled record must be examined as closely as possible. Detailed eyewitness accounts exist in the memoirs of three participants: Security Chief Phuntsok, Khenchung Tara, and a government secretary named Gegyepa Tenzin Dorje.

What was historic about this gathering was the presence of a self-appointed group of "people's representatives"[43] from among the demonstrators outside the Norbulingka, side by side with the customary assemblage of Tibetan (monk and lay) officials. These commoners had succeeded in pressuring Tibetan officialdom to allow them into the palace with their demands, and a joint assembly including them was convened. This assembly, or one similarly composed, took on a more formal aspect and title in subsequent sessions on March 11 and March 12, 1959, assuming the functions of the Tibetan National Assembly and forever changing the face of Tibetan government.

The Chinese have made several allegations regarding this assembly, which are not borne out by Tibetan sources. Although the sources vary slightly about the assembly's exact composition,[44] none support Chinese claims that cabinet ministers were present. And, the main agenda was not Tibetan independence, as the Chinese charge, but rather, to determine how best to ensure the Dalai Lama's safety. And, the assembly was not convened by the Dalai Lama, who in fact strongly opposed it.

This diverse group of government officials and people's representatives had conflicting interests, and was seriously divided. As Gegyepa relates, however, it was united in its support of the demonstrators' main concern, which was to keep the Dalai Lama from venturing into Chinese territory: "The people gathered at the Norbulingka to stop their Supreme Jewel from accepting an invitation to go, all of a sudden, to the PLA Tibet Military Command. This was his risky 'critical year,' and visiting the

Chinese was out of the question. We shared the popular sentiment, and were willing to go to any lengths necessary."[45]

The people's representatives also expressed the fear that the Dalai Lama might come to harm if he attended "a certain meeting," citing precedents from Kham and Amdo. Neither Phuntsok nor Tara specifies exactly what meeting was under discussion, but it seems reasonable to infer that it was the Second National People's Congress in Beijing, which the Dalai Lama was expected to attend.

The split between the government officials and the people's representatives emerged when it came to deciding how to protect the Dalai Lama. Fearing that the demonstrators' presence actually compromised his safety, the officials urged them to disperse, promising that his bodyguard regiment would protect him. But the mistrustful people's representatives, seeking to increase rather than reduce their role, presented a petition advocating the formation of a volunteer "people's security force" to protect the Dalai Lama when he ventured outside the Norbulingka, confining his bodyguards to functioning within the palace. Moreover, for at least some of the people's representatives, Tibetan independence was the only solution, and the cause of their anxiety was telling. Tara quotes them as saying, "We know all about Red Chinese actions in Amdo and Kham, and so we insist on discussing the issue of Tibetan independence here and now."[46]

Both Tara and Phuntsok clearly indicate that this vocal pro-independence faction did not represent the opinion of the group as a whole. Tara's account suggests that he found the independence advocates rather noisy, and he comments with evident displeasure that they "refused to go home" once they had raised their issue.[47] Security Chief Phuntsok also mentions this faction's demand for "the recovery of Tibet's independent status" from the "Chinese Communist invaders" who had "trampled" their own Seventeen-Point Agreement with the Tibetan government. He adds, however, that others present still hoped to sign a new agreement with the Chinese, causing the assembly to degenerate into a noisy, inconclusive debate.[48]

Other documents confirm this assembly's focus on the Dalai Lama's safety rather than Tibetan independence. A Tibetan record later recovered and published by the Chinese[49] states that guarding the Dalai Lama was the main agenda, and goes into some detail regarding the specific arrangements that were made for his safety.[50]

Another Chinese source also contains a document that is evidently a record of this assembly. Again, it contains no mention of declaring Tibetan independence or deciding on an action plan toward that goal. Rather, it focuses on "keeping the Treasure of the Tibetan people from falling into the hands of outsiders," and discusses increased measures for guarding the Dalai Lama. All it says with regard to "the weighty matter of independence" is that the group will "continue to submit any good conclusions that it reaches."[51]

Facts notwithstanding, the CCP Tibet Work Committee presented its own assessment of the March 10 assembly. In a cable to Beijing sent on the afternoon of March 11, the committee claimed that the gathering had declared independence, and had even chosen leaders to spearhead the movement: "the Tibetan people have formally arisen as of March 10, and . . . they have severed ties with the Central Committee and determined to 'go all the way in the struggle for Tibetan independence.' Moreover, they named Tsi-pon Shuguba, Khenchung Tara, Surkhang, and some others to lead the 'independence campaign.' "[52] This assertion, despite its inaccuracy, served to build the Party's case for the coming crackdown.

Some other matters were addressed at the March 10 Norbulingka assembly. One was the problem of dual allegiance. Many Tibetan functionaries had assumed concomitant positions in the PCART since its founding in 1956, but the people's representatives now demanded that all such individuals choose one side or the other. Those who wished to continue to serve the Tibetan government were required to sign a binding agreement to give up their posts at the PCART. Jampa Tenzin recalls that he hesitated, then picked up a pen and signed.[53]

Another major—and later controversial—development was the decision to appoint a committee to direct the general public in the crisis situation. This motion was made by Khenchung Tubten Sangpo, who nominated Tara and Tsi-pon Shuguba for starters. No one raised any objections, and four more people were added the next day. This committee assumed some coordinating functions, and it came to eclipse the cabinet's authority. Nonetheless, the cabinet continued to issue its own instructions, and the new coordinating committee had no control over the army; thus, the later Communist charge that it was a "rebel headquarters" was spurious. In fact, there was no unified command on the Tibetan side.

Like many of his officials, the Dalai Lama was concerned that the assembly at the Norbulingka might inflame the Chinese, and he still hoped to stall long enough to find a way to defuse the situation peacefully. He expressed "anger"[54] upon learning of the gathering, and he "sent instructions to the leaders stating that their duty was to reduce the existing tension and not to aggravate it."[55] He forbade any further meetings of the sort in the Norbulingka, although the group flouted his orders the next day.[56]

The cabinet, now marginalized, focused on the Dalai Lama's personal safety in the worsening crisis; it also kept Ngabo informed about developments in the Norbulingka, using Gegyepa as a conduit.[57] But the people, who had lost faith in the cabinet, insisted that they should be the ones to protect the Dalai Lama, proclaiming their willingness to die for the cause. The Tibetan soldiers ripped off their PLA insignia and uniforms. A volunteer security force was formed, with special ID passes that members had to show to gain entrance into the Norbulingka.[58]

The Tibetan colonels drew up a plan at an emergency meeting of their own. Security was to be stepped up around the Potala Palace and the Jokhang Temple. Half of Regiment 2 was to go to Drapchi Barracks,[59] and the rest to the Potala, the main armory, and Chakpori Hill. Regiment 4 was to guard the area north of the Norbulingka, Upper and Lower Gyatso,[60] and the east and west sides of the Jarak Lingka. Regiment 6's artillery camp was responsible for the downtown and Jokhang areas. Regiment 1 was in charge of the Norbulingka, including the Chensel Phodrang,[61] and an area across from the city on the opposite bank of the Kyichu River. New phone lines were to be installed to improve communications between units. The colonels submitted their plan to their commander, Lodoe Kalsang, for approval.

By 4:00 P.M., Thinley Phuntsok noticed that all but a few hundred of the demonstrators outside the Norbulingka had dispersed. He did not realize it at the time, but most of them had gone to Barkor Street, where they were marching and shouting:

> Tibet has always been free!
> Chinese Communists out of Tibet!
> Down with the Seventeen-Point Agreement!
> Tibet for the Tibetans![62]

Thinley entered the Norbulingka, gave his confidential missive to Ling Rinpoché, and walked back home.[63]

At about 5:00, Gyatsoling Rinpoché was finally granted entry into the Dalai Lama's New Palace. The Dalai Lama was sitting, anguished, with his head in his hands. Gyatsoling Rinpoché handed him the letter from General Tan Guansan.[64]

Meanwhile, a PLA driver was taking Ngari Rinpoché back to Drepung Monastery. They passed his mother's steward on the way, and he stopped the car to send the boy home instead. Diki Tsering finally breathed a sigh of relief when he got there.

The Norbulingka gate area quieted down by nightfall. Jampa Tenzin, Tenpa Soepa, and Tubten Khetsun went home, as did the crowds from Lhasa and its environs. The tumultuous day was finally over.

As midnight approached, Security Chief Phuntsok convened his lieutenant colonels and captains to patrol the Norbulingka area. His troops had built fortifications and posted armed sentries throughout the palace grounds. A large contingent of Khampas had set up tents outside the palace walls. Juchen Tubten was there, in a cluster of seven tents housing 192 compatriots from Derge, many of whom he had met in Lhasa.

The day went down in history; it was known as the "Lhasa Incident" or the "March 10 Incident of 1959" by the Chinese, but remembered forever by the Tibetans as "Tibetan Uprising Day."

: 9 :

The Undercover Men of Kham

ONE EARLY DECEMBER NIGHT IN 1957,[1] a black B-17 "Flying Fortress" bomber carrying eight strapping young men in their twenties—six Asians and two Americans—took off from Kadena Air Base in Okinawa. The Americans signaled the Asians to put on their oxygen masks, but the Asians declined with mild amusement. As Khampas, from the "rooftop of the world," the height the plane might reach was nothing to them.

This was a landmark flight, carrying the first batch of Tibetan CIA operatives in history, five Khampas on their way to parachute back into Tibet after four and a half months of intensive training on a tiny Pacific atoll. They had adopted English names for use on the American base: Athar was Tom, Wangdu was Walt, Lhotse was Lou, Dedruk was Dan, and Tseshe was Dick. A sixth member of their group named Tsewang (Sam) had been left behind in Okinawa for treatment because he had accidentally shot himself in the foot. The other Tibetan passenger on the plane was Jentzen Dondrup, Taktser Rinpoché's[2] servant, the Hindi interpreter for the mission.

The two young Americans were CIA instructors Roger McCarthy and James McElroy. With their colleagues, they had just given the Khampa trainees a crash course in basic espionage: explosives, parachuting, maps and diagrams, outdoor survival, intelligence gathering, hand-to-hand combat, disguises, translation, radio operation, and codes. The course had also included a unit on guerrilla warfare: how to organize a squad, use firearms, conduct an ambush, and give ground signals for airdrops.

The plane was headed for an interim stop at Kurmitola, a World War II airfield north of Dhaka, in East Pakistan.[3] No one on the ground knew who was on the plane, what its mission was, or where it was headed.

Five nights later, under a silvery moon,[4] the unmarked black bomber sat poised on the Kurmitola runway like a giant pterodactyl. The five

Khampas, chanting the mantra of their powerful protector, the Bodhisattva Vajrapani, approached its gangway. As they boarded, the CIA instructors shook hands with each of them, wishing them farewell and good luck.

Roaring into life, the plane took off with its load of Tibetans destined for reinfiltration into their homeland. This was their second attempt at takeoff. The first had been on a moonlit night three days earlier, but the sky had clouded up, forcing the pilot to turn back.

The crew was from Poland and Czechoslovakia, to mask American involvement in case of a crash. The mission was to parachute in a first team of men—Athar and Lhotse[5]—near Samye Monastery, about forty miles south of Lhasa, and then to head east and drop the rest of the men, a second team, into Kham.[6] After that, the plane would fly back southwest across Indian airspace to East Pakistan.

Samye Monastery had been chosen for its relative proximity to Lhasa. Aside from general reconnaissance within Tibet, Athar and Lhotse had a special assignment requiring that they be inserted near Lhasa: to notify the Dalai Lama that a formal request from the Tibetan government was a prerequisite for American aid.[7] Judging from some antiquated hand-drawn British expeditionary force maps, which was all the CIA had, the Samye Monastery area looked promising.

The CIA personnel who planned the mission had no idea what a holy site Samye Monastery was for Tibetan Buddhists such as Athar and Lhotse. As the earliest Buddhist monastery in Tibet, it traced its origins to Padmasambhava, known as Guru Rinpoché to the Tibetans, the sage who introduced Buddhism to Tibet in the eighth century. According to legend, he had designed the monastery by flying up into the air and casting a shadow with his trident on the ground. The Tibetan monarch, Trisong Detsen, had traced the shadow as a blueprint for the buildings.[8]

Athar peered through the porthole at the vast, snowcapped Himalayas, tinged an unearthly blue in the moonlight. This was the abode of the legendary *dakinis,* or "sky walkers," female deities who would manifest themselves to enlightened senior monks and take them for a spin in the sky. Athar had done a stint as a monk, although he had fallen far short of enlightenment. Yet now he too was airborne.

The pilots in the cockpit had no experience flying over Tibet, no air route maps, and no radar. Their only clues to the terrain beneath them were a few old photographs, and the antique maps, which dated back to Francis Younghusband's 1904 invasion of Tibet from British India. Because their mission had to be concealed not only from the Chinese but also from the Indians, they flew by the light of the full moon, the plane hugging the Himalayas as a screen against Indian radar. A single misstep, and they would slam into a mountainside. Once they reached the Lhokha region of Tibet, they would need to find a suitable drop zone with their naked eyes.

A broad, gleaming river came into view under the wing—the Tsangpo![9] The plane began to descend, the wide sandbanks they had seen on the old photographs growing larger as they approached. They stood up, bade their companions farewell, and prepared to leap. A supply bundle was attached by a 300-foot cord to a D-ring on Athar's harness, but the men had no backup parachutes. What was more, they had made only three practice jumps.

When the plane had descended to about a thousand feet above the ground, the hatch opened and they saw their homeland beneath them in the moonlight. Athar involuntarily patted his "L" tablet—an ampoule of cyanide taped to his leg.[10] All he had to do was bite open the ampoule to release its contents, and he would carry his secrets with him to the grave. After exchanging a grim smile with Lhotse, he flung the supply bundle down through the hatch and jumped out. Lhotse followed him.

The aircraft turned and headed stealthily east.

As Athar glided earthward, he saw the gilt statuary atop the roof of Samye Monastery—a Dharma wheel framed by a pair of deer—glowing in the light of the full moon. This was exactly where the sage Padmasambhava had flown. It was his mission to protect the religion that Padmasambhava had bestowed on Tibet.

"*Om badzar satwa hung. . . .*" He intoned the mantra of Vajrapani.[11]

In the moonlight over the high plateau, three parachutes wafted down, like pale flowers borne on the wind.

: : :

A year earlier, when Athar, a young monk at Lithang Monastery, had signed his name on a certain piece of paper, he had not realized that this act would place him on the stage of Tibetan history. His friend Wangdu Gyadotsang had approached him privately to ask whether he wanted to "learn the American art of war,"[12] and he had agreed readily. He had pressed Wangdu for the particulars, but Wangdu, after swearing him to the utmost confidence, simply promised to let him know when the time came.

Wangdu and Athar were both natives of Lithang, but from starkly contrasting backgrounds. Wangdu had grown up in the household of his rich uncle, the merchant Gonpo Tashi, whereas Athar was from a poor family. Athar's father had died when he was a small child, leaving his widowed mother to raise him and his three siblings alone. At the age of six, he had entered a wealthy household as a servant boy, and six years later had become a monk at Lithang Monastery, where he had attained functional literacy in Tibetan. Despite the hardships of his upbringing, he had grown into a splendid young man. He was energetic, smart, and eager to learn. He loved to dance in the yearly *Cham* performance at Lithang Monastery; donning the mask and sumptuous costume, he would whirl and stomp to the sound of cymbals, drums, and horns. Wangdu's younger brother Kelsang, a fellow monk, watched him from the audience, but they were just two among thousands of monks at Lithang Monastery, and they did not know each other. Had the Chinese not intervened in the region, their paths might never have crossed.

As luck would have it, Athar was assigned to the monastery's caravan team, which took him out to the wide world beyond Lithang. First he made a few round-trips to Lhasa, and then to Kalimpong. When tension in Kham began to mount in 1954, he stayed in Kalimpong instead of returning.

There were plenty of Khampas like Athar in Kalimpong, and twenty-seven young compatriots from Lithang, Bathang, and Markham gradually coalesced into a group including Wangdu and Kelsang, who arrived in the fall of 1956. They tried to support themselves with small businesses, and those who were successful helped their friends in need. Whenever there was a fresh arrival from home, they eagerly extracted the latest news and spread it around. But the news kept worsening, until one day a caravan brought reports of the bombing of Lithang Monastery. The young Khampa men began to seek a means to fight back. When the Dalai Lama was in New Delhi in 1956, his brother Gyalo Dondrup arranged for the young Khampas to meet with him, but the Dalai Lama rebuffed their entreaties for an organized resistance against the Chinese, urging nonviolence instead. The young Khampas were briefly stymied, but undeterred.

They followed the Dalai Lama to Bodh Gaya, where they met Taktser Rinpoché, who, seemingly casually, photographed each of them. Despite their willingness to fight, they knew nothing about modern guerrilla warfare. Athar had no idea that the photos were for CIA use. Gyalo Dondrup met secretly with the CIA's officer in Calcutta, John Hoskins, to choose six of the twenty-seven men for training, and they agreed to take things one step at a time.[13]

Back in Kalimpong in mid-February 1957, a messenger came to tell Athar to prepare to depart that night for an undisclosed destination.

"Don't wear a *chupa,* don't bring cash, and leave your Tibetan knife at home," the messenger instructed him. He was not to carry any objects that might provide a clue to his identity.[14]

After feasting that night, Athar and his friends changed into Indian garb and arrived punctually at a prearranged spot in Kalimpong, where they waited silently by the dark road.

At exactly 9:00 P.M., a jeep approached with Gyalo Dondrup at the wheel and his cook and Hindi interpreter, Gelung, at his side. Gyalo Dondrup gave them hushed instructions not to utter a word during the journey no matter what happened, and the jeep sped off toward Darjeeling. They made one stop for a meal, wordlessly downing a plate of chapatis and potatoes, before climbing back into the jeep. The mercury rose as the jeep wended its way down from the Himalayas, and the men, packed tight in their seats, began to sweat. After a while, Athar saw a cluster of lights on the dark plains ahead. They had reached the strategic northern Indian town of Siliguri.

A new driver replaced Gyalo Dondrup at the wheel and drove them to a spot near the border of East Pakistan. There, Gelung led them along a trail onto a tea plantation. Athar was intrigued by a small handheld device that Gelung was using to get his bearings. With the ban on speaking lifted now that they were far from human habitation, Gelung let Athar hold the device and showed him how it worked. He had never seen a compass before, always orienting himself by the stars.

After a couple of hours' hike, they reached the river that divided India from East Pakistan, which they forded, holding hands, at the shallowest section they could find. On the opposite bank, Gelung signaled them to stop by a small road. A man with a rifle approached, and Athar's heart began to pound: Was it a policeman to arrest them for the illegal border crossing?

Gelung exchanged a few words with the man, who turned out to be their Pakistani guide. He led them along a winding, deserted back road until they finally met up with some men, one of whom was Taktser Rinpoché's servant, Jentzen. His mission accomplished, Gelung handed the men over to Jentzen.

A jeep emerged from a nearby grove of trees, and the men piled in and rode to a cottage half an hour away. Eventually a man emerged to greet them. He was an imposing figure, with brown hair and blue eyes, a big nose, white skin, and blond fuzzy arms: CIA officer Edward McAllister.

So that's what Americans look like, Athar mused. McAllister's downy arms struck the young Khampas as funny, and they exchanged winks, barely able to stifle their giggles.

The jeep took them to the train station, where they were smuggled onto a first-class car in the guise of a group of prisoners and their armed guards. As the sole occupants of the car, they finally had an opportunity to stretch out and relax. Someone brought them ice water, and Athar wondered where they had gotten ice in such a warm climate. The train rattled along the track for ages to an undisclosed destination. Athar and the others got out and were bundled into the canvas-covered back of a truck, which deposited them at an airport, where they boarded a plane via a small metal staircase at the tail end. As soon as they were seated, the plane whirred into motion and shuddered down the runway. Athar felt a curious swaying sensation as the plane lifted off with a roar.

Athar looked around him with irrepressible curiosity. The cabin of a plane looked like a long narrow room with windows on both sides, he reflected. Too bad the curtains were shut so he could not get a glimpse of "heaven." Just as he tried to open the curtains for a peek, a huge American appeared and signaled him to keep them closed. After a while, someone brought him a dark-colored drink that looked like strong black tea. He was sure he saw cubes of ice in the glass, but the bubbly liquid seemed to be boiling. He took a cautious sip. It was bittersweet, with medicinal overtones. Later he learned that this peculiar fluid was called Coca-Cola.

As the plane descended, he saw a number of parked aircraft and people who looked Chinese bustling to and fro. This must be an air base in Taiwan, he surmised. He had heard of Taiwan but had never heard of Japan or seen any Japanese people, and he did not realize he was in Okinawa. The men were ushered to a small building on a hilltop where they rested briefly until some white-coated doctors came and indicated that they should strip for physicals.

The Khampa men burst into an uproar. Anyone could tell at a glance that they were perfectly healthy—what was the point of a physical? Besides, Tibetans never stripped naked! Unable to understand a word the men were saying, the American doctors were at a loss. Just then, the door opened and Athar was overjoyed to see Taktser Rinpoché.

In those days, only a handful of Americans knew Tibetan. Unable to find reliable translators, the CIA had turned to Taktser Rinpoché, who was teaching an informal Tibetan language course at Columbia University; knowing no one else who could translate, he decided to take a few months off and do it himself.[15]

Once Taktser Rinpoché appeared at the clinic and explained the instructions, the Khampas dutifully undressed and underwent the first complete physicals in their lives.

A week later, they were taken to their designated training ground, a tiny atoll where Athar first saw the sea, a boundless stretch of blue reaching to the horizon. The Khampas dug into their crash course, mastering a year's curriculum in the space of a few months.

No one told them the name of this islet with its caves, jungles, and beaches littered with ghastly white bones, and unexploded ordnance that the Tibetans were assigned to mark with little red flags for detonation. They dubbed the islet "Dursa," or "Isle of the Dead."

Not until years later did Athar learn that the islet was Saipan, and that the skeletons and bombs were relics of its horrific World War II battle.

Athar had stepped into a new world. Feeling the need to supplement his training course with English lessons, he decided to practice with the American cooks whenever he could. They would hand him a basket of potatoes and a knife, and he would sit in the kitchen peeling potatoes while he tried to converse. His first English words were all related to cooking.

More than fifty years later in New York, Athar's second daughter, Dolma Norbu, told me her father's story in fluent English. As I listened to her tale, I tried to conjure up a mental image of the man who loomed so large in my imagination.

As she finished her story, I could not help asking, "Dolma, what did your father look like?"

"Really handsome," she replied with a gentle smile. "He was on the short side for a Khampa, but he was well built."

"Roger said he was built like a fireplug,'" her sister Tsering Dolma added playfully, referring to Athar's instructor, Roger McCarthy. "He was a little hulk."

When Athar Norbu, former monk of Lithang, caravanned out to Kalimpong, little did he know that he was destined to be a "fireplug" at a turning point in history.

: : :

In the middle of the night, while the high plateau was wrapped in slumber, Athar and Lhotse landed stealthily on a sandbank near Samye Monastery.

At the sound of dogs barking in the distance, their hearts leaped into their throats, but then the barking stopped and silence was restored. They cut the parachute cords with their Tibetan knives and stood up to get their bearings. Spotting a hill about four hundred fifty yards away, they took two radio transmitters up to the top and hid them in the shrubbery. Then they headed back to their drop zone, which they found with difficulty in the dark, and made a couple of trips up the hill again to bury their gear. Aside from Tibetan clothes, a small cooking pot, a teapot, and wooden teacups, which Kelsang Gyadotsang, who was in Kalimpong, had procured for them specially from Lhasa,[16] they had wristwatches, calendars, compasses, maps of Tibet, binoculars, Tibetan telecode books, Chinese and Tibetan silver currency, and Tibetan pancakes as emergency rations. For each of them there was also a submachine gun, a pistol, a grenade, and a thousand rounds of ammunition.[17]

Exchanging their green American forest service smoke jumper suits for the Tibetan outfits, they buried everything except one of the radio transmitters and a World War II hand-cranked generator, the pistols, and some bullets. Then they stuck a few shrubs into the ground to mark the spot and sketched a map of its location.

Clambering to the peak of the hill, they radioed headquarters to report their safe arrival. Moments later they got a congratulatory reply: headquarters was going to throw a party to celebrate. Then they packed up the transmitter and surveyed the terrain beneath them. There was a forest a hundred yards away, and the gilt roof of Samye Monastery was clearly visible at a distance of about a thousand yards. About eight hundred yards in the other direction, they spotted an encampment with people milling around a large tent and several smaller ones. Athar reckoned they must be PLA soldiers.

They descended the hill onto the road, where they met a herdsman who sold them a saddleless horse and some butter and *tsampa*. Leading the horse back to their cache, they fashioned a crude saddle and reins from their blanket and parachute cords, grabbed some more supplies, and started on their way to Lhasa. The next day, they tried to radio again from Gokar Pass, but discovered that the radio was damaged, so they bought more pack animals and went back to get the spare radio and empty their cache. They took what they needed and burned the rest.

They set out again for Lhasa. This time, they were on horseback, with an extra horse and mule to carry their bulging bags, just like a couple of traveling merchants. No one would have imagined that their luggage concealed a radio transmitter, and even they had no idea that this transmitter would one day become the Tibetan government's sole link to the outside world. They happened to meet a caravan from Lithang on the way to Lhasa, and one of the riders was a friend from home. Athar asked him to notify Gonpo Tashi, who was still in Lhasa, that they had arrived and would see him in a month. Leery of the Tibetan government, they warned the friend to make sure Gonpo Tashi knew to conceal their arrival from the government officials and aristocrats.

While they were on the road, they were assigned a reconnaissance mission at Damshung Airport, which took almost two weeks. Afterward, they sent word to Gonpo Tashi that they were on their way, asking him to put them in contact with the Dalai Lama and the Tibetan government. When they reached Lhasa in early 1958,[18] Gonpo Tashi sent them a reply: he had talked to Phala and would take them to see the Dalai Lama the next day.

The next morning, Athar and Lhotse disguised themselves as monks. Gonpo Tashi sent two men to pick them up, a motorcyclist who took Lhotse on the back of his motorcycle, and a bicyclist who took Athar. Arriving separately at the Norbulingka, they entered the west gate and were shown to Phala's chambers. They were shocked at the sight of two PLA sentries at the door, until Phala explained that the sentries were in fact Tibetans. The Tibetan troops had all been incorporated into the PLA and made to wear PLA uniforms, although they still had their Tibetan army flag and separate barracks.

Phala inquired about Athar and Lhotse's training program and heaped them with praise, along with fruit and lucky talismans. But when Athar requested an audience with the Dalai Lama, Phala claimed the Dalai Lama was too busy to see them that day. Annoyed, Athar pointed out that they had important business with him, assuring Phala that they would not attract undue notice since they were dressed as monks. Phala countered that they would have to wait a couple of days for the audience, and suggested they watch the Dalai Lama from a distance while he conducted his scheduled religious rites. Athar decided to entrust Phala with the message from the United States. Did the Tibetan government have a general plan? Did it intend to resist the Chinese Communists militarily, or to strike back undercover? Athar requested that Phala and Gonpo Tashi obtain a reply from the Dalai Lama and any trustworthy government officials. He offered to relay this reply to the Americans, and to convey the American response back to Phala.

While waiting to hear from Phala, Athar and Lhotse kept moving around the Lhasa area: Drepung Monastery, Sera Monastery, and then the Penpo[19] Valley, where they spent an entire month. With no word yet from Phala, they went back to see him again, but found him unable to give them any clear answers. In fact, he had not dared to relay their questions because Tibetan officialdom was divided, and some officials could not be trusted with the secret. Athar and Lhotse decided to consult with Gonpo Tashi about how to proceed.[20] By then it was the spring of 1958, and the CCP Tibet Work Committee had started its campaign to round up illegal Han Chinese runaways from Land Reform and to "register" Tibetan refugees from Kham and Amdo. People were fleeing, and fear was in the air.

It was clearly dangerous for Athar and Lhotse to stay in Lhasa, but they had not accomplished their mission. Unsure what to do, they consulted an oracle, who advised them to leave by the twentieth day of the fourth month of the Tibetan calendar. They tried to gain another audience with Phala before their departure, but failed.

In May 1958, Athar, Lhotse, and Gonpo Tashi left Lhasa for Lhokha, and the Chushi Gangdruk Defenders of the Faith was founded there in June. Athar was summoned back to India to report on his mission, and he was still there in July, when the CIA air-dropped weapons into Tibet for the first time. After he returned to Tibet, he trained the Chushi Gangdruk and coordinated weapons airdrops, completely losing interest in the old aristocrats in the Tibetan government.[21]

On the evening of February 22, 1959,[22] a C-130 cargo plane flew above Lhokha. From the cockpit, the pilot saw a faint red glow on the ground and smoldering yak dung that gradually assumed the shape of the letter "T" as he approached, marking the spot for the airdrop.

In the plane, a few airmen known as "kickers" stood up, donned their oxygen masks, opened the hatch, and shoved out some supply bundles, which were configured so that the men waiting on the ground could load them directly onto pack animals for a swift getaway. That night, Athar and Lhotse received 150 rifles, 150 pistols, and 2 mortars, which they hid until the time came to present them to the Chushi Gangdruk forces.

On March 10, 1959, during the height of the demonstrations at the Norbulingka, Athar and Lhotse were in hiding in Lhokha, six days' journey away, and had no inkling of the turmoil in the capital.

: 10 .

Protect the Norbulingka! Protect the Dalai Lama!

THE EXTRAORDINARY DEMONSTRATIONS in Lhasa spilled over into their second day on March 11, 1959, the second day of the second month of the Earth-Hog year.

The elite of Lhasa had reached the point of no return, and the Tibetan government was virtually paralyzed. Following instructions cabled from Beijing, the CCP Tibet Work Committee moved hundreds of "patriotic Tibetans" (i.e., Tibetans employed by the Chinese) into the PCART building and other Chinese locations for their safety. Some aristocrats such as Sampo Tsewang Rigzin[1] and Phagpa Gelek Namgyal[2] were also moved, and PLA soldiers were sent to guard Ngabo's house. Their acceptance of Chinese sanctuary was emblematic of their rift with the weakened Tibetan government.

In fact, a coup d'état was taking place, although the Tibetans would have been unfamiliar with this terminology. Some officials and army officers had sided with the demonstrators to form a new political force, and established a "coordinating committee," which eventually supplanted the Tibetan government in daily affairs such as public order, guarding the Norbulingka, and directing the aroused populace.[3]

Nonetheless, the new coordinating committee did not constitute a unified Tibetan command during this time of flux. Despite their alliance, the officials and the people's representatives, who had chosen the coordinating committee, failed to see eye to eye on key questions. Neither side had a perfect grasp of the situation or a cohesive goal or plan. Even within the Tibetan military, the command seems to have been splintered. After Sampo, who had been appointed commander-in-chief in October 1958,[4] was injured by the demonstrators on March 10, Tibetan colonels evidently reported to Security Chief Phuntsok instead. Eventually, the Tibetan Army fell into disarray when Phuntsok and the commanders of Regiments

2 and 4 joined the Dalai Lama's exodus from Lhasa. As war loomed, each unit had to make its own decisions in the complete absence of intelligence regarding the Chinese deployment.

A clear sign that the Tibetan government was losing power to the people's representatives occurred early on March 11, when the latter posted six sentries near the cabinet offices inside the Norbulingka to prevent the ministers from slipping out and making private concessions to the Chinese.

The beleaguered cabinet hastily decided to try to disperse the crowd again, and called in the people's representatives. Apparently somewhat chastened, the representatives agreed to cooperate, apologized for injuring Sampo, and asked the ministers to take him some gifts as a token of their apology.[5]

A second historic assembly took place in the Norbulingka later that day. Like its predecessor on March 10, this gathering was expanded to include a number of people's representatives, whereas the traditional Tibetan National Assembly had been composed entirely of monk and lay officials. The common people had gotten their foot in the door of Tibetan governance, and by March 11, this assembly had been dignified with a formal name reflecting the change: the "Expanded Tibetan Assembly of Monk and Lay Officials [and People's Representatives]." The new name strongly suggests that the group was an emergency session—with this new twist—of the Tibetan National Assembly.[6] It continued to be a broad-based body that—despite Chinese accusations and misnomers—included Tibetans willing to cooperate with the Chinese to varying degrees. In fact, it resolved to continue working to "seek leniency" from the Chinese, and passed measures to this end in its session on the following day.[7]

No extant primary source mentions the presence of cabinet ministers Surkhang, Liushar, or Shasur at the March 11 Assembly.[8] According to Lhalu's eyewitness account, Chokteng Tubten Norsang, chief secretary of the Ecclesiastic Office, presided that day, and others present included Khenchung Tara, Kundeling Dzasa, the treasurer of Kundeling Monastery, Tsi-pon Shuguba, and former Tibetan Army commander-in-chief Khemey Sonam Wangdu.

When Lhalu arrived, the newly expanded Assembly was discussing the events of the day before and debating the measures to be taken next.

Lhalu, like some other elite leaders, advocated prudence, denouncing the killing of Sonam Gyatso on grounds that "such unseemly behavior, right at the Norbulingka, sullied the Dalai Lama's name." He opposed holding meetings at the palace, and condemned the demonstrations as counterproductive. "The PLA Tibet Military Command has more than enough cannons to put down a riot," he cautioned, "and they might destroy the Potala while they're at it."[9] Chief Secretary Chokteng Tubten Norsang echoed Lhalu's sentiments, predicting that the Tibetans would "scatter in all directions like peas"[10] under Chinese artillery fire.

Their warnings fell on deaf ears. A civil servant named Gonpo Lung Chonze and a people's representative from Amdo countered hotly that the Dalai Lama needed ironclad protection, given the abductions in Amdo.

Since the appointed time for the Dalai Lama's proposed visit to the PLA Tibet Military Command had long since passed without harm to his person, concerns had evidently shifted to a new problem: his attendance at the Second National People's Congress in Beijing that spring. In December, he had accepted the Central Committee's invitation to bring a Tibetan delegation to the Congress. However, the very idea of his going had elicited general panic in Lhasa, as it was widely believed that the Chinese would keep him hostage in Beijing to force the Chushi Gangdruk guerrillas to surrender.

No evidence of any such Chinese plot has ever surfaced. The Central Committee had not even received a name list or itinerary for the Tibetan delegation to the Congress. The pervasive Tibetan conviction that people needed to lay their lives on the line to protect the Dalai Lama was based more on reports of Chinese abuses in Kham and Amdo than it was on actual knowledge of a Chinese plot against him, and the refugees from those areas were particularly desperate to protect the Dalai Lama.

After a heated debate, the March 11 Assembly divided into smaller discussion groups based on official rank, which later submitted statements of their opinions. According to Lhalu's memoir, his discussion group went on record in support of the popular demand for independence, maintaining that Tibet was independent before 1949. The opinion statement of Lhalu's discussion group, which was far from being a resolution of the Assembly as a whole, may be among the cache of documents retrieved and published—in restricted-circulation editions—by the Chinese after the Battle of Lhasa.[11]

At this point, the Assembly appointed an enlarged coordinating committee of six. Starting with Khenchung Tara and Tsi-pon Shuguba, who had been chosen the previous day, four new members were added: Kundeling Dzasa, Khenchung Kelsang Ngawang, and two officials named Shakabpa Losel Dondrup and Lhadingse Sonam Paljor. When the Battle of Lhasa erupted later, the Chinese called this group the "Rebel Command," and labeled its usual location, the Norbulingka, as "Rebel Headquarters,"[12] which gave them a pretext for shelling the palace.

When the Dalai Lama learned of the March 11 Assembly, he decided to admonish the people's representatives himself:

> I sent for them, and all seventy of them came, and in the presence of the cabinet and other senior officials I did my best to dissuade them from their actions. I told them the Chinese general had not compelled me to accept his invitation; I had been consulted and given my consent before the invitation was issued. I said I was not in any fear of personal danger from the Chinese, and they must not create a situation which could have such serious consequences for the people.[13]

Phuntsok recalls that the Dalai Lama also urged the people's representatives "to stop holding these meaningless gatherings, which would only bring trouble," and that he exhorted them at the very least to move their venue out of the Norbulingka if they insisted on continuing to meet.[14]

In deference to the Dalai Lama's wishes, the Assembly resolved to shift its locale the next day to the Shol Scriptural Printing House, near the Potala, and to ask the demonstrators, most of whom were Khampas, to withdraw from the Norbulingka area. Not surprisingly, however, the Khampas defiantly refused to abandon their vigil. The Assembly then charged the new coordinating committee of six with all major decisions, while delegating responsibility for the Dalai Lama's personal safety to his bodyguard unit.[15]

After the meeting, the coordinating committee divided up the task of defending the palace and its surroundings. Kundeling Dzasa and Shuguba were placed in charge of the main entrance to the palace and the

Dekyi Lingka and Kundeling neighborhoods slightly to the east. Shakabpa Losel Dondrup was responsible for the north side of the palace and the Sand Dam area. Tara was assigned the road to Rama Gang ferry, to the south. Khenchung Kelsang Ngawang's authority reached from the road to Rama Gang ferry to the fields at the south gate of the security guard barracks, and an official named Lhadung took charge of the area around the west wall of the Norbulingka near the Chensel Phodrang.[16]

In consultation with Security Chief Phuntsok and the commanders of army Regiments 2, 4, and 6, it was decided that Regiment 1—the security guards—should watch over the Norbulingka and the Chensel Phodrang. Regiment 2, from Drapchi Barracks, would guard the Potala, the Shol Armory, and Chakpori Hill, atop which it had evidently been constructing fortifications for some time.[17] Regiment 6 took charge of the downtown area, and Regiment 4 had the area north of the Norbulingka.[18]

As an anti-infiltration measure, the coordinating committee added teams of trustworthy volunteers to supplement the Norbulingka's security guards. Monks from the "great three" monastic universities went to the north gate, refugees from five Amdo tribes took the west gate, Khampas from Derge, Chamdo, Gonjo, and Shuksar had the south gate, facing the river, and traders from Lhasa were on the east.[19]

At that point, the coordinating committee received a demand for weapons from the people's representatives, who asserted that arms were needed to protect the Dalai Lama because the Chinese "were surely angered by his rejection of their invitation, and might attack the Norbulingka to enforce it." The request placed Tara in a quandary: "Our government had no plans for armed resistance to the Chinese, and those of us in positions of responsibility were not empowered to distribute weapons to the people. Nonetheless, we had no choice but to consider their demand."[20]

Khenchung Gyaltsen, from the Potala Palace administration, pointed out that a room in the rear of the Potala contained some old British rifles that had once belonged to the Tibetan Army. Regulations stipulated that no one could use the rifles without permission from the Shol administration,[21] the cabinet, and army headquarters. In the current crisis, however, the group decided to bypass the regulations and load the weapons into a truck from the guard barracks under cover of night. They agreed to distribute the rifles to the people—although they had no bullets—along with instructions to defend the Norbulingka if "Chinese soldiers" approached, only firing if circumstances clearly warranted it.[22]

Meanwhile, the CCP Tibet Work Committee had just received almost identical orders. Each side believed the other was capable of attacking, and each misjudged the intention of the other. Both sides were on their guard.

: : :

The turmoil in Lhasa continued into its third day on March 12, the third day of the second month of the Earth-Hog year.

In compliance with the Dalai Lama's request, the officials and people's representatives moved their "Expanded Tibetan Assembly" outside of the Norbulingka, and held their session in the Scriptural Printing House in the Shol neighborhood. The CCP Tibet Work Committee sent a detailed report on the meeting to Beijing two days later, which suggests that its infiltrators were present. The report begins by pointing out that the people's representatives were armed: "Aside from abbots and government officials, a large number of armed rebels (about 860 of them) also attended the meeting, calling themselves 'people's representatives.'"[23] Although one should allow for possible distortions, the Chinese report provides a rare window into the dynamics of the meeting, documenting the palpable tension between the people's representatives and the Tibetan officials. Apparently, the session opened in chaos. The officials in charge arrived late, and the people's representatives chastised them:

> Suddenly everyone started jeering and cursing. Someone said there was no point in the officials' coming unless they took the meeting seriously, and suggested that they leave. An uproar ensued. The officials rose to leave, and some of them did. At this point, a so-called "people's representative" brandished his rifle at them.
>
> "Gentlemen, let's get things straight," he threatened. "We'll shoot anyone who tries to leave." At this, the officials settled down for the meeting.[24]

Once the meeting got underway, the Chinese report continues, the Tibetan officials announced that the Dalai Lama "looked haggard, was refusing to eat or speak, and kept sighing to himself," and that he wanted the group to give careful consideration to the consequences of its actions.[25] The Chinese report adds a somewhat disappointed comment that the Dalai Lama's admonishment did not go over well with the crowd. What is noteworthy about this record is its clear indication that the Chinese were aware that fomenting armed rebellion was far from the Dalai Lama's mind at this point, a fact that contradicts later Chinese charges against him.

To streamline matters, the Assembly elected a body that Tara calls the "standing committee," consisting of the coordinating committee of six people who had been selected for core leadership the day before, along with a select group of forty officials, thirty monks from Sera and Drepung monasteries, and thirty representatives from among the people.[26] Most of the standing committee members' names are unknown. The Chinese report claims that Chief Cabinet Minister Surkhang was selected for membership, although this is not corroborated in Lhalu's memoir. A separate "security committee," including Lhalu, was also named to help safeguard the Norbulingka, and instructed to start its work two days hence.[27]

Despite later Chinese claims that this March 12 Shol Assembly was a "rebel" body, using the misnomer "People's Assembly of Independent Tibet,"[28] evidence indicates that the highly vocal pro-independence faction was outnumbered and that the ultimate sense of the meeting was to seek a peaceful solution to the crisis. Moreover, the CCP Tibet Work Committee's report to Beijing reveals Chinese awareness of this fact. According to the report, the standing committee met and recommended that the Assembly as a whole ask the cabinet to negotiate a peaceful settlement with the CCP Tibet Work Committee and the PLA Tibet Military Command.[29] Lieutenant Colonel Seshing corroborates this; he recalls that the Assembly passed a motion to send a delegation to Beijing to "request leniency from the Central Committee."[30]

: : :

Meanwhile, Lhasa was dissolving into virtual anarchy, as its inhabitants splintered into interest groups with different goals, and a number of other meetings with divergent agendas were taking place. Even though the Expanded Assembly that met at the Norbulingka and the Shol seems to have been too broadly based to have passed a resolution endorsing Tibetan independence,[31] there is convincing evidence of the existence of a Tibetan independence movement in Lhasa at the time.

Some of the "reactionary documents" recovered and published by the Chinese after the Battle of Lhasa suggest the presence of such a movement. The cache from Kundeling Monastery, for example, contains a document listing ten grounds for the Tibetan demand for independence, including religious repression, false promises of autonomy, and lack of redress. The document, which lacks a precise date, indicates that an active node of independence-minded Tibetans held meetings at the monastery sometime between March 10 and March 17; however, it seems unrelated to the large Assembly sessions at the Norbulingka and the Shol.[32]

Other sources mention underground opposition groups in Lhasa at the time. According to Phuntsok's memoir, *A Life,* there were three. One—the "People's Assembly"—traced its origins to the 1952 incident;[33] another, which was organized by a young, Beijing-educated Tibetan named Ngawang Sangye, may have been the same group identified elsewhere as the "Anti-Imperialist Party of Tibet"; and the third was the secret Lhasa branch of the Kalimpong-based "Committee for Tibetan Social Welfare."[34]

The third group may have been the sender of two draft cables to the Committee for Tibetan Social Welfare in Kalimpong, dated March 16 and March 17, which the Chinese found at Kundeling Monastery and published afterward. Both contain notification to former finance minister W. D. Shakabpa that "the independent nation of Tibet was formed on the first day of the second month of the Tibetan calendar (March 10)." The exact identities of the sending organizations is controversial and enigmatic; all that can be ascertained from the blurry photocopies of the Tibetan originals released by the Chinese is that the first was sent by an organization called Bod Gerlang Tsokpa, which translates roughly as "Tibet People's Action Group." The second one may have come from the same organization or a comparable one, although the signature is almost illegible on the photocopy. In their two published translations of the first cable, the Chinese have rendered Bod Gerlang Tsokpa differently (and inaccurately) each time, attributing it to an organization they call the "Independent Assembly of Tibet" or the "People's Assembly of Independent Tibet." This inaccuracy, and the similar misattribution of the second cable, serves the propaganda purpose of confusing such underground groups with the more formal Expanded Assembly. It also gives the Chinese a pretext for accusing the Tibetan government of sending such cables and plotting a foreign-backed, armed rebellion for Tibetan independence.[35]

The cache published by the Chinese also contains the charters of two underground Tibetan independence organizations: "Basic Charter of the Independent Assembly of Tibet,"[36] and "Standing Rules of the Anti-Imperialist Party of Tibet."[37] Since both documents are available only in Chinese translation, the exact identity of these shadowy organizations cannot be confirmed with certainty.

Judging from the traditional style and heavily religious tone of the "Basic Charter of the Independent Assembly of Tibet"—in its extant Chinese translation—most of the group's members were probably rather old-fashioned Khampas and monks. It seems fairly certain that this group was distinct from the Tibetan National Assembly, as its charter castigates the Tibetan aristocracy, which traditionally dominated the Assembly, for cooperating with the "shameless, callous, evil Han Chinese" solely out of self-interest. According to a note appended to the document by the Chinese, this Independent Assembly drew its membership from the middle and lower levels of the Tibetan bureaucracy and the grass roots in Lhasa. Even though such people had elbowed their way into the formal Assembly by the early days of March 1959 (hence the term "Expanded"), they had not succeeded in overruling its entrenched caution. Moreover, the Independent Assembly was founded in 1958, a date that makes any equation of this group with the formal Expanded Assembly rather unlikely.

The "Basic Charter of the Independent Assembly of Tibet" also requires members to "try to line up aid from foreign countries opposed to the Red Chinese."[38] This tallies with the policy of the Kalimpong-based Committee for Tibetan Social Welfare, suggesting a possible connection with the Kalimpong group, and indicating that the authors of this charter may also have sent one or both of the mysterious March 16 and March 17 cables to W. D. Shakabpa. The idea of a possible connection between this shadowy group and the cables is reinforced by the similarity of the group's name (albeit in somewhat unreliable Chinese translation) to that of the sender of the first cable.

The "Standing Rules of the Anti-Imperialist Party of Tibet" does not indicate the date of the group's founding, nor does it mention seeking foreign support. Unlike the "Basic Charter of the Independent Assembly of Tibet," it is written in a clear, concise style, divided into three sections: "Conditions of Membership," "Responsibilities of Members," and "Rights of Members." It uses terms such as "revolution," "male–female equality," and "uniting the masses," suggesting that the organizers had received a Chinese Communist education. While advocating Tibetan independence, it also repudiated the "old system" of Tibet, and advocated "studying Tibetan and foreign culture and politics suitable to the times."[39]

Because the available historical materials are scant, it is difficult to pinpoint these underground organizations and their exact role in the events of March 1959 with certainty. Chinese and Tibetan sources both indicate that once the unrest began, the rifts among the Tibetans of Lhasa came to the surface, revealing a spectrum of attitudes toward the Chinese Communists and their program. Various underground organizations actively circulated their declarations, pamphlets, and statements of purpose, creating even more confusion in the city at the time. With the emergence of these competing forces, the Dalai Lama and his government lost control over the situation.

While this welter of obscure splinter groups will always present some unsolved mysteries, a few facts emerge clearly. Chinese allegations that the events of March 1959 were orchestrated from the top down by the "Dalai clique" are a gross oversimplification. Moreover, despite persistent Chinese misnomers, the unwieldy, broad-based group that met at the Shol could better be described as an emergency session of the Tibetan National Assembly; it never formally advocated independence or contained any reference to independence in its name. In fact, it is significant that the Dalai Lama ultimately designated such a body—not a "People's Assembly of Independent Tibet"—to run the country, after he had fled.[40]

: : :

As late as March 13, however, the Dalai Lama still opposed the Assembly's existence as inflammatory. According to classified Chinese materials, he received a list of participants' names that day along with a request to appoint the members formally, but he refused: "Such meetings will cause nothing but trouble, and everyone knows there is nothing to be gained from them. That's why I've expressly forbidden meetings of this sort and I refuse to designate representatives to them."[41]

This March 13 statement, which has never been released publicly in China, further attests to the Dalai Lama's continuing efforts to rein in the disturbances in Lhasa, and discredits the Chinese propaganda campaign to portray him as a ringleader. However, just one day before, Mao had issued a pronouncement showing his rather different slant on the events: "As the situation develops, we are going to be forced (but this is a good thing) to settle the Tibet question very soon."[42] Actually, the die had probably been cast as early as 1958, when Mao began to express his readiness for war in Tibet[43]—a sentiment that he explicated more fully in January 1959.[44] It seems doubtful that the Dalai Lama's efforts on March 13 could have staved off the Battle of Lhasa.

On March 14,[45] thousands of women assembled in front of the Potala in a demonstration organized by Gurteng Kunsang, a member of the aristocratic Kundeling family and a mother of six who was later arrested by the Chinese and executed by firing squad.[46] The women torched the Chinese flag, burned Mao, Zhu De, and Zhou Enlai in photo and in effigy, and marched around town shouting slogans:

> Tibet has always been free!
> Tibet for the Tibetans!
> Long Live the Dalai Lama!
> Long Live the Ganden Phodrang![47]

Proclaiming their withdrawal from the Patriotic Tibetan Women's League organized by General Tan Guansan, they formed an independent group.[48] Afterward, some of the women marched to the Indian and Nepalese consulates to request support.

: : :

One person enjoyed all the excitement at the Norbulingka: twelve-year-old Ngari Rinpoché.[49]

On March 11, a car leaving the palace gates was halted for inspection by the volunteer guards. Seeing Security Chief Phuntsok and his wife, Tsering Dolma, in the car, the guards waved it on its way to Yabshi House.

Although the immediate crisis had blown over, danger was still in the air, and the Dalai Lama, in consultation with Phuntsok, had decided to move his mother, grandmother, and little brother to a safer location inside the Norbulingka to prevent the Chinese from trying to take them into custody.

But Phuntsok and Tsering Dolma hit a snag at Yabshi House: the Dalai Lama's frail old grandmother adamantly refused to leave, insisting that the Chinese would never imprison such an old lady. It seemed risky to leave her behind, but it was clear that the hubbub at the Norbulingka would be unbearable for her, overrun as it was with armed, noisy men. Finally, arrangements were made for her to stay home under the care of another of her daughters, and Ngari Rinpoché and his mother got into the car and left. Unbeknownst to him, this was the last time he would see his grandmother, who passed away in Lhasa in 1961.

With all the adults absorbed in the crisis at the palace, Ngari Rinpoché was free to roam at will. Too young to grasp the import of the events he was witnessing, he found those days vastly more amusing than the time he had spent endlessly memorizing scriptures at Drepung Monastery, and he gladly shed his monk's habit for lay clothes. He also satisfied his fascination with guns by procuring a pistol and bullets.

Forbidden by the guards to leave the main gate, all he could do was peek outside. He saw a big tent camp filled with people: burly Khampas, weather-beaten nomads, Lhasa tradesmen, and others. A few had rifles or knives, but even those without weapons swaggered around boldly: they were the protectors of the Dalai Lama.

Huddled around campfires against the cold, some of the volunteers were brewing tea on makeshift stoves built with stones from the riverside. Men in fur hats and tall leather boots leaned against their saddles on the ground, inhaling snuff, sipping tea, and holding forth at the top of their voices.

But that evening, the rumble of an approaching convoy spurred everyone into action. Metal clinked on metal as the security guards loaded their guns and raced toward the gate. Grabbing his pistol, Ngari Rinpoché went along to watch.

In the dark, he saw thousands of people arrayed for battle, brandishing guns, knives, or even rocks in oppressive silence, ready to explode at any moment. The rumbling drew closer, and tension mounted until a long PLA convoy finally rolled by on the road north of the Norbulingka. Ngari Rinpoché could not tell what the cargo was, because it was covered with canvas. Years later, he found out that it was two companies from PLA Transport Regiment 16 delivering shells to Artillery Regiment 308.[50] That night, however, everyone thought the PLA was coming to assault the Norbulingka.

The alert was lifted once the convoy had passed, but it had been a grim reminder that danger still loomed. The people's representatives demanded proper guns and ammunition, pointing out how useless their old, empty rifles were. Ngawang Gyaltsen—a member of the Norbulingka security committee—took some men to an army storeroom on the western side of the Shol neighborhood to get bullets, which they brought back to the Norbulingka. However, they discovered the next day that the bullets, made for light machine guns, would not fit the old British rifles they had, so they returned the bullets to the storeroom. This time they found some brand-new light machine guns, still with their thick, rust-protective coating. Some of the Tibetan soldiers showed them how to melt the coating in cauldrons of boiling water and polish the guns with cloths to ready them for use.[51]

On March 13, the people's representatives cut the phone lines and barricaded the north access road to the Norbulingka to ward off any possible PLA attack.

: : :

On the morning of March 14, the fifth day of the second month of the Tibetan calendar, the tension in the city eased slightly. The cabinet instructed businesses to reopen, and issued orders forbidding citizens to bear arms, drink alcohol, or quarrel with the Chinese.[52] Meanwhile, the Norbulingka security committee appointed on March 12 showed up to take charge at the palace. The officials and the people's representatives had gone to the Shol Scriptural Printing House for a meeting, leaving only Shakabpa Losel Dondrup—a member of the coordinating committee of six—at the Norbulingka to brief the newcomers. Lhalu, a member of the new security committee, had been a lieutenant colonel in the army, and saw immediately that the Norbulingka was in chaos.

People were bustling around asking for instructions, but it was not clear who they were or where they belonged. No one seemed to know how many men were in the Khampa self-defense force, how many units it had, how many men were in each unit, or who was in charge. Lhalu assigned someone to ascertain the facts and create a roster.

A representative came from Sera Monastery to request a few hundred rifles. Lhalu learned that there was an armory at the Norbulingka, and that the man in charge, Gyaltsen Chopei, was at the meeting at the Shol Scriptural Printing House. Lhalu sent a messenger to the meeting to relay Sera's request for weapons, but those present failed to reach consensus on the matter.

Without permission to grant the Sera representative's request, Lhalu suggested an alternate method of defending the mountain behind the monastery. First, he recommended, some monks should scout around the mountaintop on the pretext of burning juniper boughs to drive away evil. If they found no PLA soldiers, they could post one hundred fifty monks to guard the mountaintop, but they should avoid conflict with the PLA.[53] The Sera monks never received the requested weapons, and remained unarmed throughout the entire Battle of Lhasa.

Security Chief Phuntsok asked Lhalu to find out whether the Tibetan Army had control of the strategic triangular hill overlooking the Rama Gang ferry on the south bank of the Kyichu River, south of the Norbulingka. This hill provided a stranglehold over the main route from Lhasa to Lhokha, and over the Norbulingka itself. After ascertaining that the Tibetan Army had no presence on the hill, Lhalu scribbled hasty instructions to Kundeling Dzasa to send scouts there, disguised as woodcutters, to make sure the PLA had not taken the area already. If not, Kundeling Dzasa was to dispatch a hundred Tibetan soldiers to do so.

That afternoon, Lhalu noticed that although there were regular sentries and Khampa volunteer guards at the front gate, the defense atop the gate was entirely inadequate: fifteen sentries and a sergeant, shielded by homemade stone fortifications, and armed with nothing more than a single mortar and a heavy machine gun. Lhalu ordered them to install sandbags and find another heavy machine gun. With their present fortifications, he reflected, the soldiers would be sitting ducks in the face of enemy shells.

As the Battle of Lhasa unfolded, he was proved right.

By that day, March 14, PLA reinforcements were transferring into Lhasa from its environs, and the Chinese war preparations were visible. Meanwhile, the Tibetans were in disarray. The demonstrators continued to meet and debate their options, but were split between hawks and doves, and even these factions were split internally about how to proceed.

That same day, Tara, a leader of the coordinating committee, received notice that Lhalu had resigned from the group in response to the demands of the Khampas, who did not trust him with responsibility for the Dalai Lama's security.[54] Nonetheless, Lhalu was arrested and imprisoned by the Chinese after their conquest of Lhasa, guilty of having served for three days as "commander-in-chief of the rebel forces."[55]

The Lhasa Incident of March 1959 was a watershed in Tibetan history: it was the first time that the common people had taken a role in politics. Most of the activists—lower-ranking civil servants, citizens of Lhasa, or battle-hardened men from Kham and Amdo—lacked both political experience and knowledge of modern warfare. Indeed, their holy city of Lhasa had never seen war, except for a few clashes with imperial Chinese troops stranded there after the fall of the Qing dynasty in 1911. These insular, naïve rebels could not have imagined how easily a government with a sophisticated military could crush their resistance.

Those assembled at the Shol Scriptural Printing House had no idea that their frantic deliberations were entirely futile. Tibet's fate was sealed. The Chinese Communists had designed their program for Tibet three years before,[56] and were merely waiting for a pretext that their propaganda machine could present to the world.

Meanwhile, Phala and the marginalized cabinet were busily making hushed plans.

: 11 :

The Gathering Clouds of War

TWO MEN, MAO AND PHALA, were ready to seize the moment. Mao, on an inspection tour of Wuhan, unleashed his military campaign in Tibet through a series of cables. Meanwhile, Phala engineered the Dalai Lama's remarkable escape, relying entirely on oral messengers sent from inside the besieged Norbulingka. Both men's schemes were covert at the time, their significance not fully apparent until years later.

As if by coincidence, both began their maneuvering on March 11, 1959.[1]

At 2:00 that afternoon, the CCP Tibet Work Committee cabled its report to Beijing on the first meeting of the officials and the people's representatives, which had taken place the day before at the Norbulingka. As this cable was seminal in the development of later Chinese propaganda, it merits close examination. First, it illustrates the erroneous Chinese view that the Tibetans, who were in fact fragmented, had coalesced into a united independence movement:

> It was resolved at the meeting that as of March 10, the Tibetan people had formally arisen and severed ties with our Party leadership, and would henceforth strive for "Tibetan independence." As leaders of the independence movement, those assembled named Tsi-pon Shuguba and Khenchung Tara (personal secretary to the Dalai Lama), along with Chief of Staff Gadrang and Cabinet Minister Surkhang or Dzasa Khemey and Vice-Commander Lodoe Kalsang of the Tibetan Army, but the list is still tentative.[2]

The cable continues with a claim that a "reactionary plot" was afoot to "abduct" the Dalai Lama, as well as a numerical estimate of the "rebel forces." These purported facts were reiterated in many Chinese sources thereafter:

> As best we can determine, more than 1,400 lamas from the "great three" monasteries had entered the city by the afternoon of March 10, and after dark, rebel elements started moving from the Lhasa environs into town in small groups of 20 to 30. Including the 2,500 to 3,000 regular Tibetan Army troops, the rebel forces in Lhasa now total between six and seven thousand men. Recent developments indicate that the reactionaries are conspiring to abduct the Dalai Lama. There is a very real possibility that this will take place.[3]

In the decades that followed, Chinese chroniclers rewrote the text of this cable repeatedly, and these figures—along with the claim that the Dalai Lama was abducted—reappeared with various embellishments. An example is the 1989 memoir of a PLA officer, which reads, "By early 1959, there were more than 20,000 armed Tibetan rebels, more than 7,000 of whom were *concentrated* in Lhasa."[4] Another key text asserts, "That night, in the name of protecting the Dalai Lama, [the leaders of the independence movement] *ordered* 1,400 *armed* lamas from the 'great three' monasteries to enter town."[5]

The CCP Tibet Work Committee got its reply from Beijing immediately. The entire text of the reply has appeared in print, although in a volume stamped "semiclassified, citation forbidden." The reply recommended giving the Tibetans enough rope to hang themselves: "It is a very good thing that the Tibetan elite has revealed its treasonous, reactionary nature. Our policy should be to let them run rampant, encouraging them to expose themselves even further. This will justify our subsequent pacification."[6] The cable further directed the CCP Tibet Work Committee to "wait patiently for at least a couple of months," stepping up its political activities while observing military restraint. Specifically, instructions were to continue to woo the elite with the United Front, to "protect Ngabo and others who are affiliated with us," to "expose the treasonous plot to abduct the Dalai Lama" to the Tibetan people, and to "gather every available scrap of evidence of our adversaries' reactionary, treasonous activities." The committee was to continue to court the Dalai Lama, but "not to fear that the reactionaries might abduct him." Beijing offered the assurance that his departure would be "no harm" to the Chinese cause, "regardless of whether or not he left of his own free will."

This cable states explicitly that the Chinese Central Military Commission was "actively preparing for the pacification," an indication that the Party leadership envisioned a military resolution, and that PLA deployments were in progress. However, the cable goes on to instruct the CCP Tibet Work Committee to let the top Party leadership determine "the right moment to strike": "Do not try to stop reactionary forces from entering Lhasa from its environs. We have nothing to fear from an extra couple of thousand foes. Any attempt on our part to block them would cast us in the role of aggressors, which would be disadvantageous to us politically. Do not occupy Chakpori Hill for now. Wait until the military campaign is formally underway."

Meanwhile, the Central Military Commission sent a number of cables to its regional military commands in Chengdu, Lanzhou, and Kunming, with orders to establish special nerve centers and prepare specific combat units to spearhead the entry into Tibet. One cable instructed Fifty-Fourth Army major general Ding Sheng to organize a center (nicknamed "Ding Headquarters") comprising his Infantry Divisions 134 and 11. Another instructed Vice-Commander Huang Xinting to take charge of Infantry Division 130, the front headquarters of Infantry Division 42, and the troops under the Chamdo Garrison Command ("Huang Headquarters"). Huang was responsible for the war effort in Chamdo, while Ding was in charge of military action in other areas of Tibet. Accompanying cables also ordered the preparation of several infantry divisions and a regiment of Air Force bombers for use in Tibet.[7]

All of these cables—the reply to the CCP Tibet Work Committee and the complex PLA mobilization orders—were dispatched simultaneously at 11:00 P.M. on March 11, only nine hours after the CCP Tibet Work Committee had cabled Beijing. Less than forty-eight hours had elapsed since the outbreak of the demonstrations on March 10, a fact which suggests that Chinese battle plans had been laid beforehand.

In Lhasa, the Chinese switched into a state of high alert for war on March 10. Work as usual was suspended, smaller units were merged into larger ones, and the CCP Tibet Work Committee began constructing earthen ramparts and bunkers in its compound. On March 11, Chinese troop units and civilian organizations around the city began round-the-clock battle preparations: digging fortifications, stockpiling ammunition and rations, and transferring silver from the banks to the CCP Tibet Work Committee compound.[8]

: : :

Mao's readiness for war in Tibet had developed over the latter half of the 1950s. As early as 1955, he had directed the CCP Tibet Work Committee to prepare Tibet for his "reforms," but his pilot program in Chamdo was met with a wave of riots.[9] Then came his offer to shelve his agenda in Tibet for six years, which Zhou Enlai transmitted to the Dalai Lama during their state visits to India. Mao did not make this offer solely out of concern for Tibet's lack of readiness for Land Reform. Since he was not yet prepared for war in Tibet, it was prudent to rely on the Dalai Lama and the Tibetan government to maintain stability for the time being. After the suppression of the Xunhua uprising Tibet in 1958, however, he turned his attention to Tibet, and to Lhasa.[10]

By early 1959, the conditions were finally ripe for completing the Chinese takeover of Tibet. China had constructed two fully functioning highways and an airport in Tibet, finished the Korean War, and begun the secret development of nuclear weapons. Moreover, the CCP Tibet Work Committee had built considerable Party strength in Tibet[11] and had also sent thousands of Tibetan youths to study in China, ensuring a source of future cadres.

By this time, there was a general yearning for war at the CCP Tibet Work Committee. Memoirist Xu Donghai recalls the mood as of March 4, 1959: "Ever since we entered Tibet, we had been waiting for the Tibetan ruling class to abandon its reactionary stance, but our kindness was repaid with ingratitude. We were running out of patience, wishing we could take up arms that very day to overturn the feudal Tibetan serf system and liberate the millions of Tibetan serfs."[12]

Mao had begun to signal his eagerness for war in Tibet. In January 1959, he received a report of unrest and serious fighting in Chamdo and Lhokha, onto which he penned the following call to arms: "This war is highly advantageous, providing us with an opportunity to mobilize the masses and temper our troops. I hope we can keep up the fight for five, six, seven, or even eight years. This will enable us to annihilate the enemy, paving the way for implementing our reforms."[13] He elaborated on these sentiments in the ensuing weeks, stating that he regarded the armed rebellion in Tibet as an opportunity for pacifying the region militarily and enforcing his policies there. "The greater the disturbance in Tibet, the better," he commented in one February message, which was transmitted to Liu Shaoqi, Zhou Enlai, Chen Yi, Deng Xiaoping, and Peng Dehuai. "It will . . . provide adequate grounds for us to suppress the rebellion and implement our reforms."[14] In a subsequent memo to Peng Dehuai, he said, "Not only are we unafraid of military engagement, but we actually welcome it."[15]

Mao no longer needed to bother with the Dalai Lama or the Tibetan government. Cultivating them had not yielded the results he wanted, and now the events of March 1959 in Lhasa presented him with a golden opportunity: a justification for military intervention that his propaganda machine could present to the world. He expounded his ideas thoroughly in a major cable to the CCP Tibet Work Committee on March 12. The text of this cable, which effectively sealed the fate of Tibet, has never been declassified in its entirety, although an excerpt has been published in a major 1995 semiclassified source. Even without the entire text, Mao's views and plans come across quite clearly:

> I have received the CCP Tibet Work Committee's cables of March 10 and 11, as well as the Central Committee's March 11 instructions to the CCP Tibet Work Committee to invite the Dalai Lama and his delegation to arrive ahead of time for the National People's Congress in Beijing. The Dalai Lama is apparently involved in a counterrevolutionary conspiracy. Its tactics are (1) to foment an uprising in Lhasa to expel us, using the Norbulingka as a stronghold. This seems to be the conspirators' initial plan. They have probably inferred from our gentle exterior and military restraint that we Chinese are cowards or that the Central Committee is powerless, and they imagine that they can expel us Chinese; and (2) to proceed on the course they have set by rupturing with our Party. They will probably continue to agitate in Lhasa, hoping to scare us Chinese away. Once they discover that they cannot, they might decide to flee to India or to establish a foothold in Shannan [Lhokha].
>
> For the time being, the CCP Tibet Work Committee should remain on the defensive militarily while taking the political offensive. Its goals should be (1) to divide the elite and bring as many as possible over to our side, including some of the "Living Buddhas" and lamas; (2) to

> educate the lower strata of society, paving the way for our work among the masses; and (3) to lure the enemy into attacking.
>
> If our foes attack, we should refrain from killing too many at the outset, and we definitely should not attack them first. It would be best to let them win a few small victories, emboldening them with the illusion that they are capable of expelling us Chinese. This will enable us to draw them into an all-out battle. Otherwise, we will have only limited military encounters, from which they will panic and flee. This would not be a bad thing, but it would be much better to hold out for a major showdown. The Dalai Lama and his cohorts are unsure of themselves. They hope for victory, but they also fear that they will be defeated and unable to escape. But we should not attempt to stop them if they do try to flee. We should just let them go, no matter whether they are headed to Shannan [Lhokha] or to India.[16]

Here we have a fuller explanation of Mao's stance—including his assertion that the Dalai Lama was conspiring to foment rebellion in Lhasa—and his strategy of luring the Tibetans into an all-out showdown. But the cable is also noteworthy for its use of explicit, highly fraught ethnic terminology. Mao's repeated references to a Tibetan desire to "expel us Chinese," or to the presumed Tibetan assumption that "we Chinese are cowards," indicate that he saw the 1959 situation as an ethnic conflict, analogous to the Tibetan government's attempt to "expel the Chinese" in July 1949.[17] His rhetoric is tinged with the same Han chauvinism that had driven the Chinese emperors of old, one of whom (Emperor Yuan of the Han dynasty) had famously said: "Anyone who offends the Great Han must be punished, even if far away." Mao may have realized this, and later delicately avoided casting the conflict in ethnic terms when speaking to non-Chinese "outsiders" such as the Panchen Lama. Instead, he substituted the pretext of "liberating the serfs," which brought his war into line with Communist dogma and endowed it with a halo of political correctness.[18]

The text of Mao's cable also helps to explain some persistent popular misconceptions on both sides. He mentions that the Chinese hoped to bring the Dalai Lama to Beijing prior to the Congress there that spring; such a proposal may have stoked Tibetan fears. He also expresses willingness to allow the Dalai Lama and his cohorts to flee Lhasa, which evidently provided the basis for later Chinese rumors that he knowingly facilitated their getaway.

On March 15, the CCP Tibet Work Committee cabled Beijing with an update on new developments and its response to the instructions received on March 11:

> It has become clear over the last few months, and especially the last two days, that the Tibetan reactionaries are in outright revolt.
>
> 1. On March 10, the reactionaries ironed out various conflicting proposals (all-out war, small battles, fight now, fight later, fight with the pen, fight with the sword) and forged an open union of all segments of their forces (the Tibetan Army, the "great three" monasteries, rebel elements from outside). While publicly rupturing with us politically, they intend to force us to strike first militarily. Over the last three days, their approach has been to engage in military preparations while stalemating us politically.
> 2. Some local government officials and so-called "people's representatives" surreptitiously declared Tibetan independence via the Indian Consulate on March 10, and the reactionaries bullied the masses into openly presenting a petition there.
> 3. They have stepped up political and military preparations, beginning by severing relations with us. Although they have not formally declared Tibetan independence, they have announced it to the masses. They have also fortified the Norbulingka, Chakpori Hill, and the Potala, and taken control of a section of the national defense highway leading into Lhasa on the north side of the Norbulingka. Moreover, they are organizing an armed volunteer army and bullying the masses into joining, while actively moving armed rebel forces into Lhasa, and so forth.
> 4. The Dalai Lama's Norbulingka Palace has been transformed into the reactionaries' headquarters.
> 5. The reactionaries have openly threatened and killed progressive individuals.[19]

The CCP Tibet Work Committee summed up the situation as follows: "The enemy is combat ready. As soon as the reactionaries formally sever relations with us, openly declaring their revolt, or if they attack us militarily, the bugle call to all-out rebellion will sound.[20]

As subsequent developments would show, this assessment was far off the mark. Moreover, Tibetan documents from this period, even those that assert the Tibetan right to independence, urge nonviolence. An obscure Tibetan document—probably a never-promulgated draft proposal from one of the Norbulingka meetings—reprinted only in a semiclassified Chinese source, is illustrative:

> All monasteries, lay and monastic officials, and all Tibetans, must firmly and unanimously uphold the righteous campaign to return Tibet to its legitimate former state of independence, *while adhering to peaceful means.* We must ensure that all local monastic and lay officials understand the importance of preserving our nationality, religion, language, and writing. Demonstrations for Tibetan independence must continue, along with widespread propaganda and education. Tibetans who have worked for the Chinese must disaffiliate from them and take a firm stand with us. We welcome any and all suggestions regarding the above. Moreover, we need to choose appropriate individuals immediately to serve as people's representatives, and bring them to Lhasa.[21]

Documents such as this one tend to be omitted from official publications intended for general Chinese readership, which harp instead on Tibetan militancy.

Ever since 1951, the key players in the CCP Tibet Work Committee had been seasoned army men such as General Tan Guansan, who made their decisions from a military standpoint. Although they probably realized that the Tibetan attempts to fortify their city were for defensive purposes, they asserted instead that the Tibetan fortifications presaged a "bugle call to all-out rebellion." Evidently aware that they lacked incontrovertible evidence to back up this pronouncement, they followed Beijing's instructions to "gather every available scrap of evidence of [their] adversaries' reactionary, treasonous activities" to prove the necessity for Beijing's "pacification" of Lhasa, in case troublesome questions arose afterward.

This task proved challenging, and even dangerous, in the chaotic atmosphere of Lhasa. Even as Tibetan officials held meetings to seek peace with the Chinese, and many Tibetans sided with them, underground Tibetan groups pushed for independence and bellicose Khampas roamed the city streets. Dai Yisheng, second in command in the Political Security Section of the CCP Tibet Work Committee at the time, recalls in a memoir that he and his men went, armed with submachine guns for self-defense, on assignment to Barkor Street to collect pro-independence posters to serve as evidence of an organized Tibetan revolt. He found himself in a standoff with two Tibetan militants armed with bayonets, but a Tibetan who had become a cadre on the Chinese side scared off the Tibetan militants with a hand grenade. At great personal risk, Dai obtained the posters, which, even if they did advocate independence, from today's perspective seem very unlikely to have been what he calls "evidence of Tibetan rebellion instigated from above."[22] If we allow for possible exaggerations and distortions, the anecdote stands as a snapshot of the urban scene in March 1959.

Surrounded by evidence of Tibetan hostility—such as the women of Lhasa burning Mao, Zhou Enlai, and Zhu De in effigy—the CCP Tibet Work Committee was plagued with rumors and paranoia. Its March 15 cable contains plans to "keep on reserve more than half a year's supply of army provisions and ammunition, in preparation for a long siege," and to take measures to secure local organs that were "scattered or poorly defended." The cable's tone reveals apprehension: "We will not be the victors unless we avoid . . . impatience and fear."[23]

: : :

On March 13, 1959, the Chinese Central Military Commission notified the ground and air forces at the PLA Lanzhou Military Command to prepare for orders to enter Tibet.

Two days later, on March 15, tens of thousands of soldiers were mobilized for deployment to Tibet. Major General Ding Sheng's "Ding Headquarters" was established in the Fifty-Fourth Army, with a staff of 305 people and the code name "Headquarters 302,"[24] along with a special command post to carry out battle plans. Regiment 401 of Division 134[25] stationed in Lintao, Gansu Province, received orders at 2:00 P.M. to start first for Lhasa, and was on the road within a couple of hours.[26] Meanwhile, Generals Zhang Jingwu and Zhang Guohua had flown from Beijing to Wuhan to receive Mao's instructions for "pacifying the rebellion and implementing reform."[27] The following day, Ding Sheng, commander of the Fifty-Fourth Army, flew to Beijing for a briefing from the Chinese Central Military Commission on the Tibet campaign.

Ding, nicknamed "The Invincible," was one of China's ace generals. Born in 1913 in Yudu, Jiangxi Province, he enlisted in the Red Army at the age of seventeen and fought in five major battles to defend the Communists' Jiangxi base area[28] against the Guomindang. His career included leading the Fifty-Fourth Army into Korea in 1953, where he distinguished himself in the Battle of Kumsong.[29] After his return to China in May 1958, the Chinese Central Military Commission sent him to Chongqing, in the PLA Chengdu Military Command, which was in charge of Sichuan and Tibet. He was a general of exceptional caliber and ferocity, and his Fifty-Fourth Army sat poised and ready to pounce on Tibet at the slightest provocation.

Freshly returned from engagements with the United Nations forces in Korea, the Fifty-Fourth Army had been dispatched immediately to quell Tibetan and Muslim uprisings in Gansu and Qinghai. The minority peoples, with their rifles, flintlocks, swords, and axes, were no match for Ding Sheng's combat-hardened Fifty-Fourth Army, whose victories in these battles have been lauded in a Chinese government-sanctioned source as "a massacre of the lambs."[30] For the Fifty-Fourth Army troops, the campaigns were a rich training ground in the tactics of their Tibetan adversaries and the demands of warfare on the high plateau.

At Ding Sheng's side was Lieutenant General Huang Xinting, vice-commander of the PLA Chengdu Military Command. Huang, who was born in 1913 in the city of Honghu, Hubei Province, joined the Communist Youth League in 1928 and the Red Army in 1931. After decades of outstanding military achievement, in 1953 he was appointed commander of the First Army of the People's Volunteer Army[31] in the Korean War.

The Tibetans did not stand a chance against this indomitable pair.

PLA Regiment 401, which had begun its journey on March 15, arrived at Lanzhou by the following morning, after having traveled through the night. In Lanzhou, it took on supplies for fighting in the cold of the high plateau, and then continued by train to the westernmost point on the Lanzhou-Xinjiang Railway, a place called Xiadong,[32] in Gansu Province. On the train, the troops underwent "thorough ideological awakening" and shared their experiences of "pacifying rebels" in the Kanlho Tibetan Autonomous Prefecture of Gansu. The political department printed up a song called "Chasing Rebel Bandits" to motivate the soldiers to behave with "firm resolve" and "conduct worthy of cadres."[33]

According to one of the participants, the indoctrination left the soldiers "raring for battle, and eager to wipe out the rampant rebel bandits."[34] But the political department had not taught the soldiers how to differentiate between "the people" and "bandits," or how to avoid civilian casualties.

Their foe was a bunch of disorganized, poorly armed Tibetan peasants, nomads, and monks.

: : :

By March 15, 1959, less than a week after the outbreak of the Lhasa Incident, the PLA was fully mobilized for its onslaught. A seasoned army regiment was hurtling toward Lhasa, and an Air Force bomber regiment was ready to go.[35]

Three infantry divisions and two infantry regiments originally belonging to the First and Fourth Field Armies[36] were also ordered to stand by for deployment on short notice to Tibet. These were finely honed units, with prior experience battling non-Han nationalities on the high plateau.

Division 130 from the PLA Chengdu Military Command would set out from Ya'an in Sichuan and take the Sichuan-Tibet Highway into Tibet, gathering first in Garzê. Its destination: Chamdo.

Led by the command post of Division 42 from the PLA Kunming Military Command, Regiment 126 would enter Tibet from the southeast and march northward, also gathering first in Garzê. Its destination: Tsakhalho. Under General Huang's command there, its mission would be to seal off the border between China and Burma, effectively cutting off the Tibetans' southeast escape route.

Regiment 162 would also gather in Garzê. Its destination: Chamdo.

Division 11 of the Independent Field Army of the PLA Lanzhou Military Command, which had been "pacifying rebellions" in the Kanlho Tibetan Autonomous Prefecture,[37] would enter Tibet via Qinghai, assembling first in Dunhuang. Its destination: Lhasa.

Division 134,[38] a unit of the Fifty-Fourth Army from the PLA Chengdu Military Command that had been used to "pacify rebellions" in Gansu and Qinghai,[59] would enter Tibet via the Qinghai-Tibet Highway, gathering first in Golmud, in Qinghai. Its destination: Lhasa.

United, the three formidable PLA garrisons of Lanzhou, Kunming, and Chengdu would envelop Tibet. The Dalai Lama and his government, lacking communications equipment or an intelligence network, had no inkling of what was in store for them. And the people of Lhasa gathered around the Norbulingka were completely in the dark.

: 12 :

A Secret Plan

THE DEMONSTRATIONS at the Norbulingka on March 10, 1959, which became known in Chinese history as the Lhasa Incident, led to Chinese military action early on March 20, the start of the Battle of Lhasa. A mere ten days elapsed between the two events, but those ten days loom large in Tibetan history, as they granted the Dalai Lama a fleeting window of opportunity for escape.

The people gathered both inside and outside the Norbulingka on March 1959 were united in their overarching concern: to protect the Dalai Lama. Yet there were worlds of difference between the satin-clad cabinet ministers on the inside and the common people in their tattered *chupas* on the outside, differences reflected in their divergent tactical choices.

While some of the Tibetan officials were meeting with the people's representatives, the cabinet ministers and top monastic officials in the Dalai Lama's inner circle were huddled over plans for the evacuation of the Dalai Lama. They did not know that Tan Guansan had mobilized for war—creating an armed militia in Lhasa within Chinese civilian organizations and dividing the city into "joint defense zones"[1]—nor did they have any inkling that the Chinese Central Military Commission was sending tens of thousands of troops in their direction. Completely cut off from the outside world, they had to base their decisions entirely on intuition and historical experience.

In the Tibetan belief system, which functions simultaneously on both the secular and the religious planes, the Dalai Lama's role is distinct from that of a king or an emperor. He traditionally heads the Tibetan government, but his spiritual role is more important. Tibetan believers revere him as a reincarnation of the Bodhisattva Avalokitesvara, a compassionate deity who descends to this world repeatedly in the person of each successive *dalai lama* to aid humans in their endless cycle of suffering. The present Dalai Lama, Tenzin Gyatso, is regarded as the fourteenth incarnation of Avalokitesvara.[2]

Given the Dalai Lama's spiritual stature, the preservation of his safety has always been of paramount importance for Tibetans, but Tibet is a small, weak nation, sandwiched between India and China. When the Fourteenth Dalai Lama was in jeopardy in 1959, the example of his predecessor naturally came to mind. The Thirteenth Dalai Lama had fled to Mongolia and then to China when Tibet was invaded by British India in 1904. After returning to Lhasa in 1908, he had evacuated to India when the Chinese (under the Qing dynasty) invaded Tibet in 1910. Even though the Chinese had issued a decree stripping him of his temporal powers, his authority was undiminished with Tibetan believers, and he resumed his rule in Lhasa in 1913, after the fall of the Qing.

Once fighting had erupted in Kham and Amdo in the 1950s, it was conceivable that the Fourteenth Dalai Lama might flee. He stopped just short of seeking asylum when he visited India in 1956. The possibility arose once again during the 1958 Taiwan Strait Crisis, when the Chinese Communists shelled the Taiwan-controlled islands of Quemoy and Matsu. The Dalai Lama was visiting Ganden Monastery, thirty miles from Lhasa, and Security Chief Phuntsok suggested that he retreat to India, but the Dalai Lama rejected his advice.[3]

The final decision to evacuate the Dalai Lama was not made until later, but by March 11, the cabinet ministers had begun work on a contingency plan: to take the Dalai Lama across the Tsangpo River into the zone controlled by the Chushi Gangdruk Defenders of the Faith, and then try to negotiate with the Chinese government from there. The cabinet authorized Phala to take care of the details, but the arrangements were kept secret from the Dalai Lama for days.

Phala was one of the most powerful Tibetans of his day. As the Dalai Lama's lord chamberlain, he screened everyone who wanted an audience with the Dalai Lama, which meant that he had a wide network of contacts. Many years the Dalai Lama's senior, he was far more experienced, and also calmer and more meticulous by nature. After he had taken on the weighty task of planning the Dalai Lama's escape, he remembered the two mysterious Khampas, Athar and Lhotse, who had called on him secretly more than a year before. They had disappeared, and he had not heard from them since, but he thought they must be somewhere in Lhokha. Realizing that their radio transmitter could provide Tibet with a precious link to the outside world, he decided to try to bring them to Lhasa right away.[4] With no modern communications equipment at his disposal, Phala had to resort to the time-honored method of sending a human messenger to find the two men. He summoned a trusted aide and gave him instructions.

That night, an ordinary-looking man led his horse out of the Norbulingka and across the broad riverbank to the ferry, which he found moored and waiting. He led his horse onto the boat, and the ferryman paddled him across to the opposite side, where he disembarked, mounted his horse, tapped its flank with his heel, and hurried away into the night.

:::

Inside the Norbulingka on March 11, the Dalai Lama was sad and careworn. This was his second major crisis in less than ten years in office. In 1950, the trouble had been in faraway Chamdo, but this time, it was right on his doorstep. His efforts to mediate between his people and the Chinese Communists for the past eight years had failed, and the anger of the populace had spiraled beyond his control.

The Dalai Lama probably understood the gravity of this crisis better than anyone in Lhasa. He had no doubt of his people's loyalty to him, or of the ruthlessness of the Chinese Communists. Zhou Enlai had warned him in 1956 in New Delhi that the Chinese government would not hesitate to suppress a Tibetan rebellion, and the precedents set in Kham and Amdo clearly demonstrated how the Chinese Communists treated those they designated reactionaries. The Dalai Lama knew that his people, armed with little more than valor, had no chance of defeating Chinese might. His top priority was to avoid escalation and prevent bloodshed. To this end, he had to soothe Tan Guansan's foul temper and persuade the impassioned masses to disperse. If he could buy enough time, the demonstrators would go home, and the Chinese would have no pretext to crack down on them.

The Dalai Lama reread the letter from General Tan Guansan that Gyatsoling Rinpoché had brought him. It was polite but cold:[5]

March 10, 1959
Respected Dalai Lama,

It is very good indeed that you wanted to come to the Military Area Command. You are heartily welcome. But since the intrigues and provocations of the reactionaries have caused you very great difficulties, it may be advisable that for the time being you do not come.

Salutations and best regards,
Tan Kuan-san[6]

The Dalai Lama penned his reply in the blank space under the Tibetan translation of Tan Guansan's letter:

Dear Comrade Political Commissar Tan,

I intended to go to the Military Area Command to see the theatrical performance yesterday, but I was unable to do so, because of obstruction by people, lamas and laymen, who were instigated by a few evil elements and who did not know the facts; this has put me to indescribable shame. I am greatly upset and worried and at a loss what to do. I was immediately greatly delighted when your letter appeared before me—you do not mind at all.

Reactionary, evil elements are carrying out activities endangering me under the pretext of ensuring my safety. I am taking measures to calm things down. In a few days when the situation becomes stable, I will certainly meet you. If you have any internal directives for me, please communicate them frankly through this messenger.

The Dalai Lama[7]
written by my own hand

The Dalai Lama evidently chose to echo Tan's diction and adopt the alien Communist lexicon in an attempt to achieve a conciliatory tone. "Anything to buy time!" he remarked later in his autobiography.[8] He also apologized graciously, but without sacrificing his dignity.

Later that day, Tan Guansan sent a courier with a second letter:

March 11, 1959
To Dalai Lama:

The reactionaries have now become so audacious that they have openly and arrogantly engaged in military provocations. They have erected fortifications and posted large numbers of machine guns and armed reactionaries along the national defence highway (the highway north of the Norbu Lingka [Norbulingka]) thereby very seriously disrupting the security of national defence communications.

On many occasions in the past, we told the *kasha* [cabinet] that the People's Liberation Army is in duty bound to defend the country and to ensure the protection of communications related to national defence; it certainly cannot remain indifferent to this serious act of military provocation. The Tibet Military Area Command has sent letters, therefore, to Surkong [Surkhang], Neusha [Liushar], Shasu [Shasur] and Pala [Phala] asking them to tell the reactionaries to remove all the fortifications they have set up and to withdraw from the highway immediately. Otherwise, they will have to take full responsibility themselves for the evil consequences. I want to inform you of this. Please let me know what your views are at your earliest convenience.

Salutations and best regards,
Tan Kuan-san

The bullying tone of the letter suggests that Tan had lost his temper. He was essentially issuing orders to the Tibetan government, orders that would surely elicit resistance from the crowds around the Norbulingka. But provoking the Tibetans, while also building up the Chinese military presence, was Mao's tactic for launching his "final showdown" without the political stigma of having fired the first shot.[9]

The Tibetan government duly transmitted Tan's orders to dismantle the fortifications to the people outside the palace, and the result was as expected. Fearing a PLA attack, they had barricaded the road north of the Norbulingka after the passage of an earlier convoy.[10] Tan's ultimatum only deepened their conviction that the PLA was planning an onslaught, and they replied defiantly. The Chinese had blocked off the road in front of the PCART building and sent soldiers to guard Ngabo's residence, so why couldn't the Tibetans protect the Norbulingka? Instead of removing the barricades, they strengthened them.

On March 12, the same day that Mao sent the CCP Tibet Work Committee his explicit instructions to "lure the enemy into attacking,"[11] the Dalai Lama sent Tan Guansan a reply:

> March 12, 1959
> Dear Comrade Political Commissar Tan,
>
> I suppose you have received my letter of yesterday forwarded to you by Ngapo [Ngabo]. I have received the letter you sent me this morning. The unlawful activities of the reactionary clique cause me endless worry and sorrow. Yesterday I told the *kasha* to order the immediate dissolution of the illegal people's conference and the immediate withdrawal of the reactionaries who arrogantly moved into the Norbu Lingka under the pretext of protecting me. As to the incidents of yesterday and the day before, which were brought about under the pretext of ensuring my safety and have seriously estranged relations between the Central People's Government and the local government, I am making every possible effort to deal with them. At eight thirty Peking time this morning a few Tibetan army men suddenly fired several shots near the Chinghai-Tibet Highway. Fortunately, no serious disturbance occurred. I am planning to persuade a few subordinates and give them instructions.
>
> Please communicate to me frankly any instructive opinions you have for me.
>
> The Dalai

Chinese sources do not mention the March 12 conflict described in the Dalai Lama's letter, but Tara's memoirs contain the following record:

> Across from our house was a depot on the Qinghai-Tibet Highway, consisting of a few Chinese-held buildings with newly added stone fortifications. At 8:00 A.M. on March 15, [the Chinese] fired a dozen rounds of machine-gun fire from these fortifications. I sent someone immediately to find out what had happened. He reported: "Soldiers from Barracks 4 say that the Chinese fired their machine guns at us from their fortifications, without provocation, and we shot back." A skirmish had actually broken

> out, but fortunately it ended right away. Two or three passersby in the Changthang Gang neighborhood [north of the Norbulingka] were injured.[12]

The Dalai Lama says there was shooting on the morning of March 12, while Tara refers to March 15. If both he and Tara are recollecting accurately, the Chinese and Tibetans clashed once or twice between March 12 and March 15, which might have sparked a full-scale war. But it did not, probably because the Chinese were not ready to escalate yet.

On March 14, the Dalai Lama consulted the Nechung Oracle. The reply: "Negotiate with the Chinese."[13]

: : :

In early February 1959, a man from Lithang named Kunga Samten stationed his squad near the ferry across the Tsangpo River in the Gongkar region of Lhokha, a key crossing point on the route from Lhasa, just over a day's travel on horseback from the city.[14]

Kunga Samten's squad of about fifty soldiers, which he headed along with two other men, belonged to the Chushi Gangdruk resistance forces, whose ranks had swelled by March 1959. Despite its aspirations to military organization, however, it was in fact a loose alliance of volunteers from thirty-seven different tribes, broken up into small, scattered guerrilla bands like Kunga Samten's, in which all or most of the men came from the same tribe.

Except for a few hundred defectors from the Tibetan Army, most of the Chushi Gangdruk fighters had no knowledge of modern warfare; they were also ill equipped and poorly coordinated. They had little in their favor except familiarity with the rugged terrain and its harsh environment, individual marksmanship, and willingness to fight to the death.

One day in March, three elders from a nearby village dropped in on Kunga Samten to say they had gotten word of trouble at the Norbulingka. Before long, Kunga Samten's own scouts brought him corroborating reports from Lhasa. He called an emergency meeting and sent messengers to the other squads in the area.

The Chushi Gangdruk had twenty regulations, one of which was that no unit could enter Lhasa without permission from headquarters. This was to prevent armed conflict from breaking out in Lhasa and jeopardizing the Dalai Lama. Kunga Samten dispatched a messenger to request permission to take his squad to Lhasa, but unbeknownst to him, Commander Gonpo Tashi was away and unaware of the problem. After the messenger had left, Kunga Samten started to worry that precious time was being lost, and set out for Lhasa right away instead of waiting for a response.

One member of Kunga Samten's squad was a young man from Lhasa named Lobsang Yeshe; barely twenty years old, he had been sent to Beijing for an education as a teenager, but had found communism distasteful and bridled at the Party's plans for Tibet. After five years in Beijing, he was sent back to Tibet as a cadre to start preparations for Land Reform, but he ran off to join the guerrillas instead. On his occasional return visits to Lhasa, he met secretly with some of his friends serving in the Tibetan government.

The morning after he got on the road, Kunga Samten divided his squad into two. Leaving the smaller group behind, he set out for Lhasa on horseback with Lobsang Yeshe, another young man named Wangchuk Tsering, and about thirty subordinates. It took until sunset to ferry the entire group across the swollen Tsangpo River on the single small coracle boat that was available. They finally reached Kundeling Dzasa's estate on the south side of the Kyichu River at midnight, and immediately sent a messenger to the Norbulingka to announce that they had arrived in Lhasa and were ready to escort the Dalai Lama to any destination if the need arose.

Meanwhile, the vanguard of Tibet-bound PLA soldiers was about to head for Lhasa from Lintao, in Gansu.

Inside the Norbulingka, Lord Chamberlain Phala anxiously awaited news of Athar and Lhotse.[15] His messenger was still scouring Lhokha for them, but they were elusive: CIA operatives shifted locations every three days to avoid detection. Phala knew that he had to remain in the palace to avoid attracting attention. He relied on subordinates to implement his plans for the impending exodus, and stayed away from the meetings at the Shol Scriptural Printing House, depending instead on regular updates from Tara.

In a tent on the Norbulingka grounds, a group of monks from Sera Monastery sat chanting prayers around the clock, with instructions that no one was to disturb them. As this was standard practice during crises, no one suspected that they were in fact surreptitiously preparing food for the Dalai Lama's journey.

The steward of Yabshi House sent some men with horses across the river, ostensibly to fetch fuel, but they left the horses at Acting Cabinet Minister Liushar's estate for later use by the escape party, on the pretext that the fuel shipment was not ready yet.

One day, Phala brought in an ordinary-looking man for an audience with the Dalai Lama. The man prostrated himself to receive the Dalai Lama's ritual touch to the crown of his head, but he did not hurry away right afterward like other commoners, nor did he keep his eyes averted in awe. Instead, he eyed the Dalai Lama carefully as if taking his measure. Two days later, Phala received a package containing trousers, a shirt, a scarf, a hat, and a thick fur-lined coat, which he put away carefully.

Another day, a messenger came to tell Phala that some men had arrived from Lhokha to see him. Phala delegated the matter to Security Chief Phuntsok. Concerned that he was too conspicuous as the Dalai Lama's brother-in-law, Phuntsok decided to send a lieutenant colonel and two captains to meet the new arrivals. Before his officers left, he made them pledge secrecy, touching a photograph of the Dalai Lama to their foreheads as a gesture of conviction.

The next morning, Kunga Samten and his party met Phuntsok's officers beside the Kyichu River to discuss the logistics of the Dalai Lama's possible departure.

Kunga Samten does not give the date of this meeting in his memoirs. Analysis of other sources indicates that it took place before March 16, probably on March 14, the day before the Tibet-bound PLA troops received their mobilization orders.

On the clear, cold evening of March 14, Phala and some soldiers went out to patrol the Norbulingka grounds in the moonlight. The hubbub had subsided at nightfall, and the palace area had sunk into an uneasy quiet. Armed sentries—both soldiers and volunteers—were guarding the main gate.

Bright flashes of light suddenly split the night like daggers.

"Who is it?" someone called.

"It is I," answered Phala.

A patrol—a captain and his subordinates with a flashlight—approached and saluted him.

Dismissing his soldiers, Phala walked alone to the door in the yellow wall[16] that led to the Dalai Lama's quarters. It was shut tight and guarded by armed men, who bowed and stepped aside for him. Seeing that the Dalai Lama's light was still on, he proceeded directly to his bedroom.

The Dalai Lama, buried in thought, looked up when he heard the door open. Phala closed the door and approached him.

"All the arrangements have been made for your departure," he said softly.[17]

The Dalai Lama was stunned. For days he had been racking his brains for a way to defuse the situation and avoid carnage. It seemed unthinkable to leave. Had things really come to such a pass?

Steadying himself, he told Phala that he had not decided whether to stay or go.[18]

The next day, the Dalai Lama consulted the Nechung Oracle again. His instructions were: to stay and continue to negotiate with the Chinese Communists.[19]

Meanwhile, Mao was meeting with his generals in Wuhan to brief them on his designs for Tibet.

: : :

At 3:00 P.M. on March 16, the Dalai Lama received a third missive from General Tan Guansan.

> March 15, 1959
> Respected Dalai Lama,
>
> I have the honour to acknowledge receipt of your two letters dated March 11 and March 12. The traitorous activities of some reactionary elements among the upper social strata in Tibet have grown to intolerable proportions. These individuals, in collusion with foreigners, have engaged in reactionary, traitorous activities for quite some time. The Central People's Government has all along maintained a magnanimous attitude and enjoined the local government of Tibet to deal with them

in all earnestness, but the local government of Tibet has all along adopted an attitude of feigning compliance while actually helping them in their activities, with the result that things have now come to such a grave pass. The Central People's Government still hopes that the local government of Tibet will change its wrong attitude and immediately assume responsibility for putting down the rebellion and mete out severe punishment to the traitors. Otherwise the Central People's Government will have to act itself to safeguard the solidarity and unification of the motherland.

In your letter, you said: "As to the incidents . . . which were brought about under the pretext of ensuring my safety and have seriously estranged relations between the Central People's Government and the local government, I am making every possible effort to deal with them." We warmly welcome this correct attitude on your part.

We are very much concerned about your present situation and safety. If you think it necessary and possible to extricate yourself from your present dangerous position of being held[20] by the traitors, we cordially welcome you and your entourage to come and stay for a short time in the Military Area Command. We are willing to assume full responsibility for your safety. As to what is the best course to follow, it is entirely up to you to decide.

In addition, I have much pleasure in informing you that it has been decided that the Second National People's Congress will open its first session on April 17.

Salutations and my best regards,
Tan Kuan-san[21]

This letter is strikingly different in tone from the previous two. While the earlier letters admonished the Tibetans in the name of the PLA Tibet Military Command, which Tan Guansan represented, this letter seems to rise above Tan's sphere of authority to threaten the "local government of Tibet" from the lofty stance of the "Central People's Government."

These nuances failed to arouse the Dalai Lama's suspicions. In the heat of the moment, he simply assumed that it reiterated what Zhou Enlai had said to him in India in 1956, without realizing it was actually an ultimatum—albeit somewhat disguised—from the top leadership in Beijing. However, when Mao's instructions regarding this correspondence were published officially years later, it was revealed that the letter was not written by Tan Guansan at all. Rather, it was written in Tan's name, at Mao's behest, by Deng Xiaoping. Deng wrote the letter on March 14 and cabled it at 11:50 that night to the CCP Tibet Work Committee. When Tan received it, he changed the date to March 15 and forwarded it to the Dalai Lama.[22] This explains how the letter can presume to speak for the central government of China. Mao also indicated that the entire correspondence "would be published in the future."[23] By this he meant that these were not merely letters to the Dalai Lama. He intended to use them in the propaganda war that would follow the pacification, as part of his master plan for "solving the question of Tibet."

For the Dalai Lama, perhaps the most significant fact about Tan Guansan's third letter was that it was delivered along with two critically important missives from Ngabo, one to the Dalai Lama and one to the cabinet, both similar in content. Ngabo's letter appalled the Dalai Lama, as it contained a request that he sketch a map of the Norbulingka, showing his own location within it so that the Chinese could spare him in case they shelled the buildings. Ngabo also said he knew of plans to remove the Dalai Lama from the Norbulingka and warned that it would be extremely risky for him to choose this course of action in the face of PLA vigilance. He added that even if the Dalai Lama did manage to escape, the current international situation would make it impossible for him ever to return to Lhasa. In sum, Ngabo's letter implied strongly that the PLA had already decided to take military action, and that it would be dangerous for the Dalai Lama either to stay in the Norbulingka or to try to decamp.[24]

One wonders about the origin and intent of this letter. Regardless of Ngabo's role, the letter's impact on Tibetan decision making could have played right into Tan Guansan's hands. Convinced a Chinese attack was imminent, the Tibetans would be more inclined to apply to Lhokha for help, requesting the transfer of the bulk of the Chushi Gangdruk forces to Lhasa to protect the Dalai Lama.

Ngabo's letter to the Dalai Lama was never published or even mentioned directly in official Chinese histories of the period. Nor do any records indicate whether Tan Guansan had any role in the issuance of this letter enclosed with his own.

Unaware that massive Chinese forces were headed toward Lhasa, the Dalai Lama took a deep breath and drafted a reply to Tan Guansan:

> March 16, 1959
> Dear Comrade Political Commissar Tan,
>
> Your letter dated the 15th has just been received at three o'clock. I am very glad that you are so concerned about my safety and hereby express my thanks.
>
> The day before yesterday, the fifth day of the second month according to the Tibetan calendar [March 14], I made a speech to more than seventy representatives of the government officials, instructing them from various angles, calling on them to consider seriously present and long-term interests and to calm down, otherwise my life would be in danger. After these severe reproaches, things took a slight turn for the better. Though the conditions here and outside are still very difficult to handle at present, I am trying tactfully to draw a line separating the progressive people among the government officials from those opposing the revolution. In a few days from now when there are enough forces that I can trust I shall make my way in secret to the Military Area Command. When that time comes, I shall first send you a letter. I request you to adopt reliable measures. What are your views? Please write me often.
>
> The Dalai[25]

The Dalai Lama's wording shows no awareness that Tan Guansan's letter had been ghostwritten. Still "buying time," he scrupulously avoids mentioning his own location in the palace, evidently hoping to forestall the Chinese attack long enough for him to disperse the demonstrators.

The Dalai Lama sent his reply to Tan, via Ngabo, enclosing a note to Ngabo with it. One official Chinese source mentions the note to Ngabo[26] but does not quote from it. This is probably because the note implies that the Dalai Lama intended to stay in Lhasa and resolve the crisis as late as March 16, as can be seen in an excerpt provided in another, little-known source:

> Thank you very much for your letter, enclosed with Commissar Tan's letter, which I received at three this afternoon. I am attaching my reply to Commissar Tan. Please read it, and then pass it along to him.

> At this point, no one has openly recommended that I leave yet. But I can see that there may be some people who would think that I should. That is why I presented detailed, specific arguments against my leaving Tibet at the meeting the day before yesterday. Now, surrounded by a mixture of enemies and friends, I know that I am in extreme danger, and I am focusing on stabilizing the situation long enough to extricate myself. Please do all you can to prevent the Chinese from acting rashly, and rest assured that you can be confident of my standpoint.[27]

The authors of the limited-edition volume probably believed this excerpt supported their claim that the Dalai Lama was abducted by a reactionary clique. It is difficult to tell what the Dalai Lama meant by these words, however, or whether we should take them at face value. Read in the context of the letter to Tan with which the note was enclosed, the Dalai Lama probably intended "extricating himself" to the PLA Tibet Military Command. Moreover, it is a fact that from March 10 on, there was chaos far beyond the Dalai Lama's control both inside and out of the Norbulingka, so he probably did feel imperiled. But his note also clearly states his focus on temporizing and "stabilizing the situation." It also seems clear from his plea to "do all you can to prevent the Chinese from acting rashly" that he was still unaware Mao had long since decided how to wrap up the Lhasa Incident.

Tensions had reached the boiling point in Lhasa. Sporadic gunfire echoed in the streets, and the PLA, which had been deploying busily, had taken up artillery positions near the Norbulingka. A Chinese memoir of the period reports that on March 13, one company of Artillery Regiment 308 moved four 120 mm mortars to the courtyard of the PLA Tibet Military Command, and established an observation point overlooking the PCART building. Meanwhile, the regimental command set up observation points in Xishan and Lhasa to supervise the artillery fire.[28] Regiment 308, which was to play a key role in the upcoming Battle of Lhasa, had been drilling for more than a year. According to a Chinese participant, the troops received pep talks from the top PLA leadership, along with an "extremely profound, realistic class education" about the "reactionary upper stratum's widespread, cruel exploitation and persecution of the serfs." The regimental Party Committee wanted to "strike while the iron was hot and apply the troops' new enthusiasm to achieving battle readiness," and in fact it had done so:

> To ensure the accuracy of our artillery, officers above the company level have made copious on-site measurements everywhere in Lhasa. Our drivers took us around the city, stopping at each target area on the pretext of repairing the vehicles, while we got out to "take breaks." We have obtained precise measurements of every spot in Lhasa within our firing range, especially those where the bandits have been or could be active, or could possibly hide.
>
> Our leadership, mindful of the weighty responsibility of our regiment in battle, has been giving these preparations its best attention. Colonel Chen Yuefang, Political Commissar Song Shengxiang, and Vice-Commander/Chief of Staff Chen Bangtai make weekly assessments of the performance of our cadres, their marksmanship, and command and adaptation abilities. They also evaluate the effectiveness of the troops' training and issue orders to raise standards. Our soldiers, like loaded artillery shells, are ready for action.[29]

People in Lhasa noticed PLA soldiers climbing the electric poles. While they might have been installing wires or propaganda loudspeakers, the Tibetans assumed they were taking measurements for artillery, and regarded it as a sign of impending war. Sandbag bunkers had appeared in front of all the Chinese buildings. Chinese flags—five yellow stars on a field of red—fluttered on the rooftops above threatening black mortars.

: : :

Inside the Norbulingka and out, people's nerves were stretched to the limit. Once he had read Ngabo's letter on the afternoon of March 16, Phala realized the die was cast. Although the Dalai Lama had not yet agreed to the evacuation from Lhasa, Phala, sensing its possible imminence, scrambled to put the final details into place.

In contrast to the turmoil outside, the garden inside the Norbulingka was an oasis of quiet in the fading daylight. The Dalai Lama describes it in his autobiography:

> There were no signs of anything untoward. The garden was quiet as usual. The peacocks strutted about with their plumes held high, uncon-

> cerned about the human turmoil; singing birds were flying from tree to tree, mixing their music with that of the fountains near the rock garden; the tame deer, the fish, and the brahmini ducks and white cranes were as placid as ever. A contingent of my bodyguard, out of uniform, was even watering the lawns and flower beds.[30]

When night fell, both Chinese and Tibetans sprang into action.

A pair of PLA officers stepped out of their headquarters on a reconnaissance mission along the riverbank outside the Norbulingka.[31]

Phala summoned the Norbulingka gate guards and warned them not to shout and shine their flashlights at him or the cabinet ministers in the palace grounds at night. Instead, he instructed them to keep their voices down, and to identify people by how they sounded in the dark. He also notified them that a "guard regiment truck" might be going to the Shol Armory near the Potala to get weapons the next night, and they should not stop it for inspection.[32]

On the east, west, and north sides of the Norbulingka, the PLA was ready for action. Its mortars were trained on the palace from all three directions, threatening war.

Many slept poorly, or not at all, that night in Lhasa. Jampa Tenzin, the lama who had resigned from the PCART business office, was in his home near Barkor Street. Ling Rinpoché's clerk, Thinley Phuntsok, was at the estate. Juchen Tubten, the Khampa from Mesho, was in his tent south of the Norbulingka. In a hideout near Drepung Monastery, Kunga Samten was waiting for news with his Chushi Gangdruk guerrilla squad.

: 13 :

Go! Go! Tonight!

THE NIGHT PASSED WITHOUT INCIDENT. At dawn, birds perched on the trees and chirped as they shook out their wings. It was March 17, 1959, the eighth day of the second month in the Earth-Hog year.

The Norbulingka gradually came to life. At the stables, the horses whinnied while the grooms' pet monkeys scampered to and fro on the long chains that bound them to the pillars. At the pond, ducks stretched their necks, quacked, and plunged into the water, as the startled fish turned tail and dived to the bottom.

The Dalai Lama's lights had been on for quite a while. As always, he had risen before daybreak, eaten the breakfast delivered by the palace kitchen, and entered his prayer room.

Normal palace activity picked up as the sky grew light. There was a changing of the guard at the gate, attendants made their rounds with breakfasts for the tutors and cabinet ministers, and gardeners came out to water the trees and flower beds.

The people camped outside the palace walls emerged, yawning, from their tents. Some circumambulated the palace chanting prayers, while others prostrated themselves in its direction. Tendrils of blue smoke from cooking fires wafted skyward, blending with the early morning mist.

Pedestrians began to appear on the streets. Ling Rinpoché's clerk, Thinley Phuntsok, finished his chores at the estate and set out for the Norbulingka, and Tenpa Soepa left his house to return to his post at the palace gates. Some independence-minded Tibetans were making their way to the Indian Consulate to cable a message to Kalimpong.

That morning, important meetings were convened in Beijing and Lhasa. In Beijing, Tibet was on the agenda at the Secretariat of the Central Committee, although few details are available.[1] Three days earlier, on March 14, Mao had summoned some of his top military officers[2] to

Wuhan to discuss Tibet policy, and the Secretariat of the Central Committee may have been anticipating an update from that meeting.

Meanwhile in Lhasa, the Dalai Lama met with his cabinet in the Chensel Phodrang, the Thirteenth Dalai Lama's palace at the Norbulingka, to discuss how to avoid war. A full week had passed since the outbreak of the unrest, and still the multitudes had not dispersed. There was reason to fear that the PLA might strike, resulting in a massacre. The only course of action seemed to be to entreat Tan Guansan, via Ngabo, not to introduce military force, thus allowing the cabinet more time to persuade the crowd to leave. The ministers drafted a reply to the letter Ngabo had sent them the previous afternoon, saying that even though the people were "foolish and impetuous," it might be possible to disperse them peaceably, and that the cabinet would keep trying.[3] They added that it would be difficult for the Dalai Lama to go to the PLA Tibet Military Command as long as the masses had de facto control of the Norbulingka, but promised that he would go once the situation improved. The letter contained a code that Ngabo was supposed to use in his reply.

It was very difficult to smuggle such a conciliatory letter past the volunteer guards, who deeply mistrusted Tibetan officialdom and searched everyone who left the palace gates for just such contraband. The cabinet ministers finally decided on a successful ruse: Minister Shasur entrusted the letter to an attendant who fooled the guards with the claim that he was going shopping.[4]

Since the beginning of the demonstrations on March 10, Ngabo had become the only channel of communication between the Norbulingka and the Chinese, and the cabinet's only possible source of information regarding Chinese intentions. However, extant materials do not indicate exactly how much Ngabo knew about the Chinese deployments; in fact, they suggest that he may have known relatively little. In his 1989 memoir, Tibetan government secretary Gegyepa recalls that the cabinet sent him to Ngabo on March 14 with a code for Ngabo to use in all future correspondence, along with an oral message: "The day before yesterday, our Supreme Jewel instructed the people's representatives to stop meeting at the Norbulingka, and he is doing his utmost to stabilize the overall situation. Please notify us what the Chinese plans are." According to Gegyepa, Ngabo replied: "This could be the end of everything. If the assembled

Lords[5] choose [to resist the Chinese], then the outcome is determined. Do not imagine that the Chinese are unprepared. I live near the Lhasa Bridge, and I hear their trucks rumbling across it day and night."[6] Ngabo's response implies that he believed the cabinet (but not the Dalai Lama) was colluding with the demonstrators. It also exhibits no awareness that the Chinese Central Military Commission had already mobilized masses of troops to converge on Tibet, as he states only that he has heard convoys on the Lhasa Bridge.

Ngabo replied to the cabinet's missive on March 17 with a hasty note via Minister Shasur's attendant, stating that he had received the cabinet's letter, he approved of the Dalai Lama's plan to go to the PLA Tibet Military Command, and would send a more detailed reply later.[7]

Now it was approximately 3:00 P.M. in Beijing. Liu Shaoqi was conducting a Politburo meeting at which PLA Chief of Staff Huang Kecheng conveyed Mao's latest instructions from Wuhan. Although the document containing Mao's orders has never been released in its entirety, its gist has been preserved in the notes of Yang Shangkun, deputy secretary-general of the Central Committee and director of its General Office. Mao had changed his tune about the Dalai Lama: now he wanted to make every effort to prevent his escape (although he still claimed the damage would not be irreparable if these efforts failed). In addition, the newly dispatched Chinese legions were to arrive at their destinations in Tibet by April 10. Upon their arrival, they were to surround Lhasa, but try to hold off on attacking until key points in Lhokha had been secured, so as to cut off the Tibetan escape route. The pacification of Lhasa and Lhokha was to be prioritized over that of other regions, and reforms were to be instituted after pacification was complete. Moreover, information about the campaign was to be kept classified.[8]

By approximately 4:00 P.M. Lhasa time, the Dalai Lama and his cabinet were meeting again in the Chensel Phodrang to formulate a reply to Ngabo's note. Suddenly, they heard a huge explosion on the north side of the Norbulingka. Tenpa Soepa, who was near the north gate at the time, states that he saw an artillery shell whistle by and splash into a marsh a couple of hundred yards away from the Norbulingka.[9] Before anyone had figured out what had happened, they heard a second explosion.

There was a momentary lull, and then panicked shouts.

"The Chinese are shelling the palace!"

"They're attacking us! War!"

From within the inner yellow wall of the palace came the sounds of people running, yelling, and cocking their guns. Some of the guards charged toward the main gate, while others hurried to the Dalai Lama's New Palace. A cabinet minister ran from the Chensel Phodrang to the main gate, shouting to the volunteer guards not to shoot back, and a pall descended over the meeting.

"This is it," everyone was thinking. The point of no return had arrived.

All present turned instinctively to look at the twenty-three-year-old Dalai Lama, the youngest monk in the room. No matter what, he had to give the word.

Should he go? It was a momentous decision for his nation. Pale and tight-lipped, he sat with his head in his hand.

"Consult the Oracle," he finally whispered after a long silence.[10]

: : :

The State Oracle of Tibet, the Thirteenth Nechung Oracle, rushed into the prayer hall with his attendants and darted into his small dressing room beside the statue of the Buddha.

There were oracles all over Tibet, but the Nechung Oracle—the portal for the Dalai Lama's principal protector deity, Dorje Drakden—was paramount. Speaking through a human medium—a monk named Lobsang Jigme—Dorje Drakden advised the Dalai Lama and his ministers regarding all major decisions.

Supported by his assistants, the medium Lobsang Jigme staggered out of his dressing room in full regalia: sumptuous brocade robes and felt boots; a round breastplate mirror; a massive headdress ringed with skulls and bells, topped with long ornamental plumes; and four flagpoles with triangular pennants on his back. The headdress alone weighed thirty pounds. All told, the eight-layer outfit weighed seventy pounds; it was so heavy that he could barely walk, even with the help of his assistants.

Monks began droning the sutras to the accompaniment of ritual horns and drums. All eyes were upon Lobsang Jigme as he drifted into his trance. Shaking off his attendants, he took a few tottering steps, drew his holy sword, and began a stately dance. His face was distorted, his eyes bulging, his breathing labored. He appeared to swell in stature, no longer struggling under the costume's weight. Suddenly he let out a piercing shriek.

"Go! Go! Tonight!"[11]

He grabbed a pen and paper in a frenzy and jotted down a clear route map. Then his assistants rushed forward and relieved him of his enormous headdress. The deity departed from his body, and he collapsed onto the floor.

During an interview with the Dalai Lama in Dharamsala half a century later, I asked, "Why do you consult the Nechung Oracle about important decisions? Are his predictions reliable?"

"I'm over seventy years old, and I've been consulting the Oracle for almost sixty years," he said. "He has never been wrong, not even once."

"In that case, is the Nechung Oracle the overriding factor in your decision-making process?"

"Not exactly," he replied. "His advice is only one of the factors that I consider. I weigh what he says against other input."[12]

: : :

On March 17, 1959, "other input" definitely meant the two explosions. Both of the Dalai Lama's published autobiographies mention them as the main precipitating factor in his decision to leave, an assertion corroborated in the memoirs of other Tibetan eyewitnesses. On April 18, 1959, in his first international press release after his arrival in India, the Dalai Lama mentioned "shells fired at the Norbulingka" as the reason for his flight.[13]

Two days after the press release, however, China's state-run Xinhua News Agency published a rebuttal titled "On the So-Called 'Statement of the Dalai Lama,'" which insinuated that the Dalai Lama's press release had been issued by someone else in his name; moreover, it vehemently denied that there had been any exploding shells at all:

> The [Dalai Lama's] statement asserts that . . . "on the 17th of March two or three mortar shells were fired in the direction of Norbu Lingka Palace." This is a brazen, outright fabrication. The fabricator, however,

> leaves a backdoor open for himself: "Fortunately the shells fell in a nearby pond!" But if the People's Liberation Army really wanted to attack, why was it that it only fired two or three mortar shells and did not venture to fire one more shell after they fell in a nearby pond?[14]

Since China denied having fired the shells, there was no need to present any reasons for having done so, and the question remained unresolved for decades.

In 1991, a Chinese account finally shed some light on the subject. While alleging that the Tibetans initiated the conflict, it acknowledges for the first time that two shells were indeed fired; it also reveals that they were fired by a militiaman who did so without permission: "On March 16 and 17, the armed rebels at the Norbulingka shot at the Lhasa Depot of the Qinghai-Tibet Highway, firing more than thirty artillery shells at the fuel tanks. Without seeking permission, a militiaman at the depot fired two 60 mm mortar shells back at them."[15] The presence of the militia and such weaponry at the Qinghai-Tibet Highway depot, opposite the Norbulingka, strongly suggests that it had become a paramilitary facility.

Writing in 1993, Ji Youquan basically corroborates this account; however, his version asserts that the shells were fired by a policeman:

> [On the morning of March 17,] the armed rebels fired three provocative rounds at the Lhasa Depot of the Qinghai-Tibet Highway. Their intense rifle fire damaged several doors and windows at the depot. This was an act of brazen aggression. An economic policeman[16] at the depot, Zeng Huishan, was angered by the provocation of the armed rebels. Without seeking permission, he lobbed a couple of 60 mm mortar shells back at them. The shells landed and detonated in a spot a few hundred yards north of the northern wall of the Norbulingka.[17]

Ji does not attempt to explain why a civilian unit such as this depot was equipped with a 60 mm mortar, or why an "economic policeman" was able to use it.

A subsequent official source, published in 1995, retells this story with some noteworthy embellishments:

> On [March] 16, the armed rebels at the Norbulingka suddenly started shooting continuously at the Lhasa Depot of the Qinghai-Tibet Highway, which they saw as a hindrance because it obstructed a semicircle of

> rebel strongholds that included the Norbulingka, the Potala, and Chakpori Hill. On [March] 17, the crowd of armed rebels on the north side of the Norbulingka started firing at the depot again, lobbing more than thirty artillery shells at the fuel tanks and pillboxes. Without seeking permission, Zeng Huishan, an economic policeman at the depot, fired back with two shells from a 60 mm mortar, which landed a few hundred yards north of the northern wall of the Norbulingka.[18]

As in the 1991 account, the Tibetan provocations are magnified here: they are charged with having assaulted the depot on two days instead of only one, and with firing more than thirty artillery shells at it. Despite this alleged large-scale, unilateral Tibetan artillery assault, the Chinese are described as having refrained from retaliating in kind.

A Chinese source in a semiclassified compilation published in 1995 also mentions that there were two shells, and it refers to Zeng Huishan (without naming him) as a militiaman rather than an "economic policeman,"[19] which again suggests the possible paramilitary nature of the highway depot.

A key 2008 official compilation repeats this information and embellishes the account still further, claiming that the Tibetans unilaterally attacked not only the depot but also PLA camps and civilian installations:

> On [March] 17 . . . the armed rebels stepped up their provocations, firing continuously at PLA camps and local civilian enterprises. Among them, the Lhasa Depot of the Qinghai-Tibet Highway received particularly intense fire. More than thirty artillery shells struck the fuel tanks there, a serious threat to its safety. At 3:00 P.M., Zeng Huishan, who was a militiaman and a policeman at the depot—in violation of military regulations—shot back without permission at the armed rebels at the Norbulingka with two 60 mm mortar shells, which landed a few hundred yards outside of the northern palace wall.[20]

If the Tibetans were really guilty of such serious provocations as those the Chinese have alleged since the 1990s, then how could these charges have been omitted from the original Xinhua press release in April 1959? That was the moment when China most needed to legitimize its "pacification" of Tibet in the eyes of the world. The emergence of the magnified accusations several decades after the fact seems highly suspect.

No military code of discipline would tolerate a militiaman's jumping the gun during a hostile standoff. In this particular case, the militiaman's action could have been detrimental to the Chinese, whose hurried deployments were not quite complete. It seems reasonable to assume that there would have been a thorough military investigation of the incident, but no record of any such investigation is available.

No Tibetan sources—whether published in China or in exile—mention Tibetan attacks on the Chinese highway depot on March 16 and 17. In fact, Chinese allegations of unilateral Tibetan attacks on Chinese civilian and military installations on those days seem dubious, since such actions could have imperiled the Dalai Lama while he was in the Norbulingka. Nevertheless, for Zeng Huishan to have suddenly fired shells at the Norbulingka with no particular provocation makes no sense either. The incident will probably remain murky unless further information comes to light.

The fact remains that the two artillery shells moved the Tibetans and Chinese beyond their impasse and spurred the Dalai Lama to leave. Once he was gone, he reasoned, the people would no longer perceive a need to guard him, and they would clear out of the Norbulingka area. He hoped his departure would prevent a bloodbath.

: : :

Tales of fleeing monarchs are the stuff of high drama, and as such, stories like those of the Dalai Lama's flight in 1959 have always been popular in literature, theater, and film. Many different versions have emerged over the years, both in China and abroad, but the endless retellings have tended to obscure the facts.

One unresolved question is the exact number of people in the Dalai Lama's escape party, including all the attendants and guards. The memoirs of the participants tend to be vague on this point, probably because of the haste of the occasion, and because the detailed logistics had been delegated by Phala to several different individuals. In fact, fewer than 100 people left the Norbulingka with the Dalai Lama on the night of

March 17, corresponding roughly to the number that eventually crossed the Indian border.[21] Various accounts suggest that the escape party later swelled to more than 400, including Tibetan Army soldiers and Chushi Gandruk guerrillas who joined the group as escorts.

Later Chinese accounts, on the other hand, give a variety of inflated, unsubstantiated estimates. One claims that more than six hundred people went with the Dalai Lama that night:

> Cloaking themselves in the excuse that the PLA had fired mortar shells [at the Norbulingka] and that they were acting for the Dalai Lama's protection, the armed rebels abducted him and took him south across the Lhasa [Kyichu] River toward Shannan [Lhokha] under cover of night, along with an entourage of more than six hundred of the elite leaders of the armed rebel clique.[22]

This figure can also be found in another major Chinese source.[23]

The Rama Gang ferry across the Kyichu River was equipped with only one rectangular wooden boat with a capacity of thirty people (not including horses), and three or four coracle boats, each with a capacity of ten. One round-trip took at least thirty minutes. At the rate of seventy people per hour, it would have taken more than eight hours to get six hundred people across.[24] Moreover, even if these six hundred people had tried to sneak out of the Norbulingka in small groups, it would have been nearly impossible for such a large total number to slip by the Tibetan crowds and the PLA without setting off general alarm.

Perhaps to compensate for the unreasonable estimate of "more than six hundred," a 2008 Chinese source reduces the number to one hundred fifty, but it embroiders in other respects: "On [March] 15 . . . the elite reactionaries stepped up their preparations to abduct the Dalai Lama: they planned their route and composed the name list for an entourage of one hundred and fifty people. They also chose seven decoys, monks the Dalai Lama's age who could pass for him, and outfitted them in clothing similar to his."[25]

The "seven decoys" ploy seems improbable. No source is given for it, nor is it mentioned in the memoirs of Phala and Phuntsok, who planned the escape. As far as numbers go, this Chinese estimate of one hundred fifty may include attendants and guards. It nonetheless conflicts with Tibetan sources, which indicate that guards for the Dalai Lama were designated on March 17, and not beforehand.

Another source of confusion is the report in the memoirs of Roger McCarthy, the CIA instructor who trained Athar and Lhotse's group on Saipan, that the Dalai Lama had two decoy detachments to throw his pursuers off the trail.[26] He states that he got this information from personal interviews with Gonpo Tashi and Athar, but neither of the two was involved in the escape plans. Gonpo Tashi did not see the Dalai Lama until he himself slipped away to India much later, and Athar joined the Dalai Lama's group on the road, almost a week after it had departed the Norbulingka. Moreover, neither of the two mentions this detail in his memoirs. It is known, however, that Phala made arrangements for both a vanguard and a rear guard. McCarthy may be referring to these, while seemingly misunderstanding their purpose.

As soon as the two mortar shells detonated on the fateful afternoon of March 17, a Tibetan participant recalls, some people's representatives rushed into the Norbulingka to speak to the cabinet. It was their opinion that the PLA was testing its mortars as a prelude to an imminent attack on the Norbulingka. They demanded that the cabinet arrange for the Dalai Lama to seek asylum abroad.[27]

At any rate, the Nechung Oracle had spoken. The question now was not whether to evacuate the Dalai Lama, but how.

The cabinet, Chief of Staff Gadrang, Lord Chamberlain Phala, and Security Chief Phuntsok called an emergency meeting to discuss the people's representatives' demand and the logistics of the exodus. The key was to sneak past the crowds guarding the Norbulingka. If people got wind of what was happening, they would rush forward to help protect the Dalai Lama. The ensuing commotion could set off a PLA massacre, defeating the Dalai Lama's original purpose in choosing to leave. Thus, speed and stealth were essential. In addition to the Dalai Lama's family and tutors, his entourage would include Lord Chamberlain Phala, Security Chief Phuntsok, Chief of Staff Gadrang, cabinet ministers Surkhang, Shasur, and Liushar, and a few other important officials. To avoid attracting attention, they planned to divide into three groups to cross the river, and to wait approximately an hour between crossings.

There were two routes to Lhokha from the Norbulingka. One was to cross the Kyichu River at the Rama Gang ferry south of the palace. The other was to follow the highway north of the Norbulingka, eventually turning west toward Chushul or Gongkar. After discussion, they chose the former. It was not without its dangers, as the PLA's August First Farm faced the river, but it seemed the safer of the two options. The route north of the palace would take them right past the Chinese transportation depot, but if they took the southward route, a PLA posse would have to cross the river to catch up with them. And even if the Tibetan crowds realized what was happening, it would be difficult for large numbers of people to follow them across the river with their horses.

Once the group had made these preliminary decisions, the remaining details were left to Phala. He and Phuntsok decided that Phuntsok would appoint guards and escorts, and that Colonel Junpa of Regiment 2 and Kundeling Dzasa would take charge of the Dalai Lama's safety on the road. Plans were made for evacuating the Dalai Lama's family members. All preparations had to be completed by that night.

A group including Acting Cabinet Minister Liushar, Grand Secretary Tenzin Lobsang Dondrup, and Potala representative Lobsang Dondrup went to the Potala treasury and withdrew a large gold brick, fifty gold elephant coins, forty gold Tibetan coins, two golden crab figurines, a golden goblet, and 141,267 Indian rupees, to use on the road.[28]

Kundeling Dzasa found Tenpa Soepa, who was helping to guard the north gate, swore him to confidentiality, and asked him to find some horses for the group. He managed, with difficulty, to get five from the palace stables, although he could not get saddles. Later that evening, he would take the horses home for safekeeping until they were needed. Deciding it would be risky to try to smuggle dozens of horses from the palace stables to the other side of the river, Kundeling Dzasa instructed his steward to prepare more horses at his estate on the south bank.

Phala told the Dalai Lama's chef to go to the Rama Gang ferry with cooking equipment, and swore him to secrecy with the Buddha as his witness. Kunga Samten's squad received word to wait for the group at the ferry that night. After dark, they moved from their hiding place near Drepung Monastery to one near the ferry.

Phuntsok told Colonel Junpa to have his men carry grain and weapons to the riverside and wait there, and to post guards along the route and around the ferry area.[29] He also instructed Colonel Dokharsey and Lieutenant Colonel Sonam Tashi to set out on the following night with a rear guard of more than a hundred of their best soldiers to shield the Dalai Lama from possible PLA pursuers. Most of Regiment 1, the Dalai Lama's security guard unit, was assigned to stay behind to guard the Norbulingka instead of going on the trip. Despite some confusion about the date, Lieutenant Colonel Seshing's memoir provides a vivid description of Phuntsok's parting instructions:

> At approximately 8:00 P.M. Lhasa time on March 8 [*sic*], Colonel Phuntsok Tashi came running in and called all the lieutenant colonels and captains . . . to a meeting.
>
> "I have an important announcement today," he said. "But first I want everyone to swear to secrecy in front of the gods."
>
> Everyone made the required pledge.
>
> "The Dalai Lama is very worried about the current situation," he continued, "and he has asked to be temporarily evacuated. After he leaves, you will be in charge of making sure everything here is taken care of properly." . . .
>
> "Cavalrymen who are going on the trip should prepare now for departure," he concluded, "and you should distribute their advance pay immediately. Your families had best relocate to the countryside, and you should flee too if things take a turn for the worse."
>
> With these words, he turned and hurried back into the palace.[30]

Since Seshing goes on to describe the departure of the Dalai Lama "that night," it seems clear that he is relating the events of March 17, despite his use of the mistaken date of March 8. He had probably confused the Tibetan and Western calendars, as the date of the Dalai Lama's exodus was the eighth day of the month according to the Tibetan calendar. His memoir continues: "At approximately ten o'clock that night Lhasa time, the Dalai Lama, his mother, his sister Tsering Dolma, and others passed through the Norbulingka guard headquarters and fled Lhasa via the Rama Gang ferry. I did not have a chance to say good-bye to the Dalai Lama because I was too busy distributing advance pay to the cavalry in his escort."[31] Although Seshing's memoir unfortunately does not specify the number of cavalrymen concerned, the fact that he was apparently distributing their pay at the moment of the Dalai Lama's departure suggests that they may have been members of a rear guard, thus corroborating Phuntsok's account.

At approximately 5:00 that evening, Phala sent a civil servant, Khenchung Tubten Tsepal, to the Indian Consulate with an oral message for the consul, Major Chiba: "As you know, the situation is dire, and the Dalai Lama may have to evacuate Lhasa. We will continue to negotiate with the Chinese. If we cannot come to an agreement with them, India is our only possible haven. Please report this to your government." Major Chiba asked when and where the Dalai Lama would be crossing into India. Tubten Tsepal made a second trip to the Indian Consulate with Phala's reply, which Major Chiba forwarded to the Indian government. All Phala could say, however, was that this rough preliminary notice would have to suffice because they had not worked out the details yet, and they would have no way to contact the consul again once they had left Lhasa.[32]

The sun sank slowly in the west and the sky grew dark. The turmoil of the day finally subsided.

All of a sudden, gunfire rang out at the riverside, startling Phuntsok, who was patrolling the palace grounds. He glanced at his watch. It was almost time for the first group of evacuees to slip out of the palace: the Dalai Lama's mother, his sister Tsering Dolma (Phuntsok's wife), his uncle, and his little brother Ngari Rinpoché were supposed to leave the south gate of the Norbulingka on the pretext of visiting a convent. Phuntsok hurried to their living chambers.

The garden was an oasis of peace. The birds had gone to roost, the fish lay low in the pond, and the green prayer flags fluttered in the breeze. Stars glimmered among the clouds in the sky.

Outside the Norbulingka, the multitudes—some in their tents and others in the open air—got ready for another sleepless night.

: 14 :

The Night Ferry

AT APPROXIMATELY 8:00 P.M., a servant opened Ngari Rinpoché's door and told him his mother wanted to see him.

He went to her room. She looked nervous, and his sister Tsering Dolma was there.

"Go get dressed quickly," his mother told him, trying to control the quaver in her voice. "We're going on a trip."[1]

Ngari Rinpoché caught on right away. "To India?" he asked.

"No," she replied. "We're visiting a convent across the river."

Ngari Rinpoché turned to leave.

"Don't breathe a word of this to anyone!" she called after him.

Ngari Rinpoché had seen his elder brother the Dalai Lama only once in the last few days, and he had looked a bit haggard. Still, despite his furrowed brow, his years of religious practice graced him with an aura of calm. The exploding mortar shells had convinced him: he had to flee. Once he reached Lhokha, he would be effectively beyond the reach of the Chinese army. Then he could continue south toward the border of India and try to negotiate with the Chinese once more from the safety of distance.

In his room, Ngari Rinpoché shed his maroon monk's habit for an ordinary coat and trousers, and slipped his pistol into his pocket. Then he sat twiddling his thumbs, aching to share the secret. Was Fat Old Man going too, he wondered?

Bounding down the stairs, he pushed open the door of a small room. "Fat Old Man" was sitting inside in his monk's habit, his head bowed over some needlework, with a heap of white curtains beside him. He was Ngari Rinpoché's paternal uncle, formerly Regent Taktra Rinpoché's secretary. Ngari Rinpoché had always called this genial fellow Fat Old Man, and had never learned his real name.

"What are you doing?" Ngari Rinpoché asked.

"Get out of here!" his uncle snapped. "I'm making sacks for *tsampa!*"

That meant he must be going, too.

On his way back upstairs, Ngari Rinpoché bumped into one of his mother's maids.

"Hey, guess what!" he shouted. "We're going to India!"

She glared at him. "Shh! Don't let anyone hear you!"

Irritated, Ngari Rinpoché went to his mother's room to see if people were ready yet. All the lights were on, and the servants were helping his mother and sister dress for the trip. Removing their long gowns, striped aprons, jewelry, and talismans, they laid them on the table and donned Khampa soldiers' clothes, which looked so funny that Ngari Rinpoché burst out laughing. The ladies exchanged glances and joined him in a chorus of giggles.

There was a knock on the door. Ngari Rinpoché opened it, and an officer named Captain Lobsang entered, followed by a guard with a submachine gun. The time had come. Ngari Rinpoché's sister handed him a heavy scarf and a fleece hat, and they set out in haste, forgetting the talismans and gold earrings on the table. Ngari Rinpoché raced down the stairs to say good-bye to the servants on the veranda.

A crisp night wind was blowing, and stars peeked out between the clouds. As he descended the stairs in the darkened building, Ngari Rinpoché heard gunfire from the direction of the river. Gun at the ready, the guard ran to the doorway and peered outside. The shooting stopped. The guard motioned them to follow him, and they made their way silently through a dark grove of trees to the south gate of the Norbulingka.

There they paused in the shadow of the palace wall while Captain Lobsang told the guards to open the gate, claiming that the group was going to the river on a patrol mission. The gate swung open, and the little band of "Khampa soldiers" filed out. Perhaps too overwhelmed by the events of the day, the guards failed to notice that the "patrol" included a child. The group left the Norbulingka without looking back.

Outside the gate, Ngari Rinpoché saw a sea of tents and smelled snuff in the air. Some people were asleep inside their tents, while others were huddled in their fur robes on the ground outside, guns in hand. None of these volunteers noticed anything unusual about this particular "patrol," since such groups left the palace routinely every night.

The Kyichu River was straight ahead. Tsering Dolma had to help her arthritic mother limp down the rocky, weed-choked riverbank. Watching them, Ngari Rinpoché suddenly realized that he was the "man of the family." He patted the pistol in his pocket. Someone brought his mother a horse, which she mounted, while everyone else walked alongside. A soldier had two sacks that Fat Old Man had made, now filled with *tsampa,* meat jerky, and butter. At the riverside they found two waiting coracle boats, with twenty soldiers standing in silent guard. The little group boarded the boats and they pushed off the bank. Standing in his boat, Ngari Rinpoché looked back at the Norbulingka. The gilt statuary on its roof—a Dharma wheel framed by a pair of deer—was gleaming faintly in the night. With a splash of its oars, the boat carried him away.

They disembarked quickly at the south bank, where Kunga Samten and thirty Khampa guerrillas awaited them with horses. The men greeted the Dalai Lama's mother and sister with deep respectful bows, while the boat turned around immediately for its next load.

Suddenly remembering his grandmother back in Yabshi House, Ngari Rinpoché turned to his mother.

"What about Grandma?"

She bit her lip, and her eyes filled with tears.

Ngari Rinpoché's heart sank. His grandmother, too old and frail to make the journey, had been left behind in Lhasa with his aunt.

He walked alone for a while, and then stopped and gazed back at the other side of the river. To the west of the Norbulingka he saw a cluster of lights in the Nordo Lingka area: the PLA's August First Farm, with its hospital and barracks. Tucked into the mountainside north of the farm, he barely discerned a complex of buildings: Drepung Monastery, where he had spent his childhood. Sadly, he pressed his palms together and performed three prostrations in its direction.

: : :

As Phuntsok entered the inner palace courtyard, someone brought word that the first group had safely made its escape. With a sigh of relief, he headed toward the glowing yellow windows of the Dalai Lama's New Palace. There was only an hour left until the appointed time. He found

Phala, who told him that preparations seemed to be on schedule for the later evacuees.

Once the decision to flee had been made, the Dalai Lama had stopped fretting and turned his attention to preparing for the trip.[2] Summoning several of the key people's representatives, he told them that he and the cabinet had to leave Lhasa temporarily, and asked them to conceal his departure and take care of crowd control. While sad to see him go, the representatives were relieved that he would be safe, and promised their cooperation. Once they had gone, the Dalai Lama sat thoughtfully at his desk for a while, and then picked up a pen and wrote a letter. Afterward, he went out to synchronize his watch with Gadrang's and Phala's, and to pray in the palace shrines.

At 9:30 P.M., he returned to his room to dress for the trip. Layman's garments were neatly folded for him on his bed. He had not worn such attire in almost twenty years. Alone in the dim lamplight, he shed his monk's habit for the simple coat and trousers, and then stepped into his prayer room. The sacred *thangka* of Palden Lhamo[3] on the wall, dating from the Second Dalai Lama's time, caught his eye. Feeling the need of its protective powers, he removed it from the wall and rolled it up. Then he took a white silk prayer scarf and went to the Temple of Mahakala.

Ascending the staircase, he reached an imposing, ancient red wooden door and gave it a forceful shove. As it creaked slowly open, the smell of incense greeted him. He paused at the threshold, bathed in the golden lamplight, silently surveying the familiar scene. The temple was dimly lit by rows of small butter lamps, which flickered on the table in front of the statue of Mahakala. The sacred blade in the deity's hand glinted in the lamplight like a bolt of lightning. A monk was scooping butter for the lamps from a large urn behind the statue, his face half hidden in its shadow. A row of monks sat in front of the statue solemnly reciting sutras, heads bowed. All sensed his presence, but no one looked up. A duo of monks accompanied the prayers with clashing cymbals and a plaintively wailing horn.

Standing before the statue, the Dalai Lama unfolded the prayer scarf, bowed deeply, and laid it at the deity's feet as a gesture of farewell. Mahakala, a wrathful manifestation of the Buddha's compassion, had a crown of skulls, bulging eyes, and an aura of flames. He stood for the conquest of demons and noxious forces within oneself, and for complete, fearless devotion to the benefit of all living beings. Despite his fierce exterior, his heart was merciful, and he was the Dalai Lama's protector.

The Dalai Lama pressed his palms together in prayer, and then sat down to read from the sutra, which he flipped open to a passage about "confidence and courage." Steadying himself, he focused on the text. The future was completely unknown, and all was in the hands of the Buddha.

At 10:00 P.M., Phuntsok went to the Dalai Lama's room as planned, and found him standing in the dim lamplight, wearing a long coat, with his rolled-up *thangka* under his arm. When he saw Phuntsok, he turned off the lights and walked out the door. His chamberlains pressed their palms together in farewell. He asked them to darken the building and then followed Phuntsok outside. A dog came to greet him, sniffing him and wagging its tail. He patted it on the head, and it sat down to watch him and Phuntsok make their way across the inner courtyard. A lieutenant and a foot soldier joined them and brought up the rear. Phuntsok had been leading night patrols around the palace every night for a week, so the little group attracted no particular attention. When they arrived at the Kelsang Phodrang, the Seventh Dalai Lama's palace, they found Phala, dressed in simple lay clothing and waiting in front of the darkened building.

The Dalai Lama paused at a shrine to offer a prayer and visualize his eventual return to Lhasa. Then they crossed the garden toward the gate in the yellow wall, where Chief of Staff Gadrang, also in plain clothing, was waiting along with some guards. As the Dalai Lama approached, a soldier handed him a rifle, which he slung over his shoulder. He removed his glasses and put them into his pocket. Gadrang whispered to him that he must be sure to stay with the group, no matter what happened. At the south exit from the palace, Phala told the guards to open the gate for his "night patrol." Some people volunteered to join them, but he declined. "You go that way," he told them, "and we'll go this way, and we'll be sure to meet up."[4]

The little "patrol" swished past as they spoke.

As the Dalai Lama stepped out of the Norbulingka, he sensed the presence of the crowd, which was a blur without his glasses. It was late at night after a long hard day, and people were too tired to pay any attention to the little "night patrol." Crossing the wide path that encircled the palace, the fugitives descended onto the riverbank and wended their way through the scrub until they met Kundeling Dzasa with an army captain and a few heavily armed soldiers, who were waiting in the dunes. The captain had a horse for the Dalai Lama.

"What's your name?" asked the Dalai Lama.

"Kelsang Dramdul."

"An auspicious name," commented the Dalai Lama, mounting the horse.[5] Kelsang meant "good luck," and Dramdul meant "to subdue." With the captain guiding the horse by the reins and guards on all sides, the little group proceeded in silence toward the ferry. Clouds had shut out the moonlight, and the overgrown shrubs loomed like enemy soldiers in the dark. Slowly, the group proceeded across the rough terrain toward the water's edge.

Chief of Staff Gadrang kept his hand on his sword, warily eyeing every clump of bushes. Juchen Tubten was also there with three of his countrymen. They spread out behind the Dalai Lama to form a rear guard, rifles at the ready, keeping a tense lookout for enemy lying in ambush.

When they reached the river, they found Regiment 6 standing guard, and the wooden boat and a coracle awaiting them. The Dalai Lama, Gadrang, Phuntsok, and some soldiers rode in the coracle, while the rest of the group boarded the wooden boat with the horses.

The primeval nighttime stillness of the valley and the soft gleam of the ripples on the water created the illusion of safety. But the lights were still blazing at the PLA August First Farm facing the river, even though its mortars and machine guns were shrouded in darkness.

Juchen Tubten and his men stood on the riverbank watching the boats disappear into the night.

On the other side, the group found Colonel Junpa, along with Kunga Samten, Lobsang Yeshe, and their band of Khampa warriors, one of whom stepped forward and bowed, presenting a white prayer scarf to the Dalai Lama.

"What's your name?" asked the Dalai Lama.

"Tenpa Dhargye," the man replied.

"An auspicious name," the Dalai Lama said again, observing that Tenpa Dhargye meant "promote the Dharma."[6] Putting his glasses back on, he noticed the lights of the PLA camp back across the river. Suddenly they seemed too close for comfort.

: : :

Earlier that evening at the Norbulingka, Tenpa Soepa had met with Kundeling Dzasa and Colonel Junpa, who were part of the Dalai Lama's group. They had assigned him thirty soldiers, and said they would signal him with gunfire when they reached the south side of the river with the Dalai Lama at about 10:30 that night.[7] It would be his job to provide horses for the third and last group of escapees—the cabinet ministers and tutors—and escort them to the river. They also said that if Tenpa Soepa did not see the ferry when his group arrived at the river, he should signal them with a flashlight wrapped in red cloth, and they would shine a regular flashlight from the south bank to let him know the ferry was on its way. Then they split up. Kundeling Dzasa and the colonel instructed their servants that anyone who came to find them should be told that they had gone to patrol the hill by the Rama Gang ferry. Tenpa Soepa and his servant took the soldiers, and the horses from the palace stables, back to his home in the Kundeling neighborhood. There was an alley behind his house, with a bridge at its entrance. Tenpa Soepa's instructions were to wait for the gunfire signal and then to proceed to the bridge and wait there for a truck to arrive.

Gunfire shattered the stillness of the night around 10:30. Ling Rinpoché, the Dalai Lama's Senior Tutor, came out of his room in the Norbulingka, dressed in layman's clothes. His clerk, Thinley Phuntsok, who had gone to the window, turned at the sound of Ling Rinpoché's footsteps, and was surprised to see him in such attire. Ling Rinpoché motioned to him to remain silent. Somewhat perplexed, Thinley escorted Ling Rinpoché to the main gate, where Ling Rinpoché stopped and shook hands with him.

"Take care," he whispered.

Thinley watched Ling Rinpoché walk toward a waiting truck, suddenly realizing that the Senior Tutor was going on a long journey. A pilgrimage, perhaps? Or was he going to Lhokha? As he stood there in confusion, his heart began to pound: Was Ling Rinpoché running away? Did that mean the Dalai Lama was leaving too?[8]

At that moment, Tubten Khetsun, the teenage clerk, was on night shift at the gate. He had been at the Norbulingka ever since his appointment to guard duty on March 13. Just after 10:00 P.M., he saw cabinet ministers Surkhang, Shasur, and Liushar patrolling the grounds in plain clothing. Surkhang warned him and his fellow guards to increase their vigilance just before dawn, when it was "customary for the Chinese to attack."[9]

Before long, he saw a truck with a tarpaulin over its back emerge from the palace grounds. Phala had instructed the guards the preceding day that there was no need to inspect a guard regiment truck exiting the palace, and the gates swung open to let the truck out. The watchful crowds around the gate saw the truck but never imagined that the tarpaulin concealed the Dalai Lama's two tutors, Ling Rinpoché and Trijang Rinpoché, Cabinet Ministers Surkhang, Liushar, and Shasur, and some servants. The truck sped toward Tenpa Soepa's neighborhood.

Tubten noticed that the Dalai Lama's personal bodyguards seemed to have disappeared. Although this struck him as odd, he did not dwell on the thought at the time. At the end of his shift, he went back to his quarters, where he saw his uncle and brother whispering to each other. They fell silent at his approach, and he asked them what was wrong, but they replied tersely that he would find out soon.

Tenpa Soepa heard the gunfire at 10:30 P.M., his prearranged signal that the Dalai Lama had safely crossed the river. Pretending to go for a stroll, he went out to the alley near his house, where he saw a few idle passersby. He shooed them away and returned to his house, instructing his soldiers to guard the alley and keep people out.

At about 11:00 P.M., a truck pulled into the alley. The soldiers lifted the tarpaulin so the occupants could climb out. Tenpa Soepa led the arrivals into his courtyard and helped them mount their horses. Then he divided his soldiers into a vanguard and a rear guard, and they set out for the river.

When the three cabinet ministers had arrived for their day's work at the Norbulingka on the morning of March 10, 1959, they had no idea they would be trapped in the palace for a week, never to go home again, or that commoners would encroach on their authority as hereditary aristocrats for the first time in history. Their exchange of the sumptuous robes of officialdom for ordinary clothing signified the end of an era. Tibet's isolation had been shattered, and now it would have to adapt to the modern world.

These entrenched aristocrats, dubious of change in general, were especially wary of the draconian Communist reforms. As they saw it, Tibet was in the path of a deluge, and it was their job to try to preserve the Dalai Lama—the soul of Tibet—and follow him into an uncharted future.

The group arrived at the river, where they found more Tibetan soldiers waiting for them. Seeing that the ferry had not arrived, Tenpa Soepa took out his red flashlight and signaled the opposite bank. A faint white light gleamed in response. Twenty minutes later, he heard the splashing of oars as the wooden boat appeared.

The men and their horses boarded, the ferryman pushed off from the bank, and the boat glided silently across the river.

: : :

The Dalai Lama's party spurred their horses westward as fast as they could. The mountain range lining the river valley towered on their left, with only a tiny road snaking its way to the top. They had entered the most perilous stretch of the journey. The lights of the August First Farm glared at them from the other side of the river, so shallow at this spot that PLA vehicles could drive right across it. Trucks often came to the sandbank in the middle of the river to load sand and gravel for PLA construction projects. A truck might arrive at any moment, catching the fugitives in its headlights, and the bald barrier ridge along the river would provide no cover for their getaway. With their horses' hooves clattering as loud as thunder, they struggled to make out the stony path in the darkness. The short stretch of road seemed endless to the Dalai Lama, who had never been so scared in his life.[10]

Kunga Samten's guerrilla soldiers, mostly unaware of whom they were escorting that night, chattered noisily as they went, consulting each other at forks in the road. At one such fork, the Dalai Lama took the wrong direction. When he quickly turned and retraced his steps, he noticed some torches, as if people were pursuing them, but his guards assured him it was only his Khampa escort.

They plodded on for a few miles until they reached a sandbar, where those in the lead paused and waited for stragglers. This was another hazardous spot where PLA vehicles could ford the river. Phuntsok ordered a few dozen soldiers to stay there to foil Chinese pursuers, should they come.

Relief had swept over Phuntsok the moment he disembarked from the ferry. Sleep deprivation suddenly caught up with him, and he kept dozing off as they trudged along on horseback. Lord Chamberlain Phala was personally leading the Dalai Lama's horse, to make sure the Dalai Lama, with his poor eyesight, did not take another wrong turn.

The mountains cast a dark veil over the little band as they trekked across the ridge and disappeared among the peaks beyond.

Meanwhile, the ferry carrying Tenpa Soepa, the tutors, and the cabinet ministers reached the south shore, where the steward of the Kundeling estate had horses ready for them. They mounted quickly and plunged into the night to catch up with the Dalai Lama's group.

During a short rest break before they reached Che Pass, Tenpa Soepa saw Kundeling Dzasa from the Dalai Lama's group riding back to meet them. He had an important mission for Tenpa Soepa. Handing him the letter the Dalai Lama had written just before their departure, he instructed Tenpa Soepa to return to Lhasa and deliver it first thing in the morning to Khenchung Tara, who was still in the Norbulingka. Tenpa Soepa slipped the letter into the folds of his robe, and he and his servant headed back the way they had come.

: 15 :

Into the Himalayas

THE DALAI LAMA and his entourage emerged into the peaceful wilderness on the other side of the ridge, relieved to be out of danger for the moment. Gazing out at the dark mountains stretching into the distance, they wondered where they might find a place to stop for a rest.[1]

It was bitterly cold at this high altitude, and they had left in such a hurry that the Dalai Lama had not even had time to eat. Phala sent Kunga Samten and some of his men ahead as scouts. They found an estate called Namgyal Gang a couple of hours away, and asked the owner to prepare a room for the Dalai Lama. Delighted, the man and his family set to work cleaning a room and stoking the kitchen fires.

After many hours without rest, the Dalai Lama barely had the strength to keep trudging ahead in the numbing cold. At 3:00 A.M. he saw the faint lights of a settlement and heard dogs baying in the distance. Finally, the group reached the Namgyal Gang estate, where Kunga Samten opened the door for them.

The Dalai Lama's hosts welcomed him with white silk prayer scarves and ushered him into their worship room, which they had prepared for his use. He collapsed in exhaustion. Phala suddenly realized that in his haste he had forgotten to bring any bedding. He had an attendant fetch a saddle blanket, which he fumigated with incense and draped over the Dalai Lama's legs. As the estate was barely twenty miles from Lhasa, they dared not rest more than an hour, and they set out again just as the sky was beginning to glow in the east, bringing the morning of March 18, 1959.

The entourage reached the foot of Che Pass at around 8:00 A.M. The sun was up but it was still freezing cold. The cabinet ministers and tutors had caught up with them, expanding their group to a few dozen people. Someone had brought a mule with bedding and some sacks of *tsampa* and jerky, and the group took a rest break at the foot of the pass before ascending. The servants and guards quickly gathered wood and kindling, built a fire, and made breakfast. "Che Pass," or "Sandy Pass," was aptly named. Sand blanketed the slopes and swirled in the stinging winds, which robbed the travelers' tea of its warmth and peppered it with grit. They gulped the tepid brew down as best they could, cherishing its faint heat. Then they packed up their utensils and got ready to ascend the pass. The sun had reached the height of the mountain peak, bathing the plains behind them in its brilliant light.

Just then, an old man leading a white horse with a fine saddle emerged from the golden morning haze. Presenting the Dalai Lama with a white silk prayer scarf, he introduced himself as Tashi Norbu, from nearby Shedrong Village, and said he had been a groom at the Norbulingka in the Thirteenth Dalai Lama's day. Hearing that the Dalai Lama was approaching Che Pass, he had come to offer his favorite horse. With a deep bow, he handed the reins to the Dalai Lama, who accepted gratefully. To the travelers, the auspicious white horse seemed a godsend.

The old man advised Phala that it would be safer for them to avoid Che Pass, which would be crowded with pilgrims headed for Samye Monastery this time of year, and to take the more secluded Lumbala Pass instead, even though it was steeper.[2]

Bidding the old man farewell, they began their ascent of the sheer, dark side of the mountain. Fat Old Man's saddle came loose and slipped down around his horse's belly, leaving him clinging to the horse's mane, and Ngari Rinpoché could not stop laughing at the sight.

Phala rode in front of the Dalai Lama and led the Dalai Lama's horse by the reins. The travelers dismounted during the steepest stretches of road to spare their horses. At the top of the pass, an elevation of more than sixteen thousand feet, Phala turned and told the Dalai Lama to take one final look at Lhasa.

Dismounting, the Dalai Lama gazed down at the faraway ancient city. From this distance, all seemed quite normal. There was no sign of the PLA artillery trained on the palace, or of any impending doom. He pressed his palms together in prayer for Lhasa, and got back on his horse to descend the opposite side of the mountain into the Tsangpo River Valley. Beneath them to the southwest, the broad, jade-green river snaked its way along the valley floor.

There were no settlements at the foot of the pass, and it was about six miles to the only river crossing: Pantsa ferry. On the opposite bank was a village called Kyishong, or "Happy Valley."

Although the descent took the entourage down the sunny side of the mountain, the slope was steep and coated with slippery sand. The travelers dismounted and ran downhill holding hands, while their attendants led their horses. Whole groups fell down together, their companions laughing at them as they scrambled to recover their footing and their scattered belongings. All told, this arduous stretch of the journey took them more than three hours.

Just as they were beginning to worry that the PLA might be lying in wait at the foot of the pass, a sudden spring sandstorm began pelting their faces, but they took comfort in the idea that it would also blind any possible Chinese pursuers.

After Kunga Samten and his men had ridden ahead to ascertain the coast was clear, the group proceeded to the ferry. They crossed in small groups, the oarsmen struggling against the wind.

By then the sky was awash with the rosy sunset, setting the mountain landscape aglow. The villagers of Kyishong were lined up along the river, their faces streaming with tears as they bowed low with their white prayer scarves. Bluish tendrils of juniper incense wafted up from the riverbank to merge with the clouds above. Among the crowd were Khampas from the Chushi Gangdruk forces, some of whom wore the white or yellow armbands of new recruits.

The Dalai Lama stopped for a respite in the village, while the local people filed by to pay their respects. The weary travelers had been on the road almost continuously for eighteen hours, but they still had miles to go before reaching camp.

Misty-eyed, the villagers watched them disappear into the dusk.

: : :

As the Dalai Lama and his band trekked across the Himalayas, the idea that they were creating a legend was far from their minds. News of the Dalai Lama's disappearance reached the outside world on March 21, 1959, and from then on, all eyes were riveted on Tibet, as people wondered where he had gone. His astounding reappearance more than a week later inspired both Han Chinese and Tibetans to try to reconstruct the story, which gradually assumed epic proportions.

Not surprisingly, the Chinese and the Tibetan versions of the story differed markedly. According to the Tibetans, the Chinese had been plotting to kidnap the Dalai Lama, but the gods had intervened: he had slipped out of the Norbulingka undetected, and the sky had been so heavily overcast during the next two weeks that the Chinese pilots could not catch him.

In contrast, there were two major Chinese variants of the story. The first, used widely in propaganda intended for foreign consumption—despite the Dalai Lama's constant denials—was that the reactionary Tibetan elite abducted him to India. The story held that "counterrevolutionaries" in Lhasa had initiated a carefully orchestrated insurgency on March 10, 1959, intending to split Tibet off from the motherland. The PLA had exhibited admirable self-restraint for ten days, after which it had followed orders to strike back, but the reactionaries had kidnapped the Dalai Lama in the meantime. A second Chinese variant of the story emerged in official publications in the 1990s (although it had been passed along the grapevine for years before), mostly in domestic propaganda: that Mao facilitated the Dalai Lama's getaway, which would have been impossible otherwise. Both versions are still circulating in China today, in official media and by word of mouth.

Aside from Mao's March 12 cable to the CCP Tibet Work Committee—in which he said, "We should not attempt to stop them if they do try to flee"[3]—the strongest evidence that Mao facilitated the Dalai Lama's escape seems to be a quote that the historian Ji Youquan attributes to General Li Jue, former vice-commander of the PLA Tibet Military Command: "On the night of March 17, 1959, we had our artillery trained on the Dalai Lama and his entourage when they were getting ready to cross the Lhasa [Kyichu] River. If we had chosen to fire, not one of them would have left that riverbank alive. But the Central Committee had not ordered us to obstruct their escape, so we sat quietly amongst the trees, watching by the light of the moon as they fled to the opposite shore in boatloads."[4] The historical value of this quote is dubious. Li Jue was not in Lhasa at all during the time in question, a fact that the historian Ji

Youquan neglects to mention. In 1957, Li Jue had been appointed chief of the Nuclear Weapons Bureau, a confidential unit known publicly only as "Bureau Nine," and he had been in "Nuclear City" in Qinghai since August 1958 to oversee China's early experiments with the atomic bomb.[5] At best, then, Li Jue may have been repeating some hearsay about the episode. Moreover, the quote does not even appear in any available sources on Li Jue,[6] and Ji Youquan also fails to document his quote, casting its reliability further in doubt.

Ji Youquan adds the following passage in support of the theory that the Chinese willingly allowed the Dalai Lama's party to get away: "Tan Guansan's troops were prepared long in advance, and had encircled Lhasa way ahead of time. He had a reinforced company of guards headed by Zhu Xiushan, as well as a company of armored vehicles. If the Central Committee had ordered him to thwart the Tibetan officials' escape, then not one of them would have been able to leave Lhasa."[7] Ji Youquan begs the question here. Tan Guansan may have had such reinforcements, but Ji has not proven his contention that the Central Committee deliberately withheld their use. Zhu Xiushan has published a memoir, but it makes no mention of the ferry area; indeed, he does not discuss the night of March 17 at all.[8]

Ji Youquan further maintains that PLA troops stationed in a trench near the ferry witnessed the Dalai Lama's escape. He adds the following detail in support of his quote from Li Jue: "Tan Guansan's soldiers were sitting along their trench, guns at the ready, watching by the light of the moon as the Dalai clique crossed the Lhasa [Kyichu] River and hurried away toward Shannan [Lhokha]."[9] This story seems unlikely. Ji does not specify the location of the trench, but if the PLA had clearly witnessed the Dalai Lama's escape close-up on March 17, it should have been reported to Beijing right away. However, Beijing was not notified until two days later, on March 19.[10] Moreover, even the mention of bright moonlight does not tally with the recollections of Tibetan eyewitnesses, who recall an overcast sky.[11]

Since the Dalai Lama did not make up his mind to flee until March 17,[12] Li Jue and Ji Youquan's claims could not be true unless there were PLA troops guarding the Rama Gang ferry continuously for several days around that time. If there were, no Chinese PLA men have left firsthand accounts. There is an eyewitness memoir by a PLA officer named Chen Bing, but—like Zhu Xiushan—he omits March 17 entirely. Instead, he offers a vague description of the peaceful scene at the riverbank near the Norbulingka on the night of March 16, which contains no mention of a PLA presence, and then skips ahead to March 18.[13]

In a later publication, Ji Youquan backpedals from his claim that the PLA knowingly allowed the Dalai Lama to cross the river on March 17, saying instead that the PLA watched the party get away but did not realize who it was:

> Tan Guansan had just received a letter that the Dalai Lama had smuggled out to him, and he was trying to find a way to bring the Dalai Lama to the PLA Tibet Military Command quickly, to protect him from danger in general, and from possible abduction by the rebel clique. He had no idea that the Dalai Lama had left Lhasa that night.
>
> Ever since the start of the upheaval in Lhasa, the PLA Tibet Military Command had been sending intelligence-gathering teams to all the ferry points and major thoroughfares in Lhasa to report on enemy movements.
>
> Our intelligence agents stationed at the ferry secretly observed a few hundred people crossing the river and heading south in the middle of the night on March 17. However, they did not realize that these people were the rebel clique leaders and the Dalai Lama and his family.[14]

Why hadn't the PLA taken control of the Rama Gang ferry before the Dalai Lama's escape on March 17? The explanation that the PLA deliberately left the ferry area unsecured fits with the standard Party line that Mao, ever infallible, intended to let the Dalai Lama cross the river, and most Chinese chronicles fail to explore the question much beyond that. In fact, the Central Committee's March 11 instructions to the CCP Tibet Work Committee made no mention of closing the ferry crossing, and Mao did issue bold instructions on March 12 not to try to stop the Dalai Lama and his cohorts if they tried to flee. But it is less well known that Mao's position had changed by the afternoon of March 17, when he had issued new instructions to the Politburo to "make every effort to prevent the Dalai Lama's escape."[15]

Meanwhile, at virtually the same time that Mao announced his change of mind on March 17, the Dalai Lama was, unbeknownst to either Mao or Tan Guansan, deciding to leave Lhasa that very night. While it is not possible to pinpoint exactly when Tan Guansan learned of Mao's new instructions, we do know that the Chinese lacked reliable intelligence about the Dalai Lama during the critical days of March 16 and 17. The rare, semiclassified memoir of Zhang Xiangming, vice-chairman of the United Front Bureau of the CCP Tibet Work Committee, states this quite clearly: "Although we had information about the Dalai Lama from March 10 to March 15, we had no one who could get near him on March 16 and 17. Thus, we had no accurate source of reliable information with regard to his escape on March 17."[16] This explains why the CCP Tibet Work Committee was unable to confirm the Dalai Lama's escape until March 19, and even then was uncertain whether he had left on March 16 or March 17.[17]

There were also other, purely military factors at work in this complex tale. Another semiclassified memoir by a cadre in the CCP Tibet Work Committee at the time suggests a tactical reason Tan might not have wanted to close off the ferry area:

> A leading comrade announced at a meeting one day that the rebel armies were converging on Lhasa from all directions, and that there was certain to be an armed uprising in the city. We made up our minds to do battle with the rebels in Lhasa. The plan was to ensnare them with the [traditional Chinese] "bagging" tactic: first we would post our troops strategically so that they could enter—but not exit—the city. Then, once they entered and began their armed uprising, we would resolutely, thoroughly, and completely wipe them out.[18]

Since the Rama Gang ferry was a key entry point for potential foes to enter Lhasa from Lhokha, Tan Guansan probably left it open to "bag the rebels," luring them into the city before ultimately closing off the "mouth" to prevent their exit. Given this plan, and Mao's earlier instructions not to worry about the Dalai Lama's escape, it would have made sense for Tan to leave the ferry unsecured for the time being. Moreover, closing off the Dalai Lama's river escape route involved a great deal more than simply occupying the Rama Gang ferry, which was actually not a ferry in the modern sense of the word, but merely a relatively easy crossing point. There were other, somewhat less convenient places to cross, but trying to guard the entire river would have spread Tan's troops too thin.

Either course posed additional risk for Tan because he was operating under explicit instructions from Beijing to await further orders—possibly even for "at least a couple of months"—before beginning to fight. By March 11, Mao had begun to mobilize his legions of reinforcements, and Tan was supposed to wait until they arrived, which would take time.[19] Thus, he had to avoid provocative acts that could have sparked premature confrontations, such as cutting off the Rama Gang ferry right under the noses of the angry Tibetans surrounding the nearby Norbulingka.

Later Chinese assertions that the Dalai Lama's escape was actually a good thing tend to blur the issue of how he could have gotten away. In September 1959, for example, months after the Dalai Lama had gone, General Zhang Jingwu offered the following justification: "It's no problem for us that the Dalai Lama, his entourage, and tens of thousands of Tibetans have fled to India. Now we can mobilize the masses and implement the Democratic Reforms unimpeded, and India has the burden of dealing with all of those refugees. Actually, it was not a bad thing to let the Dalai Lama escape."[20] It is easy to see how after-the-fact statements of this sort could be misinterpreted as representations of official CCP policy at the time of the escape.

The claim that the Party deliberately allowed the Dalai Lama's escape was perpetuated as recently as 2008, in a major official compilation that contains several misstatements: "The PLA Tibet Military Command had perfect grasp of the movements of the Dalai clique at all times. It followed the Central Committee's directions to refrain from obstructing the escape, and promptly reported it to the Central Committee."[21] In fact, the PLA Tibet Military Command lacked intelligence on the Dalai Lama's whereabouts on March 16 and 17, it reported his escape belatedly, and the Central Committee had become newly concerned about trying to keep him in Lhasa. This official source goes on to quote a directive that Mao issued to his personnel in Lhasa *after* he had been notified, probably on March 20.

One major official Party history inadvertently contradicts the frequent assertions of Communist Party omniscience. It tells of a fourth letter Tan Guansan supposedly sent to the Dalai Lama in the Norbulingka, but after his escape; the story suggests that Tan was still in the dark, possibly as late as March 18: "The letter, which expressed Tan's hope that the Dalai Lama would keep his promises to cooperate with the Party and curb the rebellion, was delivered to the Norbulingka by former cabinet minister Kashod Choekye Nyima. But by the time he arrived at the Norbulingka with the letter, the Dalai Lama had already escaped."[22] Although this source does not specify the date when this letter was supposed to have been delivered, it was probably March 18, because the Dalai Lama was in the Norbulingka until late at night on March 17. This "fourth letter" was never published, nor was it ever mentioned in any other sources.

There is convincing evidence that the CCP Tibet Work Committee did not notify Beijing of the Dalai Lama's escape until quite late on March 19, even though he had been gone for two days by then. No less a figure than Yang Shangkun, the highly placed deputy secretary-general of the Central Committee and director of its General Office, mentions receipt of this notice in his records of the proceedings of the Secretariat of the Central Committee for the evening of March 19; moreover, his wording makes it clear that the CCP Tibet Work Committee had not yet ascertained whether the Dalai Lama had escaped on March 16 or March 17.[23] That the notification was not sent until the night of March 19 is corroborated by a semiclassified insider's memoir, which states unequivocally that the CCP Tibet Work Committee "did not report the Dalai Lama's escape to the Central Committee, or notify its local militia and PLA troop units, until the night of March 19."[24] Even a major 1995 source, written with enough hindsight to date the Dalai Lama's departure correctly to the night of March 17, readily acknowledges that there was a lapse of two days before the Central Committee received notification on March 19.[25]

This testimony casts further doubt on any claim that the CCP Tibet Work Committee had been certain of the Dalai Lama's departure in real time on March 17. If it had, why would it have waited until March 19 to notify the Party? Ji Youquan's description may be closer to the truth. PLA intelligence teams may have observed the Dalai Lama crossing the river without realizing who it was, even though Ji's estimate of an entourage of "a few hundred" people seems overblown.

The appeal to the Chinese imagination of the story that Mao deliberately opened the doors for the Dalai Lama is evident in a 1982 memoir by Xu Jiatun, former chief of the Hong Kong Bureau of Xinhua News Agency, who sees it as proof of Mao's brilliance as a tactician:

> Mao Zedong had an unusual turn of mind, and he often came up with extraordinary ideas. Here is an example that I remember. In 1959, Commander Zhang Guohua was in charge of quelling the Tibetan rebellion, and the Dalai Lama was trapped inside the Potala Palace. Mao sent a cable to Zhang and the CCP Tibet Work Committee, which I saw. . . . It contained instructions from Mao to Zhang Guohua to enable the Dalai Lama's withdrawal to India by freeing up an escape route for him all the way from the Potala to the Indian border. Mao provided detailed directions for Zhang Guohua about what to do and when to do it, and even proposed some locations for staging fake attacks. He thus induced the Dalai Lama to flee to India.
>
> This episode exemplifies Mao's knack for thinking a step ahead of most people. He realized that the Tibetans revered the Dalai Lama as a Living Buddha. What would he have done with the Dalai Lama if he had captured him alive? And assassinating him would have been even worse. This shows what a superior strategist Mao was.[26]

The errors in this passage cast doubt on its overall reliability. Zhang Guohua was not in Tibet at the time, nor was the Dalai Lama "trapped in the Potala Palace." Moreover, the Dalai Lama did not have his entire route to India planned when he left the Norbulingka. During the first portion of his journey, he and his officials still entertained the possibility of negotiating with the Chinese and remaining in Tibet.[27] They determined the next day's route spontaneously at nightly meetings on the road, depending on the circumstances, and (although it must have been discussed sooner) the final decision to enter India via Tsona was made much later in the journey, on March 26.[28] Like Li Jue's spurious reminiscences, Xu Jiatun's account cannot be cited as proof of the theory that Mao enabled the Dalai Lama's getaway.

Ji Youquan's chronicle also devotes considerable space to an assessment of the Dalai Lama's escape by intelligence chief Jiang Wenqi of the PLA Tibet Military Command, whose version of the events of the night of March 17 borders on the fictional: "Our concealed intelligence agents at the ferry reported that five or six hundred people armed with rifles came out of the Norbulingka, waded across the river, and headed south from there."[29] This description bears no resemblance to the facts of the escape, although it vaguely suggests a completely different episode that occurred during the subsequent Battle of Lhasa.[30]

The other Chinese explanation of the Dalai Lama's disappearance—that he was abducted—was evidently spread by Mao himself for propaganda purposes. In a history of the period published in 1993, Ji Youquan quotes the (undated) directive Mao sent to the CCP Tibet Work Committee after he had been notified of the Dalai Lama's escape, probably on March 20. It strongly suggests that the abduction story was manufactured:

> It is a very good thing that the Tibetan cabinet clique has openly committed treason, the Dalai Lama has fled, the rebel bandits have attacked our military installations, and the Tibetan political situation has become completely clear. But we may be able to use the Dalai Lama's prestige to our advantage. For now, we shall not announce publicly that the Dalai Lama has fled, or name him as a ringleader. We shall stick with the story that the traitors have abducted him. This may help undermine the enemy's calls to the people to rebel in the Dalai Lama's name. If the Panchen Lama joins the rebels, it is forbidden to kill him, and completely out of the question to allow him to escape to a foreign country.[31]

Evidently convinced that the notion the Dalai Lama was abducted by traitors would help to undermine the Tibetan resistance, Mao had the story put into propaganda pamphlets in Tibetan and widely distributed at the time.[32]

Oddly, when an official, semiclassified version of the excerpt from Mao's directive appeared in 1995, it had censored out Mao's opportunistic statements about using the Dalai Lama and the Panchen Lama.[33] This suggests that Ji Youquan may have committed an error in including them in his history, which had been released to the general public two years earlier; evidently, the Communist Party preferred to remove such matters from the record.

In 2008, the Communist Party finally produced a modified version of Mao's instructions for the general public:

1. If we proclaim [the Dalai Lama] a traitor, he won't be able to return unless he acknowledges his guilt and repents.
2. If we proclaim that he was abducted, there is still hope that he may disengage from the rebel cause and return soon, in which case he would be restored to his positions in the Norbulingka and in the National People's Congress.[34]

At the time of the Dalai Lama's flight in 1959, he was a deputy chairman of the Standing Committee of the National People's Congress, and was recognized internationally as the religious and temporal leader of Tibet. China had to satisfy world opinion on a thorny question: Why would a man of such stature abandon his people for exile in a foreign land? The theory that he had been abducted thus appeared early. In his first public press release after the escape, the Dalai Lama stated "categorically that he left Lhasa and Tibet and came to India of his own free will and not under duress,"[35] but Xinhua News Agency promptly issued a refutation, which insinuated that his press release had been written in his name by his abductors.[36] Nonetheless, the abduction story lost credibility internationally, as the Dalai Lama became a public figure again and spoke freely on the subject.

On the other hand, the fascinating tale that Mao—ever infallible—ushered the Dalai Lama to India has proved an effective propaganda tool within China; I heard it time and again in my youth. Despite its frequent repetition, it remains improbable. By March 17, Mao had issued instructions to prevent the Dalai Lama's escape, and in fact any professed indifference to the matter may have been a public mask for his own awareness that he probably would not have been able to stop the Dalai Lama, even if he had tried. Tibet was vast, its border long, and his total troop strength in Tibet was not sufficient to guard all possible exit routes.[37]

In addition, if Mao had actually wanted to facilitate the Dalai Lama's escape, he would have had to issue specific orders to this effect, but no evidence of this has surfaced to date. Thousands of members of the PLA and the militia in Lhasa would have needed official warnings not to open fire on the Dalai Lama and his entourage, as any slipups would have ruined Mao's plan. However, no mention of any such orders appears in any memoirs of Chinese eyewitnesses or participants. We encounter the story only in the writings of people who were not in Lhasa at the time, and not even they cite instructions from on high to facilitate the escape. In fact, no memoir of any Chinese commander on the spot states that he actually witnessed the Dalai Lama's escape party or anything resembling it.[38]

It was entirely feasible for a prominent Tibetan religious leader to slip away against Mao's will, and the Dalai Lama was not the only one who did so. The Sixteenth Gyalwa Karmapa[39] also fled, entering Bhutan a few days before the Dalai Lama reached India, but no one bothered to present theories to account for his escape.

: : :

After a long day on March 18, the travelers arrived at a small monastery known as Ra-me, their first overnight stop. The Dalai Lama went to his tiny room on the second floor and then sent for his little brother, Ngari Rinpoché.

The mood of the group was grim, but its youngest member, Ngari Rinpoché, was having fun. All the adults excused his childish antics, letting him gallop around on his horse without admonishing him to behave in a manner more befitting a brother of the Dalai Lama. Kunga Samten recalls sensing that the little boy was oblivious to the gravity of the situation. Decades later, Ngari Rinpoché remarked mirthfully, "I've heard the Dalai Lama say, 'My little brother was the only one of us who went gaily into exile!' "[40]

That night, Phala, Gadrang, Kundeling Dzasa, Phuntsok, the three cabinet ministers, and Kunga Samten met to map their course. Kundeling Dzasa said the route through Bhutan would be the shortest, but Kunga Samten objected that it would require them to go around the west side of Lake Yamdok Youtso, bringing them within striking distance of PLA strongholds in Gyantse and Shigatse. Kunga Samten also reminded them it would be difficult to find suitable places to spend the night along the Bhutan route, since it traversed a great deal of pastureland. He said it would be safer to head eastward, and find the Chushi Gangdruk resistance forces, whom he had notified by messenger that the Dalai Lama was on his way. The group finally agreed to go to Chonggye,[41] wait for more news from Lhasa, and then proceed from there.[42] This meeting was also Phala's first opportunity to announce that he had alerted the Indian Consulate in Lhasa of the Dalai Lama's possible need for political asylum in India.

Worried about the Dalai Lama's safety in Lhokha, those assembled also decided to issue some orders in the name of the Tibetan government: (1) Regiment 5 was to be transferred from Tingri to Gyantse,[43] (2) the commanders of Regiments 3 and 4 were to be transferred from Shigatse and Gyantse to Lhasa, and (3) the governor of the northern region was to destroy Damshung Airport and the highways and telephone lines in the north.[44] These orders were not carried out; it is not known whether they were even received.

That night, the rear guard of approximately one hundred soldiers led by Dokharsey and Sonam Tashi caught up with the group, providing welcome reinforcements, and a new security plan for the Dalai Lama was drawn up. There would now be three tiers of guards: an inner tier of the Dalai Lama's bodyguards, a middle tier of Tibetan Army soldiers from Regiment 2, and an outer tier of Chushi Gangdruk guerrillas, with approximately 100 in each of the first two tiers and 200 in the third. Then the discussion turned to whether to travel by day or by night; the decision was made that it would be safer to move by day.[45]

On the morning of March 19, the Dalai Lama composed a letter to the Panchen Lama, explaining that sudden developments had necessitated his temporary departure from Lhasa for Lhokha, and that he hoped the Panchen Lama would do his best to maintain Tibet's spiritual and political welfare. When he had finished writing the letter, he stamped it with his jade seal and dispatched it via messenger to Shigatse. The cabinet ministers also wrote to their colleagues Ngabo and Sampo Tsewang Rigzin, who had stayed in Lhasa, saying: "All of us hope for liberty. Please do your best to maintain the spiritual and political missions of the Ganden Phodrang and the welfare of the people."[46] It is not known whether these letters ever reached their designated recipients.

Meanwhile, on the same day in Shigatse, the Panchen Lama cabled General Tan Guansan to express his willingness to cooperate with the Shigatse Work Committee and the PLA to "crush the armed rebellion."[47]

From that point on, the party traveled in three groups. The Dalai Lama's mother and sister rode in front, guarded by Chushi Gangdruk soldiers, while the Dalai Lama kept Ngari Rinpoché by his side in the middle group so the women could travel faster. The cabinet and tutors brought up the rear. Without modern communications equipment, the groups had to rely on messengers to interact with each other. And with so many tiers in the escort, some of those on the periphery were unaware of whom they were escorting.

They spent the night of March 19 in the nearby village of Chitesho, renowned throughout Tibet for its serge cloth. The Dalai Lama slept in a monastery there called Dophu Choekor Ling.

The travelers got an early start on the morning of March 20, along a winding road of hairpin turns, so tight in some spots that they could barely squeeze by, and so steep that they often had to dismount.

As it turns out, Tibetans were streaming across the Himalayas in an unprecedented mass exodus during this period. Sources agree that their numbers were legion, although figures are imprecise. In mid-May 1959, the *New York Times* described the scene at Foothills, India, and reported an early Indian government tally:

> The first party of Tibetan refugees arrived at the Indian reception center today and told of Communist Chinese brutalities and machine-gunning. . . .
>
> The Indian Government has announced that 11,500 Tibetan refugees had crossed the border into the rugged uplands of India's Assam Province and were headed for Foothills and hut camps set up for their care. The exodus from the Himalayan kingdom began after the Communist Chinese overlords put down an uprising in Lhasa, Tibet's capital, with heavy casualties.[48]

This preliminary figure applies only to refugees who had been counted at Indian entry points by the date of the report, omitting those who went to Nepal, Bhutan, or Sikkim. The Chinese have cited an overall figure of more than twenty thousand refugees by 1961, and the Tibetan government-in-exile has put the number at eighty-five thousand by 1969. These estimates do not account clearly for the multitudes who died on the way or in the refugee camps after their arrival.[49]

Nomads from Lake Qinghai herded their livestock across the Yellow River; peasant families from Kham crossed the Drichu River; groups of monks traveled together. Many had no idea where to go; they just wanted to elude "the Chinese." In desperation, they sought advice from senior monks they encountered on the road, but the monks were refugees themselves, and could offer little more than prayer and vague comfort.[50] These aimless small bands of refugees sometimes merged into bigger groups, forming conspicuous targets for the PLA. Many were slaughtered in air raids,[51] and many more were captured. If taken alive, it was ruled that they had been coerced into leaving, and they were forcibly repatriated. Countless lives were lost and families rent asunder.

Not all refugees were poor. Upper-class Tibetans—those whom the Communists had courted as preeminent religious personages and United Front Targets were faced with the same wrenching choices: some stayed with the Chinese Communists, others clung to the Dalai Lama, while still others simply fled on their own.

During his journey, the Dalai Lama did not know that the Sixteenth Gyalwa Karmapa and his entourage were also on their way out through Bhutan. In fact, the spiritual leaders of all four major schools of Tibetan Buddhism fled Tibet for India at around this time.[52]

By March 20, word had spread that the Dalai Lama was in Lhokha. The faithful tried to pay homage to him along the way, but often could not pick him out of the group in his layman's disguise.

The Dalai Lama has expressed appreciation for his guards, who had little more than their own bodies with which to shield him.[53] Sometimes small bands of Khampa guerrillas would appear to pay their respects, big men in high leather boots, fur hats, and bulky coats, with a motley assortment of weapons. Often visiting under cover of night, they would leave their weapons at the door and then enter, performing three prostrations before bowing deeply to receive his touch on the head. Then they would bow again as they exited, retrieve their weapons, and disappear into the night.

: : :

At dusk on Friday, March 20, the Dalai Lama's party reached a manor called Gyango Gyasang at the foot of Sabo Pass. Ngari Rinpoché and the Dalai Lama stayed in the manor house, but it was so small the rest of the group had to spread out around the village.

In the predawn hours of March 21, the group began its ascent of Sabo Pass, a three-hour climb and too steep to do on horseback. The sun was just rising as they reached the crest of the pass, where they paused briefly to wonder at the magnificent view of snowcapped peaks jutting into the sky. Then they descended, reaching Chenye Monastery, about thirty miles away, just before sunset.

At about this time, news of the events in Tibet was finally breaking in the United States, with a front-page story from New Delhi in the *New York Times*. The Dalai Lama's eldest brother, Taktser Rinpoché, who was in New York, learned that violence had broken out in Lhasa and that the Dalai Lama's "whereabouts [had] not been revealed."[54] He picked up the phone and called his brother Lobsang Samten, who was also in the United States. Lobsang Samten had already heard about the trouble in Lhasa, and he flew to New York that night. The Dalai Lama's teenage sister, Jetsun Pema, who had left Lhasa at the age of nine, heard the news at her convent school in Darjeeling.

Meanwhile, the Dalai Lama's group was having its nightly planning meeting far away at Chenye Monastery. Phuntsok turned on his battery-powered radio and picked up a crackly Voice of America broadcast.

"Thousands of people have risen up against the Communists in Lhasa," an announcer said. "The Dalai Lama, the spiritual and political leader of Tibet, has disappeared."[55]

At last, the world has noticed our suffering, thought Phuntsok, somewhat encouraged. But then his heart sank: What was happening in Lhasa?

Meanwhile, Athar was on his way to Chonggye. He and Lhotse had been training Chushi Gangdruk guerrillas in Lhokha when a messenger arrived with the letter Phala had dispatched from the Norbulingka after the initial outbreak of the Lhasa Incident. The letter informed Athar and Lhotse that the Dalai Lama intended to go to Lhokha, and asked them to head toward Lhasa to help. They gathered an escort of Khampa guerrillas, packed their radio transmitter and air-dropped weapons, and got onto the road. On the way, they received word that the Dalai Lama had escaped the Norbulingka, at which point they divided into two groups. Athar raced ahead with the transmitter and a few dozen soldiers to find the Dalai Lama, leaving Lhotse to follow with more soldiers, the pack animals, and weapons.[56]

On the morning of March 22, the Dalai Lama said his prayers at Chenye Monastery, donated alms to the monks, and set out for Chonggye. Four days out of Lhasa, and they had covered only about sixty miles.

By the time news of the developments in Lhasa finally broke in the United States, eleven days had passed since the start of the unrest on March 10, and the Battle of Lhasa was virtually over.

But the Dalai Lama, deep in the wilderness, did not know this yet.

: 16 :

Battle at Daybreak

JUST BEFORE DAWN on Wednesday, March 18, 1959, Tenpa Soepa woke up on the south side of the river and spurred his horse back to the ferry to deliver the Dalai Lama's letter to Tara in the Norbulingka. The Tibetan soldiers guarding the area stopped him for his ID, but he had not brought it with him, never imagining a need to return to Lhasa. Fortunately, his servant Gyalpo's ID satisfied the soldiers, and they went to get him a boat. While he was waiting, a Khampa volunteer commander named Ngawang Senge asked him to bring home some weapons and ammunition from the government armory, which Ngawang's men would pick up that night.

Tenpa Soepa sat down on a rock and stared glumly at the river. Lhasa, bereft of its Dalai Lama, was on the brink of war, and now he had to go back! He might not get another chance to escape, he reflected, and he toyed with the idea of sending his servant Gyalpo to deliver the letter alone. Pulling the letter out of the folds of his robe, he found that it was not sealed, so he opened it.[1] It was an announcement that began: "To all high reincarnate lamas, monks, and personnel of Drepung, Sera, and Ganden monasteries, all monastic and lay government officials, and all Tibetans from every walk of life. . . ." Grasping the import of the letter immediately, Tenpa Soepa read on. "Although Tibet has historically been an independent country," the Dalai Lama continued, "the Chinese have subjugated us because we are weak." The reason for the current upheaval, he said, was widespread Tibetan distress over "the destruction of monasteries, slaughter of innocent people, expropriations of property in Kham, and pernicious slander of the Buddha in the newspaper in Garzê."[2] The Dalai Lama reiterated that he had done his utmost to calm the situation, but without success. Now, perceiving that his own life was imperiled, he had fled temporarily with his key officials, but he promised to issue further instructions once he had reached safety in Lhokha. His wording indicates that he was unaware of Mao's war plans, and that he hoped to go into hiding only temporarily, until a peaceful settlement had been negotiated with the Chinese.

The key question here is, to whom did the Dalai Lama delegate matters of state in his absence? In his letter, he specified that they were to be handled until further notice by "the Expanded Tibetan National Assembly currently holding sessions at the Shol Scriptural Printing House." This was the broad-based body that had begun its meetings at the Norbulingka before switching its venue to the Shol, a body that had—despite a vocal independence faction—resolved to seek peace with the Chinese. Evidently, his choice of this group was a conscious one, made in full awareness that there were other, more radical organizations also vying for recognition.[3]

Tenpa Soepa knew what he had to do. The letter was too important to entrust to Gyalpo. He boarded the ferry and crossed the river.

Gunfire suddenly rang out as he was walking along the river toward the Norbulingka. This had become an everyday occurrence by then, so he ignored it and pressed on. Then a bullet whizzed right by him, and he flung himself down onto the gravel in terror. When the shooting paused, he jumped up and ran to the palace, where he found Tara, gave him the letter, and conveyed Ngawang Senge's request for weapons.[4]

Phuntsok had invited Tara to join the escape, but Tara had declined, lest his absence from his visible position at the Norbulingka be noticed, creating suspicion that the Dalai Lama had fled and jeopardizing his safety.

After reading the letter, Tara authorized Tenpa Soepa to withdraw the weapons and hurried off to consult with the rest of the coordinating committee. Tenpa Soepa and a few helpers hauled a few dozen rifles and some ammunition from the palace armory to his house.

When Tara showed the Dalai Lama's letter to his colleagues, they were overjoyed to learn the Dalai Lama had gotten away safely. All agreed that it would be better to wait a couple of days before announcing the contents of the letter, to give the Dalai Lama time for a head start before the PLA learned of his escape.[5] Tara sent a messenger to ask former acting prime minister Lobsang Tashi, whom the Dalai Lama's letter had appointed to negotiate a peaceful settlement with the Chinese, to come to the palace.[6]

While the Dalai Lama's letter underscored his hope to forestall violence, it also warned Tibetans to keep up their guard: "Do your utmost to protect the Jokhang Temple, the Potala and the Norbulingka, and the great three monastic universities, while preserving the safety of all the . . . Tibetan people."[7]

In response to a request from Tara for volunteers, Juchen Tubten offered to take some men to guard the Rama Gang ferry. Equipping himself with an extra rifle from the palace guard arsenal, he went to round up some men.[8]

: : :

Meanwhile, the PLA Tibet Military Command was putting the finishing touches on its checklist for battle, which included completing a trench from its August First Farm, on the north side of the Kyichu River, to a crossing point on the river. This could be used in conjunction with Artillery Regiment 308's existing trench on the south side of the river to create crossfire and choke off the Tibetans' escape route from Lhasa to the Lhokha region.[9] Vice-Commander Deng Shaodong sent a couple of officers to inspect Artillery Regiment 308 and discovered to his great satisfaction that it was "ready for combat on a mere three minutes' notice." As one of the officers, Chen Bing, recollects:

> The artillery was properly positioned, with shells neatly stacked in place. The soldiers, full of fighting spirit, were waiting at their stations. "We're all ready," they declared. "We've got precise measurements for all our targets, and all the data we need. We're just waiting for the word from above."[10]

The PLA had a battle plan, which Chen outlines as follows:

> We were determined to unleash the full power of people's war. . . . The city was divided into eight defense zones under one umbrella command. We had superior artillery and weaponry with which to neutralize the enemy in Lhasa: thirteen infantry companies drawn from Regiment 155 (minus Battalion 3), Regiment 159 (minus Battalion 1), and

> the security guard battalion from the PLA Tibet Military Command, with flexible support from Artillery Regiment 308, an armored vehicle company, and a platoon of flamethrowers.[11]

In typical Communist jargon, Chen's reference to "the full power of people's war" is a statement that the people of Lhasa, that is, the Tibetans, were eager for liberation by the Chinese. His bias is blazoned in the title of his memoir, "Death to the Traitors."

Thinley Phuntsok spent the entire day of March 18 in the Norbulingka trying to keep up the pretense that the Dalai Lama and his entourage were still there. When someone brought prayer beads and a talisman for Ling Rinpoché's blessing, Thinley took the objects inside and had them blessed by someone else, as if Ling Rinpoché had not fled.[12]

Only a handful of people inside the Norbulingka knew of the Dalai Lama's departure, and the crowds outside had no inkling of it yet.

That night, thirty Chushi Gangdruk soldiers came to Tenpa Soepa's house to pick up the weapons and ammunition. He had planned to leave Lhasa with them but was overcome with exhaustion and decided to get some sleep instead.

Meanwhile, PLA Transport Regiment 16 received orders to seal off the Rama Gang ferry. With Company 2 in the vanguard, training battalion commander He Guodong set out with Company 1, toting two heavy machine guns and six light machine guns.[13]

Juchen Tubten led sixty men to defend the ferry. He stationed twenty of them in a village at the bottom of the hill on the south side of the river, twenty in the middle, and twenty at the top, and assigned them to rotate in shifts.[14]

: : :

On Thursday, March 19, Major General Ding Sheng transferred the "Ding Headquarters" of his Fifty-Fourth Army by train to Lanzhou, the quickest gateway into Tibet.[15]

Meanwhile, all the Tibetan civil servants reported to the Norbulingka as usual for the morning tea service, but pandemonium broke loose when they discovered that the Dalai Lama, the cabinet, and the tutors were missing. Tara announced that the Dalai Lama had gone, leaving a letter with instructions. Lobsang Tashi, who had arrived by then, was stunned by the news.[16]

The Assembly the Dalai Lama had authorized to act in his absence continued to meet at the Shol Scriptural Printing House on March 18 and 19. Information about the proceedings is scant, and the Chinese have not released any captured Tibetan documents from those two days. According to Tsewang Gyurmey Majha, an Assembly member who later escaped to India, various proposals were put forth, including a hawkish faction's motion to start guerrilla warfare and seek foreign support, which was not passed. Six men were selected to draft a resolution for submission to the Chinese, but the Assembly ran out of time before any actual decisions could be made.[17]

In a little room in Tan Guansan's office on the morning of March 19, Vice-Commander Deng Shaodong chaired an urgent meeting of high-ranking officers. Tan Guansan gave a report and issued combat assignments, while emphasizing that the PLA should avoid appearing as outright aggressors:

> Staff Officer Yu Shutang of the War Department said that war would probably be necessary to resolve the problem in Lhasa.
>
> "We should not be the ones to fire the first shot," cautioned Tan Guansan. "We must remain on the defensive until conditions are ripe. This will expose our enemy as evil and bring the Tibetan people over to our side, so that we can stamp out the rebellion completely."
>
> Next it was decided that Vice-Commander Wu Chen of Regiment 159 would lead a company of troops that night to take up positions on the hill near the ferry.[18]

After reaching the ferry, the soldiers from PLA Transport Regiment 16 were ordered to watch for three green flares, which would be the signal to "counterattack."[19]

Tenpa Soepa slept straight through the night and into the afternoon. Finding himself with nothing in particular to do when he woke up, he went to the Norbulingka. By then, the palace was buzzing with rumors about the Dalai Lama's escape, although his letter had not yet been presented publicly.

"I heard that Gyalwa Rinpoché isn't here anymore. Is that right?" someone asked him in hushed tones.

"What? Of course he's here. Where else would he be?" Tenpa Soepa replied, keeping his vow to secrecy.[20]

The news had not yet spread beyond the palace walls. Tara and the coordinating committee had decided to wait until the following day, March 20, to publicize the Dalai Lama's letter. Once the announcement had been made, all those who had flocked to the palace area would be asked to disperse.[21]

The CCP Tibet Work Committee may have gotten wind of the Dalai Lama's escape by the morning of March 19 (probably through secret informers inside the Norbulingka). What is known for certain, however, is that it had learned the news by that evening, when it relayed its report to Beijing. Extant records omit all cable correspondence between the committee and Beijing from March 17 to March 19, however, disclosing only the Panchen Lama's March 19 loyalty statement, which had been written at Mao's request.[22] Thus, the Central Committee's initial reaction to the momentous news of the Dalai Lama's escape, as well as its instructions to Tan Guansan, have remained obscure to this day.

Tibetan sources make it painfully clear that the Chinese could have avoided war in Lhasa, had they been so inclined. The picture would have changed radically if they had waited until the public announcement of the Dalai Lama's letter on the morning of March 20. The Dalai Lama's main motivation for leaving was his hope that the volunteer protectors around the Norbulingka would disperse once he was gone, leaving the Chinese no ostensible reason for attack. But Chinese materials indicate that Mao was determined to find a pretext for war[23] and carry out his plans. The PLA was ready for action by the time the Dalai Lama's escape had been confirmed. Once he was gone, there was no longer any need for restraint, and time was of the essence.

Lieutenant Colonel Seshing, who had taken charge of the Norbulingka guards in Phuntsok's absence, was not gearing up for war on March 19 and 20. He spent those days on routine tasks such as distributing regular pay to his men, and he even sent three hundred of them (about half of his regiment) off-site to grind *tsampa*.[24]

Meanwhile, the Chinese, now aware of the Dalai Lama's departure, were mobilizing PLA and militia units all around Lhasa on the evening of March 19. Xu Donghai, a militia member at the CCP Tibet Work Committee, recalls that his compound was fully prepared for battle by that time. Pillboxes—under construction since March 10—had sprung up on all sides, three lines of defense had been drawn, and stockpiles of arms were at hand. Xu states that his militia unit had a machine gun and nine submachine guns, all with plenty of ammunition, and a great many hand grenades. He writes that all members of his unit were "immediately ordered to their battle posts" when the following urgent orders arrived from militia headquarters at approximately 8:00 P.M.: "We have reliable reports that the Dalai Lama and his principal cabinet members fled Lhasa on March 17, leaving behind only the die-hard rebels. . . . All signs indicate a high possibility that they will launch an armed attack on us tonight."[25] Wang Qixiu, a Post and Telecommunications Office employee, recalls receiving similar orders that night: "We have reliable reports that the rebels are going to strike tonight. Militia members are not to undress and go to bed. They must maintain extraordinary vigilance, prepare for battle, and defend themselves resolutely."[26]

Battalion Commander Zhu Xiushan of the PLA guard unit states that he returned to his office at around 8:00 P.M. with a battle plan from above, and he and his officers fine-tuned their combat assignments. He recalls:

> All of us—officers and men—had a hunch that the war was about to start, and no one could sleep that night. As I was mulling this over, the telephone rang. It was Section Chief Zou Fengming from headquarters.
>
> "Are you ready, Commander Zhu?"
>
> As soon as I replied, he continued: "The leadership is concerned about your readiness. Number Two [Tan Guansan] just asked me about you again, and I told him not to worry."[27]

At 9:00 P.M. on March 19, Wu Chen, vice-commander of Regiment 159, and Zhu Xiaogang, vice-commander of Battalion 3, loaded a company of men and two mortars onto trucks and rumbled across the Lhasa Bridge to join Artillery Regiment 308 on the south side of the river.

Too exhausted to go home, Tara spent the night in the Dalai Lama's physician's room at the Norbulingka.

After a full day at the palace, Tenpa Soepa took his friends' advice that it would be safer to stay there overnight than to go home, and he slept in a small guardroom about ten yards from the Dalai Lama's New Palace. Jampa Tenzin, who was keeping an eye on the situation from his home near Barkor Street, had not yet heard about the Dalai Lama's flight. Tubten Khetsun, who was helping to guard the palace gate, had planned to go home to see his mother, but had to stay at his post overnight instead. To contain the news of the Dalai Lama's escape, no one was allowed to leave the Norbulingka.

Regiment 4 of the Tibetan Army and the PLA Tibet Military Command's guard regiment were neighbors, separated by only a wall. That evening, the Tibetan soldiers undressed and went to bed as usual, unaware of the excitement next door, but PLA and Chinese militia units everywhere in Lhasa stayed awake all night, weapons at hand.

Juchen Tubten and twenty of his men were sound asleep in the village at the foot of the hill near the ferry. His other two groups were at their stations, one at the top and one at the middle of the hill, with bonfires to keep them warm. It did not occur to them that the bonfires made them easy targets.

Vice-commander of PLA Regiment 159 Wu Chen and his men arrived at the artillery regiment camp on the south bank of the river and prepared to complete their mission: to seal off the ferry with cannons "to corral the rebels."[28]

The Battle of Lhasa was about to start.

Meanwhile, the Dalai Lama was in a village too small to be found on any map, and CIA radioman Athar was on his way to join him. Apart from the Indian government, which got updates from its consulate in Lhasa, and the Soviet government, which may have had satellite monitoring of Tibet or received reports from the Chinese,[29] the outside world had no idea of the pivotal developments in the secluded capital of the "land of snows."

: : :

Determining the accuracy of numerical comparisons of Chinese and Tibetans in the Battle of Lhasa has always been problematic. Tibetan sources, which interpret the uprising as spontaneous, provide no detailed statistics on the number of Tibetans involved. Many Lhasans went home a few days after the initial upheaval on March 10, leaving mostly out-of-towners from Kham and Amdo camped outside the Norbulingka. The people inside the Norbulingka, however, were predominantly local, including civil servants, attendants, Tibetan soldiers, and their families. A number of Lhasan civilians, along with some Tibetan soldiers, monks, and Khampas, were at key sites such as Chakpori Hill, the Potala, the Jokhang Temple, and Ramoche Temple. But they were so mobile it is difficult to confirm their numbers.

Chinese sources vary wildly on the subject. The most popular rendition of events is the legend that "one thousand PLA soldiers neutralized seven thousand rebel bandits." This story derives its estimate of the number of Tibetan "rebels" from a 1959 cable from the CCP Tibet Work Committee,[30] but it was not widely circulated in China until more than thirty years later. In 1995, a roughly comparable estimate first appeared in the initial overview chapter of a semiclassified compilation bearing the imprimatur of two committees of Communist Party editors in the TAR, which states: "The PLA, with only a thousand men, killed, wounded, or captured more than 5,300 armed rebels and seized large quantities of weapons and ammunition."[31]

This is probably the first Chinese source to state specifically that the PLA numbered about one thousand in Lhasa in March 1959, although somewhat incomplete lists of PLA units in Lhasa had been provided by Chen Bing in 1989 and by Ji Youquan in 1993. According to Ji's account, the PLA had "thirteen infantry companies from Regiment 155, Regiment 159 (both incomplete), and the PLA Tibet Military Command guards, one company of light armored vehicles, and Artillery Regiment 308."[32] Ji neglects to mention two other key units, however: the battalion of mechanical engineers and Transport Regiment 16, both of which participated significantly in the fighting despite their supposed noncombat status. An official 2008 compilation also lists Infantry Regiments 155 and 159, the PLA Tibet Military Command guard battalion, and Artillery Regiment 308. Although it mentions Transport Regiment 16 and the mechanical engineers' battalion, it does not give the number of troops, and it omits the armored vehicle company.[33]

A somewhat greater head count of PLA soldiers was given in 2008 by Major General Xu Yan, a PLA National Defense University professor whose research specialty is the suppression of the Tibetan resistance. However, his vague estimate of "fewer than three thousand"[34] is, like Ji's, flawed by its omission of Transport Regiment 16 and the mechanical engineers' battalion. He mentions only the "thirteen infantry companies from Regiment 155, Regiment 159, and the PLA Tibet Military Command guards, along with one armored vehicle company and three battalions from Artillery Regiment 308."

Chinese claims regarding the number of armed Tibetan "rebel bandits" are inflated and inconsistent, and tend to perpetuate the notion that there were at least seven thousand, or even many more. Ji Youquan claims that there were more than nine thousand "Khampa bandits" at Chakpori Hill alone,[35] although he does not exceed ten thousand for his estimate of the total number of "bandit forces" in Lhasa. Xu Yan practically doubles this figure, bringing it to almost twenty thousand: "When the rebellion in Lhasa began on March 10, more than seven thousand rebel bandits from Kham and other places surged into the city, and approximately ten thousand lamas and local citizens were given weapons and organized into combat units."[36] Another major source sticks with the earliest estimate: "By the night of March 19, seven thousand armed rebels had entered Lhasa from various places. About five thousand of them had entrenched themselves around the Norbulingka."[37]

Chinese sources roughly concur that there were a few thousand regular Tibetan Army troops in Lhasa at the time. The PLA probably had a fairly accurate gauge of the number of Tibetan Army regulars because Tibetan officers were given PLA rank in 1955 and Tibetan soldiers were issued PLA uniforms. The CCP Tibet Work Committee's cable to Beijing on March 11 gives the number as between 2,500 and 3,000. PLA officer Chen Bing provides a comparable figure, stating that in 1959 the Lhasa rosters of the Tibetan Army included Regiment 1, with 645 men; Regiment 2, with 1,023 men; Regiment 4, with 489 men; and Regiment 6, with 375 men. According to Chen, then, the force thus totaled 2,532, including noncombatant monk-chaplains.[38]

However, we know that the Tibetan Army presence in Lhasa had shrunk somewhat by the time of the battle. Hundreds of Tibetan soldiers deserted and joined the rebels after the special National Assembly session at the Norbulingka in November 1958,[39] and one to two hundred of them left to escort the Dalai Lama on his escape, mostly in his rear guard.

The Chinese forces were swelled by militias in addition to regular PLA troops. Overall numbers are unavailable. In fact, the only numbers to be found are those for one unit, the Lhasa Post and Telecommunications Office, provided in a 2008 memoir by Wang Qixiu, a Chinese employee:

> The CCP Tibet Work Committee had instructed all . . . offices to organize all cadres and employees into militias. All work units were divided into companies and platoons, and the work units united in twos or threes into battalions. I was the political instructor of the militia company at my workplace, the Lhasa Post and Telecommunications Office. The militia comprised all ninety-nine regular employees, regardless of gender or ethnicity. . . . We selected a core platoon of veteran soldiers and young men, which was equipped with several light machine guns, and everyone had either a rifle or a submachine gun and four hand grenades.[40]

The Tibetans pouring into Lhasa in those days were by no means all Chushi Gangdruk soldiers, as the Chinese claim. Most were refugees from Kham and Amdo, including inexperienced, poorly equipped resisters such as Juchen Tubten. While Chinese sources tend to downplay the number of Chinese forces by omitting supposedly noncombatant units and militia, they inflate the number of Tibetans by including exaggerated numbers of alleged Chushi Gangdruk forces, even counting the monks who accompanied the army.

In terms of equipment, the two armies were far from evenly matched. The PLA had "vehicle transport and Soviet-style 122 mm howitzers, 76 mm cannons, and 120 mm mortars," as well as armored vehicles and flamethrowers.[41] The Tibetans had far less. If Chen Bing's figures are correct, they had 32 cannons, 9 heavy machine guns, 122 light machine guns, 266 submachine guns, and 2,300 rifles. If there were 2,600 Tibetan soldiers, these numbers suggest that some of them even lacked rifles.[42]

Artillery was the centerpiece of the Chinese battle plan, and they had absolute superiority in this respect. The PLA had been importing artillery into Lhasa for a long time, and by March 1959, its artillery units were completely ready for action. The Chinese expected a foregone conclusion for the Battle of Lhasa, and this was proved correct.

In a conflict between a standing army and a popular uprising such as this one, the long-range capabilities of artillery endow it with a psychological impact beyond its physical destructive power. The enormous explosions ignited by an enemy too far away to be seen created terror among the Tibetans and sapped their morale.

According to Chen Bing's memoir, PLA troops were in place all over Lhasa by the night of March 19, the eve of battle:

> Battalion 1 of Regiment 155 was awaiting orders at "Hospital 49" at the August First Farm in the western suburbs, and Battalion 2, the mechanics' battalion, was ready to go where needed. Battalion 2 of Regiment 159 was at the PCART and the United Front Bureau, and Battalion 3 was at the Lhasa Muslim Elementary School. Spare soldiers from the PLA guard battalion were also available.

Perhaps even more important, Chen relates that the PLA Tibet Military Command unveiled its formal three-stage battle plan at an officers' meeting on the night of March 19:

1. Artillery Regiment 308 is to cover Battalion 2 of Regiment 159 while it attacks Chakpori Hill and isolates the Norbulingka from the city.
2. Regiment 155 (minus Battalion 3) is to execute a pincer attack from the east and west on the Norbulingka, wiping out the bulk of the armed rebels, while Regiment 159 deploys some of its forces to coordinate with this attack, and the rest to take Kundeling.
3. Regiment 155 (minus Battalion 3) and Regiment 159 (minus Battalion 1), along with the available forces from the guard battalion, are to surround and neutralize the remaining enemy in the city.[43]

On the Tibetan side, however, the top officers—Phuntsok, Sonam Tashi, Junpa, and Dokharsey—had left with the Dalai Lama, thus incapacitating the Tibetan Army's command structure. Tara, Shuguba, and Shakabpa Losel Dondrup's group of civil officials and monks in the Norbulingka knew nothing of war, yet now faced a thoroughly galvanized modern army.

At midnight on March 19, Vice-Commander Wu Chen of PLA Regiment 159 set out with a company of ground troops on a three-hour march in the dark from the artillery regiment encampment on the south side of the river to the hill by the Rama Gang ferry. He found the area quiet, with bonfires and people on the hillside, but they failed to notice his arrival. He assigned one squad to occupy the ferry, one platoon to take the foot of the hill, and another platoon to cover the hill itself. He also set up a mortar, reminding his soldiers that it should be used only with the utmost care and precision.[44]

Juchen Tubten and his twenty men were asleep at the bottom of the hill, unaware war was about to begin.

Wu gave the order to start the action at 3:10 A.M., and his men streamed toward their assigned destinations with their bayonets. Half an hour later, gunfire seared the predawn calm. The Battle of Lhasa had begun.

The "first shot" was fired on the hillside, or what Ji Youquan calls the "second hill." Twenty Khampas were standing guard. According to Ji Youquan, the Chinese soldiers assigned to occupy the hill had made their way past the midpoint when the Khampas challenged them to identify themselves. They remained silent, and the Tibetans opened fire. The message was cabled right away to Beijing: the Tibetans had fired "the first shot."

In an attempt to seize the moral high ground, the Chinese have always insisted that the Tibetans initiated the clash. Here is a typical description, taken from a major Party source: "A PLA company was in control of the Rama Gang ferry. . . . At 3:40 A.M., the armed rebels fired on us there."[45] Truth has been stood on its head: in fact, the Tibetans were in control of the ferry and the Chinese were the aggressors.

There had been prior armed skirmishes, but the Chinese had not seized upon them as "the first shot" in the Battle of Lhasa, because Beijing and the CCP Tibet Work Committee had not been fully prepared for war. By March 19, however, when Deng Shaodong ordered Wu Chen to march to the hill at Rama Gang, the Chinese were ready: a regiment of Division 134 of the Fifty-Fourth Field Army was approaching Lhasa; troops from three PLA Military Command Regions were waiting to invade Tibet; and the Chinese had even printed official announcements of the battle to be posted all around Lhasa. Under these conditions, the predawn clash at Rama Gang was the pretext the Chinese sought.

Chinese allegations did not stop with charges that Tibetans fired the first shot. That shot, the Chinese claimed, had been the start of a planned, citywide war of rebellion. This accusation, however, tends to be poorly backed up with specific evidence. Historian Ji Youquan's 1993 account is illustrative:

> At 3:40 A.M. on March 20, 1959, Vice-Commander Wu Chen of Regiment 159 exchanged fire with the rebel bandits at Rama Gang. Within two minutes of firing the first shots at the hill, the rebel bandits, who were also besieging our civilian and military installations all around town, launched simultaneous attacks throughout the city. The rebel Tibetan government clique had unleashed its war against the CCP Tibet Work Committee and the PLA in Tibet.[46]

The Chinese elaborated this story in 2008, claiming that Tan Guansan refrained from giving the orders for a "counterattack" until 10:00 that morning, after "the reactionary Tibetan government and elite reactionary clique" had initiated "all-out attacks" around Lhasa. This source, however, provides paltry evidence of Tibetan provocations. First were three alleged attacks on the Lhasa Depot of the Qinghai-Tibet Highway, just north of the Norbulingka. No time is given for the first one,[47] the second one was at "approximately 6:00 A.M.," and the third one is not described at all; the latter two cannot be verified in Tibetan sources. It also cites the clash at the Lhasa Construction Office near Ramoche Temple "at 8:00 A.M."[48] All are described as conflicts between the "armed rebels" and Chinese militia. "Armed rebels" is the blanket Chinese term for any armed Tibetans, army regulars or not.

The historian Ji Youquan and PLA guard battalion commander Zhu Xiushan present widely divergent accounts of the outbreak of the battle. Here is Ji Youquan's version:

> When the artillery company of Regiment 155 at the Heroes' Memorial Park west of the Norbulingka heard gunfire [at the ferry], they interpreted it as the start of the counterattack. Their commander ordered the troops to their posts, and they started to fire loudly at the Norbulingka, continuing until they received a questioning telephone call from the PLA

> Tibet Military Command, where the artillery fire had been heard. A few minutes later, the rebel bandits launched a simultaneous attack on the PLA installations they had long besieged.[49]

PLA guard battalion commander Zhu Xiushan has a different tale to tell about that morning:

> Shortly before daybreak on March 20, rapid gunfire broke out west of the Norbulingka. Comrade Du Zhi, commander of Company 3, burst into battalion headquarters.
>
> "Let's fight, Commander!" he blurted out.
>
> I heard earsplitting artillery fire from the west side of town. Deciding that there was no time to lose, I gave the order.
>
> "Attack, and make it snappy!"
>
> When Commander Du had gone, I had someone connect me to main headquarters. Chief Zou of the War Department took my call.
>
> "I've given the orders for Company 3 to attack," I told him.
>
> "Fine. Keep me posted," Chief Zou replied.
>
> I hung up the phone and ordered all companies to take up their positions and resolutely attack the enemy aggressors. Within a few minutes, Company 3 began shooting in the yard right next door to me! I heard brief bursts of grenade fire, followed by strafing with rifles, machine guns, and submachine guns, hissing flames from flamethrowers, and soldiers' battle cries. My commanders' ferocity and speed instantly sapped the enemy's capability to resist. Within a few minutes, my men had completely exterminated the enemy defense and declared a victory in their first engagement of the Battle of Lhasa. One obstacle was out of the way.[50]

Zhu adds in conclusion that his Company 3 "was able to neutralize an enemy more than twice its size" thanks to its "political consciousness and valor."

Despite Zhu's assertion that the Tibetans were "enemy aggressors," his story reads overall more like a description of a unilateral attack than of a defensive action. Moreover, he maintains a telling silence about why the fighting takes place "in the yard right next door," and neglects to specify which Tibetan unit was his adversary.

In 2008, an official Chinese compilation approvingly summarized this story, while unwittingly discrediting Zhu's account and providing essential missing information. It reads: "The PLA guard battalion's bold, powerful attack made short work of Tibetan Army Regiment 4 to the north."[51] This seems to be an acknowledgment that Zhu's soldiers initiated the attack, and that their adversary was Tibetan Army Regiment 4. In a significant revision of Zhu's account, however, the Tibetans are not described as having been "right next door." Instead, in wording that creates the illusion of distance, this version places them vaguely "to the north." Still, we know from other sources that Tibetan Army Regiment 4 and the PLA guard battalion were neighbors, separated only by a wall, and that the Tibetans were unprepared for battle.

In fact, the Tibetans were sound asleep. This crucial detail is omitted by Zhu Xiushan and the official retelling, but Ji Youquan supplies it, further undermining Zhu Xiushan's insinuation that the Tibetans were the "aggressors":

> As soon as Zhu Xiushan received his orders, he realized that he should start by neutralizing Regiment 4, because they shared one compound, separated only by a wall, and they often threatened him. He secretly organized his men in the middle of the night, and a few dozen of them smashed the dividing wall at dawn on March 21 and attacked through the opening while the Tibetan soldiers were still asleep. They hopped out of bed when they heard the wall crashing down, but it was too late—Zhu Xiushan's troops had already entered their courtyard. The Tibetans tried to resist, but Zhu Xiushan disposed of their whole regiment after an hour of fierce combat.[52]

Ji Youquan places this battle on March 21, the day after the fall of Chakpori Hill and the Norbulingka on March 20. It seems unlikely—although not entirely impossible—that Tibetan Regiment 4 would have been sleeping quietly next door to the PLA at that point. No matter what the date was, however, Ji makes it clear that the PLA initiated the attack. Furthermore, Ji's estimate that the sleepy Tibetans held off the PLA for an hour of "fierce combat," if it is correct, shows Zhu Xiushan's account in a somewhat boastful light.

Xu Donghai, a memoirist from the CCP Tibet Work Committee, has yet another version of the episode: "Under Zhu Xiushan's command, the PLA guard battalion quickly scaled the wall into Tibetan Army Regiment 4 barracks. . . . Not a single shot was even fired, but the wicked Tibetan soldiers, trembling with fear, surrendered their arms, got dressed, and docilely allowed themselves to be taken prisoner."[53] Xu's account dispels any notion that the Tibetans instigated this clash.

The major Communist Party history of the period claims that after the "armed rebels" fired the first shot in the wee hours of the morning at Rama Gang, they followed up immediately with all-out attacks on more than ten institutions around Lhasa, including the PCART office building, People's Hospital, the People's Court, the People's Prosecutor's Office, the Meteorological Bureau, the Tibet Trading Company, the Post and Telecommunications Office, the *Tibet Daily,* and the Tibet branch of Xinhua News Agency.[54] However, while there were some sporadic exchanges of fire around the city that morning, the Chinese claim of a massive, synchronized Tibetan attack seems suspect, and is not corroborated in any available memoirs of the employees in the Chinese units that the Tibetans supposedly attacked. Moreover, according to one major Chinese Communist history of the period, General Tan Guansan had ordered his preapproved, pretranslated announcements of the battle posted around the city by ten in the morning on March 20,[55] but the announcements claimed that the rebels had launched full-scale attacks on the night of March 19, and that the PLA Tibet Military Command had received orders from above to suppress the rebellion.[56] This is problematic because the announcements were posted before Tan Guansan's battle plan had been approved by the Chinese Central Military Commission, and they had already been printed before the alleged attacks took place. The reference to the night of March 19 is also puzzling.

After the predawn clash at Rama Gang on March 20, the PLA artillery camp on the west side of Lhasa started firing shells at the Norbulingka. One of them flew over the interior yellow wall, grazed the roof of the Dalai Lama's New Palace, and exploded in the courtyard, shattering the windows and littering the ground with shards of glass. Tenpa Soepa leaped out of bed, grabbed his gun, and charged out of his room.[57]

In the absence of specific orders, Tubten Khetsun and the palace guards at the south gate waited helplessly after the shelling began. Then they heard Khampa battle cries outside the gate, and assumed the PLA must be attacking the palace. Tubten went outside for a look once the shouting had subsided, but there was no sign of an encounter: the

Khampas had apparently been yelling to boost their own morale. Before long, he heard the Tibetan guards in the Norbulingka firing their cannons back at the PLA artillery camp to the west in a futile attempt at self-defense.[58]

Asleep in the Dalai Lama's physician's room, Tara "heard what seemed to be artillery fire." He too sprang out of bed and ran to the palace meeting hall as the shelling mounted in intensity. There he saw people frantically trying to telephone the Shol Scriptural Printing House and the Potala, but the phone lines had been cut. Reminding people to guard their posts, Tara stepped outside to survey the situation.[59]

Awakened by the gunfire near Rama Gang ferry, Juchen Tubten and his men leaped up and charged toward the hilltop with their guns. Some were killed and wounded in the hail of gunfire, while others ran away. Juchen Tubten and two others took a circuitous route, dodging Chinese fire, reaching the small fortification at the top of the hill as the sky was turning light. From there, they looked down at the PLA arrayed beneath them, and saw machine guns and artillery trained on the Norbulingka, phone lines along the riverbank, and trenches at the foot of the mountains. It was suddenly clear to Juchen Tubten how well prepared the Chinese forces were.[60]

15. Chushi Gangdruk guerrillas, with the organization's flag in the background. Note the traditional garment, known as a *chupa*.

16. The White Palace, overlooking Deyangshar courtyard at the Potala. The Dalai Lama watched the *Cham* dance performance with the high-ranking Chinese officials from his chambers on the top floor; the highest Tibetan officials watched from the next level down; and the low-ranking Tibetan officials watched from the level beneath that. The common people stood under the porticos lining the courtyard.

17. The Dalai Lama in scriptural debate during his final examinations for the *Geshe Lharampa* degree at the Jokhang Temple in February 1959.

18. Athar Norbu, early Tibetan CIA (Central Intelligence Agency) agent, in 1956 or 1957.

19. The Gyadotsang brothers. *Right to left:* Wangdu, Burgang, and Kelsang.

20. Demonstrators in front of the Norbulingka on March 10, 1959.

21. Chakpori Hill topped with the Chakpori Tibetan Medical Institute, viewed from the Potala, circa 1950.

22. Chakpori Hill, former site of the Chakpori Tibetan Medical Institute, topped today with a television tower. The billboard caption reads: "General Secretary Xi Jinping is connected heart to heart with all the peoples of Tibet."

23. The Dalai Lama and his youngest brother, Ngari Rinpoché, on the Himalayan crossing.

24. Establishment of the provisional government of Tibet at Lhuntse Dzong on March 26, 1959.

25. The Dalai Lama's entry into India on March 31, 1959.

26. Early Tibetan refugees in India.

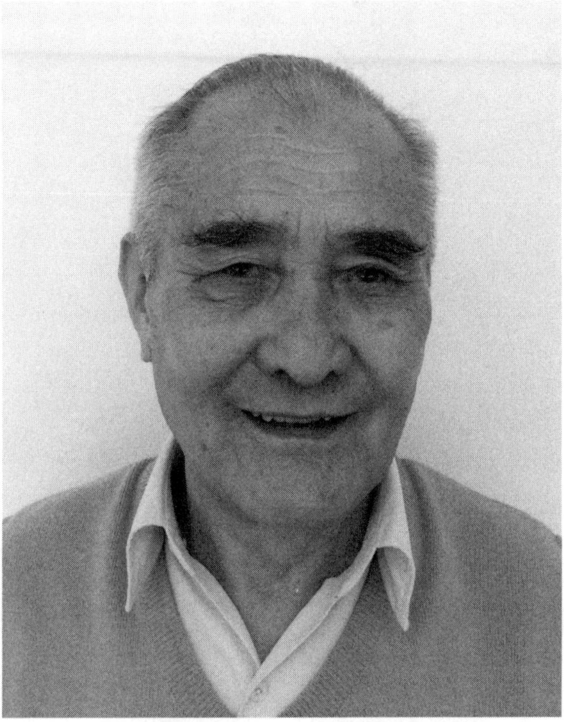

27. Tenpa Soepa in recent years.

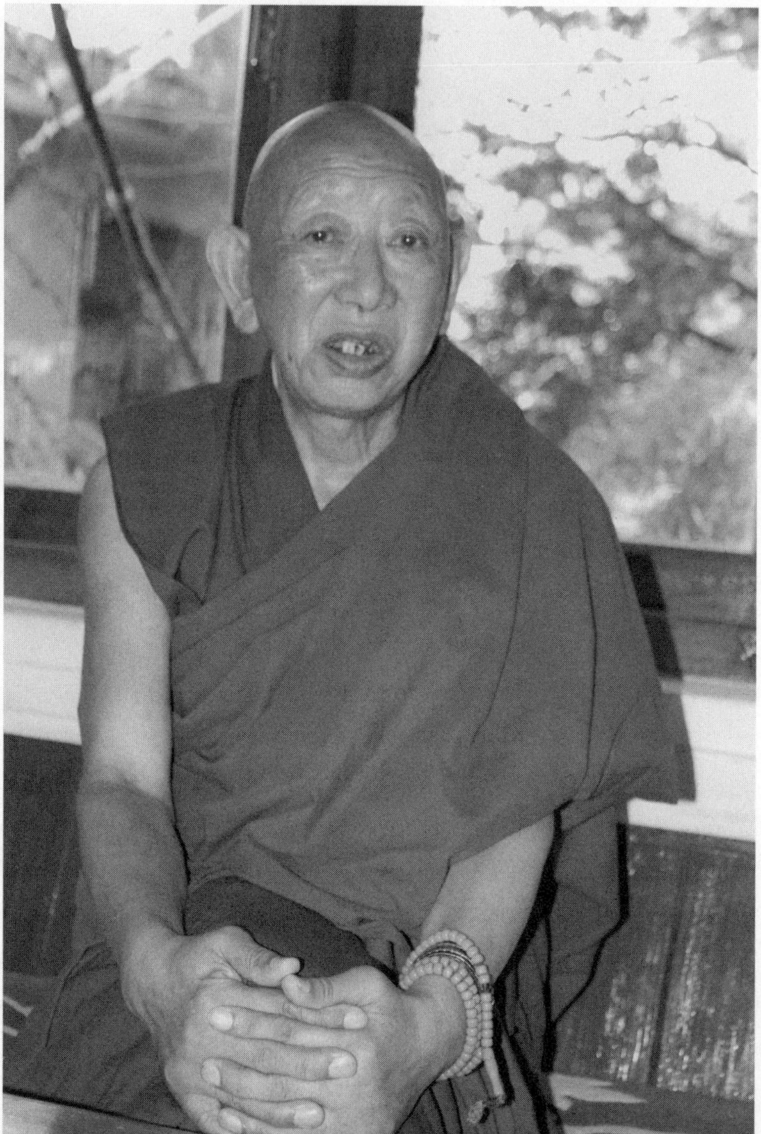

28. Jampa Tenzin in 2009.

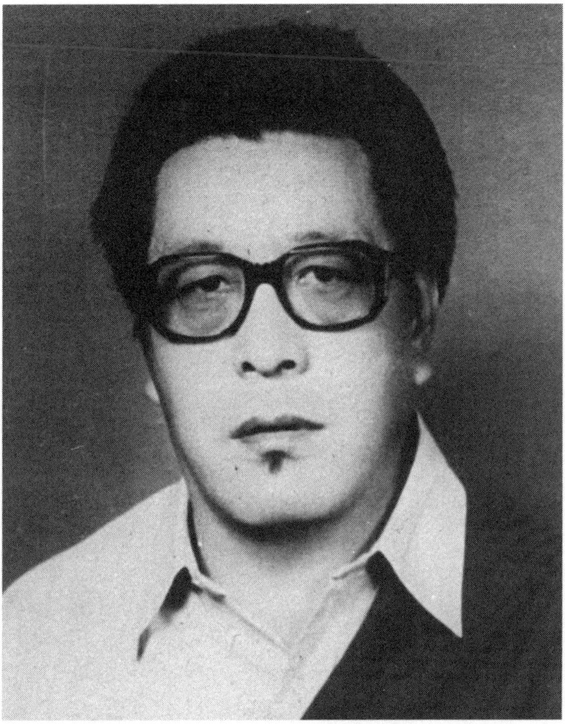

29. Juchen Tubten in the 1960s.

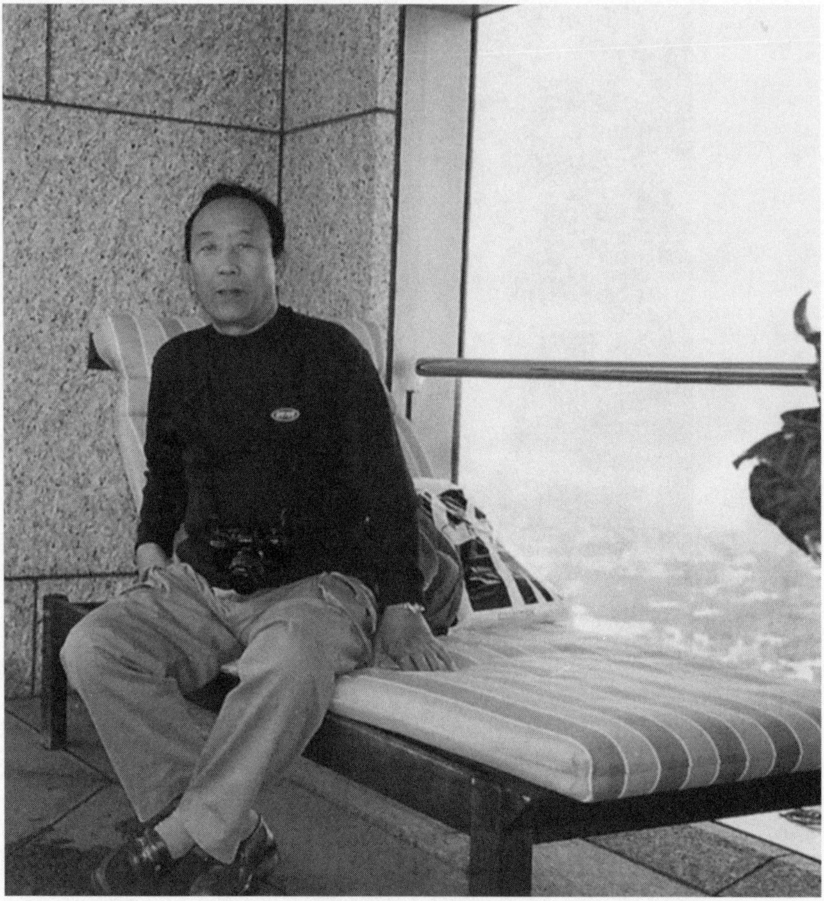

30. Thinley Phuntsok in the 1980s.

: 17 :

The Death of the Medicine Buddha

AT 5:00 A.M. ON MARCH 20, 1959, the conference room at the PLA Tibet Military Command in Lhasa was packed with officers in their red-starred caps.[1] These men—Political Commissar Tan Guansan, Vice-Commander Deng Shaodong, Vice-Political Commissar Zhan Huayu, and their chief subordinates—held the fate of Tibet in their hands.

During the night, the Chinese Central Military Commission in Beijing had received the cabled news of the Dalai Lama's decampment and the outbreak of war in Lhasa and forwarded it to Mao, still on his inspection tour in Hubei, for his instructions. An unexplained delay of a few hours in this roundabout cable communication with Mao meant that Tan Guansan conducted his meeting in the absence of Mao's specific orders.

Tan knew from cable exchanges on March 11 and 12 that Mao had already mobilized his troops; thus, the question for Tan that morning was not whether to go to war, but when. He believed the moment had come, and it was time to decide on the strategy. A recent official history lauds his "bold" initiative at this point:

> Displaying bold statesmanship and the courage to stand by his convictions before the Party and the people, Tan Guansan . . . announced his decision on the spot: it was too late to wait for PLA reinforcements, he said, and the counterattack should begin at 10:00 A.M. that day. First they would take Chakpori Hill, Lhasa's commanding peak, [thus] dividing the enemy. Then they would make a concerted attack on the Norbulingka and wipe out the rebel headquarters there. Finally, they would proceed to destroy the rebel positions all around the city. They would spare the Potala, a heritage site, by besieging the rebels there instead of striking them directly. This counterattack plan was immediately cabled to the Chinese Central Military Commission and Chairman Mao.[2]

This analysis strongly suggests that Tan knowingly flouted orders from Beijing to wait for the PLA reinforcements before striking, especially as Mao had specified in his March 12 cable that the Chinese should "hold out for a major showdown." More detail about Tan's decision is provided in a valuable primary source, a semiclassified 2006 memoir by Zhang Xiangming, vice-chairman of the United Front Bureau of the CCP Tibet Work Committee in March 1959. He recalls:

> After the Dalai Lama had left, the PLA Tibet Military Command turned its attention to the question of when to launch the counterattack to pacify the rebellion. The Central Military Commission had issued orders to draw all the rebels into Lhasa, and to wait until the reinforcements from China arrived before wiping out all of the rebels at once within the city. There were already a great many rebels in Lhasa—perhaps more than ten thousand—but after the Dalai Lama fled on March 17, they started trickling out toward Shannan [Lhokha]. A directive from the PLA Tibet Military Command expressed concern that the rebels might all escape before the reinforcements arrived from Lanzhou. But Beijing had ordered us to wait, so everyone was anxious. We spent all night on March 19 trying to figure out what to do. The consensus of those present—including Political Commissar Tan, Vice-Commander Deng, and a number of cadres and officers—was that all the rebels would escape if we delayed any longer. We agreed that there was not enough time to obtain authorization from Beijing, and that we would launch our counterattack in the predawn hours of March 20. Political Commissar Tan made the final decision to adopt this course of action, saying that if necessary he would take the blame for disobeying orders from the Central Military Commission. That is how the matter was decided.[3]

This passage suggests a reason for Tan Guansan's impatience for military action early that morning: he knew that the Tibetans who had gathered in Lhasa to protect the Dalai Lama would leave the area once the Tibetans announced his escape to the crowds outside the Norbulingka. Time was not on his side.[4]

The exaggerations of Tibetan strength in Zhang Xiangming's account notwithstanding, Tan and his colleagues had lived in Lhasa long enough to know that the Tibetan forces were no match for them, as Ji Youquan explains:

> After some analysis, the consensus was that we had absolute military superiority. The rebel troops were splintered into bands from Yunnan, Sichuan, Qinghai, Kham, and various regions of Tibet, with only a loose coalition to bind them together. We could prevail easily by taking advantage of this flaw and destroying the individual bands one at a time. This knowledge is what convinced Tan Guansan to decide to counterattack the Tibetan government rebel clique . . . with the forces he already had at hand.
>
> The idea was to surround the rebels: the training battalion on the north; Transport Regiment 16 and Infantry Regiment 155 on the west; Regiment 159 and part of the guard battalion on the southeast. Regiments 155 and 159 would swoop in together to mop up each pocket of rebels one by one.[5]

Tan decided to execute the three-stage master plan drafted the night before: to take Chakpori Hill first, then the Norbulingka, and to conclude by mopping up in the remainder of the city.[6] This was to include the Jokhang Temple, Ramoche Temple, and the Potala, making a total of five main battle sites. Meanwhile, the armored vehicle company would post the preprinted announcements justifying the Chinese military intervention. Once the plan was settled, it was cabled immediately to the Central Military Commission for approval. However, Tan Guansan chose not to wait for a reply: he knew war had already broken out, regardless of whether the Central Military Commission authorized it.

: : :

Extant memoirs fill in the picture of escalating Chinese-Tibetan strife on the night of March 19, which may have begun even before the "first shot" had been fired in the predawn hours of March 20. Huang Shaoyong, an officer in PLA Transport Regiment 16, attests that the members of his regiment who had been sent to the ferry area exchanged fire with the Tibetans earlier that night. His account begins:

> On the morning of March 19, headquarters notified us that three green signal flares would be our orders to counterattack. But the enemy was sending up signal flares all night, so it was hard to tell whether the flares we saw were theirs or ours. We ordered our troops to implement the

> original battle plan, mobilizing Company 1 of the training battalion to prepare to attack the rebel bandits.

This passage is problematic: the battle had not yet begun on the morning of March 19, yet headquarters was formulating orders to "counterattack." In other words, the PLA must somehow have been certain that the Tibetans would attack first. Not surprisingly, Huang's story does claim that this happened:

> In an attempt to break out of our encirclement and cross the river, at midnight [on March 19] a large group of rebel bandits assaulted our soldiers who were guarding the ferry. Led by the battalion commander, Company 1 of our training battalion strafed them with light and heavy machine-gun fire until they skulked away in defeat, leaving more than a hundred corpses behind. By the approach of dawn on March 20, the city was reverberating with gunfire, and the Battle of Lhasa had formally begun.
>
> Meanwhile, the ravine west of the city had been swarming all night with more than a thousand noisy rebel bandits and their whinnying horses. They tried repeatedly to bring reinforcements in through the pass there, but our troops were standing guard, and everyone at the July First Farm and other units in the area was armed and ready, so the rebels had to abandon their rash plans.[7]

Huang seems to be describing a serious battle that supposedly occurred at midnight, before the early morning encounter between Wu Chen's troops and the Tibetans at the riverside. He also offers a snapshot of a hostile standoff west of the city. Although his tale of conflict at the ferry is not corroborated elsewhere,[8] the tension and chaos of the night of March 19 are palpable in his account.

We also have a memoir by Lhalu, who was at home in Lhasa:

> On the tenth, by the Tibetan calendar [March 19], the sound of gunfire persisted into the latter half of the night.
>
> On the morning of the eleventh, by the Tibetan calendar [March 20], I still heard guns and artillery fire from the direction of the Norbulingka. The roads were barricaded and impassable. In the distance, I could see flashes of gun and artillery fire atop Chakpori Hill.[9]

Here Lhalu may be referring to an unsuccessful PLA assault on Chakpori Hill early on the morning of March 20, which Juchen Tubten has also mentioned.[10] Other noteworthy exchanges of fire had also preceded Tan Guansan's fateful decision. There had been hostilities at the Rama Gang ferry, and Zhu Xiushan's "victory" before dawn, which had "neutralized" the soldiers of Tibetan Regiment 4 in their sleep.[11] There had also been other sporadic clashes.

Against this backdrop, Tan Guansan moved quickly to implement his preplanned "counterattack," prompted by fear that this unique opportunity to crush the rebels assembled in Lhasa would slip away.

: : :

Chakpori, which means "Iron Hill" in Tibetan, stands southwest of the Potala Palace and is one of Lhasa's main attractions despite its relatively modest height. Looking down on it from the nearby Potala, its shape suggests a swimming dragon; from the faraway Dekyi Lingka it looks like a crouching tiger; and from across the river, it is an imposing, craggy dome.

This hill, holy to the Tibetans, was crowned with a temple to the Medicine Buddha, Bhaisajyaguru, and the renowned Chakpori Tibetan Medical Institute, founded in 1696 by the Tibetan statesman, scholar, and physician Desi Sangye Gyatso. The Institute boasted an invaluable collection of artworks and medical texts, and a long, distinguished tradition of the training and preparation of monastic medical students, including the personal physicians of the successive *dalai lamas*.[12]

At 10:00 A.M. Beijing time on March 20, with no reply from Beijing, General Tan Guansan issued orders to launch the first stage of the formal plan for the Battle of Lhasa, the shelling of Chakpori Hill.

Five minutes later, red, green, and white signal flares streaked across the pristine highland sky. The soldiers of Artillery Regiment 308, camped on the south side of the river, had 76 mm cannons and 122 mm howitzers at the ready. They watched as their trial volley of three shells blew up a round stone building on Chakpori Hill, and then proceeded with concerted shelling using a group of forty-two cannons. The practice drills, careful measurements, and calculations that had begun before

March 10 now paid off: the bombardment went like clockwork. Shells screeched across the river one after the other, destroying their target, the Chakpori Tibetan Medical Institute, with supreme accuracy.[13]

Bursts of flame erupted on the hilltop in the dazzling morning sun. The signboard of the medical institute collapsed, its pillars snapped, and its roof caved in, and it finally crumbled to the ground. Statues of mighty, benevolent deities, including Vajrapani, the thousand-armed Avalokitesvara, and Padmasambhava, shattered as smoke billowed skyward, its black tendrils drifting along the river and past the Potala, finally blending with the clouds on the horizon.[14]

Wang Guozhen, commander of the regiment's Company 3, watched in admiration. His memoir, with a title that translates roughly as "Thunderbolt from the Heavens Punishes the Fierce Outlaws," describes his impressions:

> From our lookout post, I saw every volley land precisely on target. Chakpori Hill was ablaze, and debris swirled in the air. Our artillery fire increased in precision and intensity, shells flying faster and faster! I felt the earth shaking, and the sky itself seemed to be on fire. With nowhere to hide, the rebel bandits scattered in confusion. I relentlessly ordered our men to keep shelling the bandits as they fled.
>
> "That'll teach you, you rebels!" our men whooped as they fired.
>
> What an outlet for our hatred![15]

Forty-nine years later, Professor Xu Yan of the PLA National Defense University penned the following description of the barrage: "In the hour that followed, more than a thousand rounds of artillery fire whizzed through the air and landed on the hill, gutting all of their pillboxes and trenches before they had a chance to shoot back. After 11:00 A.M., a company of PLA Regiment 159 charged up the hill, reaching the summit in an hour without encountering resistance, and discovered that the rebels who had not been obliterated had all fled."[16] Xu does not give a Tibetan body count, but historian Ji Youquan claims the round stone building that crumbled under the first trial volley was the "command headquarters for nine thousand Khampa rebel bandits on the hill."[17] As Chakpori Hill is relatively small, this number seems highly unlikely. It is difficult to determine whether Ji was simply in error, whether the PLA Tibet Military

Command exaggerated the lineup before the battle, or whether the number was meant to encompass all the rebels in Lhasa, in which case it would still seem inflated. Nonetheless, it is the only figure ever to appear in Chinese sources.

There are memoirs by Tibetan survivors of every battle except Chakpori Hill, for which we have only a passing mention in the blog "Shadow Tibet," by Tibetan exile writer Jamyang Norbu. He cites an oral interview with "the only survivor who escaped from the hill," who states that it was defended by seventy-seven soldiers from the Drapchi Regiment.[18]

Far from being "bandits preparing for rebellion" as Chinese sources assert, the Tibetan soldiers on Chakpori Hill were simply fulfilling their regular duties to guard key points around the city, in the spirit of Mao's 1952 instructions to "let them [the Tibetan government] do all the dirty work."[19] Maintaining public order, with its potential for causing friction with the populace, fit into Mao's notion of "dirty work," and the CCP Tibet Work Committee had charged the Tibetan government with the unwanted task.

From their perch on the other side of the river, Juchen Tubten and his men witnessed the destruction on Chakpori Hill: "The bombardment continued nonstop for two hours. A curtain of smoke surged up from the mountain, blocking our view of the Potala. As the air cleared, we saw that all the buildings atop Chakpori Hill had been leveled, but the Potala was still intact."[20] He watched in dismay as a gigantic smoke plume blew across the river on the wind.

After the shelling of the hill, Vice-Battalion Commander Zhang Fuchen and Political Instructor Cao Zhikai[21] began their charge up its south and southwest slopes. Vice-Commander Zhang started by ordering a volley of light and heavy machine-gun fire as cover for his vanguard, which then cautiously approached its "targets," namely, the shrubs on the hillside, torching all "obstacles" with flamethrowers. Heavily armed soldiers charged to the summit without pausing or meeting any resistance on the way. Everything went so smoothly that it was anticlimactic. Although he was glad to have conquered the hill, Tan Guansan was disappointed that his troops had taken no prisoners.[22]

Historian Ji Youquan states that all the buildings on Chakpori Hill were leveled in the Chinese bombardment, but neglects to mention the

Tibetan Medical Institute by name. In fact, no memoir published by any Chinese veteran of the Battle of Lhasa—PLA or militia—has ever specifically mentioned the destruction of the Medical Institute, with its irreplaceable art collection and library of scholarly medical texts. Furthermore, no one will ever know how many medical students, faculty members, and staff may have been caught in the indiscriminate bombing that day, as there were apparently no survivors from the Institute. Commander Wang Guozhen, who ascended the hill after the shelling, describes only "smashed enemy fortifications and a dozen or so dead donkeys lying splayed in their pens,"[23] as if these were the only casualties.

For two and a half centuries from the institute's founding, its ritual music had wafted out over the city from the hilltop. According to the folk song:

> The song of the golden *dungchen*[24]
> Rings out from the Potala.
> The song of the brass *dungchen*
> Resounds from Chakpori.

On March 20, 1959, the holy strains of the *dungchen* were silenced.

: : :

The destruction on Chakpori Hill brought all of Lhasa within striking range, and once PLA artillery was installed on the hill, sites such as the Norbulingka and the Jokhang Temple became easy targets. Artillery Regiment 308 moved its lookout post to the west slope of the hill, the highest point east of the Norbulingka.

The PLA artillery gunners turned their attention to the Norbulingka before the smoke had cleared over Chakpori Hill. All the heavy artillery of Regiment 308, plus the recoilless rifles and 60 mm and 82 mm mortars of Regiment 155 were trained on the Norbulingka from the west, south, and east. By then, armored vehicles were blocking the main streets of Lhasa and PLA trucks were circulating with huge loads of artillery shells in preparation for the next offensive. [25]

Chakpori Hill and the Norbulingka were the two main encounters in the Battle of Lhasa. Both took place on March 20 and followed a similar pattern: heavy shelling of the target for some hours, followed by infantry assault. Determining the exact duration of either encounter is problematic, however, because existing sources provide conflicting sets of information, especially regarding the start times. While the general outlines of the Chakpori Hill battle (roughly, from 10:00 A.M. until noon) are relatively clear despite the discrepancies among the sources,[26] it is particularly difficult to pinpoint the span of the shelling of the Norbulingka. Nonetheless, it is worthwhile to try to do so.

All sources basically concur that the Norbulingka shelling ended with the Chinese infantry charge, at approximately 7:30 P.M. Moreover, several sources agree that the shelling began soon after the PLA had taken Chakpori Hill. Wang Guozhen, a commanding officer at Chakpori, attests that his regiment turned its entire firepower on the Norbulingka almost immediately after the fall of the hill. He also relates that the Tibetan resistance at the palace was sapped after two hours of shelling, although the barrage continued beyond that point.[27] Historian Ji Youquan gives the duration of the shelling as five and a half hours, beginning at 2:00 P.M.[28] Tibetan eyewitnesses recollect intermittent bombardment of the Norbulingka beginning early in the morning on March 20, but they agree that the heavy shelling started between 1:00 and 3:00 P.M., reaching a peak in the late afternoon.[29]

Given these accounts, it seems likely that the shelling of the Norbulingka lasted several hours, starting shortly after noon and ending before the infantry assault. As a modern scholar has stated that more than a thousand rounds of artillery fire were lobbed at Chakpori Hill within a single hour,[30] we can speculate that the Norbulingka was subjected to an even more ferocious bombardment.

Perhaps this seemed overly brutal to the compilers of the official Chinese Communist Party account in 2008, who simply omit the mention of any starting time for the shelling.[31] The story was distorted even further in March 2009, when the Xinhua News Web posted its "Internet Photo Gallery in Commemoration of the Fiftieth Anniversary of the Democratic Reforms of Tibet." The website contains a photo with the following caption, in both English and Chinese: "Around 2:00 P.M. on March 20, 1959, PLA forces launched an attack on the rebellion command in Norbulingka, and occupied it at 8:30 P.M."[32] This abbreviated explanation does not mention the shelling, and misleads the reader into thinking that the PLA conducted a six-and-a-half-hour infantry assault beginning at 2:00 P.M.

The silence of official sources regarding the bombardment of the Norbulingka speaks volumes. Moreover, as will be shown, the official historiography omits the backstage communication between Beijing and Tan Guansan that motivated his unbridled attack.

: 18 :

River of Blood

AS SOON AS THE FIGHTING BROKE OUT on March 20, 1959, in Lhasa, the Chinese Central Military Commission tightened the deadlines for its Tibet-bound infantry reinforcements:

- Division 134 will proceed as soon as possible after assembling in Golmud and arrive in Lhasa by March 30.
- Division 11 will proceed as soon as possible after assembling in Dunhuang and arrive in Lhasa before April 2.
- Regiment 162 will set out from Garzê on March 31 and reach Chamdo on April 2.
- Division 130 will leave Ya'an, assemble in Garzê, and reach Chamdo before April 10.
- Regiment 126, led by the command post of Division 42 from the PLA Kunming Military Command, will reach Tsakhalho, south of Chamdo, before April 15.[1]

The PLA reinforcements were closing in, but Lhasa was already at war.

The next target after Chakpori Hill was the Norbulingka, which was surrounded on all sides: the PLA Tibet Military Command on the east; Company 7 from Regiment 159's Battalion 3, and Artillery Regiment 308, both on the south bank of the river; Regiment 155's howitzer company on the west, near Heroes' Memorial Park and the August First Farm; and forces at the Lhasa Depot of the Qinghai-Tibet Highway on the north.[2]

When the first intermittent shells started to hit the Norbulingka in the predawn on March 20, Tenpa Soepa heard an explosion near his little room behind the Dalai Lama's New Palace.[3] Grabbing his rifle, he ran to the fortifications at the north gate and tried to shoot at the Chinese highway depot across the way, but no bullets came out. Someone told him that the rifle was still clogged with its rust-protective factory coating, and took it away to clean it. Tenpa Soepa switched to his pistol instead, but the muzzle jammed up with loose dirt when he aimed it through the holes in the walls of the earthen fortifications.

After a lull, sporadic shelling resumed at approximately 6:00 A.M., although it did not build to full intensity until much later. The palace guards returned fire toward the east and the west, but then a huge salvo arrived from the west, knocking out the Tibetan gunners on that side. The guards at the main gate fled, leaving it unprotected.

With no battle plan or command structure, the Norbulingka was reduced immediately to chaos: some people ran helter-skelter around the palace; others tried to make a dash to the river. The casualties mounted quickly. Phuntsok and the best soldiers had gone with the Dalai Lama, leaving Lieutenant Colonel Seshing in charge of defending the Norbulingka. At a loss, he phoned Tara to ask what to do. "You'll have to figure that out yourself," Tara replied. Seshing relates what happened next: "We . . . decided to try to defend ourselves. I hauled out a cannon and a heavy machine gun and took some gunners out the back door on the south side of palace guard headquarters. We had just set up the cannon . . . and were preparing to fire it when a powerful shell from the other side of the river blew up right near us. As soon as the dust settled, I opened my eyes and found that my gunners had fled back inside headquarters."[4]

Probably sometime that morning, Ngabo's gate guard, Rigyon Tashi Wanggyal, arrived with a letter from Ngabo to the cabinet, and asked Secretary Gegyepa where to deliver it. Gegyepa told him to take it to Tara, who found it was written in an undecipherable numerical code and discarded it.[5] Unfortunately, Ngabo has never mentioned this letter in his writings, and its contents remain a mystery. One can only wonder what he might have said to the cabinet at that point.

Secretary Gegyepa recalls a document he composed as the shelling escalated that day:

> Tsi-pon Shuguba and Lobsang Tsewang, a fourth-rank official, called me to headquarters and asked me to draft a notice with the following text: "Stand up, Tibetans, in defense against the Red Chinese Communist attackers. For the preservation of our faith and polity, all Lhasans . . . between the ages of sixteen and sixty are hereby called upon to come forth posthaste to reinforce our defenses. Bring your own weapons

> and rations." I wrote it up, made fifteen copies by hand, and stamped them with the official seal, but a mounting hail of mortar shells and bullets prevented me from ever disseminating the notices.[6]

Although Gegyepa never managed to distribute this document, the Chinese published a similar one they discovered at the Norbulingka after the battle:

> The armed struggle of the Khampas and Tibetans, monks and lay, against the Communists and for the independence of Tibet is underway. All citizens of our holy realm must join the army to defend the Dharma. All between the ages of eighteen and sixty must enlist and report immediately to Lhasa for duty. Bring your own weapons, ammunition, rations, and other supplies. Shirking your duty is impermissible. Remember: those who place their own lives above the cause of preserving the faith will be subject to court-martial.[7]

When the Chinese first released this document in a classified publication in the spring of 1959, it was undated and attributed to the Tibetan National Assembly. However, when they later reprinted it in a semiclassified edition, they dated it to March 13 and attributed it to the "People's Assembly of Independent Tibet,"—their generic misnomer for the Tibetan National Assembly—as proof that "the Tibetan government plotted the armed uprising." The Chinese editors give no explanation for the decision to date the document to March 13, which seems far too early. The "armed struggle" had not yet begun, and the Tibetan Assembly at the Shol Scriptural Printing House had resolved just the day before "to ask the cabinet to negotiate a peaceful settlement with the CCP Tibet Work Committee and the PLA Tibet Military Command."[8] This latter-day Chinese attribution seems improbable, therefore, although the document could be some version of the notice that Gegyepa wrote and "stamped with the official seal," but never distributed, during the battle on March 20.

Frightened, young Tubten Khetsun went to his uncle's room during the shelling of the Norbulingka that afternoon. From there he was called to a meeting of the twenty-odd civil servants who remained in the Norbulingka, where Tara reported that he had been caught in the PLA bombardment at Chakpori Hill, but had fortunately escaped unharmed. "Staying inside the Norbulingka, you have no way to fight back and will just be slaughtered," he announced. "It would be better to find a way to get outside, and you should combine your strength to do that by any means." However, Tubten recalls, there was "no discussion about how to unite," and people were left to their own devices.[9]

Tenpa Soepa and the others abandoned the fortifications at the north gate and scattered in all directions.

The shelling intensified as the afternoon progressed, reaching a crescendo in the late afternoon.[10] Tibetan survivors describe the shells with the identical phrase: "pelting down like rain."[11]

The Norbulingka found itself virtually defenseless.

: : :

The official Party history glosses over the ruthless bombardment of the Norbulingka, a sacred Tibetan heritage site, describing it vaguely as "an intense barrage."[12] Ji Youquan goes into somewhat more detail:

> The attack on the Norbulingka began at 2:00 P.M. The entire artillery force of Regiment 308 [south of the river] joined with the 60 mm cannons, 82 mm mortars, and recoilless guns of Regiment 155 at Heroes' Memorial Park [west of the palace]. This was an all-out artillery strike. They used a rolling barrage strategy, steadily inching the line of fire forward in fifteen-yard increments from east to west and driving the fleeing rebel bandits ahead of the advancing line of exploding shells.[13]

Although Ji Youquan lists the relatively small artillery weapons of Regiment 155, he omits the details about Artillery Regiment 308's heavier weaponry. A few decades later, Xu Yan disclosed the following:

> The key battle in the suppression of the Tibetan rebellion was the Battle of Lhasa in March 1959, in which PLA artillery provided the brunt of the firepower. Because of the challenging topography of the region, the PLA Tibet Military Command had only one artillery regiment: No. 308, with its vehicle transport. Equipped with Soviet-style 122 mm howitzers, 76 mm cannons, and 120 mm mortars, it functioned as the "fist" of the PLA campaign. . . .
>
> When the PLA attacked the rebel bandit stronghold in the Dalai Lama's Norbulingka Palace on the afternoon of March 20, the artillery

> had Central Committee orders to spare the palace itself. Therefore, 122 mm howitzers were used in a rolling barrage strategy to strafe the rebel bandits who were outside the buildings. An intense line of explosions steadily advanced in fifteen-yard increments, flushing thousands of rebel bandits out of the Norbulingka. The shells, as if equipped with eyes of their own, chased the bandits and blew them and their horses to pieces, crushing the backbone of the rebellion.[14]

A regiment subsumed two or three battalions, each of which had twenty-four to thirty-six howitzers. Evidently, Artillery Regiment 308 (on the south side of the river), which must have had dozens of mighty 122 mm howitzers, provided the main firepower in the attack on the Norbulingka, while Regiment 155 on the west was only an auxiliary force.

The most telling Chinese description of the bombardment of the Norbulingka is provided by Wang Guozhen, commander of Artillery Regiment 308's Company 3:

> After we took Chakpori Hill . . . we turned our regiment's whole firepower onto [the Norbulingka], almost immediately.
>
> Well in advance of the battle, we had divided the palace area into several firing zones, which we swept methodically from the south with rapid, perfectly choreographed salvos.
>
> Most of the rebel bandits entrenched [at the Norbulingka] were cavalrymen from Qinghai, Gansu, Kham, and Yunnan, tough opponents who were willing to die for their cause. Having lost Chakpori Hill, they were itching for a fight with us, and were counting on their sheer numbers, extensive weaponry, and formidable palace walls. To their surprise, however, those very walls made them as easy to snuff out as turtles trapped in a jar.
>
> Our first round of fire, like boiling water dumped into an ant's nest, or a torch set to a beehive, threw the rebels instantly into chaos. They ran pell-mell, but we tore them apart no matter which way they went. They wailed like demons and howled like wolves, but there was nowhere to hide.[15]

"Cavalrymen" is a misleading term here. The nomads who had come to Lhasa from Kham and Amdo may have had horses, but they were not trained soldiers, much less "cavalry."

Wang Guozhen claims to have had Chinese intelligence reports that there were "more than five thousand rebel bandits" in and around the Norbulingka during the shelling,[16] but this estimate is premised on the misconception that all the Tibetans present were "rebel bandits," a dehumanizing label that serves to justify their slaughter. In fact, Tibetan accounts indicate there were plenty of ordinary civilians at the Norbulingka that day, including townspeople, military families, gardeners, grooms, servants, monks, government officials, and civil servants.[17]

Tenpa Soepa bumped into the Dalai Lama's photographer, Jigme Taring, during the peak of the artillery barrage.

"Come with me," Jigme Taring said during a lull. "Let's go into the palace and get a camera to document this for all the world to see. Then we'll try to escape with the film, but we'd better shoot each other if they catch us!"

They got the camera and returned to the garden, where they were about to start taking pictures when a shell suddenly hurtled by overhead, separating them. In the scramble to dodge the intensifying bombardment, they never found each other again, or managed to record the destruction in photographs.

Tubten Khetsun and a few others had sought cover in a palace building within the interior yellow wall of the Norbulingka. Just as they were opening their little silver amulet cases to imbibe the sacred contents for protection, a shell hit the building. They panicked and darted outside, scattering under a hail of shells. Tubten suddenly felt a stabbing pain in his left leg: a piece of shrapnel. Then a second piece grazed his right cheek. Dripping with blood, he tried to escape via the stable when an exploding shell brought down the doorway, crushing many people inside. He heard the wails of wounded men and the whinnying of frightened horses.

Tubten's head began to reel from the loss of blood. The din around him faded into a distant buzz, and the fallen trees, shards of glass, and dismembered bodies all shrank to tiny specks on a blood-red background. Overcome with thirst, he staggered into the office of the stablemaster, who quickly poured him a glass of water, stirring in some pills that had been blessed by a senior monk. Tubten drained the potion in one gulp as shells continued to burst, shaking the building to its foundations. Then he emerged dazedly from the office amid the booming cannon fire.

Lieutenant Colonel Seshing went to move his family out of immediate danger and returned to guard headquarters. One of his captains burst in with news that the aristocrats were performing a divination to see whether they should surrender or not. A group of guards decided to try divination as well; they went to their shrine and placed two balls of *tsampa* in front of the sacred statue, each containing a slip of paper. One said, "flee," the other said, "surrender." The deity's instructions were to surrender.[18]

Tara made his way toward the Temple of Mahakala, where he found about a hundred bewildered people crowded at its threshold. After urging them to disperse and run, he entered the building. Three days earlier, when the Dalai Lama had paid his farewell visit here, he had found the monks from Namgyal Monastery impassively chanting their prayers; they were still doing so now, despite the bombardment. The faint golden light of the tiny butter lamps, flickering with each explosion, illuminated their faces as they sat, eyes cast downward, lips moving gently. Standing at the altar, Tara pressed his palms together in prayer, slipped a ball of sacred *tsampa* into the folds of his robe, and left in silence.

Shells continued to crash around him, raising clouds of smoke and debris. Tara looked back at the temple. The gilt Dharma wheel on its roof glittered in the sunlight and green prayer flags flapped wildly in the sooty air. He heard the piercing clang of a prayer bell, its echo seeming to spiral heavenward.[19]

After he lost Jigme Taring, Tenpa Soepa ran into his faithful servant Gyalpo, who had brought him something to eat. Spotting a colleague nearby, Tenpa Soepa invited him to share, but just then an explosion knocked the colleague dead. Tenpa Soepa tried to get a grip on himself. If I'm fated to die today, then it's no use running, he thought. He stood his ground and ate his fill.

"Gyalpo," he said, turning to his servant, "you're dismissed. You can't be expected to take care of me now. Run for your life!"

After watching Gyalpo disappear, Tenpa Soepa went to the stable to try to commandeer a horse for a getaway, but found a throng of people, all desperate for horses. Suddenly, a Khampa militiaman whipped out his pistol and pressed it against Tenpa Soepa's chest.

"I'm going to blow you up!" he yelled. "Damn you officials! We've been begging you for weapons all along, but you wouldn't give us any! This is all your fault! You're going to die for this!"

Under the circumstances, Tenpa Soepa felt unable to explain to him that the Dalai Lama and the government had been trying to negotiate a peaceful settlement. Before he could reach for his pistol, a shell blew up nearby.

The blast flung Tenpa Soepa to the ground, and he found himself unable to stand up once the smoke cleared. He struggled to his feet, using his rifle as a cane, and was hobbling into an adjacent room when a shell hit the building and destroyed the roof. A large chunk of debris landed on top of him, pinning him to the ground and crushing his left leg. He screamed for help, but no one came: everyone around him was either wounded or dead. Somehow he managed to free his leg. Shells were bursting in the garden outside, but he was beyond fear. He had only one thought: water.

He crawled back into the stable and gulped greedily from the horses' trough. All the people were gone, leaving only panicky, rearing horses. He could barely dodge being trampled, and he realized he was in no condition to mount a horse. Losing hope, he crept painfully toward the yellow wall. If he had to die that day, he wanted to take his last breath on the hallowed ground where the Dalai Lama had spent his days. He inched his way along in the dirt, leaving a long bloody trail behind him. Beside a pond in the garden, he gave up and flopped down on his back, gazing up at the smoke-filled sky and waiting quietly for a shell to hit him and put an end to his life.

After emerging from the stablemaster's office, Tubten Khetsun stood amid the bursting bombs and flying shrapnel, wondering if his uncle and brother were still alive, and where he should go. He noticed one of the grooms' pet monkeys, still chained to its pillar in front of the stable, trying wildly to escape the explosions. It had somehow managed to wrap its head with a torn shred of awning. Tubten limped over to it to set it free, but the terrified monkey scampered to the top of its pillar at the sight of him and sat there trembling, burying its face in the cloth as the shells continued to explode.

Tara arrived at the now-unguarded main gate of the palace, where a group was waiting for him: his nephew Sonam Tsering and a servant, two couriers, a monk from Gyuto Lower Tantric College, and a young soldier from Regiment 2. They had Browning rifles, bullets, and two horses, one of which was for him. Tara took out the sacred *tsampa* ball from the temple and gave everyone in the group a piece to swallow for protection. Then they exited the Norbulingka and headed toward Chakpori Hill.[20]

Behind them, the palace was shrouded in smoke.

: : :

Tibetan sources belie Wang Guozhen's assertion that the Tibetans at the Norbulingka were "itching for a fight" with the Chinese after the fall of Chakpori Hill. Aside from the "first shot," specific Chinese allegations of Tibetan provocations on the morning of March 20 are paltry: three attacks on the highway depot north of the Norbulingka, and one on the Lhasa Construction Office near Ramoche Temple. Why, then, did Tan Guansan bombard the Norbulingka so brutally? In his memoir, Wang Guozhen states that he issued specific orders to kill as many people as possible, ensuring that there were no survivors:

> I was directing the shelling from atop Chakpori Hill, enjoying the scene below.[21] Suddenly I noticed more than a thousand rebel bandit cavalrymen cowering in an area sheltered by the high palace walls at the south gate, which our artillery had missed because we were firing northward from the south bank of the river. I made sure they got their comeuppance.
>
> "Fire from east to west, as rapidly as you can!" I ordered immediately. "Aim your line of fire at the area within the south wall!"
>
> The rebel bandits, who had imagined themselves safe, were blown to bits immediately. People and horses were splayed on their backs, and blood and flesh hurtled through the air.[22]

To account for the ferocity of the assault on the Norbulingka, we must look beyond the official historiography to examine Tan Guansan's interchanges with Beijing just before and during the battle.

Tan Guansan finally received his reply from the Chinese Central Military Commission late in the morning of March 20, and it was disconcerting. Sent at 9:30 A.M., it arrived at 11:07[23] and read: "Fighting has begun in Lhasa and the Dalai Lama has fled. These developments are advantageous to settling the question of Tibet. Your policy for now should be: Control all key points to prevent the enemy forces from escaping to the north or the south. Corral them in Lhasa until our main forces arrive to wipe them all out."[24]

The cable, signed by Defense Minister Peng Dehuai, arrived during the bombardment of Chakpori Hill, beyond the point of no return for Tan Guansan. Half an hour later, Tan was still in a quandary when he received another cable with instructions from Mao: "Keep the enemy in Lhasa, and try to draw the rebels from all over Tibet into the city and ensnare them until we can eradicate them all at once. If they escape from [premature] confrontations now, we'll have even more trouble with them later."[25]

According to Ji Youquan, Tan Guansan "broke out into a sweat" when he read these messages from on high. He was fully aware he had given the order to go to war without first obtaining approval from the Chinese Central Military Commission, and now he had specific instructions to wait. If things went wrong, his status as a veteran Party member meant he could be subject to even harsher treatment than a class enemy. He had just witnessed the fall of his colleague Fan Ming, deputy secretary of the CCP Tibet Work Committee, and he knew his own fate might be even worse. As part of the nationwide Rectification and Anti-Rightist Campaigns, the CCP Tibet Work Committee had recently undergone a major purge, conducted in a slew of meetings between April and November 1958. Fan Ming had been in charge for the first month, when the main target had been Li Jue, former vice-commander of the PLA Tibet Military Command.[26] The winds soon shifted, however, when Zhang Jingwu and Zhang Guohua returned to Lhasa from Beijing with new instructions from Mao. Old rivalries resurfaced as these two generals from the Southwest Bureau turned the campaign against Fan Ming, who was from the Northwest Bureau.

The result of this drawn-out campaign was the identification of the "Fan Ming anti-Party clique." Although he was disliked for his swagger, Fan Ming was a soldier-scholar whose record of Communist achievement included leading a PLA march into Tibet in 1951 to escort the new pro-Beijing Panchen Lama to Shigatse and install him there. Now he was forced to stand onstage and endure humiliation before his subordinates for five months. Ultimately branded an "ultra-rightist,"[27] he was expelled from the Party and the army, and punished severely, bringing his associates and his family down with him.[28] His rapid fall from grace sent shock waves through the CCP Tibet Work Committee.

On the surface, this purge looked like infighting between Fan Ming and his two adversaries from the Southwest Bureau. However, it reflected the hesitation of the Central Committee, and Mao in particular, regarding the proper strategy for Tibet. Fan Ming evidently did not realize that his vision for Tibet, no matter what its motivation, was diametrically opposed to Mao's,[29] or that he could be accused of undercutting Mao's plans.

The Lhasa Incident flared up while the memories of this campaign were still fresh. Tan Guansan, who had just survived the purge, must have been quaking at the parallels between his transgression and Fan's. Ji Youquan attempts to re-create Tan's decision process at this point:

> Disrupting Mao Zedong's battle strategy might worsen matters in Tibet, in which case it would be hard to answer to Mao. But now that the fighting had begun, what was he to do? After mulling the problem over, Tan realized that he might be able to compensate for his mistake by obliterating the rebels, making sure that as few as possible escaped with their lives. In simple terms, victory was essential.
>
> He was outnumbered by the enemy, so victory was not certain. Should he continue to fight? If he stopped at this point, the armed rebels would take to the hills, leading to bigger trouble in the future. Finally deciding to defer to the judgment of the top leadership, he reported the situation to the Central Committee and the Central Military Commission, who immediately cabled his message to Mao. Meanwhile, he ordered all of his troops to prepare to attack.[30]

Ji Youquan adheres to Party line in his assertion that Tan Guansan believed he was outnumbered—and in the overestimation of Tibetan strength that it implies—although he may have been deliberately exaggerating to the Central Committee to protect himself in case he failed. Ji also seems to invoke the specter of potential foreign aid to the Tibetans, an angle the Chinese Communists played up after the battle. His description seems perceptive overall, but we will never know precisely what was going through Tan's mind at the time.

Here is Mao's reaction, as described by Ji Youquan:

> "What a blockhead!" Mao raged when he learned what Tan Guansan had done.
>
> But there was no stopping now that the battle had already begun. Focusing on the need for victory, Mao cabled back his assent to go to war, but he warned Tan Guansan that defeat would be unacceptable. Tan knew he would have to answer to Mao if he lost.
>
> Realizing that Mao was giving him a chance to prove himself, Tan chose the Norbulingka as the linchpin of his strategy. Conquest of the palace would give him dominion over Lhasa, and victory would be his. He issued orders to attack the Norbulingka, commanding his troops around the city to keep all enemy reinforcements away, regardless of the sacrifice involved. He also ordered Artillery Regiment 308 and the artillery of Regiment 155 to pound the enemy at the palace, not allowing the rebels to catch their breath.[31]

Tan Guansan knew that only a stunning victory could save him from court-martial, and that he would be judged by the number of "armed rebels" he killed. Fortunately for him, he had already taken Chakpori Hill, but after the shelling of the Norbulingka had begun he also obtained "license to kill" from above, a cable from the Chinese Central Military Commission. It appears in full in a semiclassified source:

> Now that we have taken Chakpori Hill, the rebels have two possible options:
>
> 1. They might stay in Lhasa and continue to do battle with us.
> 2. They might attempt to break out of our encirclement under cover of night, either individually or as a concentrated force. The latter is the most likely scenario.
>
> If the rebels stay and fight, you should capture as many as possible of their strongholds one by one, shrinking them into one small area, and then concentrate your firepower to wipe them out.

> If they try to break out of our encirclement after dark, either as individuals or as a concentrated force, you should crush them all resolutely, no matter what it takes.[32]

An openly published official history, however, offers only an expurgated summary of this cable, downplaying its merciless tone:

> At 6:00 P.M. the Central Military Commission sent instructions that if the rebels continued to fight in the city now that our troops had taken Chakpori Hill, we should capture as many as possible of their strongholds one by one. The message went on to say that our troops should make multiple attacks on the Norbulingka, taking over the rebels' command headquarters in a swift blitz before closing in on the city.[33]

Tan Guansan had passed the point of no return, and Beijing had given him free rein. If he branded all the Tibetans congregated at the Norbulingka "rebel bandits," he could sacrifice them without a qualm. The crackdown on the Xunhua Incident of 1958,[34] widely trumpeted as a model among Party ranks, provided adequate precedent for the massacre of civilians. Tan knew that he must shrink at nothing,[35] but the official Chinese histories maintain strict silence on this point.

: : :

Juchen Tubten and his men lay flat on their bellies atop the hill near the Rama Gang ferry, surveying the scene below. On the hillside beneath them was a small artillery camp, with its cannons pointed at the Norbulingka and its machine guns aimed at the riverbank.

After daybreak, a few dozen Tibetans tried to make a dash from the Norbulingka to the river, hoping to cross it to safety. Vice-Commander Wu Chen gave the order to fire, and his machine gunners mowed everyone down. A second group tried to escape the same way and met the same fate.

Juchen Tubten and his men had no machine guns or grenades. They used their obsolete British rifles to fire at the PLA beneath them, but to no avail.

At dusk, thousands of people darted out of the Norbulingka and ran toward the river. To get there, they had to cross a wide, stony expanse of riverbank, dodging potholes, dunes, and shrubs.[36]

Commander Wang Guozhen was watching from his lookout post on Chakpori Hill:

> After the second and third round of bullets [*sic:* should read "shells"] rained down, the rebel bandits burst out of the south gate, whooping wildly, in a death-defying dash to break out of our encirclement and reach the river crossing. I ordered our gunners to use their shells to block them with a deadly firewall. The terrified rebels turned to run back to the palace, but I gave orders to track them with artillery: "Send out a line of fire, as fast as you can!" Our shells screamed toward their targets and blew up right in the middle of the crowd of bandits.[37]

Ji Youquan corroborates the story:

> A couple of thousand rebel cavalrymen and several hundred infantrymen made a dash for the Lhasa [Kyichu] River crossing. Wu Chen immediately told Miao Zhongqin to use his heaviest artillery fire to reinforce the area.
>
> "Comrade, support the ferry area right now. Here come thousands of the goddamned rebels. Pound them as hard as you can!"
>
> Miao Zhongqin immediately turned the entire regiment's artillery fire on the ferry area. As shells exploded in continuous waves in the river and on its banks, the rebel bandits were beaten back to the north bank.[38]

Juchen Tubten watched from the hilltop as waves of people surged out of the Norbulingka toward the riverbank.[39] Totally inexperienced in warfare, they had no idea that they were positioning themselves squarely in the crosshairs of PLA soldiers with orders to be merciless, and that the rank and file was pumped full of "class hatred."[40]

Wang Guozhen describes the carnage: "The bullets [*sic:* should read "shells"] terrified the bandit hordes, ripping their chests open, beheading them, and laying their horses flat. The bandits were screaming, and their horses were whinnying amid the smoke and dust of the explosions as they fell one after the other. Wounded horses were stampeding, while panicky bandits ran helter-skelter."[41]

Tara's memoirs contain the following:

> For about two hours starting at 3:00 P.M., shells rained down on the riverbank leading to the Rama Gang ferry from the south gate of the Nor-

bulingka. Hundreds of men and horses were running pell-mell amid the smoke of the explosions. They included ordinary people who were trying to protect the Norbulingka, some of whom had just obtained getaway horses inside the palace. Thousands of people were massacred in this bombardment. . . .

Why was everyone trying to flee that day? It was mainly because they had heard the Dalai Lama was gone. Besides, they knew they did not stand a chance against the brutal Chinese artillery.[42]

The expanse of riverbank south of the Norbulingka became a killing field. People continued to press ahead against the artillery fire, trying in vain to save themselves by crossing the river, or to hide from the machine-gun fire and artillery shells coming from the south bank of the river. Commander Wang Guozhen made sure his men pressed in to dispose of them all: "I noticed that some of the rebel bandits who had retreated to the north bank were gathering near the Receiving Pavilion,[43] and I could not tell if they were planning to counterattack or to flee. Without pausing to find out, I gave the order to fire, exterminating them all on the spot. Our comrades in the infantry were literally jumping and whooping with joy."[44] Some people managed to wade into the river, but the relentless firestorm from the hillside followed them. As the bullets struck, plumes of spray rose from the water, and swirls of blood dyed it red.

Finally, the racket ceased, and time seemed to come to a standstill. The sun sank slowly in the west, bathing the drab peaks along the river valley in the rosy glow of an early spring sunset, and dappling the river with points of dancing light.

Juchen Tubten surveyed the scene in shock. Not a single person was left standing, and the valley was enveloped in a deathly silence. Untold numbers had fallen, with only the mountains and river as mute witnesses. The pure, snow-fed river was clogged with corpses, which bobbed along past the mountains on waves of red. Everything looked red to Juchen Tubten: the sun, the sky, the water, the riverbanks, even the snowy peaks in the distance.

The brief silence was shattered by a piercing screech, as another salvo of shells struck the Norbulingka. Juchen Tubten looked up at the palace. Its gilt roof, with its statuary of the Dharma wheel and pair of deer, was glowing, as if with holy golden light, against the smoke-filled sky.[45]

: : :

Under the cover of fierce artillery fire, Regiment 155, Transport Regiment 16, and a portion of Regiment 159 stormed the Norbulingka from all sides.

Crowds of people surged out of the smoking palace to the north, but Vice-Commander Deng Shaodong ordered Regiment 308 to drive them back in and pound them to death with heavy artillery.[46]

At 7:30 P.M., PLA soldiers charged into the unguarded main gate.[47] The shelling was over. By 8:30, the Norbulingka had fallen.

Other troops blew up the palace walls with dynamite and marched in. They combed the buildings one by one, kicking the bodies on the ground to see whether they were dead. Although they encountered sporadic resistance, there was no real battle.[48] Lieutenant Colonel Seshing ordered his surviving men to lay down their weapons and stack them in the courtyard of guard headquarters in preparation for surrender to the PLA.

After three brushes with death, Tenpa Soepa was lying unconscious in a heap of corpses.

Tubten Khetsun had joined the crowd trying to reach the river. When the people in front of him started dropping in the machine-gun fire, he darted back into the Norbulingka and hid in the stables. Everyone there surrendered that night.

As darkness descended on the city, Juchen Tubten and his men crept down the hill and slipped away through the mountains toward Lhokha.

After leaving the Norbulingka, Tara and his companions tried to head north via the Jarak Lingka, Kundeling Monastery, Lhalu Marsh, and Sera Monastery, but they lost each other while running from Chinese pursuers. Finding the northern route blocked, Tara turned south on his own. He reached the river at dusk, along with some survivors he encountered outside the south gate of the Norbulingka.

"Quick, lie flat on the ground before the Chinese soldiers shoot you!" someone shouted.[49]

Tara saw that a number of people had crawled into shallow pits on the riverbank, waiting to flee after dark. After nightfall, the silvery moon flooded the river with light. Then, as if in answer to Tara's prayers, a cloud finally arrived and darkened the sky. Everyone rose and hurried west to a shallow river crossing. A hundred more people appeared just as they were about to strip and wade in, and they all forded the river together holding hands.

Tibetan casualties at the Norbulingka were uncounted, but the Chinese reported five or six hundred people taken captive.[50] Following Central Committee orders, the PLA troops withdrew promptly from the Norbulingka and proceeded directly to the city itself. The Battle of Lhasa would now move to Ramoche Temple, the Potala, and the Jokhang Temple.

That night the moon beamed as usual on the river as it flowed along the valley in solemn silence, its sandy banks soaked with blood.

: 19 :

Inferno

THE PEOPLE OF LHASA awoke on the morning of March 21, 1959, to a vastly transformed cityscape.

The PLA had sealed the assets of the Norbulingka during the night, and Chinese soldiers were patching the battered palace walls with chunks of rubble. All captives, including the wounded, had been carted off to makeshift detention centers.

The Indian Consulate had been caught in the cross fire on the preceding day, but no one was hurt, and a report of the fighting was promptly cabled to New Delhi.

On March 17, the day of the Dalai Lama's escape, Indian Prime Minister Nehru had addressed his parliament about Tibet, but he had continued to downplay rumors of armed conflict: "I would not say that there has been large-scale violence there—although there have been scattered eruptions. . . . At this time I would term the conflicts ideological rather than military or physical."[1]

On March 21 Lhasa sank into radio silence for several days, and when broadcasts resumed, the Chinese Communists controlled their content. It was not until the first batch of refugees arrived in India in May that the story began to emerge in detail.

Meanwhile, early reports of the fighting had leaked out, and by March 21 the *New York Times* had blazoned headline news that "open warfare against the Chinese Communist overlords of Tibet" had broken out in Lhasa. Indian newspapers were also beginning to carry the story. But Nehru was dilatory in his reports to Parliament, probably not addressing the truth there until March 23 and March 30, and then only superficially.[2]

The events in Tibet attracted attention in the West, where memory was fresh of the Soviet invasion of Hungary less than three years earlier. But the people of Lhasa had no idea that the world had taken notice, and the fighting raged on.

At a strategic planning meeting at the PLA Tibet Military Command at 8:00 A.M. on March 21, Vice-Commander Deng Shaodong summed up the victories of the previous day. Stages 1 and 2 of the battle plan—to occupy Chakpori Hill and the Norbulingka—had been accomplished. It was time for Stage 3: mopping up the pockets of "rebel bandits" around the city. Some troops would surround the Potala, the Jokhang Temple, and the "great three" monastic universities, awaiting orders to attack, while others would stamp out resistance elsewhere.

The fighting reached another peak at approximately 10:00 that morning, when the PLA artillery began blanketing Lhasa with shells from the south side of the river, and armored vehicles rolled into the streets, crushing Tibetan defense. The PLA took Kundeling House, the Lhalu estate, Yabshi House, Tsarong House, and Taring House, set buildings ablaze with flamethrowers, and blew up the dividing walls between people's houses to make passageways for the troops.[3]

The fighting started so suddenly that civilians had no chance to evacuate. Chinese sources have maintained complete silence on civilian casualties, but Tibetan witnesses attest that there were many. One especially valuable memoir is provided by the Fifth Yulo Rinpoché, a monk at Gyuto Upper Tantric College and organizer of the defense of Ramoche Temple,[4] who says that "the Chinese Communists shot Tibetans indiscriminately, whether they had taken part in the resistance or not, and ambushed and killed many Tibetans who ran to Ngabo's house for sanctuary."[5] Another witness, Jampa Tenzin, has stated in a personal interview that he saw fleeing beggars and children slain near Ramoche Temple, a report corroborated in other Tibetan memoirs.

Ramoche Temple and the Potala Palace both fell on March 21. Sources from both sides indicate that Ramoche Temple was the site of intense close-range combat, the most serious engagement after Chakpori Hill and the Norbulingka. The official Chinese historiography, however, has very little more to say about either clash. Ji Youquan describes the Potala battle in relative detail but sheds little light on the conflict at Ramoche. In particular, Chinese sources provide few facts about Tibetan numbers, weapons, or organization at either site. Yulo Rinpoché's memoir, when corroborated with other sources, provides an eyewitness perspective on Ramoche and helps to fill this gap.[6]

: : :

On March 20, Yulo Rinpoché, asleep in his room at Gyuto Upper Tantric College, was awakened by earsplitting gunfire before dawn. He hopped out of bed, pulled on his monk's habit, and ran to the rooftop of Ramoche Temple, the college assembly hall. Artillery shells were streaking across the dark sky between the Potala and the PLA Tibet Military Command. The air was redolent with incense, and he heard the intoning of prayers from within the temple during lulls in the gunfire.

Returning quickly to his room, Yulo Rinpoché changed into layman's clothes, strapped on an ammunition belt, picked up his rifle, and went to see the head monk, Gedun Gyatso, to ask whether he had weapons and ammunition. He had none, Gedun Gyatso sighed, adding that he had requested weapons at the Norbulingka and at the Shol Scriptural Printing House, but had been told that the Dalai Lama had expressly forbidden their issuance to monks from Gyuto Upper and Lower Tantric Colleges.

The Dalai Lama had singled these monks out because they were the cream of the crop. Gyuto Upper Tantric College, a highly selective institute of advanced Buddhist studies founded in 1485, required applicants to demonstrate mastery of the Buddhist canon through a rigorous entrance examination. Only five hundred monks could be admitted; Drepung Monastery, by comparison, had about ten thousand. The taking of human life in combat would negate years of practice for these exceptional monks, at great cost to the transmission of the Buddhist faith.

However, things had come to such a pass that it was no longer possible to pursue a quiet Buddhist practice in Lhasa. Yulo Rinpoché and a group of his colleagues made the excruciating decision to defend their monastery.

That was the morning of the shelling of Chakpori Hill. While the Tibetan Medical Institute crumbled, one hundred and twenty monks of Gyuto Upper Tantric College were conducting a solemn ceremony in Ramoche Temple. Lined up in rows before the oldest, holiest statue of the Buddha in Tibet,[7] they renounced their Vinaya monastic vows, which forbade the taking of life.

This was the temple where they had prayed, prostrated themselves, and meditated every day. But now there was no time to sound the bells, drums, or horns, and the brightly colored prayer flags hung motionless. The monks stood in quiet unity, with gunfire audible outside. Rows of butter lamps flickered on the altar, bathing the temple in a golden glow and reflecting the statue of the Buddha with his half-closed eyes and beneficent smile.

After the ceremony, the monks filed out across the threshold in silence, just as they always did after religious assemblies, but their world had changed. They knew they might never cross that threshold again.

Without military training or adequate equipment, they had to fall back on sheer instinct. They decided to set fire to the Lhasa Construction Office, which bristled with fortifications and armed militia right nearby. Taking gasoline, a pump, and cotton, they rushed to the construction office compound. Their plan was to spray gasoline in over the wall with the pump and then toss in burning cotton, but the wall turned out to be too high. Two monks hacked a hole in it with picks, squeezed their way through, and were immediately shot and killed on the other side. Other monks crawled in after them, smashed the windows of a storehouse, sprayed in some gasoline, and set it ablaze. As the smoke billowed, they beat a hasty retreat under a hail of gunfire.

A Chinese source describes the encounter as follows: "The armed rebels entrenched at Ramoche Temple attacked the construction office with more than a thousand men. They breached our compound and were repulsed by the brave action of our militia."[8] This account stands in contrast to Yulo's memoir, which states that only a few people were involved in the attack on the construction office, and that there were—all told—a few dozen Tibetan soldiers and 120 monks at the temple that day.[9]

Back at the temple, Yulo divided the monks into squads of six or seven, with only one rifle for each squad, to be borne by the designated squad leader. Yulo assigned the armed men to lookout duty on the scriptural debate platform, while dispatching the others to offer prayers in the temple, prepare food with the army men, or help transport ammunition. In the afternoon, he heard that the men he had sent to the Potala for weapons had been thwarted in their mission by PLA barricades in the streets. A little later, a lieutenant colonel stationed at the Jokhang Temple sent some men with two cannons and six crates of shells. By this time, Yulo had heard about the Dalai Lama's escape, but he kept the news from his compatriots.

The PLA was too preoccupied with Chakpori Hill and the Norbulingka during the day to pay attention to Ramoche Temple. After the fighting finally died down late that night, an eerie silence descended over the Lhasa Valley, and Yulo patrolled the roof constantly in the biting wind.[10]

The next morning, March 21, the Tibetans of Ramoche Temple clashed with the Chinese from the nearby construction office and People's Hospital.[11] Tibetans avoid touching the dead and wounded in battle, fearing that one's protective talisman will lose its power through contact with blood. Such a taboo was untenable, however, given the weapons shortage. Yulo retrieved the bloodstained rifles, rinsed them with holy water from the temple, and redistributed them to the monks. Accompanied by local civilians, they charged toward the hospital with shouts of "Resist the invaders!"[12]

"Watch out! The Chinese are coming!" a Tibetan army captain suddenly shouted through a megaphone.

Yulo and a few others climbed up onto the temple roof. Dense ranks of Chinese soldiers were approaching.

Yulo and his compatriots fired down from the rooftop, but they were completely outgunned. According to a Chinese source: "Our troops attacked the die-hard rebels from Qinghai and Kham at Ramoche Temple at 1:06 P.M. on March 21. They hoped their sturdy building would protect them in their last-ditch struggle, and even hoisted their 'snow-lion flag,' planning to resist to the bitter end. We hit them hard with close-range weapons, including explosives, flamethrowers, grenades, and submachine guns."[13]

Explosives smashed the gilt roof and the top story of the building, with its monks' quarters and guest chamber for the Dalai Lama. Yulo and his men came down from the roof. The scriptural printing press was on fire. Pressing forward through the thick smoke, the PLA encircled the temple. Then armored vehicles rolled through the gates and into the courtyard. Yulo threw himself to the ground amid the corpses and played dead. A PLA soldier came over and kicked him, but no one discovered that he was alive: "When the soldiers left, I got slowly to my feet, brushed myself off, and readied my gun. Then I [left Ramoche Temple], headed [south] through the Desar complex, and arrived at Gaden Khangsar Palace. Many of my compatriots were doing the same. . . . The steps of nearby Tsemonling Temple were strewn with so many corpses that there was nowhere to walk."[14] After more than two hours of fierce combat, the defenders of Ramoche Temple succumbed at 3:30 on the afternoon of March 21, with heavy Tibetan casualties and extensive damage to the ancient building. Yulo's story is confirmed by the eyewitness account—released only in a semiclassified publication—of a member of the Chinese cleanup team of militia and soldiers dispatched to the temple after the battle: "When we arrived at Ramoche Temple, we found the premises deserted except for one lama at the gate named Phuntsok, who let us in. The roof of the main hall was still on fire, and the grounds were littered with a great many rebel corpses. We set to work at once to extinguish the fire, and the PLA sent engineers to dispose of the unexploded artillery shells and trucks to clear away the corpses."[15]

: : :

Jampa Phuntsok was in cloistered practice at Namgyal Monastery, at the Potala Palace, when the demonstrations began in Lhasa on March 10. Sensing that monastic seclusion was untenable as the crisis escalated, the abbot dismissed the monks, and Jampa returned to everyday life at the Potala, continuing his daily Buddhist study and practice on his own. He went only once to the Norbulingka during this period.[16]

At the sound of gunfire before dawn on March 20, the soldiers and monks at the Potala sprang from their beds and peered out the windows. The city was in chaos, with both sides shooting at random. The PLA headquarters exchanged a few rounds of desultory fire with the Potala, but the formidable palace walls sustained only superficial damage, while the obsolete Tibetan cannons had little impact on the PLA buildings. When the bombardment of Chakpori Hill began, Jampa recalls, the Tibetans at the Potala could only watch as their beloved landmark went up in smoke.

Realizing that they could not defend the huge Potala Palace with only a handful of soldiers and a couple of hundred monks, the Tibetans considered running away. Some of the monks did flee after witnessing the fall of the Norbulingka that night, but Jampa and the others hesitated. As monks of Namgyal Monastery, longtime residents of the Potala, they could not bear to desert it in its time of trouble, although none of them could even fire a gun. Jampa had been a monk since the age of eight, starting at Sera Monastery, and then moving to Namgyal four years later. He had never touched a gun in his life.

Just as they were starting to look around for some weapons, a large group of monks from Sera Monastery arrived. Their heads and hands were wrapped with strips of cloth, and they were wielding swords and lances. These, however, were merely old weapons, abandoned in their temple by believers who had piously renounced violence. Jampa was glad to see them, thinking they had come to help.

"Where are your guns? What have you been doing all this time?" they scolded.

Jampa and the others finally found some weapons of their own. The soldiers showed the monks how to pull a trigger, but no one had found any bullets.

At a strategy meeting late that night, someone suggested attacking the PLA Tibet Military Command and its artillery camp on the south bank of the river, but no one volunteered to go. After a long, ineffectual debate, they finally resolved that anyone else who tried to flee would be summarily executed. Some people deserted that night nonetheless, but others, including Jampa, remained.

The next morning, March 21, the PLA turned its artillery onto the Shol neighborhood, in front of the Potala, as well as targets on both of its sides. Commander Wang Guozhen provides the following description:

> First we shelled the Shol area along the front of the Potala to take out the fortifications there. Afraid to return our fire, the rebel bandits abandoned their dead and wounded and retreated into the Potala.
>
> On the left side of the Potala was the rebel artillery camp, which was a serious threat to us, as the rebels had used it to fire at the offices of the PCART, the Public Health Committee, and the PLA Club. We turned

our artillery directly onto this camp instead of pursuing the enemy forces that were fleeing from the Shol area into the Potala. The overconfident rebel bandits fired back at us but soon fell completely silent. Once they were subdued, we directed our artillery fire immediately to the right side of the palace.[17]

Commander Zhu Xiushan is even more succinct: "Company 1 of our battalion, with the support of an armored vehicle platoon and Artillery Regiment 308, occupied the cluster of Tibetan buildings beneath the Potala relatively smoothly."[18] In plain language, this means that heavy artillery fire and armored vehicles cleared the way for Company 1 to take over the area beneath the Potala, probably inflicting massive casualties in the Shol area. A drawing by an anonymous Tibetan published in CIA instructor Roger McCarthy's *Tears of the Lotus* provides a unique visual record of the attack.[19]

Wang Guozhen's account of the assault on the Potala is laconic in comparison to his lavish descriptions of the strikes on Chakpori Hill and the Norbulingka. Moreover, both he and Zhu Xiushan confine their descriptions to the PLA bombardment around the palace, omitting mention of the PLA firing at the palace itself, apparently to create the impression that the PLA had acted in keeping with a directive from Zhou Enlai to spare the Potala as a "major cultural heritage site."[20]

There was, however, Chinese fire directed at the Potala, although the Chinese apparently chose somewhat smaller weaponry here than they had used at Chakpori Hill, in keeping with Zhou's instructions. Ji Youquan's account is illuminating:

> Artillery Regiment Chief of Staff Miao Zhongqin recommended the use of recoilless rifles to knock out the enemy weapons. Tan Guansan asked whether this technique would damage the building. It would not, Miao assured him, as recoilless rifles killed and wounded efficiently, with minimal explosive impact. Tan Guansan then ordered Regiments 159 and 155 and the PLA Tibet Military Command guard battalion to deliver all their recoilless rifles so that Miao Zhongqin could establish a recoilless rifle battalion.
>
> Miao set up his encampment in a vacant field on the north bank of the river near the PLA Tibet Military Command compound.

"Let's see you fire a couple of rounds to show them a thing or two," said Deputy Chief of Staff Fu Tingxiu.

Miao scrutinized the Potala through his field glasses and spotted a window that was emitting gunfire. He gave the order for a recoilless rifle to shoot at the window, silencing the enemy fire.

Miao proceeded to shoot at every window that emitted gunfire, striking his target without fail each time, while Fu Tingxiu applauded his accuracy. A single shell from a recoilless rifle could destroy a whole room full of bandits. Miao went to the Potala to assess the damage when the battle was finished, and found he had hit all six or seven bandits in each room that his shells had struck, while leaving the building intact.[21]

The claim that the palace survived "intact" seems exaggerated. The 57 mm recoilless rifles used in this strike[22] delivered shells weighing almost three pounds, which must have taken a toll on the building and its contents.

The Chinese strike was viewed quite differently by the Tibetans. Even if the Potala was left standing, it was sacred, and any damage was a sacrilege. Jampa, who was inside the building, recalls that the chant master of Namgyal College led religious rites during the shelling, and describes the Tibetan defenselessness against the long-range PLA artillery: "There was nowhere to hide. Their shells followed us everywhere. We couldn't see them, so we couldn't fight back." Unwilling to abandon the Potala, they considered holding out for a chance to confront the enemy face-to-face, as the palace had a year's stockpile of food and water. Jampa barely knew how to shoot a gun, but he tried: "We fired out of the windows in self-defense. Someone said there were Chinese soldiers, but I don't know if we hit any of them."[23]

However, the monks changed their minds as the PLA shells continued to penetrate the palace, deciding, "although it would be shameful to abandon the Potala, it seemed like the lesser of two evils, as it would be razed to the ground if we continued to try to defend it."[24] To them, the Potala was far more than what the Chinese called a "cultural heritage site": it was Tibetan heritage itself. Tracing its origins to the seventh century, it was holy ground, home of *dalai lamas* since the seventeenth century, and of eight sacred stupas containing their remains. Having seen the Chakpori Tibetan Medical Institute and the Norbulingka gutted, the defenders of the Potala had no doubt that it could suffer a similar fate.

Once the decision to capitulate was made, some people fled through the rear gates of the palace. The others hung white prayer scarves out the palace windows the following morning, March 22.

Seeing the white flags of surrender, Wang Guozhen's "eyes brimmed with tears of elation." His gunners, however, who had shelled seventeen targets in Lhasa in two days, were exhausted:

> Pumped full of hatred and fighting spirit during battle, they accompanied the booming of the cannons with their own battle cries.
>
> "That'll teach you, you rebels!" "You'll never get away!" "Let that be a lesson to you!" "Take that!"
>
> They yelled themselves hoarse. Some of them had loaded hundreds of rounds of ammunition without pausing, until their arms were swollen.[25]

Meanwhile, only the trembling white prayer scarves at the palace windows seemed to give voice to the Tibetans' anguish.

: 20 :

Surrender, and Save the Temple!

JAMPA TENZIN WENT ABOUT HIS BUSINESS as usual throughout the tumult that had begun on March 10, 1959.[1] As a young, entry-level civil servant, he went to tea service every morning at the Norbulingka, attended meetings there and at the Shol, and then returned to his home near Barkor Street. Beyond his decision to resign from the PCART, he had been relatively uninvolved in the strife. But extraordinary times often thrust ordinary individuals into unexpected roles.

Before dawn on March 20, he was jolted from a sound sleep by the booming of guns and mortars. He jumped out of bed, pulled on his monk's habit and ran to the door with his rifle, but then stopped, wondering where to go. Since he was living at home, he was out of touch with events around town. He found his parents standing terrified in the yard, straining to decipher the sounds outside: people running and yelling, doors banging, artillery from far away, and gunfire nearby. He stood with his rifle and watched the fiery bursts in the dark, smoke-filled sky. His mother was bowing and praying loudly as she stoked the censer, its little door emitting a red glow that danced on her gray hair. The air was pungent with a curious mixture of incense, charred *tsampa,* and gunpowder.

The artillery grew louder during the morning, with continuous explosions coming from the direction of the Potala. As his parents knelt at the household altar and prayed for the protection of the Dalai Lama and the city, Jampa glanced at them uneasily. His father was grimly silent, while his mother kept dabbing at tears.

The explosions eventually stopped,[2] and Jampa heard footsteps in the street again, along with cries of "Protect the Jokhang Temple!" Then came an urgent knock at the door. It was one of his friends, bearing a rifle.

"Come on! Let's go to the Jokhang," he said.

Jampa went into his room, changed quickly into layman's garb, and hurried out with his friend, rifle in hand. People from all along Barkor

Street were running toward the Jokhang, afraid it might meet the same fate as the temple on Chakpori Hill. Armed with rifles, knives, clubs, and various household implements, the people hastily barricaded the east and west access to the temple with everything they could get their hands on: boards taken from street stalls, stones, bricks, sacks of *tsampa,* and assorted merchandise.[3]

Jampa and his friend found the temple courtyard thronged with local citizens, along with some Tibetan soldiers, chaotically debating what to do. With no clear chain of command, most people eventually took up positions on their own, some in the courtyard, others on the roof or in the upstairs passageways. A few hundred people planted themselves at the main gate, ready to serve as human shields for the building.

Jampa and a group of civil servants decided to divide up among the temple entrances, and he went to the south gate along with two soldiers. Directly across Barkor Street loomed the Chinese Public Security Bureau, the guns on its fortified roof pointing straight at the temple.

Soon they heard popping gunfire, and shells landed in Barkor Street. One hit the main gate of the temple, blowing up a slab of flagstone and inflicting heavy Tibetan casualties. Another struck the cooking area on the west side of the building, igniting the firewood there. Chinese militia fire from the neighboring rooftops shattered the gilt temple roof, but Jampa ordered his two soldiers not to shoot back lest the Chinese respond with grenades, harming civilians in the packed downtown neighborhood. According to a semiclassified Chinese memoir,[4] however, Tibetan snipers picked off the PLA soldiers from a rooftop across the street during the battle.

Late that night, Jampa went out with a colleague and found Barkor Street littered with the dead and wounded. Fifty or sixty corpses lay strewn around the main entrance to the temple.

: : :

Jampa spent the next day, March 21, on guard at the Jokhang. By that night, the main action of the Battle of Lhasa was winding down, although there was still some fighting in the streets. From his post at the south gate of the temple, Jampa heard approaching gunfire. Chinese troops had sealed off the gate with machine-gun fire from their rooftops across the street, continuing to strafe it periodically, and they had torched a nearby building with flamethrowers. Jampa's recollections are largely corroborated by those in the semiclassified Chinese memoir:

> On the afternoon of March 21, under the cover of heavy machine guns from the PLA Tibet Military Command, some PLA soldiers charged the building across the street from the Jokhang and set it ablaze with flamethrowers. More PLA soldiers stormed nearby buildings, set up machine guns, and began to strafe the Jokhang. The Tibetans were still firing from the windows on the south side of the temple's main gate, and the PLA troops set one corner afire with flamethrowers.[5]

Panic-stricken people were running toward the temple in search of refuge, but the number of Tibetan temple defenders had dwindled. There had been almost a hundred casualties at the main gate, and many people had fled. At this point, Jampa and his friend ran into an acquaintance, a former *tsedrung* named Tubten Kasha who had gone to school in Beijing and returned to Lhasa after graduation. The three of them went into the main hall, with its hallowed Jowo Rinpoché statue of the twelve-year-old Sakyamuni. In the flickering light of the butter lamps on the altar, the young men pressed their palms together in prayer for the fallen.

There they met a monk from Drepung Monastery—one of the people's representatives—who brought good tidings: the Dalai Lama had left Lhasa a few days ago. It was the best news Jampa had ever heard in his life.

"Even if we seem to have lost this battle," he exclaimed joyfully, "this means we have won!"

Now that he knew the Dalai Lama was safe, Jampa's thoughts turned to self-preservation. His little group decided to perform a divination with hand-drawn trigrams in front of the Jowo Rinpoché statue, but they could not find a pencil and paper. Instead, they took two pieces of grain from a dish on the altar, a white one signifying "don't surrender," and a black one for "surrender." Then they pinched off two balls of *tsampa* from the ritual food offering in front of the statue, wrapped each piece of grain in a ball, dropped both balls into a talisman box, and shook the box. If they drew the black grain, the plan was to go outside with white prayer scarves. The grain they drew turned out to be white, ruling out surrender, and leaving them with only one option: to flee. Jampa had a friend who lived nearby, so they decided to try to reach his house.

They crept out of the main hall at 2:00 A.M., leaving their guns behind, and took a back route to the shrine of the Bodhisattva Tara, where they waited for an opportunity to make a dash onto Barkor Street. The burning building had collapsed into embers. The PLA had captured most of the houses along the street, and soldiers were streaming from them toward the Jokhang Temple. Gunmen on the rooftops tracked the three young men as they flitted down the dark, deserted street. Suddenly a flare exploded, spotlighting the fugitives in its blinding glare. Jampa faltered, while soldiers on the rooftops peppered the streets with machine-gun fire. Out of the corner of his eye, Jampa saw one of his companions stumble, stagger a few steps, and fall to the ground, faceup. The flare faded, returning the street to darkness.

Jampa ran for his life. Another flare burst, flooding him with light. Gunfire echoed around him, and bullets ricocheted on all sides. A bullet penetrated his thick cotton gown and underwear, and he felt its heat against his skin. One of his comrades had fallen and the other had disappeared, and he found himself alone. Hugging his chest in desperation, he touched a reassuring lump under his clothing—his protective talisman—and made a dash for the darkness in the distance.

When the next flare lit the sky, he darted into an alley, but there he stopped in his tracks, confronted by a row of rifles aimed directly at him.

He was trapped.

: : :

Armored vehicles rolled into Barkor Street just before daybreak on March 22. Traversing the improvised barricades with ease, they pulled right up to the Jokhang Temple. Behind them came ranks of soldiers, who surrounded the temple, rifles cocked and awaiting the order to fire.

Machine guns were trained on the Jokhang from rooftops all around, and soldiers waited, ready to respond to the slightest resistance with a torrent of gunfire.

The Jokhang Temple stood serene in the predawn darkness. The guns, and the entire world, had fallen silent. Inside the temple, butter lamps gleamed, while soft hymns of praise floated outward.

As the sun rose, the pair of deer and Dharma wheel on the rooftop sparkled in the morning light, and multicolored prayer flags fluttered against the smoky sky.

A male voice shattered the silence. A Tibetan official with a megaphone on one of the armored vehicles was bellowing calls for surrender.

There was no response from inside.

He gave up and was replaced by a senior lama, who continued to shout exhortations, still with no response.

Finally, some PLA soldiers forced a man with a weary face and unkempt hair—a people's representative they had captured at the Norbulingka—to take the megaphone. With rifles pointed at him, he shouted hoarsely:

"Surrender now! If you don't come out, the PLA will raze the building. Surrender, and save the temple!"

Still no response.

The man kept shouting through the megaphone. "Surrender, and save the temple. . . ."

Finally, a snow-white prayer scarf appeared on the rooftop in the faint dawn light. The Tibetans had lost the battle, but the temple still stood.[6]

: 21 :

The Aftermath

RELIEVED, GENERAL TAN GUANSAN lost no time in cabling a report of his triumph to the Central Committee on the morning of March 22, 1959.[1] He had done more than simply oust the Dalai Lama and his government. His application of the techniques of modern warfare in the ancient city—a grand-scale replication of the model developed in Sichuan and Qinghai—had demonstrated Chinese Communist determination and military might to the vacillating Tibetan elite, clearing the way for the Communists to achieve their ends in Tibet. "Pacifying rebellion" supplied the ideal pretext for casting off the restrictions of the Seventeen-Point Agreement, imposing Land Reform, and incorporating Tibet solidly into the motherland.

Even as the battle was still raging on the preceding day, March 21, 1959, the General Political Department of the PLA issued a detailed directive to Lhasa, setting the course for the PLA's political and propaganda tasks after the battle was won.[2] It probably took some time to draft such a document; at any rate, its appearance before the battle was over stands as further evidence that the Chinese were confident of victory, and had already planned their next moves.

The Central Committee issued a similar directive to the CCP Tibet Work Committee one day later, on March 22, but it is significant that the earliest instructions came from the PLA. Tibet had essentially been under military rule ever since the Communists had first invaded Tibet at the beginning of the 1950s, and the CCP Tibet Work Committee was a de facto military regime.

The PLA directive, published in a censored version for the general public in 2008, began by "defining the nature" of the events in Lhasa, as a setup for its new draconian stance:

> The activities of the Tibetan reactionary clique are planned, organized, counterrevolutionary, and treasonous, instigated and supported by American imperialism and other reactionary foreign forces. We may define this as a sharp class struggle waged by the Tibetan reactionary clique against the will of the people, in the name of ethnicity and religion, in order to support its feudal rule and serf system.

Despite the claim that the uprising was "against the will of the people," the directive acknowledged:

> At the beginning of the rebellion, inevitably some—and perhaps even the majority of—the masses were forced into joining, or did so because of their low political consciousness.

Nonetheless, even this fact could be explained according to Communist dogma:

> Most of the Tibetan people still lack political awareness because they have been deceived for ages by their feudal rulers and their religion, and because of the historical estrangement between the Han and Tibetan peoples.

The directive makes it quite clear that the Party regarded the "rebellion" as ample justification for its decision to impose its "reforms" simultaneously with the "pacification" campaign:

> In the past, the Central Committee was planning to wait until the time was ripe before implementing peaceful, gradual reform to solve the Tibet question. Now that the Tibetan reactionary clique has torn up its agreement with us regarding the peaceful liberation of Tibet, openly betraying the motherland, we have no choice but to change our policy and resolve the Tibet question ahead of our original schedule.[3]

What this meant in actuality was that the PLA would be authorized to conduct Land Reform at gunpoint in the guise of "pacification," as it had in the Tibetan regions of Sichuan in 1956. This fact was to be concealed by a propaganda effort, however, as the PLA directive states explicitly in a passage tellingly omitted from the public version of the document: "Our policy is to use the slogan of pacification of rebellion as an umbrella term that includes the Democratic Reforms. Therefore, in our propaganda, we should speak only of pacifying rebellion rather than of reform."[4] As in the analogous campaigns in the Tibetan regions of Sichuan and other provinces earlier in the 1950s, the term Democratic Reforms in this passage refers to the Party's imposition of Land Reform, "religious reform," and the mass arrest and sentencing or execution of "counterrevolutionaries."[5]

On March 22, the policies set forth by the PLA were echoed by the Central Committee in its directive, which opened with the declaration:

> The local government of Tibet[6] has torn up the Seventeen-Point Agreement, betrayed the motherland, and unleashed all-out rebellion in Tibet. Circumstances compel us to initiate our showdown with the Tibetan reactionary elite separatist elements ahead of our original schedule, and to implement a pacification campaign to resolve the Tibet question once and for all. Under these circumstances, the Central Committee's original policy of postponing the reforms for six years has naturally become untenable.

The Central Committee directive added that implementing the Democratic Reforms and "guiding Tibet onto the road of socialism" would serve to "thoroughly eradicate treasonous separatist activities."[7] After more than eight years in Tibet, the Chinese Communists knew that the only way to take full control of the region was to remodel it forcibly to align with the rest of China.

The Central Committee directive also reiterated the call for subterfuge in public propaganda regarding PLA involvement in Land Reform: "To make full use of our present advantageous situation . . . and to isolate the enemy as much as possible, our public slogans should pertain only to pacifying rebellion, without mention of implementing the Democratic Reforms."[8] Like those in the PLA directive, these instructions appeared only in a semiclassified publication, and highlight the ulterior motive behind China's use of force to "pacify" the "rebellion."

The Communists moved quickly ahead with their plan.

On March 23, the PLA Tibet Military Command announced the dissolution of the municipal government of Lhasa and the establishment of a Lhasa Military Control Committee to take its place. The city of Lhasa, along with the rest of Tibet, was thus placed under military rule.[9]

On March 24, Major General Ding Sheng, commander of the Fifty-Fourth Army, flew to Lhasa with his political commissar, Xie Jiaxiang, and some other officers. These were the men of "Ding Headquarters," the original nerve center for the Tibet-bound forces from the PLA Chengdu Military Command.[10]

On the same day, an "Order of the State Council of the People's Republic of China" was drafted and sent to the State Ethnic Affairs Commission to be translated into Tibetan.[11]

On March 26, Commander Zhang Guohua flew back to Lhasa to take charge of the CCP Tibet Work Committee.[12] Its task had shifted from maintaining the United Front to "pacifying the rebellion" and "mobilizing the masses."[13] It was also in charge of receiving the surrendering Tibetan troops, assuming political power, and sealing or confiscating the assets of the Tibetan government and hostile members of the elite.

On March 27, the remaining officers of "Ding Headquarters" flew from Lanzhou to Lhasa, and Xinhua News Agency delivered the "Order of the State Council" to Tibet by special plane.

On March 28, Premier Zhou Enlai promulgated the "Order of the State Council," dissolving the "local Tibetan government" and supplanting it with the PCART. The order also dismissed from the PCART eighteen people deemed "traitors," and appointed the Panchen Lama to replace the Dalai Lama—who had been "abducted"—as its chairman.[14] On the same day, Regiment 401, the vanguard of Major General Ding Sheng's Tibet-bound reinforcements, arrived in Lhasa.[15]

On March 29, *People's Daily* published the "Order of the State Council." Nineteen days after the eruption of the Lhasa Incident and a week after the news had broken around the world, the Chinese people finally learned what had happened in Tibet, or at least they were told the official Chinese Communist Party version of the story. They were the last in the world to hear, even though it was supposedly "domestic news."

: : :

On March 28, 1959, Xinhua News Agency released an official communiqué regarding the Lhasa Incident, defining it as "an armed rebellion deliberately instigated by the reactionary clique of the upper social strata," who "had the effrontery to carry off the Dalai Lama by force from Lhasa on March 17."[16] But this announcement came too late. The international community had heard that the Dalai Lama was safe, and therefore had little interest in manufactured tales of his abduction. By that time, reporters from all over the world had rushed to India to hear the Dalai Lama's own side of the story.

The communiqué did not mention the casualty toll on either side, confining itself to the less sensitive subject of prisoners, with the claim that "more than four thousand rebel soldiers" had been captured by March 23.[17] The probable reason for this glaring omission was the decision to conceal the heavy bombardments of the Norbulingka and other sites. It is not surprising that early Chinese sources tended to follow the communiqué's example.[18] Later ones, however, have presented widely disparate numbers.

In 1993, decades after the fact, Ji Youquan seems to have been the first historian in China to approach the question of casualties, although he mentions only the Chinese side, asserting that "63 PLA officers and men were killed and 210 wounded." He adjusts the number of Tibetan captives given in the early communiqué, placing it at "5,360 soldiers and officers."[19]

A semiclassified source published in 1995 hints at Tibetan casualties, but still masks the number of deaths: "With a mere thousand-odd men, the PLA killed, wounded, or took captive more than 5,300 armed rebels."[20] A Party history published two months later finally gives the first public, official Tibetan body count: "More than 5,300 rebels were neutralized, including 545 killed and more than 4,800 wounded or captured."[21] A 2008 official compilation repeats the Tibetan death toll as 545, while fine-tuning the number of wounded and captured to 4,815.[22]

These are the only Tibetan casualty figures that China has officially released to date. They evidently represent a determination to stay within the CCP Tibet Work Committee's oft-cited 1959 estimate of seven thousand Tibetan "rebels."[23]

However, these numbers do not tally with those suggested elsewhere in Chinese sources. While avoiding a direct statement of the overall Tibetan casualty toll, Ji Youquan claims that there were "nine thousand Khampa rebel bandits" at Chakpori Hill alone, and hints at the number of dead with the assertion that none of the defenders of the hill survived the PLA bombardment. His estimate is suspect to say the least,[24] but it is a far cry from the officially released tally of 545 Tibetan dead in the entire Battle of Lhasa.

The trend toward downplaying Tibetan casualties in Chinese government sources over the years can also be seen in the figures pertaining to the shelling of the Norbulingka. According to company commander Wang Guozhen's eyewitness account, published in 1989, there were "more than five thousand rebel bandits" at the palace that day. He states that he personally gave the order to shell the crowd of thousands who were trying to flee to the north of the palace, and he claims to have "wiped them all out on the spot." He also takes evident pride in his descriptions of lethally bombarding thousands of Tibetans fleeing in other directions or cowering in the gaps in artillery coverage.[25] Ji Youquan echoes him.[26] If there is truth to these claims, they again contradict the official figure of only 545 Tibetans killed in the entire Battle of Lhasa.

The official compilation released in 2008, however, whitewashes the bloodshed: "After losing Chakpori hill, the rebels occupying the Norbulingka were shaken by heavy PLA artillery fire. More than two hundred rebel cavalrymen tried to escape across the Lhasa [Kyichu] River, but were beaten back by Company 7 from Regiment 159. More than a thousand of them also tried to flee to the north, but were thwarted by Regiment 308's forceful artillery. Most of them had to retreat to the Norbulingka."[27]

Chakpori Hill and the Norbulingka were only two of the many sites that the PLA pummeled during the Battle of Lhasa. Casualties at the others—Ramoche Temple, the Jokhang Temple, Andrugtsang House,[28] Kundeling House, and the Shol neighborhood near the Potala—are not specified in Chinese sources, but it is impossible that there were none.

For reasons which may be inferred, Tibetan eyewitnesses of the Battle of Lhasa have not left precise casualty statistics; we have little except Tara's rough estimate that "thousands were massacred" in the bombardment of the Norbulingka.[29] Moreover, it should be noted that untold numbers of Tibetan lives were destroyed in ramifications of the battle. Some Tibetans tried to flee to the Penpo Valley, but were mowed down by PLA pursuers. Others languished for years or died later behind bars. Right after the battle, the Chinese converted a number of buildings—such as Drapchi Barracks, the guard unit headquarters at the Norbulingka, and various aristocrats' estates—into makeshift prisons for captives. Some were kept as conscript laborers in the Lhasa environs and put to work on such construction projects as the Lhasa Stadium, the Ngachen Hydroelectric Power Station, and the PLA Tibet Military Command Hospital. Other captives were shipped off to harsh labor camps on China's frontiers.[30] Many were locked up for as long as twenty years, and not granted amnesty until just before the Dalai Lama sent his first official fact-finding delegation to Tibet in 1979.[31]

Questions surround the Chinese appropriation of Tibetan property in the aftermath of the Battle of Lhasa. It was official Party policy to "confiscate the rebel elements' land, buildings, livestock, grain, and agricultural implements, and redistribute them to the peasants."[32] This is not what happened, however. The army, state-run farms, and various institutions took over the fields, livestock, and pastureland, while municipal bureaus and the army absorbed the buildings appropriated from the aristocrats. With regard to these buildings, the Central Committee expressly stipulated: "in cases where they are being used by various organizations or the army, they should continue to be used as they are, and not be redistributed to the masses."[33] When it came to confiscated belongings, the Central Committee presented guidelines for "delineating clearly between what should be public property and what should be distributed to the masses," ruling that valuable items should be turned over to the government for handling, including "large quantities of foodstuffs, butter, tea, gold and silver, merchandise, automobiles, automobile parts, construction materials, and luxury consumer items such as watches, radios, cameras, bicycles, and sponge cushions."[34]

It has never been revealed how much wealth the government and cadres derived from these appropriations. Although the campaign was conducted in the name of "liberating the serfs" and "striking down the local tyrants and distributing their land," very little actually reached the masses. What was left to be "divided equally" among them, according to the Central Committee decree, were "all ordinary household items such as clothing, bedding, mats, and furniture, no matter what their condition."[35]

The total value of the property confiscated in Lhasa, and its ultimate fate, remain a mystery.

: : :

When the battle was over, Tan Guansan went to inspect the damage at the Norbulingka. He found the palace grounds littered with rubble and corpses. PLA soldiers had patched some of the holes in the walls and tidied up the outside of the Dalai Lama's New Palace, picking up shattered flowerpots and righting fallen apple trees. Finally free of the onerous Tibetan formalities, which had forbidden him entrance into the Dalai Lama's quarters without due ceremony, Tan Guansan entered the deserted New Palace and surveyed it in his capacity as its new keeper.

Meanwhile, the women of Lhasa were scouring the town for their missing menfolk, crowding around the makeshift jails to scan each arriving group of fettered Tibetan captives.

After Jampa Tenzin was captured near the Jokhang Temple, he was taken to a detention center at a mansion on Barkor Street. The Chinese forces had run out of handcuffs, and lashed the prisoners together with rope instead. The next day, he was transferred to a center near Ramoche Temple, which gave him occasion to witness the destruction there. Corpses and unexploded shells were strewn on the ground in front of the temple and along its walls. The gilt roof was battered, and the nearby houses were still smoldering, their walls riddled with bullet holes.[36]

Thinley Phuntsok was at Ling Rinpoché's estate throughout the battle. He had no part in the fighting, but was rounded up nonetheless.[37]

Tubten Khetsun and some other civil servants were taken to the PLA Tibet Military Command and locked up in a small jail there. His uncle and his sister, a nun, were also arrested; his uncle died in prison.[38]

On the morning after the shelling of the Norbulingka, Tenpa Soepa was awakened by a racket: Chinese soldiers were searching the palace. He crawled to his feet and went to surrender. Large groups of captives were sitting on the ground in the yard. Since he was still bleeding, he was sent into a big prayer hall with the rest of the wounded, many of whom were dead or dying. They were kept there without medical care until the following morning, when he was finally taken to a hospital to treat a shattered bone in his left foot.[39]

Juchen Tubten and about a dozen men crossed the Tsangpo River and headed for Gongkar, where they paused for a few days to make further plans.[40]

After Tara crossed the river late on March 20, he traveled south all night toward Lhokha. The next day, he crossed Che Pass and the Tsangpo River, took a brief rest stop, and arrived at Kyishong Village, where he found his younger sister. At that point, he wrote to the Dalai Lama to report the fighting in Lhasa and warn him that he was still at risk of PLA capture. He recommended that the entourage proceed to India, and asked to join them. He also wrote to the Chushi Gangdruk commanders, requesting that they guard all river crossings and main routes.

After delegating his sister to find someone to deliver the letters, Tara left Kyishong at 3:00 A.M. on March 22. On March 23, he caught up with Kundeling Dzasa and Colonel Dokharsey, who had a dozen soldiers with them. They told him that the Dalai Lama might go to India, and hearing that, the little band headed directly for Tsona, near the Indian border.[41]

: 22 :

The Eternal Crossing

ON MARCH 22, 1959, Athar Norbu rode into Chonggye on horseback with his radio transmitter and Chushi Gangdruk guerrilla escort, and climbed a hill to peer around with his field glasses. Spotting the Dalai Lama's entourage approaching Riwo Dechen Monastery[1] from afar, he raced down to meet them.

At 2:00 P.M., the local people—officials, citizens, and six hundred monks—formed a long receiving line, bearing offerings of incense and white silk prayer scarves. First to arrive were the Chushi Gangdruk guerrillas, the outer tier of the Dalai Lama's protection. Next came the bodyguards, led by Colonel Junpa. At about three o'clock, the Master of the Robes, the Master of Religious Ceremonies, Ling Rinpoché, and Lord Chamberlain Phala arrived, heralding the arrival of the Dalai Lama. The local people bowed low in reverential welcome. Yet many of them failed to recognize the Dalai Lama, a bespectacled young man in a common maroon robe and fur cap, mistaking a well-dressed senior lama in the group for him instead. Security Chief Phuntsok and his fifty soldiers brought up the rear of the procession.[2]

Athar met with the Dalai Lama and briefed him on his mission. Then Lhotse arrived, bringing the extra soldiers and luggage. Phala introduced the two of them to the cabinet ministers, whom they joined on a hillside for a tête-à-tête. Humble commoners such as Athar and Lhotse had never before enjoyed such intimacy with Tibetan noblemen. No one had ever imagined that these cabinet ministers would be the last vestiges of Tibetan nobility, or how their world would change forever the moment they left Lhasa.

As the entourage had made its way from Chenye to Riwo Dechen Monastery, the Dalai Lama's guards had been alarmed at the sight of an approaching posse of horsemen, but one of the riders had turned out to be Tsi-pon Namseling,[3] who brought appalling news: he had heard that

Chinese forces had bombarded Lhasa but knew few details. The Dalai Lama listened to Namseling's report in dismay, wondering about the extent of the destruction.

Soon afterward, Tara's courier arrived at Riwo Dechen and presented Tara's urgent letter to Phala, asking him to give it to the Dalai Lama as soon as possible. In his chambers on the top floor, the Dalai Lama read the letter, and learned of the catastrophes at Chakpori Hill and the Norbulingka.

Devastated, the Dalai Lama reflected that his years of effort had amounted to nothing: he had not been able to prevent the outbreak of war. The Chinese had moved on to a new phase, he realized, discarding their veneer of cooperation with him and cautious "management" of Tibet.[4] Apparently undaunted by the prospect of world disapproval, they had shut off any possibility of dialogue with him. The handwriting was on the wall for Tibet, and for him: now he had no choice but to cross directly into India, abandoning his original plan to try to negotiate with the Chinese again.

That evening, Athar radioed the CIA to report that he had found the Dalai Lama. The congratulatory reply came instantly. Five days after leaving the Norbulingka, the Dalai Lama had finally established contact with the outside world. This radio exchange was also the US government's first confirmation of his whereabouts.[5]

The Dalai Lama spent a comfortable night at Riwo Dechen Monastery, but it was not safe to linger. The largest PLA garrison in Lhokha was barely twenty miles away, in Tsethang. The escape party would have to press on toward Lhuntse Dzong, near the Indian border, where they planned to announce a provisional government.

The next morning, March 23, a group of Chushi Gangdruk guerrillas arrived for an audience with the Dalai Lama. He found himself caught in a moral quandary: on the one hand was the massacre and suppression of his people, but on the other was his religion's tenet of nonviolence. Resistance was suicidal, but renouncing it entirely would mean helplessly awaiting the worst. At a loss for substantive recommendations for the guerrillas, he exhorted them simply to preserve themselves and avoid provoking the Chinese. Next, his officials consulted with the guerrillas about the PLA threat to the Dalai Lama in Lhokha and the arrangements for his rear guard. After this conversation, Kunga Samten and his men left the Dalai Lama's escort and headed back to Gongkar to stave off any PLA pursuers.[6]

By that time it was noon, and the travelers pressed on. Ahead loomed a forbidding peak called Dongkar, or "White Conch Mountain," which they ascended in the bitter cold for two hours. Finally, they arrived at a pristine glacier on top, and slid across treacherous ice to the other side.

After Dongkar, they came to Dhargye Ling, which was Ling Rinpoché's home monastery, and he had gone ahead to make arrangements. There they fortified themselves with a good night's rest before attacking the infamous pass at Yarto Tag, a snowy peak that juts up into the sky like a gleaming sword, reaching almost twenty-two thousand feet above sea level.

They were on the road again at five the next morning, March 24. Braving snow, wind, and thin air, they plodded to the top of the steep slope, where they found a broad vista of lush pastureland and an icy lake mirroring the sun.

After an eleven-hour trek, the weary travelers reached Eh Chumdogyang,[7] a tiny hamlet of a few hundred people known only for its foul weather and barren soil. A Tibetan saying goes, "Better to be born an animal in good pastureland than a human in Eh Chumdogyang."

Here Athar and Lhotse distributed their cache of airdropped weapons to the Tibetan soldiers in the Dalai Lama's inner tier of guards. Each received a rifle with a hundred bullets and a handgun with thirty bullets. There was also a mortar, one of the two that had arrived in the second CIA airdrop on February 22. The other had gone to the Chushi Gangdruk forces.[8]

The cabinet ministers drew up plans for the new provisional government and sent some men ahead to Lhuntse Dzong to make arrangements for the consecration ceremony.

That night the travelers could barely find room to sleep in the tiny village, and some of them had to spend the night in the livestock sheds.

On March 25, the group crossed Shobo Tag Pass and reached Kathang Monastery.

The grueling journey failed to put a damper on Ngari Rinpoché's high spirits. He was fascinated by Athar and Lhotse, with their advanced weapons, mysterious box, and team of special guards. When the travelers arrived at camp each night, everyone else set about refreshing themselves, but these two always disappeared right away with their box. Eventually they would reappear and join the others in tea and conversation, never letting the box out of their sight. Ngari Rinpoché found them very odd, but it was beyond his comprehension that these two men were making it possible for the American CIA, on the other side of the globe, to update President Eisenhower daily on the Dalai Lama's progress.[9]

: : :

At 8:00 A.M. Lhasa time on Thursday, March 26, the Dalai Lama's entourage arrived at Lhuntse Dzong, the last district in Tibet on the way to the Indian border. They had been on the road for nine days.[10]

The Tibetan system established by the Fifth Dalai Lama in 1642 had been reduced to this tiny band of a few dozen officials, three cabinet ministers, a few high-ranking army officers and their men, a senior lama, and the Dalai Lama's two tutors. Now that Lhasa had fallen, the Dalai Lama sensed that the very survival of the Tibetan people depended on his own survival and that of his government.

The consecration ceremony was conducted with great fanfare at the small castle in Lhuntse Dzong. A long line of thousands of local people greeted the Dalai Lama with white prayer scarves, singing and dancing, and loud blasts on longhorns and conch shells. Then the Dalai Lama and his tutors shared the traditional bowl of buttered rice and silverweed root with the local monks, after which they held services in the prayer hall on the second floor and went back downstairs.

Decked out in his official finery, Chief Minister Surkhang stood at the top of the stone steps of the castle, flanked by Shasur, Liushar, Phala, and other officials. Beneath him stood the governor of Lhokha, the commissioner of Lhuntse Dzong, the lamas and abbots of the eight monasteries in the district, hundreds of Tibetan soldiers, and thousands of local people. Because of the events in Lhasa, Surkhang intoned, and on the orders of the Dalai Lama, he hereby repudiated the Seventeen-Point Agreement and established the provisional government of Tibet, with Lhuntse Dzong—renamed "Victory Lhuntse"—as its temporary capital. Surkhang also announced the appointment of Lukhangwa, who was in India, and

Lobsang Tashi, who had stayed in Lhasa, as acting prime ministers. The Dalai Lama affixed his official signature to the proclamation. Then the local people sang celebratory songs and Lhotse fired the mortar into the air three times. The ceremony concluded with a prayer service for the Dalai Lama's health, longevity, and success.

At Lhuntse Dzong, the Dalai Lama wrote letters to Lukhangwa, Lobsang Tashi, and Chushi Gangdruk commander Gonpo Tashi.

His letter to Gonpo Tashi cited his exceptional valor and contributions to the Tibetan religion and polity, bestowed him with the esteemed rank of *dzasa,* and presented him with a set of prayer beads and a holy figurine. Gonpo Tashi had been so busy trying to organize his scattered resistance forces that he had not learned of the events in Lhasa until March 22, when he caught an All-India Radio news broadcast while he was in a remote part of Tibet.[11]

Athar reported the provisional government's formation to the CIA, and received a prompt reply with congratulations and an offer to send people to help with any specific plans. Athar relayed the message to Phala.

"Can the United States send an airplane to rescue us if we have trouble on the way?" Phala asked.

This reply brought Athar's long-standing exasperation with the Tibetan government back to the fore. Ever since the onset of trouble in Kham in 1956, the Tibetan government had passively clung to its shrinking mandate, unable to adapt and respond to the swiftly developing challenges of the times.

He told Phala that he and Lhotse had already chosen two sites, one suitable for an airdrop and the other for an airplane landing, adding that the Americans had made repeated offers to help, but had been hamstrung by the Tibetan government's lack of concrete plans.

After a moment's pause, Phala replied that the news of the fighting in Lhasa had prompted the decision to proceed directly to India instead of staying in Lhuntse Dzong to try to negotiate with the Chinese. He told Athar to ask the US government to arrange with India for the Dalai Lama's asylum, and Athar radioed the request immediately to the CIA.[12]

In Washington, DC, CIA director Allen Dulles reported to President Eisenhower that he was fairly certain the Dalai Lama would soon cross the border.[13]

: : :

They spent the night at Teulhey[14] Monastery, slightly beyond Lhuntse Dzong. There they had another planning meeting. The urgency of the situation now demanded that they take the quickest route to India, through Tsona, abandoning all thought of traveling through Bhutan. Since they had been cut off from communication on the road, however, Phala did not know whether the Indian government had granted them asylum. Two fourth-rank officials—Tsangchen Kelsang Tubten and Phala's brother, Phalasey Wangchuk—were sent ahead to the border to seek official permission for the Dalai Lama to enter. Their orders were to bring back a reply as soon as possible, without stopping anywhere along the way.

All agreed there was no time to lose, as the Chinese might be close behind. The Dalai Lama sent his mother and sister ahead.

The entourage set out from Teulhey Monastery before dawn on March 27. This was a formidable stretch of mountainous road. The travelers lost sight of the path in the thick blanket of snow, trudging in the wrong direction for hours before finally retracing their steps to their original starting point. Lacking snow goggles, most people shielded their eyes with their hair or strips of dark cloth. Their breath froze, dusting their beards with frost. They crossed Lagoe Pass, where gloomy clouds enshrouded the snowcapped peaks and a piercing wind chilled them to the bone, walking close beside their horses to keep warm. On the other side of the pass, the weather improved and the snow started to melt. Finally they reached the village of Jhora in the late afternoon. India was getting closer, and all breathed a sigh of relief.

The next morning, Saturday March 28, they left Jhora at daybreak and continued toward Tsona via Karpo Pass. The sky was a brilliant blue, but the wind was biting, and the sun glare blinded them as they filed across the vast snowy landscape.[15] The Dalai Lama and his cabinet had no idea that Chinese premier Zhou Enlai promulgated an "Order of the State Council" dissolving their government on that very day. Nor did they know that the *New York Times* was carrying headline news dated March 27 from Kalimpong: "Tibetans' Revolt Said to Be Failing; Dalai Lama Flees." The article said the Chinese had imposed a dawn-to-dusk curfew and were issuing official radio broadcasts from Lhasa, and that former cabinet ministers Ngabo and Sampo Tsewang Rigzin were disseminating "appeals to the populace to cooperate with the Chinese authorities." The article concluded with tragic detail: "According to one report received here today, Chinese troops were on continuous duty for twelve hours burning the bodies of the fallen on the banks of the [Kyichu] River."[16]

While they were crossing Karpo Pass, the travelers heard a roar in the sky. A silvery unmarked dual-engine plane was approaching from the southwest.

"A plane!" someone shouted. Everyone panicked and scattered in all directions. Some people ducked behind boulders and others dropped flat to the ground.

The Dalai Lama, Ngari Rinpoché, Chief of Staff Gadrang, and Security Chief Phuntsok, who happened to be near each other, stood on a thawed patch of ground and prayed to the Three Jewels—the Buddha, the Dharma, and the Sangha (monastic community)—for protection. Some of the Chushi Gangdruk guerrillas cocked their rifles at the plane.

"Don't shoot! We don't know who they are!" shouted Phala.

All eyes were on the plane as it flew straight northwest and vanished like a mirage, leaving the travelers to wonder as they collected themselves and resumed their trek. Everyone was convinced the plane had been looking for the Dalai Lama, although some thought it was from the Indian government and others were sure it was from the Chinese Communists. There was no indication that it had spotted them.[17] No nation has ever claimed responsibility for the unmarked plane, and it has remained a mystery ever since.

There were people standing in the snow on the other side of Karpo Pass: an official welcoming group from Tsona, who burst into sobs at the sight of their beleaguered ruler.[18]

In the middle of the night on March 28 in Washington, DC, an urgent cable arrived for Desmond Fitzgerald, head of the CIA Far Eastern Division. It was from Athar, with a request that the US government negotiate asylum for the Dalai Lama in India. Normally such matters needed approval from the top echelons of government—even the president—before they could be acted upon. But Fitzgerald realized that the chain of command could be dangerously slow in this case, especially since it was a weekend. Instead, he forwarded the request to the American embassy in New Delhi, flagging it as urgent.

Six hours later, Fitzgerald received his reply: Prime Minister Nehru was ready to welcome the Dalai Lama and his entourage into India.[19]

: : :

New challenges presented themselves once the escape party reached Tsona. Which of the five routes to Tawang[20] would be best? Who should go with the Dalai Lama into India? What kind of rear guard should be put into place after he had left Tsona? The risks seemed heightened by the possibility that an outpouring of refugees into Lhokha might draw PLA pursuers into the area, yet no one in the Dalai Lama's entourage had enough military experience to be sure of what to do.

They finally chose to travel via the village of Mangmang; the other four routes, while shorter, were hazardous at that time of year. They also decided that a small contingent of soldiers would escort the Dalai Lama into India, while most stayed behind as a rear guard.[21] All civilians were to go with the Dalai Lama.

Once these questions were resolved, Chief Cabinet Minister Surkhang sat down by candlelight and drafted an initial press statement for the Dalai Lama to release from India.[22]

The next morning, March 29, the local people cleared the road of snow, and the group left Tsona. As they traveled southward, they gradually descended from the rugged Himalayas into a lush, green valley.

Mangmang, inhabited by the Monpa, an ethnic minority, was the last Tibetan outpost before the border. There the Dalai Lama found the two men he had sent ahead to obtain permission for him to enter India, and they had accomplished their mission: Indian officials were on their way to welcome him at the border outpost of Chhuthangmo.

Mangmang was the first place the Dalai Lama felt safe from the PLA since leaving Lhasa. The little village was packed with Khampa guerrillas and Tibetan Army soldiers, all standing guard. But the weather was hot and humid, and the Dalai Lama ended up sleeping in a leaky tent in the rain. After a poor night's rest he awoke with a fever and dysentery, but his physician had been left behind in Lhasa. Luckily, Security Chief Phuntsok had brought along another dose of the pills that had cured the

Dalai Lama during his *Geshe* examinations at Ganden Monastery a few months earlier. Phuntsok gave the Dalai Lama a pill and took him to a nearby hut to rest. However, with livestock pens on the ground floor, roosters crowing on the roof, and barking dogs everywhere, the Dalai Lama endured a second sleepless night.

It was Tuesday, March 31, the twenty-second day of the second month of the Earth-Hog year. Although Mangmang seemed safe, it was time to move on.

Just north of the border, the Chushi Gangdruk guerrillas and the Tibetan Army soldiers stood in formation for a farewell salute.[23]

Athar asked Phala if he had brought enough money from the government coffers in Lhasa, and Phala replied that he had not. Athar donated all the cash he and Lhotse had. Then he watched the Dalai Lama disappear into the distance, and climbed a hill with his radio to send a final message: "The Dalai Lama and his officials arrived safely at the India border March 31 . . . XXXX will return from the Indian border to Tsona Dzong, 1 April. . . . Please inform the world about the suffering of the Tibetan people. To make us free from the misery of the Chinese Communist operations. . . ."[24]

This was a watershed moment in history: the Tibetan people were forever divided into two.

Ashen-faced and racked with dysentery, the Dalai Lama approached the border astride a yak. He had reached the homeland of the Buddha.[25]

Behind him in Lhasa, his people faced ruin. Ahead of him lay a vast, unfamiliar world.

Epilogue

MAO'S PLA REINFORCEMENTS arrived in Tibet after the Battle of Lhasa to complete his plans and "pacify the rebellion." The strife continued and the casualties were legion: a classified PLA Tibet Military Command publication boasted that the PLA "neutralized" more than 87,000 "rebel bandits" between March 1959 and October 1960.[1] On April 14, 1959, two weeks after the Dalai Lama reached India, the PLA sealed off the route he had used through Tsona. Nonetheless, Chushi Gangdruk commander Gonpo Tashi managed a harrowing escape into India soon afterward with 126 of his guerrillas and 40 Tibetan Army soldiers from Regiment 2.[2]

After dissolving the Tibetan government in Lhasa on March 28, the Chinese State Council proceeded to disband the Chamdo Liberation Committee on April 20. In late May, the CCP Tibet Work Committee drafted comprehensive plans to redraw Tibetan administrative regions, replace Tibetan currency with Chinese yuan, impose Communist policies on the monasteries, and confiscate weapons. The CCP Tibet Work Committee grouped 120 cadres into 12 task forces to take over local administrations around Tibet. The PLA Tibet Military Command also sent 800 cadres into the local administrations, and dispatched 5,700 cadres and soldiers, divided into task forces, to enforce Communist policies.[3] Tibetan refugees continued to pour by the tens of thousands into neighboring countries, as the Chinese Communists embarked on a series of political campaigns in Tibet—from Land Reform through People's Communes and the Cultural Revolution—analogous to those conducted in China. In the midst of this process, in September 1965, the Tibet Autonomous Region was established, making Tibet formally a province of China.

In 1966 the Cultural Revolution reached Tibet. All but 529 of its 2,676 monasteries had been devastated between 1959 and 1961,[4] and the rest were mostly damaged or destroyed during the Cultural Revolution. Tibetan culture itself—language, religion, and way of life—was placed in jeopardy of extinction. Even the Panchen Lama ended up in jail from 1966 until 1975; although the Chinese had anointed him chairman of the PCART in the Dalai Lama's place in 1959, expecting him to continue to serve as a puppet, he eventually spoke out against Chinese ill-treatment of the Tibetans.[5]

The Chinese Communists may have thought they had subjugated Tibet, and that its people were well on the road to assimilation. But they underestimated the strength of Tibetan religious convictions and sense of ethnic identity.

After decades without contact, Deng Xiaoping initiated a dialogue with the Tibetan government-in-exile in 1979, and the Dalai Lama sent his first fact-finding delegation to Tibet. Wherever it went, Tibetans poured by the thousands into the streets to pay their respects.[6]

: : :

The refugee crisis was the first challenge the young Dalai Lama faced after his arrival in India. Tibetans continued to pour across the border, many fleeing empty-handed, without any prospects. Thousands perished of infectious disease and heatstroke while employed in road construction in northern India, but still the numbers grew. The Dalai Lama worked with the Indian, Nepalese, Sikkimese, and Bhutanese governments to create refugee settlements; by 1969 there were twenty-four settlements in India and a number in neighboring countries, and more settlements were added in later years.

The Dalai Lama's main task, however, was to model a Tibetan path to modernity as a counterweight to that presented by the Chinese Communists. Long convinced that Tibet should be governed "through democratic institutions based on social and economic justice,"[7] he founded the Tibetan government-in-exile at Dharamsala, with a modern constitution and an elected Parliament, and he eventually vested all executive authority in the elected prime minister.[8] The new government enacted religious reforms and created a comprehensive educational system from kindergarten through high school. The "great three" monastic universities—Sera, Drepung, and Ganden—were reestablished in southern India with updated curricula, while Tibetan youth also began to seek higher education in colleges abroad.

The Dalai Lama received the Nobel Peace Prize in 1989 for his advocacy of "peaceful solutions based upon tolerance and mutual respect in order to preserve the historical and cultural heritage of his people."[9] He has become a spiritual leader of world stature, fostering a rebirth of Tibetan culture and religion and bringing them from relative obscurity to worldwide attention. While the Dalai Lama does not—despite Chinese rhetoric to the contrary—personally advocate outright independence for Tibet, recommending instead a "middle way," his activities have garnered widespread international support for the Tibetan cause.[10]

The Dalai Lama's advocacy of peace and compassion has stood in sharp contrast to the Chinese Communist ideology of class struggle for more than half a century. In an unexpected turn of events for Mao and his followers, their violent tactics did not resolve "the Tibet question." In fact, Tibet has grown so much in importance that China now defines it as a "core interest": an issue of China's sovereignty, territorial integrity, and national stability. Despite all efforts to stop them, Tibetan refugees continue to flee across the Himalayas, while Tibetan protestors within China set themselves on fire and turmoil erupts periodically in Lhasa. Almost sixty years have passed since the Dalai Lama escaped from Lhasa. His picture is banned there, yet his spirit has never left the "land of the snows."

: : :

The March 1959 events in Lhasa altered not only the course of Tibetan history, but also the fates of many individuals.

Tenpa Soepa was captured after the fall of the Norbulingka and imprisoned for twenty years, until March 14, 1979. In May 1980, he obtained permission to go to India, and soon left for Dharamsala, taking along his most prized possession: a recent professional photograph of himself with his aging father.[11] He served in the Dalai Lama's government-in-exile until his retirement in 1995, and died in 2011 at the age of seventy-eight.

Jampa Tenzin was jailed during the battle at the Jokhang Temple and did twelve years of hard labor in prison work gangs in Lhasa, building the Lhasa Stadium and the General Hospital of the PLA Tibet Military Command. He completed his sentence in 1971, but was then detained in labor camps for ten more years. As a man of forty-five, he finally returned to his home near Barkor Street. In 1983, he obtained permission to go to

India, where he reentered the monastic fold and assumed a post in the Dalai Lama's private office.[12]

Tara caught up with the Dalai Lama at Tsona, although he stayed behind with the rear guard for a few days after the Dalai Lama proceeded to India. Then he followed the Dalai Lama to Dharamsala, where he continued to serve as his personal secretary until his retirement in 2001.[13] He died in 2013 at the age of ninety-three.

Juchen Tubten had slipped away across the hills south of the Rama Gang ferry on the night of March 20, and spent the next few months as a guerrilla in Lhokha. In June, he led approximately seventy guerrillas into India, eventually arriving in Dharamsala. He served the government-in-exile in a number of distinguished positions, including minister of information and speaker of the Parliament. As a member of the Dalai Lama's first fact-finding delegation to Tibet in August 1979, he saw his long-lost wife and children. They had had no news of each other for more than twenty years, and Juchen Tubten had remarried in India. He died in New Delhi in August 2011, at the age of eighty-two.[14]

After escorting the Dalai Lama to the Indian border, Athar and Lhotse continued to coordinate CIA airdrops into Lhokha until the resistance effort failed, when they left Tibet. Lhotse died in the 1960s. Athar spent a number of years in Nepal and Darjeeling; later he helped train Tibetan CIA agents at Camp Hale in Colorado and worked to aid the guerrilla efforts that continued from Mustang, Nepal. He immigrated to the United States in the 1990s and died in August 2001 in New York. The youngest of the first batch of Tibetan CIA trainees, he was the last to pass away. In compliance with his wishes, some of his ashes were scattered in Dharamsala and the rest in Lithang, his homeland.[15]

Thinley Phuntsok, who was at home on Ling Rinpoché's Lhasa estate when it was captured on March 21, was arrested, jailed, and released, but then imprisoned again as a "counterrevolutionary" from 1970 to 1980. In 1983, he escaped to Dharamsala, where he worked for the government-in-exile until his retirement. He moved to the United States in 2008.[16]

Upon reaching India with the Dalai Lama, Ngari Rinpoché attended an English-language boarding school in Darjeeling. Later he fulfilled his long-held dream of the soldierly life by enlisting in the Special Frontier Force of the Indian Army, a unit comprised mostly of Tibetans at the time.[17] He was an early organizer of the Tibetan Youth Congress, a major pro-independence NGO. He stayed in Dharamsala, the only member of the Dalai Lama's family to remain by his side all along.

Tubten Khetsun surrendered at the Norbulingka and spent four years in "reform through labor," working on a series of construction projects in and around Lhasa. Released in 1963, he stayed in Lhasa for the next twenty years, spanning the Cultural Revolution. In 1983, he went to Nepal, and later immigrated to the United States.[18]

Sampo Tsewang Rigzin, the Tibetan cabinet minister who had been injured by stone-throwing demonstrators on March 10, 1959, recovered and participated in the Chinese Communist government after the fall of Lhasa. He was nonetheless denounced during the Cultural Revolution in 1967 on charges of having been a "leader of the armed rebellion" in March, 1959. He died in disgrace in 1973, and was posthumously rehabilitated six years later.[19]

Former cabinet minister Ngabo stayed in Tibet at first, eventually moving to Beijing. On March 28, 1959, he was appointed deputy chairman and secretary general of the PCART, and later held a number of other positions of authority, including president of the TAR and deputy chairman of the Standing Committee of the National People's Congress. Zhou Enlai himself shielded him from attack during the Cultural Revolution. When he died in Beijing in 2009 at the age of ninety-nine, both Beijing and Dharamsala eulogized him for his service.[20]

In Dharamsala, Phuntsok Tashi continued to serve in the Tibetan exile government. In 1964, his wife Tsering Dolma—the Dalai Lama's eldest sister—passed away, and he later remarried; his second wife, Kesang Yangkyi Takla, was also a Tibetan government figure. Phuntsok wrote a valuable three-volume memoir, *A Life;* he also went to Tibet as a member of the Dalai Lama's first fact-finding delegation in 1979. In 1989 he moved to London, and he passed away in Dharamsala in 1999.[21]

Lord Chamberlain Phala, with his extraordinary organizational skills, became the Tibetan exile government's first diplomat: the official representative at the Dalai Lama's first foreign Tibet Office, established in Geneva in 1964.[22] He died in Switzerland in 1985.

: : :

General Tan Guansan's premature military action—undercutting Mao's plan to eradicate the opposition all at once—meant that it took China three more years to crush the resistance in outlying areas. Nonetheless,

Tan escaped punishment thanks to his stunning victory in Lhasa, and was appointed first vice-president of the Supreme People's Court in 1966. He was persecuted as a "capitalist roader" during the Cultural Revolution, however, finally resurfacing in a sinecure as advisor to the PLA Chengdu Military Command in 1978. He died of illness on December 6, 1985, and his ashes were interred at the August First Farm in Lhasa, one of the artillery camps he used to shell the Norbulingka.[23]

After being purged as an "ultra-rightist" in 1958, General Fan Ming was incarcerated for the next twenty-two years, starting in a labor camp in the Changbai Mountains on China's border with North Korea. He was transferred to another camp at Dali in Shaanxi Province because of illness, and then thrown into Qincheng Prison in Beijing in September 1962 on charges of associating with the "Peng Dehuai anti-Party clique."[24] In 1980, he was rehabilitated and appointed deputy chairman of the Shaanxi Committee of the Chinese People's Political Consultative Congress. He died of illness on February 23, 2010, in Xi'an. His memoir, published in Hong Kong shortly before his death, provides a wealth of information about the behind-the-scenes workings of the Chinese Communist outpost in Lhasa during the 1950s.[25]

General Zhang Guohua was appointed chairman of the Sichuan Revolutionary Committee during the Cultural Revolution, and then served as governor of Sichuan until his sudden death from heart disease while chairing a meeting on February 20, 1972, at the age of fifty-eight.[26]

General Zhang Jingwu, China's top-ranking official in Lhasa, stayed there in 1959 to impose Land Reform in Tibet. After the TAR was established in 1965, he was transferred to Beijing to serve as deputy minister of the United Front Work Department of the Central Committee. He and his wife Yang Gang were cruelly persecuted during the Cultural Revolution. Yang Gang was incarcerated at Qincheng Prison in Beijing and coerced into making "confessions"; eventually, she lost her mind. In 1967, Zhang Jingwu was sent to a May Seventh Cadre School[27] and then locked up in Qincheng Prison, where he suffered savage beatings, finally committing suicide by hunger strike on October 27, 1971. His body was cremated behind closed doors, his ashes were "lost," and his family was not notified of his death until two years after the fact. The Central Committee and the Central Military Commission exonerated him in 1979 and held a memorial service in his honor. With no remains, not even a cinerary urn, the officials in attendance had only a large photograph of him before which to place their wreaths.[28]

Zhang Jingwu was the first high-ranking Chinese Communist and PLA general to cross the Dalai Lama's path. They had met in Dromo on July 16, 1951, when the Dalai Lama was barely sixteen years old, and Zhang was a seasoned, forty-five-year-old general. More significant than the age gap, however, was the enormous disparity in their worldviews. Yet the Dalai Lama recalls Zhang as a man who, although blunt and cantankerous, may nonetheless have been "a good person underneath."[29]

Zhang was a staunch Communist and a firm believer in class struggle, as evinced by his 1960 pronouncement on the "pacification" of Tibet: "[This] . . . was not an 'ethnic war.' It was a class war, instigated by a handful of ultrareactionary feudal lords to prevent the Communist Party from leading the large serf class to freedom. This was a class war with no room for compromise."[30] Little did he know that a few years later he himself would be the victim of a similarly uncompromising "class war."

: : :

On May 27, 2009, I interviewed His Holiness the Dalai Lama at his residence in Dharamsala. I asked him what he thought of General Fan Ming.

"A very conservative man," he said with a smile.

I told him that Fan Ming had resumed the practice of Chinese medicine after his release from prison, and had treated many patients gratis in his old age.

"That's very good," he commented, smiling again.

I started to tell him that Zhang Jingwu had been hounded to death during the Cultural Revolution, but he interrupted me.

"I know, I know," he said quietly.

I glanced up at him. His face was sad, and his eyes gleamed with tears.

Ngari Rinpoché, Tenpa Soepa, Jampa Tenzin, and the Dalai Lama's three secretaries all fell silent.

A solemn hush descended over the room.

NOTES

Note: Tibetan-language sources are generally listed by their English titles, without page numbers.

PREFACE TO THE ENGLISH EDITION

1. Established by the Nationalists (Guomindang) in 1939 and dissolved by the Communists in 1955, Xikang was a province largely corresponding to Kham, although it also included portions of Ngaba (in traditional Amdo), and Liangshan (inhabited by the Yi nationality). Chamdo, nominally also part of Xikang, was ruled by Lhasa from 1918 until the Chinese Communists took it over in 1950. Kham is divided by the Drichu (Chinese: Jinsha) River; to the west is Chamdo (in today's TAR), and to the east are the ethnically Tibetan areas of Garzê (in today's Sichuan), Yulshul (in today's Qinghai), and Dechen (in Yunnan). During the 1950s, the Chinese created the Ngaba, and the Garzê, Tibetan Autonomous Regions in Sichuan. (See Map 2.)
2. Chinese: Dege, Baiyu, and Muli.
3. Chinese: Zhuoni.
4. https://en.wikipedia.org/wiki/Seventeen_Point_Agreement_for_the_Peaceful_Liberation_of_Tibet.
5. *Zhonggong Xizang dangshi dashiji, 1949–1966*, 70.
6. For an early (1957) exposition of this policy, see "Zhonggong dui 'Xizang gongwei guanyu jinhou Xizang gongzuo de jueding' de pishi," *Xizang de minzhu gaige*, 61.
7. There are no precise numbers for these refugees, but the Dalai Lama is on record as having said to Zhou Enlai that "tens of thousands" of them had crossed the border into Tibet in the first half of 1956 alone. Jiangbian Jiacuo (Jampel Gyatso), *Mao Zedong yu Dalai, Banchan*, 187–188.
8. I present more detailed research on the tactics—including the military—used by the Chinese to impose their policies on the Tibetan regions of China during this early period in my book, *Dang tieniao zai tiankong feixiang, 1956–1962: Qingzhang gaoyuan shang de mimi zhanzheng.*
9. Apei Awangjinmei (Ngabo), "1959 nian '3 yue 10 ri shijian' de zhenxiang." See the Bibliography for different editions.
10. The title *rinpoché* is used for highly venerated teachers or reincarnate lamas.

11. Dhargye, the late governor of the Golog Tibetan Autonomous Prefecture of Qinghai.
12. There are, however, a number of cases where it seemed sensible to retain the Chinese terms at times, for example: Shannan (Lhokha), the Lhasa River (Tibetan: Kyichu), the Jinsha River (Tibetan: Drichu), Xunhua (Tibetan: Yadzi), Hainan (Tibetan: Tsolho), and Haidong (Tibetan: Tsoshar).
13. Haidong, for example, became a prefecture in 1978, and most of the current administrative divisions in the TAR date to 1960, although they are continually being updated.
14. Such variations are found, for example, between Chen Guangsheng and An Caidan, *Changjian Zangyu renming diming cidian* and Tsering Wangyal Shawa, *Tibet Township Map and Place Name Index.*
15. "Guanyu Dalai Lama huiguo de wutiao fangzhen," Renminwang, at http://cpc.people.com.cn/GB/64184/64186/66702/4495501.html.

PROLOGUE

1. Jamchen Chokhor Ling (often referred to as "Lithang Monastery"), one of the largest monasteries in Kham (present-day Sichuan), was established in 1580 by the Third Dalai Lama, Sonam Gyatso. See Chapter 1 for more on the destruction of the monastery, which occurred in 1956.
2. The source of this story is my 2009 interview with Geshe Lobsang, who was born after the events he narrates. "Geshe" is a title indicating that one holds the *Geshe* degree, an advanced academic degree in Tibetan Buddhism.
3. "Rebel bandits" (or simply "rebels") is the standard Chinese Communist label for Tibetans who rose up against their policies.
4. Yorupon was the title of Sonam Wangyal, the latest in a centuries-old lineage of headmen in the Bumyak grasslands of the Garzê (Chinese: Ganzi) Tibetan Autonomous Prefecture in Sichuan (in the traditional Tibetan province of Kham).
5. The ages given in this book may reflect the Tibetan system, in which one is considered to be one year old at birth.
6. The suffix "la" is the customary Tibetan respectful form of address.
7. Ratuk Ngawang, *The Fearless Defense of Lithang by Monastics and Civilians against Invasion (1936–1959).*
8. *Ganzi zhouzhi*, 50.

1. THE SEEDS OF WAR

1. This story is based on personal interviews with Juchen Tubten, who became an official in the Tibetan government-in-exile after the events de-

scribed in this book. His account of this episode is also largely corroborated in an official Chinese source: *Dege xianzhi*, 25–28, 311.

2. Chinese: Kangding.
3. In his seminal speech of February 1958, Li Weihan, head of China's United Front Bureau, designated "Democratic Reforms" as the formal term to be used in the minority regions, but specified that the process was analogous to "Land Reform" in the Han areas.
4. The Guomindang (The Chinese Nationalist Party, or "Nationalists") governed China from 1928 until 1949, when they were defeated by the Chinese Communists in the Chinese Civil War and retreated to the island of Taiwan.
5. Qin Heping, "Cong fandui tusi dao jieshou minzhugaige—guanyu Xiakedaodeng de yanjiu," 75.
6. Author interview with Juchen Tubten, September 22, 2009.
7. Philip C. C. Huang, "Rural Class Struggle in the Chinese Revolution," 105 (Huang Zongzhi, "Zhongguo geming zhong de nongcun jieji douzheng," 66).
8. Chinese: Jinsha River. The Tibetan syllable "chu" in Drichu denotes a river, so the translation "Drichu River," while readable, is redundant.
9. *Dege xianzhi*, 23; Qin Heping, "Cong fandui tusi dao jieshou minzhu gaige—guanyu Xiakedaodeng de yanjiu," 67.
10. Qin Heping, "Cong fandui tusi dao jieshou minzhu gaige—guanyu Xiakedaodeng de yanjiu," 74.
11. Mao Tse-tung [Mao Zedong], *Selected Works of Mao Tse-tung*, 5:35.
12. *Ganzi Zangzu zizhizhou minzhu gaigeshi*, 40–41; *Dangdai Zhongguo minzu gongzuo dashiji, 1949–1988*, 1:75.
13. The source of this story is an unpublished 2013 personal interview with distinguished Tibetan Communist Yangling Dorje, who was present and shared this sentiment, even to the point of writing a letter to Liao Zhigao to express his concern about the haste of the Chinese program.
14. Qin Heping and Ran Linwen, *Sichuan minzu diqu minzhu gaige dashiji*, 33. The proposal also included the Tibetan Autonomous Region of Sichuan (soon to become Ngaba).
15. *Ganzi Zangzu zizhizhou minzhu gaigeshi*, 48.
16. Ibid., 45.
17. *Zhongguo gongchandang Sichuansheng Degexian zuzhishi ziliao, 1950–1993*, 16.
18. *Dege xianzhi*, 26.
19. Li Weihan's announcement was made at the Fifth National Congress for United Front Work (Qin Heping, *Sichuan minzu diqu minzhu gaige ziliaoji*, 78).
20. Zhang Xiangming, *Zhang Xiangming wushiwunian Xizang gongzuo shilu*, 69.
21. This was a Qing dynasty administrative unit used in the Tibetan regions until it was abolished by the Chinese Communists.

22. "Living Buddhas" is the English translation of the Chinese term for *tulku* (Tibetan: sPrul sku; Sanskrit: Nirmanakaya), the reincarnation of a recently deceased lama, recognized by his disciples and installed as his successor. Some, such as the successive *dalai lamas,* are considered to be bodhisattvas. Although the Chinese rendition of the term is inaccurate, it will be translated literally into English in direct quotations of Chinese sources.
23. Qin Heping and Ran Linwen, *Sichuan minzu diqu minzhu gaige dashiji,* 79.
24. Mao's advocacy of the violent treatment of "class enemies" pervades his writings. For example: "A revolution is not a dinner party. . . . A revolution is an insurrection, an act of violence by which one class overthrows another." "Report on an Investigation of the Peasant Movement in Hunan" [March 1927], Mao Tse-tung [Mao Zedong], *Selected Works of Mao Tse-tung,* 1:28.
25. For a standard Chinese Marxist exposition dated September 15, 1956, see Liu Shaoqi, "Liu Shaoqi zuo zhengzhi baogao," at http://cpc.people.com.cn/GB/64162/64168/64560/65452/4526551.html. For a recent critical exposé, see Dikötter, *The Tragedy of Liberation.* See also Xie Youtian, *Xiangcun shehui de huimie.*
26. Jamyang Norbu, *Warriors of Tibet,* 110–111.
27. According to official statistics, the total population of the Tibetan regions of Sichuan in 1950 was 580,000. In 1958, it was 686,234. I deduced the 1956 figure for the total population from those of 1950 and 1958. See *Sichuan Zangzu renkou,* 23–24.
28. Qin Heping, *Sichuan minzu diqu minzhu gaige ziliaoji,* 42.
29. Chinese: Seda.
30. Chinese: Baiyu.
31. The area traditionally known as Chakdu (Tibetan: Nyarong) was renamed Xinlong County when the People's Liberation Army (PLA) took it over in July 1957.
32. *Ganzi zhouzhi,* 49.
33. The sixteen thousand Tibetan rebels had eight thousand guns. *Ganzi Zangzu zizhizhou junshizhi,* 185.
34. Jamyang Norbu, *Warriors of Tibet,* 105.
35. *Xinlongxian wenshi ziliao diyiji—jianguo wushinian Xinlong zhi bianhua zhuanji,* 54.
36. Author interview with Lodi Gyari, May 14, 2009. Lodi Gyari is Dorje Yudon's son; she and her husband, Gyari Nyima, eventually escaped to India.
37. Chinese: Aba. This area is now known as the Ngaba Tibetan and Qiang Autonomous Prefecture.

38. These numbers reflect the March 13 and 18 uprisings in Troskyab and Barkham, in the Ngaba region, but they do not reflect uprisings that occurred from April onward. *Aba Zangzu Qiangzu zizhizhou junshizhi,* 542–543.
39. *Sichuan shengzhi junshizhi,* 295.
40. *Luqu xianzhi,* 328; *Deqin xianzhi,* 9. In addition, there were significant uprisings among the Yi minority in Sichuan and Yunnan at this time, but these are beyond the scope of this book.
41. Mao personally gave the orders for this military action. See *Yunnan shengzhi,* 49:369.
42. Lithang Monastery was bombed on March 29, 1956, and the battle there was concluded the following day. Two thousand four Tibetans are known to have been involved, of whom 311 were killed and 80 were wounded; the rest of this number either surrendered or were captured. The monastery at Chathreng was bombed on April 2. Eighty people inside the monastery are known to have perished in the bombing, but there is no record of the total number of casualties. The monastery at Bathang was bombed on April 7, but casualty figures are unavailable. See *Sichuan shengzhi junshizhi,* 297; *Ganzi Zangzu zizhizhou junshizhi,* 188; and *Yunnan shengzhi,* 49:370. See also my *Dang tieniao zai tiankong feixiang.*
43. Qin Heping, *Sichuan minzu diqu minzhu gaige ziliaoji,* 89.
44. Although the Seventeen-Point Agreement promised to preserve the existing Tibetan system, the PCART—which reported directly to Beijing—in fact overrode the Tibetan government, the Dalai Lama, and the Panchen Lama. It has been described by Mikel Dunham (*Buddha's Warriors,* 139) as "a giant wedge, to be driven into, and fatally crack, Tibet's governing system." The TAR was not formally established until 1965.
45. Jiangbian Jiacuo (Jampel Gyatso), *Li Jue zhuan,* 158–160.
46. The corvée laborer system was a complicated, often abusive, system of unpaid labor levied by local lords, monasteries, and aristocrats on farmers and herdsmen, sometimes as a method of repaying debts.
47. The term "districts" refers to the old Tibetan administrative divisions known as *dzong.*
48. "Jiu jiji xiezhu xiuzhu Kang-Zang gonglu yishi Xizang difang zhengfu gei XX zong bing simiao de tongzhi," *Xizang wenshi ziliao xuanji,* 9:127.
49. "Jinzang riji zhaichao zhi san (5/3/1952–7/25/1952)," ibid., 90.
50. See Tsering Shakya, *The Dragon in the Land of Snows,* 102–103 and 108–111.
51. See "Bada zizhong, gaxia, sandasi daibiao yu Zhang daibiao, Zhang siling jiu 'Guanyu chexiao liang sicai zhiwu he qudi "renmin huiyi" bufa

huodong wenti' jinxing huishang de beiwanglu," *Xizang wenshi ziliao xuanji,* 9:128–129.

52. "In 1953, the Central Committee approved the establishment of two separate song and dance troupes, one for the Dalai Lama and one for the Panchen Lama. After the March 10 Incident of 1959, the two troupes were merged into one, the Tibet Song and Dance Troupe." Jiangbian Jiacuo (Jampel Gyatso), *Mao Zedong yu Dalai, Banchan,* 201. Le Yuhong's diary also mentions the Panchen Lama's troupe. See *Xizang wenshi ziliao xuanji,* 9:85.
53. Chinese texts routinely speak of the Dalai Lama and the Panchen Lama as "Dalai" and "Panchen," omitting the title "Lama." While this is nowhere explained explicitly, it can have subtly contemptuous overtones, and is grating to the Tibetan ear. However, since Chinese usage is inconsistent—and its nuances variable and elusive—"Dalai Lama" and "Panchen Lama" (which are more familiar to English readers) have usually been substituted in this translation.
54. "Jinzang riji zhaichao zhi san (5/3/1952–7/25/1952)," *Xizang wenshi ziliao xuanji,* 9:96.
55. Mao Zedong, *Jianguo yilai Mao Zedong wengao,* 6:113–114.
56. Phuntsok Wangyal (1922–2014), from Bathang County, was the founder of the Tibetan Communist Party, and served as Tibetan-Chinese translator for high-level negotiations such as the Seventeen-Point Agreement and the Dalai Lama's visit to Beijing in 1954. He held a number of important posts in the Chinese administration of Tibet until being imprisoned in 1958. He was rehabilitated in 1978.
57. Phuntsok Wangyal submitted his findings via United Front head, Li Weihan, and the party secretary of Mongolia, Ulanhu. Melvyn Goldstein, Dawei Sherap, and William Siebenschuh, *A Tibetan Revolutionary,* 209–210.
58. Mao Zedong, *Mao Zedong Xizang gongzuo wenxuan,* 147.
59. Zhou Enlai, "Guanyu xibei diqu de minzu gongzuo," *Zhou Enlai tongyi zhanxian wenxuan,* 323–328.
60. *Zhonggong Xizang dangshi dashiji, 1949–1994,* 65.
61. *Xin Zhongguo guofang dashiji, 1955–1960,* at http://www.gf81.com.cn/second_link/gfls/5.html. According to *Sichuan Zangzu renkou,* the Tibetan population of Sichuan was 686,234 in 1958.
62. Dalai Lama, *Freedom in Exile,* 111–112; author interview with the Dalai Lama, June 30, 2009.

2. SUMMIT IN DELHI

1. The Nechung Oracle at the time was the thirteenth, a monk named Lobsang Jigme. In Chinese, Dromo is known as Yadong.

2. Dalai Lama, *Freedom in Exile,* 110–111.
3. According to the system of rankings promulgated by the Chinese State Council in 1956, the Dalai Lama was in the second tier of administrative officialdom, on a par with a vice-premier of the nation, while Zhang Jingwu, Zhang Guohua, and Tan Guansan were provincial military officers in the sixth tier. See Jiangbian Jiacuo (Jampel Gyatso), *Mao Zedong yu Dalai, Banchan,* 124. Fan Ming was probably in the sixth or seventh tier. However, in the three separate (and seemingly parallel) hierarchies of Chinese rank—administrative, military, and Communist Party—the guiding principle was that Party membership outweighed all other considerations.
4. An example of Fan Ming's objectionable behavior is Tibetan Communist Phuntsok Wangyal's story of his arrival with his troops in Lhasa on December 1, 1951. Evidently, Fan insisted on parading his troops around the Barkor despite Zhang Guohua's admonitions that such flaunting of Chinese military power would offend the Tibetans and make the Chinese seem like conquerors rather than friends. Melvyn C. Goldstein, Dawei Sherap, and William Siebenschuh, *A Tibetan Revolutionary,* 166–167.
5. Shi Zhe and Li Haiwen, *Zai lishi juren shenbian,* 380. Mikoyan's memoir does not include this statement by Mao. Shi Zhe was the interpreter at the meeting.
6. Mao Zedong, *Mao Zedong Xizang gongzuo wenxuan,* 4.
7. Ibid., 6.
8. Fan Ming and Hao Rui, *Xizang neibu zhi zheng,* 370.
9. Ibid.
10. The traditional Tibetan province of Kham was divided by the Drichu River between Tibet (Chamdo) and China (Sichuan). For Tibetans, all was "Kham."
11. Zhang Xiangming, *Zhang Xiangming wushiwunian Xizang gongzuo shilu,* 67–68.
12. *Neibu cankao,* September 7, 1956, 187; Cheng Yue, ed., *Zhongguo gongchandang Xizang Changdu diqu lishi dashiji, 1949–2009,* 58.
13. *Zhonggong Xizang dangshi dashiji, 1949–1994,* 70. In the Chinese document, Markham, Dzogang, and Tsakhalho are referred to by their Chinese names: Ningjing, Zuogong, and Yanjing.
14. Dorje Pandatsang ultimately changed his mind and ended up supporting the Communists again.
15. Mao Zedong, *Mao Zedong Xizang gongzuo wenxuan,* 150.
16. Buddhism is considered to have three main branches: Tibetan Buddhism is classified as Vajrayana, or Tantric Buddhism. The other two are Theravada and Mahayana.

17. The Chinese had installed Choekyi Gyaltsen, the Tenth Panchen Lama, as a pro-Beijing puppet in Shigatse, taking advantage of the historic enmity between the courts of Lhasa and Shigatse.
18. Nanjing was the Chinese capital under the Guomindang.
19. Author interview with the Dalai Lama, June 27, 2009.
20. Andrugtsang Gonpo Tashi, *Four Rivers, Six Ranges,* 49–50, 57.
21. Author interview with Kelsang Gyadotsang, May 10, 2009.
22. For the *Tibet Mirror,* see http://goo.gl/C3lWvA.
23. Author interview with Kelsang Gyadotsang, May 10, 2009.
24. The Kyichu River, otherwise known as the Lhasa River, runs along the south side of the city.
25. Sikkim was a British protectorate from 1890 until 1975, after which it became a state of India.
26. Geshe Sherab Gyatso (1884–1968) was born in Xunhua County, Qinghai. He served as vice-governor of Qinghai and also had national standing as a member of the Second National Committee of the Chinese People's Political Consultative Conference.
27. "Tsang Tibet" refers to the region controlled by the Panchen Lama's Administrative Council at Shigatse. At the time, Tibet was divided into three regional administrations; the other two were the Chamdo Liberation Committee and the Lhasa government. All were subsumed under the State Council of China and the PCART.
28. All quotes from Nehru are in his original English wording. This passage and the following one are from *Selected Works of Jawaharlal Nehru,* 2nd ser., 35:520–521.
29. "Suzerainty" is the English term used by Nehru. See ibid.
30. *Zhou Enlai yu Xizang,* 329–333, 387–395. Zhou made the journey to India twice between late November 1956 and January 1957. In order to pressure the Dalai Lama to return to Lhasa, he met with the Dalai Lama three times there, and with his family members and key officials twice.
31. Ibid., 146.
32. The Common Program, an interim constitution of the People's Republic of China, was adopted in 1949 and remained effective until the ratification of the 1954 Constitution.
33. Jiangbian Jiacuo (Jampel Gyatso), *Mao Zedong yu Dalai, Banchan,* 187–188.
34. *Zhou Enlai yu Xizang,* 146.
35. Zhou had a number of private conversations with Nehru during this visit, but formal records are not available.
36. Author interview with the Dalai Lama, June 28, 2009.

37. *Pingxi Xizang panluan,* 111.
38. Mao Zedong, *Mao Zedong Xizang gongzuo wenxuan,* 152–153.
39. The Chinese had infiltrated the Tibetan government and the émigré community in Kalimpong with spies. The CCP Tibet Work Committee and the PLA Tibet Military Command both had Intelligence Committees, which reported separately to the Central Committee. Fan Ming chaired the one at the CCP Tibet Work Committee, while Li Jue was in charge of the one at the PLA Tibet Military Command. See Jiangbian Jiacuo (Jampel Gyatso), *Mao Zedong yu Dalai, Banchan,* 173.
40. In *The Dragon in the Land of Snows,* Tsering Shakya points out (156) that He Long's words must have seemed all the more menacing because of his role as one of the architects of the 1950 invasion of Tibet. Translation of the proverb here is from *My Land and My People* (152), where the Dalai Lama also recalls this anecdote. With the hindsight of history, this episode seems ironic; for all of his swagger during the 1950s, He Long died a miserable death in jail during the Cultural Revolution.
41. Author interview with the Dalai Lama, June 30, 2009.
42. The "Five Principles of Peaceful Coexistence" is a reference to a portion of the Agreement on Trade and Intercourse between India and the Tibet Region of China; this was an outgrowth of the 1914 Simla Accord between British India and Tibet.
43. Nehru, *Selected Works of Jawaharlal Nehru,* 2nd ser., 36:587–603.
44. Ibid., 610–616.
45. *Pingxi Xizang panluan,* 112–115. Here Zhou uses the anachronistic term "Xikang," although the old province had been dissolved.
46. Nehru, *Selected Works of Jawaharlal Nehru,* 2nd ser., 36:610–616.
47. For the McMahon Line, see Map 4.
48. The Agreement on Trade and Intercourse between India and the Tibet Region of China was signed in Beijing on April 29, 1954. (The note quoted is from the original text in *Selected Works of Jawaharlal Nehru.*)
49. Nehru, *Selected Works of Jawaharlal Nehru,* 2nd ser., 36:600–601.
50. For more on the McMahon line, see Lamb, *The McMahon Line,* or Yang Gongsu, *Cangsang jiushinian,* 198–241.
51. Nehru, *Selected Works of Jawaharlal Nehru,* 2nd ser., 36:601.
52. Ibid., 35:598; Patterson, *Requiem for Tibet,* 163.
53. *Pingxi Xizang panluan,* 118–119.
54. Lukhangwa, the anti-Chinese former acting prime minister of Tibet who was forced to resign during the "People's Assembly" episode of 1952, was an exile in Kalimpong. See Chapter 1.

55. *Pingxi Xizang panluan*, 118–119.
56. Gyalwa Karmapa, Rangjung Rigpe Dorje (1924–1981), was the sixteenth successive reincarnated head of the Karma Kagyu sect.
57. Author interview with the Dalai Lama, June 30, 2009.

3. TRAGEDY AT LAKE QINGHAI

1. *Qinghai Zangzu renkou*, preface, 1. The Tibetan presence in Qinghai has now dwindled to approximately 21 percent.
2. In Chinese, respectively: Hainan, Huangnan, Haibei, Guoluo, and Yushu.
3. Tibetan: Tsonub.
4. *Qinghai shengzhi*, 75:87.
5. Tibetan: Yadzi.
6. Later published as "On the Co-operative Transformation of Agriculture," in Mao Tse-tung [Mao Zedong] *Selected Works of Mao Tse-tung*, 5:184–207.
7. See http://books.google.com.hk/books/about/Decisionsonagriculturalcooperation.html?id=pEeyAAAAIAAJ.
8. Qin Heping, *Sichuan minzu diqu minzhu gaige ziliaoji*, 497–503.
9. According to Marxist-Leninist orthodoxy, the transformation was supposed to be a two-stage process.
10. "Wei chedi wancheng Qinghai Sheng muyequ shehui zhuyi geming er douzheng," *Minzu zongjiao gongzuo wenjian huiji, 1949–1959*, 2:1072.
11. Dajie, *Guoluo jianwen yu huiyi*, 112–113.
12. See Jiangbian Jiacuo (Jampel Gyatso), *Shishi Banchan Lama zhuanji*, 98–99. Casualty figures are taken from "Guanyu Xunhua feiluan qingkuang he jinhou yijian de baogao," *Minzu zongjiao gongzuo wenjian huiji, 1949–1959*, 2:1037–1039. The number of deaths comes from "Qinghai shengwei guanyu Xunhua Salazu zizhixian fangeming wuzhuang panluan shijian de jiaoxun de baogao," ibid., 993–999. On April 30, 703 of the arrested were released, and another 400 scheduled for release on May 1. The fate of the rest is unknown (ibid., 1037–1039).
13. "Xunhuaxian dangyuan he zongjiao guanxi de yixie qingkuang," ibid., 555–558.
14. Quotations in this and the preceding paragraph are from "Guanyu Xunhua feiluan qingkuang he jinhou yijian de baogao," ibid., 1037–1039.
15. Chinese: Xinghai.
16. *Xinghai xianzhi*, 346.
17. Ibid.
18. Ibid., 24.
19. "Qinghai shengwei guanyu jiejue 1958 nian pingpan douzheng kuodahua yiliu wenti de qingshi baogao," *Sanzhong quanhui yilai zhongyao wenxian huibian*, 2:960. See also Dajie, *Guoluo jianwen yu huiyi*, 112–113, and Jiangbian

Jiacuo (Jampel Gyatso), *Shishi Banchan Lama zhuanji*, 98. Many statistics and individual cases can also be found in the "Biographies" and "Redress of Injustice" sections of the annals of the autonomous Tibetan prefectures and counties.

20. The "Three Red Banners" were the General Line of Socialist Construction, the Great Leap Forward, and the People's Communes. People's Communes, introduced at this time, were the next level of collectivization after "higher-level Agricultural Producers' Cooperatives." They were large units combining many of the previous cooperatives, in which private ownership was abolished, and the commune managed all labor and land. Communes were divided into "production brigades," which were further divided into "production teams."
21. "Guanyu muyequ shengchu rushe wenti de zhishi," *Minzu zongjiao gongzuo wenjian huiji, 1949–1959*, 2:1115–1118.
22. *Qinghaisheng Zangzu Mengguzu shehui lishi diaocha*, 19.
23. The denouncement was made by Ji Chunguang, chairman of the Qinghai United Front Bureau, at the Twelfth Expanded Meeting of the Qinghai Party Committee in 1959. "Chedi suqing youqing jihuizhuyifenzi Zhang Guosheng tongzhi zai tongzhan gongzuo shang youqing touxiangzhuyi de sixiang yingxiang, jianjue guanche dangde tongyi zhanxian gongzuo wei shehuizhuyi fuwude fangzhen!" *Minzu zongjiao gongzuo wenjian huiji, 1949–1959*, 1:428.
24. "Guanyu muyequ renmingongshe shengchandui, xiaodui de guanli tizhi he jingying guanli zhong jige wenti de zhishi," ibid., 1122–1125.
25. *Xinghai xianzhi*, 346.
26. Tibetan: Tsolho.
27. "Guanyu geng guangfan geng shenrudi kaizhan zhengzhi zhengqu gongzuo de jidian yijian," submitted to the Central Committee on May 24, 1959. *Minzu zongjiao gongzuo wenjian huiji, 1949–1959*, 2:1004–1005.
28. A *dri* is a female of the yak species.
29. "Guanyu geng guangfan geng shenrudi kaizhan zhengzhi zhengqu gongzuo de jidian yijian," submitted to the Central Committee on May 24, 1959. *Minzu zongjiao gongzuo wenjian huiji, 1949–1959*, 2:1003.
30. The calculations herein are based on the statistics found in *Xinghai xianzhi*, chapter 6 of "Dilizhi" and section 3 of "Jingjizhi," which contain puzzling discrepancies.
31. "Guanyu geng guangfan geng shenrudi kaizhan zhengzhi zhengqu gongzuo de jidian yijian," *Minzu zongjiao gongzuo wenjian huiji, 1949–1959*, 2:1006.
32. Gao Feng, "Jixu kefu youqing baoshou, guzu ganjin wei jinnian gengda, geng hao, geng quanmiande yuejin er fendou," ibid., 1:310. The report was

delivered at the Tenth Meeting of the Second Plenum of the Qinghai Party Committee.

33. *Xinghai xianzhi*, 169, 225.
34. "Guanyu zai shaoshu minzu zhong jinxing zhengfeng he shehuizhuyi jiaoyu wenti de baogao," *Minzu zongjiao gongzuo wenjian huiji, 1949–1959*, 2:938–957.
35. The "backyard steel" campaign during the Great Leap Forward required people to melt down their metal possessions in backyard furnaces to make steel. Because the results were usually substandard, the campaign contributed to the economic disaster at the time.
36. Careful scrutiny of Chinese statistics reveals that the Tibetan casualty toll had increased by the end of 1960 and strongly suggests that most of the "neutralized rebels" were unarmed or poorly armed. "By the end of 1960, after more than 3 years of pacifying the rebels, we had fought 108 battles, neutralizing 8,609 rebel bandits, and confiscating 2 machine guns, 5 submachine guns, 30 handguns, 1,613 assorted rifles, 296 flintlocks, 45,200 rounds of ammunition, 5,269 knives, and 14 field glasses" (*Xinghai xianzhi*, 346). The source of the information regarding indiscriminate shooting in "rebel areas" (which also included Golog and Yulshul) is my interview with Dhargye, former governor of the Golog Tibetan Autonomous Prefecture.
37. The Four-Antis Campaign, conducted only in ethnic regions of China, ostensibly targeted "rebellion, law-breaking, privilege, and exploitation."
38. For "Qinghai shengwei dui quansheng zhenya panluan wenti de zhishi," and Mao's comments, see *Minzu zongjiao gongzuo wenjian huiji, 1949–1959*, 2:989–992.
39. Quotations in this and the preceding two paragraphs are from "Qinghai shengwei guanyu Xunhua Salazu zizhixian fangeming wuzhuang panluan shijian de jiaoxun de baogao," ibid., 993–999.
40. "Zhongyang pizhuan 'Qinghai shengwei Guanyu Xunhua Salazu zizhixian fangeming wuzhuang panluan shijian de jiaoxun de baogao,'" ibid., 992–993.
41. "Qinghai shengwei guanyu Xunhua Salazu zizhixian fangeming wuzhuang panluan shijian de jiaoxun de baogao," ibid., 993–999.
42. Du Hua'an, "Guanyu Qinghai sheng minzu gongzuo qingkuang he jinhou yijian de fayan," ibid., 1:468. The speech was given at the Eleventh Conference for National United Front Work on December 18, 1958.
43. Zhang Lihe, "Chuan xibei gaoyuan de Zangchuan fojiao xianzhuang," 44–45.
44. Chinese: Gannan.

45. The four remaining monasteries were Labrang, Tingzin Dhargye Ling, Tso Gompa, and Ganden Shedrup Pekar Drowa Ling.
46. *Zhongguo gongchandang Gannan lishi, 1921.7–2003.7,* 216, 234, 243.
47. Chinese: Ledu.
48. *Ledu xianzhi,* 19.
49. *Mawlas* were leading religious personnel.
50. *Ledu xianzhi,* 310. The report also notes: "We destroyed 9,875,400 clay Buddhist statues, along with sutras and assorted religious objects, confiscated 5,313 rooms, 239 horses, 59 mules, 1,418 cows, and 609 sheep . . . and sent the copper Buddhas and religious objects to be melted down."
51. *Huangzhong xianzhi,* 238.
52. "Wang Feng tongzhi yijiuwubanian shiyue qiri zai lamajiao wenti zuotanhui shangde jianghua," *Minzu zongjiao gongzuo wenjian huiji, 1949–1959,* 2:785.
53. "Wei chedi wancheng Qinghai sheng muyequ shehuizhuyi geming er fendou," ibid., 1070.
54. "Wang Feng tongzhi yijiuwubanian shiyue qiri zai lamajiao wenti zuotanhui shangde jianghua," ibid., 2:784.
55. "Chedi suqing youqing jihuizhuyifenzi Zhang Guosheng tongzhi zai tongzhan gongzuo shang youqing touxiangzhuyi de sixiang yingxiang, jianjue guanche dangde tongyi zhanxian gongzuo wei shehuizhuyi fuwude fangzhen!" ibid., 1:432.
56. Reference to "religious activities going underground" can be found in an official Chinese source, *Jianguo yilai zhongyao wenxian xuanbian,* 14:836. The specific activities described in this paragraph come from several sources, including Dawa Cairen (Dawa Tsering), *Xueji xueyu,* 565–566, Ciren Donzhu (Tsering Dondrup), *Chifeng huxiao,* 97–98, and my interview with Dhargye, the late governor of the Golog Tibetan Autonomous Prefecture, on August 22, 2012.
57. "Guanyu geng guangfan geng shenrudi kaizhan zhengzhi zhengqu gongzuo de jidian yijian," *Minzu zongjiao gongzuo wenjian huiji, 1949–1959,* 2:1002–1007.
58. Yin Shusheng, "Jinyin Tan zhitong," 44.
59. Ibid.
60. *Hainan Zangzu zizhizhou zhi,* 32.
61. Chinese: Tongde.
62. "Guanyu geng guangfan geng shenrudi kaizhan zhengzhi zhengqu gongzuo de jidian yijian," *Minzu zongjiao gongzuo wenjian huiji, 1949–1959,* 2:1002–1007.
63. Chinese: Jianzha.

64. Chentsa County of Malho Tibetan Autonomous Prefecture was comprised of the Angla, Dangshun, Jiarang, and Chatsaithang areas.
65. *Jianzha xianzhi,* 1:413, 520.
66. Chinese: Jiuzhi.
67. Dajie, *Guoluo jianwen yu huiyi,* 223.
68. Chinese: Huangzhong.
69. The Dalai Lama was born in the Amdo village of Taktser (Chinese: Hongya), Shihuiyao Township, in present-day Tsongkha (Chinese: Ping'an) County, Haidong Prefecture, Qinghai Province.
70. *Huangzhong xianzhi,* 240. Also, all but five of the eighty-five mosques in Rusar County were closed down in the September 1958 "reforms" of Islam.
71. Baba Phuntsok Wangyal, et al., *Witness to Tibet's History,* 45.
72. The Seventh Rongpo Drubchen, Lobsang Thinley Lungtok Gyatso, was head of Rongpo Monastery, a post held by a succession of reincarnate high lamas harking back to the seventeenth century. Arrested on June 16, 1958, he died in prison on November 30, 1978, and was posthumously rehabilitated on October 4, 1980. See *Huangnan Zangzu zizhizhou zhi,* 1544.
73. *Dangdai Zhongguo minzu gongzuo dashiji, 1949–1988,* 1:274.
74. An eyewitness of the repression of 1958 in Qinghai and a resident of the United States since 1998, Arjia Lobsang Tubten Rinpoché is one of the foremost Tibetan Buddhist leaders to have escaped into exile.
75. An early Tibetan Communist and Red Army recruit, Tashi Wangchuk (1913–2003) was a Long March veteran who rose to the position of vice-governor of Qinghai and other national positions of authority. Toppled in 1958, he made a brief comeback until being redisgraced in 1964, and was rehabilitated and restored to posts of distinction in 1979.
76. Han Youren, *Yichang bei yinmoliaode guonei zhanzheng,* 56–57, 159–162.
77. "Zhonggong zhongyang dui Qinghai shengwei 'Guanyu jiejue yijiu wuba nian pingpan douzheng kuodahua yiliu wenti de qingshi baogao' de pifu," *Sanzhong quanhui yilai zhongyao wenxian huibian,* 2:958–964.
78. Ajia Luosangtudan (Arjia Tubten Lobsang Rinpoché), "Xu" (foreword) to Li Jianglin, *1959: Lhasa!* and Pingcuo Wangjie (Phuntsok Wangyal), "Huiyi Zhaxi Wangxu tongzhi," in *Pingdeng tuanjie lu manman,* 355.
79. "Guanyu shengwei sanji ganbu huiyi de baogao," *Qinghai shengzhi,* 81:796. Actually, the pronouncement had been made in 1961 by Gao Feng's successor, Wang Zhao, but remained unpublished until 2003. Meanwhile, Wang had been tortured to death in the Cultural Revolution. Although the 2003 document collection that published Wang's pronouncement is not classified, it is obscure, and Chinese websites for the general public present a censored version of Gao Feng's story. The following URL, for example, which omits

the year 1958 entirely, also omits the fact that he was removed from his post (largely because of the famine) and states instead that he was sent to study in a Chinese Communist Party "school": http://baike.baidu.com/subview/304835/8949779.htm.

80. "Wei chedi wancheng Qinghai sheng muyequ shehuizhuyi geming er fendou," *Minzu zongjiao gongzuo wenjian huiji, 1949–1959,* 2:1067.
81. Mao's term. See Mao Zedong, *Mao Zedong wenji,* 7:1.
82. See Dikötter, *Mao's Great Famine,* or Yang Jisheng et al, *Tombstone.*
83. *Huangzhong xianzhi,* 18.
84. Dajie, *Guoluo jianwen yu huiyi,* 117; Ma Wanli, ed., *Jingjian,* 199.
85. *Zhonggong Xizang dangshi dashiji, 1949–1994,* 72–73.
86. Chinese: Haiyan.
87. The exact number of Mongolian and Tibetan nomads forcibly relocated was 9,325 (1,715 households); approximately half of them were sent to areas hundreds of kilometers away. At least 704 people died en route. Seven hundred thirty-four proactive arrests were also made "to prevent rebellion." "Zhonggong zhongyang dui Qinghai shengwei 'Guanyu jiejue yijiu wuba nian pingpan douzheng kuodahua yiliu wenti de qingshi baogao' de pifu," *Sanzhong quanhui yilai zhongyao wenxian huibian,* 2:958–964.
88. See Yin Shusheng, "Jinyin Tan zhitong," and Tie Mu'er, "Zai Kukunao'er yibei."
89. "Mao zhuxi pizhuan Qinghai shengwei 'Dui quansheng zhenya fangeming panluan wenti' de zhishi," *Tongzhan zhengce wenjian huibian,* 3:1787.
90. *Dangdai Zhongguo zhuangjia bing,* 227.
91. *Jiefang Xizangshi,* 346.
92. Land Reform officially began in the Dechen Tibetan Autonomous Prefecture of Yunnan in August 1956. In March 1957, Tibetan rebellion broke out in Gyalthang, and the PLA rolled in soon thereafter. In May, the Central Committee issued instructions to "pacify the rebellion swiftly" to prepare for "reforms." Land Reform was resumed in September and declared complete in all Tibetan regions of Yunnan by the end of 1958. In some areas, collectivization was imposed simultaneously with Land Reform rather than in two separate, more gradual stages, as Marxist orthodoxy prescribed. See Le'anwangdui, *Diqing Zangzu zizhizhou zhi,* 33–36, 479–480, and *Dangdai Yunnan Zangzu jianshi,* 44–47.
93. According to an official Chinese source, the Communist Party admitted in 2003 that things had gone too far in Gansu in 1958, and exonerated 24,900 people, many of them posthumously. In the fighting that took place between March and November 1958 in Kanlho, 3,076 Tibetans (including 32 distinguished lamas and local leaders) were killed, 1,015 were

wounded, 2,065 were taken captive, 4,371 fled the battlefields, and an unknown number surrendered. More than 300 Chinese PLA soldiers also died. Land Reform was enforced under the policy of "simultaneous fighting and reform." In late 1958, "more than 1,200 anti-Party, antisocialist bad elements and counterrevolutionaries were made to thoroughly pay for their crimes . . . in more than 2,000 struggle sessions . . . and they were paraded through the streets and countryside for further struggle." Fifteen percent of the household property in the region was confiscated, and 31.5 percent of the nomads were blacklisted as "members of the exploiting classes." By 1961, 8.6 percent of the Tibetan population of Kanlho had been arrested; with a starting population in early 1958 of 158,400, this amounted to 13,622 people. *Zhongguo gongchandang Gannan lishi, 1921.7–2003.7,* 232, 234–235, 356.

4. UNEASY SPRING IN LHASA

1. Princess Wencheng was sent by China's Tang dynasty as a consort to Tibetan king Songtsen Gampo, in a diplomatic settlement between their two countries. The priceless statue, said to have been personally blessed by the Buddha himself, was part of the princess's dowry.
2. In the complex traditional calendar system, the years rotate through a cycle of five elements in combination with twelve zodiac animals.
3. One's risky "critical year" (*skag*) recurs every twelfth year, along with one's zodiac animal.
4. Sometimes rendered as a "doctorate in Buddhist studies," the attainment of a *Geshe Lharampa* degree requires mastery of an extensive curriculum in Sanskrit, logic, Buddhist philosophy, and Tibetan medicine, art, and culture.
5. Chinese: Cuomei, Shannan. Today, Cuomei is a county and Shannan (Lhokha) is a prefecture.
6. Chushi Gangdruk, or "Four Rivers, Six Ranges," is the traditional name for the Kham region. The four rivers are the Drichu (the Jinsha, the upper reaches of the Yangtze), the Salween, the Mekong, and the Yalong. Six mountain ranges form the watersheds for these river systems: the Tsawagang, the Markhamgang, the Zelmogang, the Poborgang, the Mardzagang, and the Minyak Rabgang.
7. Author interview with Kelsang Gyadotsang, May 10, 2009.
8. Xu Hongseng, "1958 nian qiba yuejian Zhang Jingwu tongzhi tong galunmen de jici tanhua jianlu," *Xizang wenshi ziliao xuanji,* 24:202.
9. The traditional Tibetan government included both monastic and lay officials in a hierarchical seven-rank system, with the seventh rank at the bottom. A *tsi-pon* (often rendered as "finance minister") was a fourth-rank lay official.

10. Tubten Khetsun, *Memories of Life in Lhasa under Chinese Rule,* 21.
11. Ibid.
12. Sexin Luosangdunzhu (Seshing), "Yuan Zangjun jingweituan jingweiying de jianzhi ji youguan wo ren jingwei yingzhang shi fasheng panluan de qingkuang," 135.
13. *Zhonggong Xizang dangshi dashiji, 1949–1994,* 85.
14. Sexin Luosangdunzhu (Seshing), "Yuan Zangjun jingweituan jingweiying de jianzhi ji youguan wo ren jingwei yingzhang shi fasheng panluan de qingkuang," 135.
15. Author interview with Tenpa Soepa, September 9, 2009. For the Reform Bureau, see *Xizang wenshi ziliao xuanji,* 9:20–26, 13:28.
16. See "Guanyu genju 'Xieyi' gaige Xizang shehui zhidu de bugao" (printed from a handwritten document), *Xizang wenshi ziliao xuanji,* 9:137–141.
17. Gyalwa Rinpoché is an honorific Tibetan term for the Dalai Lama.
18. Author interview with Tenpa Soepa, September 9, 2009.
19. Minister Yuthok had stayed in India in 1957. See Chapter 2.
20. Available sources strongly indicate that Zhang Jingwu was not in Lhasa during the Lhasa Incident and the Battle of Lhasa. The Dalai Lama recalls that in the late winter of 1958 Zhang brought him an invitation from the Central Committee to the Second National People's Congress in Beijing that spring. However, he may be remembering incorrectly (unless Zhang made a brief visit to Lhasa), as *Zhonggong Xizang dangshi dashiji, 1949–1994* says the messenger was Tan, who was in charge during Zhang's absence.
21. *Zhonggong Xizang dangshi dashiji, 1949–1994,* 79.
22. Author interview with Tenpa Soepa, September 9, 2009.
23. Ibid.
24. Wang Qixiu, "Qinli 1959 nian Xizang pingpan," http://dangshi.people.cn/GB/8339083.html; see also Zong Zidu, "Niliu fangun de rizi," 125.
25. *Zhonggong Xizang dangshi dashiji, 1949–1994,* 85.
26. Ibid.
27. The commander of the Tibetan Army was known as the Magchi. Since Tibetan ranks and units were not a precise match for modern ones, close approximations have been chosen for translation. Under the Magchi were the "Dapon," translated as "colonel/regiment." Next were the "Rupon" (lieutenant colonel/battalion). Then came the "Gyapon" (captain/company), followed by the "Dingpon" (lieutenant/platoon).
28. There are various, conflicting accounts of the shadowy meeting. Based on information he derived from an interview with a participant, Tsering Shakya (186) says that the middle- and lower-level bureaucrats "vowed to protect the Dalai Lama and the Tibetan polity," but Seshing's account of the

meeting does not mention this pledge. Chinese sources seem to confuse this secret meeting with the special plenary meeting of the Tibetan National Assembly at the Norbulingka in November 1958. *Xizang gemingshi* (119–120) claims that there were six of the secret sessions and that Surkhang, Phala, Kundeling Dzasa, and other high officials attended them, but this does not tally with Seshing's memoirs. See Sexin Luosangdunzhu (Seshing), "Yuan Zangjun jingweituan jingweiying de jianzhi ji youguan wo ren jingwei yingzhang shi fasheng panluan de qingkuang," 136. The meeting attended by Surkhang and the others was the special meeting of the Tibetan National Assembly, which Surkhang chaired. See *Zhonggong Xizang dangshi dashiji, 1949–1994*, 85. In addition, *Neibu cankao* (May 27, 1959, 15–17) contains a letter found at the Norbulinkga that seems to refer to the secret meeting.

29. *Jiefang Xizangshi*, 347–349.
30. *Xizang dangshi tongxun*, vols. 1 and 2 (double issue), 25.
31. *Xizang wenshi ziliao xuanji*, 4:33.
32. Phuntsok Tashi was married to Tsering Dolma, the Dalai Lama's eldest sister.
33. See Melvyn C. Goldstein, Dawei Sherap, and William Siebenschuh, *A Tibetan Revolutionary*, 224.
34. The Tsedrung Lingka was a garden park used by *tsedrungs*, who were monastic civil servants.
35. The Shuktri Lingka was the meadow in front of the Potala Palace, named after a teaching throne built for the Seventh Dalai Lama.
36. Xu Donghai, "Pingxi Lasa wuzhuang panluan muduji," 9. The fighting in Jomda dates to July 1956; the highway battles were in August–September 1956; Tramok was on January 4, 1959; Tengchen was on January 24, 1959; Tsethang was on October 1958 and on January 25, 1959. The Dalai Lama also mentions the fighting at Tsethang in his *Freedom in Exile*, 127.
37. The Tsangpo River is the portion of the Brahmaputra River that flows through Tibet.
38. Author interview with Juchen Tubten, September 22, 2009. Sershul is a pastoral region bordering Qinghai and the TAR, corresponding roughly to today's Shiqu County in Sichuan, although it is somewhat larger. The traditional Tibetan name for the region was Dzachuka; Sershul is probably a modern Tibetan transliteration of the Chinese "Shiqu." The war zones included Derge, Palyul, Bathang, Drongthra, Jomda, and Markham.
39. The airport was in Yulshul County (now called Yulshul City), which is to be distinguished from the Yulshul Tibetan Autonomous Prefecture.
40. *Qinghai shengzhi*, 56:803. Official Chinese sources such as this one tally only the airdrop missions, preserving a telling silence on the number of combat

missions. The latter must be derived from Chinese pilot memoirs such as "Xueyu jiaofei ji" by Hong Weiquan, for example, who says that his unit flew 224 of them.

41. See Li Jianglin, *Dang tieniao zai tiankong feixiang,* 443–444.
42. Hong Weiquan, "Xueyu jiaofei ji," 15.
43. Author interview with Dhargye, late governor of the Golog Tibetan Autonomous Prefecture, August 22, 2012.
44. Zhang Pingzhi, "Gaoyuan hongying," at http://kong25.bokee.com/275102737.html.
45. This terminology pervades Chinese sources. See Ding Sheng, Jin Guang, and Yu Ruxin, *Luonan yingxiong,* 302; *Xinghai xianzhi,* 346.
46. Zhang Guoxiang, as recorded by Lin Rusheng, "Zhongguo tu-4 chuanqi," 32.
47. *Qinghai huabao,* nos. 5–6 (December 1958) (no page number).
48. See, for example, Jiang Dasan's memoir, "77 sui laofeixingrenyuan de boke."
49. Author interview with Juchen Tubten, September 22, 2009.
50. *Jiefang Xizangshi,* 350.
51. The Chinese had purchased the Sampo and Kyitö mansions, near the Jokhang Temple, to house various offices.

5. THE EXORCISTS' DANCE AT THE POTALA PALACE

1. Although there are some variations in the performance of this ritual dance, overall its contents are similar. Descriptions in this chapter are based on sources such as Cao Yali, "Qinghai Ta'ersi qiangmu yuewu qianxi," *Qinghai minzu xueyuan xuebao* (shehui kexue ban), no. 1 (1999): 49–51.
2. "Disciplinarians" (Tibetan: *she-ngo*) were fierce monastic police, with awe-inspiring costumes and face paint.
3. *Zhonggong Xizang dangshi dashiji, 1949–1994,* 87. For more on the Chinese military preparations, see Chen Bing, "Panguo biwang," 39.
4. The four states of mind in Buddhism are variously interpreted, but as explicated by Namgyal Monastery in Dharamsala they include loving-kindness, compassion, joy, and generosity.
5. Apei Awangjinmei (Ngabo), "1959 nian '3 yue 10 ri shijian' de zhenxiang," *Zhongguo Zangxue,* no. 2 (1988): 3.
6. Apei Awangjinmei (Ngabo), "1959 nian '3 yue 10 ri shijian' de zhenxiang," in Zhang Xiaoming, ed., *Jianzheng bainian Xizang,* 1:175.
7. The original Tibetan term for the Dalai Lama's chief of staff is *chikyab khenpo,* a third-rank monastic official in the Dalai Lama's inner circle, sometimes rendered as "chief official abbot." He was responsible for the Dalai Lama's everyday life, and for transmitting petitions and memorials to the Dalai Lama.

8. Chi Haotian, preface to *Jiefang Xizangshi*, 2.
9. *Jiefang Xizangshi*, 354.
10. Ji Youquan, *Baixue*, 483.
11. Ji Youquan, *Xizang pingpan jishi*, 79.
12. The Dalai Lama was a deputy chairman of the Standing Committee of the National People's Congress at the time.
13. Jiangbian Jiacuo (Jampel Gyatso), *Mao Zedong yu Dalai, Banchan*, 200.
14. Luo Liangxing, "Yichang tebie de yanchu," 136.
15. Author interview with the Dalai Lama, June 30, 2009. The Dalai Lama seems to have remembered incorrectly who watched the performance with him. In his two autobiographies, he mentions Tan Guansan and Zhang Jingwu, but Zhang Jingwu was not in Lhasa at the time. Most sources, including the memoir of the Dalai Lama's brother-in-law, Security Chief Phuntsok, confirm that Tan was not present.
16. Mount Wutai, located in Shanxi, is the most famous of the Four Sacred Mountains in Chinese Buddhism. It was the legendary abode of the Bodhisattva Manjushri, often depicted in Tibetan art as an old man seated on a ferocious tiger.
17. The *lingga* (Sanskrit), a ceremonial object with roots in ancient shamanistic tradition, is a doll made of *tsampa* (roasted flour) dough. In the described ritual, evil is driven symbolically into the *lingga,* which is then destroyed as an exorcism.
18. The *vajra* (Tibetan: *dorje*) is a ritual weapon symbolizing power and enlightenment, as well as Vajrayana Buddhism in general.
19. Phuntsok Tashi (Phuntsok), *A Life,* vol. 2.
20. Ji Youquan, *Xizang pingpan jishi,* 80. Ji Youquan is a generally reliable latter-day source of the official Chinese position. As executive secretary of the Propaganda Department of the PLA Tibet Military Command (stationed there from 1974–1996), with the rank of assistant regimental commander, he had access to top-secret PLA archives, and he provides many details regarding Chinese politics, military affairs, propaganda, and warfare. The definitive 2008 Chinese Communist compilation discussed above, which bears the imprimatur of Chi Haotian, draws heavily on his work, a sign of official sanction.
21. See Chapter 1.
22. *Zhonggong Xizang dangshi dashiji, 1949–1994,* 41–42.
23. The *torma* is a stupa-shaped offering made of *tsampa* and decorated with multicolored butter sculptures.

6. PERIL AT THE PRAYER FESTIVAL

1. Gama Quyang, "Dalai lama de shanshi jigou," 94–127.
2. *Platycladus orientalis* is a conifer in the cypress family. While Chinese arborvitae is often given as its common name, juniper is in fact a closer relative, although neither is fully botanically accurate. Tibetans burn it as incense, often crushed or mixed with other fragrant plants such as cumin or barley flour. See Farjon, *A Monograph of Cupressaceae and Sciadopitys,* 415–419.
3. Known as the *Ashtamangala,* the Eight Auspicious Signs include the umbrella, the pair of fish, the conch, the vase, the lotus, the infinite knot, the victory banner, and the wheel.
4. Beneath the cabinet there were two major administrative divisions, the Yigtsang (Ecclesiastic Office) and the Tsikhang (Finance Office), each administered by four fourth-rank officials. The Yigtsang officials were monk-secretaries, called *drung-yigs;* they were responsible for religious affairs. The Tsikhang officials, the *tsi-pons* (finance ministers), took charge of lay affairs of state.
5. The Holder of the Ganden Throne is the nominal head of the Gelug school of Tibetan Buddhism, a position held by the abbot of Ganden Monastery. In 1959, this was Tubten Kunga, the ninety-sixth in a lineage reaching back to the beginnings of the Gelug school in the fifteenth century.
6. Jiangre Awangcibai, "Dalai Lama chuxing yishi," 1–9.
7. *Zhonggong Xizang dangshi dashiji, 1949–1994,* 5. The CCP Tibet Work Committee was formally declared (but only to Communist Party members) in Lhasa in early 1952, although the strategic decision on how to disguise the committee's entry into Lhasa was made on June 11, 1950. See *Zhongguo gongchandang Xizang zizhiqu zushishi ziliao, 1950–1987,* 11.
8. *Zhonggong Lasa dangshi dashiji, 1951–1966,* 1; *Lasa zai qianjin,* 7, 10.
9. See *Zhongguo gongchandang Xizang zizhiqu zuzhishi ziliao, 1950–1987,* 36.
10. Ibid.
11. Ibid., 67. Cadres need not be party members.
12. In this book, times will be given in the local Lhasa time unless Chinese sources are being cited, in which cases they will be given in Beijing time. It is worth noting that although the People's Republic of China today spans an area equivalent to five time zones, all—including Lhasa and other outlying minority regions—are required to use Beijing time, despite the inconvenience this may cause to the locals.

13. *Xizang gongzuo wenxian xuanbian, 1994–2005,* 70.
14. For Tibetan Regiment 6, see Chen Bing, "Zangjun shilüe," 91. The PLA built the Lhasa Bridge soon after it first entered the city.
15. Luosang Pengcuo, "Guanyu Zhebangsi tiebang lama de youlai jiqi zhiquan," 61.
16. *Pingxi Xizang panluan,* 70.
17. *Neibu cankao,* April 26, 1959, 9.
18. *Pingxi Xizang panluan,* 71.
19. Tibetan: *Kyerab Gyatsa.*
20. At this yearly holiday event, gorgeous multicolored sculptures carved in butter were displayed in a competition in which the Dalai Lama was supposed to choose the winner.
21. Dalai Lama, *Freedom in Exile,* 130; Phuntsok Tashi (Phuntsok), *A Life,* vol. 2.
22. *Pingxi Xizang panluan,* 73.
23. After the Dalai Lama's escape, the entire Monlam Prayer Festival was banned until 1986, when it was held again (presided over by the Tenth Panchen Lama), but it was banned anew in 1990, and has been severely restricted ever since.
24. Now referred to as the president of the People's Republic of China rather than the chairman, this is a largely ceremonial position.
25. Author interview with the Dalai Lama, June 30, 2009.
26. The Dalai Lama's *Freedom in Exile* (130) mentions "two junior Chinese officials." Security Chief Phuntsok's memoir says that it was Vice-Commander Chen Mingyi of the PLA Tibet Military Command who came to ask for the date. *Jiefang Xizangshi* (354) says that He Zuyin and Li Zuomin went to the Norbulingka on March 1, 1959, to ask the Dalai Lama to set a date, but the Dalai Lama was not at the Norbulingka on March 1. He did not move back from the Jokhang until March 5.

7. THE DALAI LAMA MAY NOT BRING BODYGUARDS!

1. Author interview with the Dalai Lama, June 30, 2009.
2. The Dalai Lama's "New Palace," formally known as the Takten Migyur Photrang (Eternal Palace), was added to the Norbulingka in 1956.
3. A *dra-tsang* is a monastic college. All three sites are in today's Lhokha Prefecture of Tibet.
4. Tubten Khetsun, *Memories of Life in Lhasa under Chinese Rule,* 23.
5. *Jiefang Xizangshi,* 355; *Xizang gemingshi,* 122. The former mentions Li Zuomin by name, while the latter refers to him simply as a "United Front section chief."

6. Under the aegis of the CCP Tibet Work Committee, the Patriotic Tibetan Women's League was open to all, and many of Lhasa's aristocratic women joined it.
7. Dalai Lama, *My Land and My People,* 163; Tarawa Tenzin Choenyi (Tara), *Introducing Myself.*
8. The Lhasa Youth and Women's Council was a Communist Party organization. Non-Party members could participate in its activities, but could not hold leadership positions.
9. Taring Rinchen Dolma, *Daughter of Tibet,* 256.
10. Jigme Taring, a prince of Sikkim who lived in Tibet, was the Dalai Lama's photographer. His wife, Rinchen Dolma, was a member of the aristocratic Tibetan Tsarong family.
11. Phuntsok's story comes from his memoir, Phuntsok Tashi, *A Life,* vol. 2.
12. Phuntsok had served as a translator during the negotiations for the Seventeen-Point Agreement, and as the Dalai Lama's Chinese tutor.
13. This quote—and all in the following seven paragraphs—comes from Phuntsok Tashi (Phuntsok), *A Life,* vol. 2.
14. Security Chief Phuntsok headed the Dalai Lama's security guards, Tibetan Army Regiment 1.
15. A *khenchung* was a fourth-rank monastic official.
16. Sexin Luosangdunzhu (Seshing), "Yuan Zangjun jingweituan jingweiying de jianzhi ji youguan wo ren jingweiyingzhang shi fasheng panluan de qingkuang," 132–161.
17. Ibid., 137.
18. *Xizang gemingshi;* Re Di, et al., comp. and ed., *Xizang geming huiyilu,* vol. 4; *Jiefang Xizangshi.*
19. *Pingxi Xizang panluan,* which is a collection of carefully selected Chinese and Tibetan documents.
20. Apei Awangjinmei (Ngabo): "1959 nian '3 yue 10 ri shijian' de zhenxiang," in Zhang Xiaoming, *Jianzheng bainian Xizang,* 1:176.
21. *Dzasa* was a title meaning "commander," the third-highest rank in the Tibetan government.
22. *Xizang gemingshi,* 122.
23. *Zhonggong Xizang dangshi dashiji, 1949–1994,* 88.
24. *Jiefang Xizangshi,* 355.
25. Jiangbian Jiacuo (Jampel Gyatso), *Mao Zedong yu Dalai, Banchan,* 206.
26. There were significant connections between the Dalai Lama's bodyguard unit and the PLA, stemming from the Seventeen-Point Agreement, which stipulated that the Tibetan Army would be subsumed gradually into the PLA. After 1951, the Central Committee designated

Regiment 1 of the Tibetan Army, which was stationed at the Norbulingka, as the Dalai Lama's security guards, and granted the unit a Chinese government subsidy. In 1955, the PLA awarded rank to Tibetan army officers. Security Chief Phuntsok became a lieutenant colonel, and was promoted to colonel the following year. It is also worth noting that the Dalai Lama's title of deputy chairman of the Standing Committee of the National People's Congress accorded him the status of a national leader of China. Therefore, local officers such as Tan Guansan had technically overstepped the limits of their power in making a policy decision about the Dalai Lama's bodyguards.

27. Phuntsok Tashi (Phuntsok), *A Life,* vol. 2.
28. Ibid.
29. Sojong rites are monthly or bimonthly rituals for renewing monastic vows.
30. Tsering Shakya, *The Dragon in the Land of Snows,* 187.
31. Tarawa Tenzin Choenyi (Tara), *Introducing Myself.* This is also the source for the following four paragraphs.
32. Apei Awangjinmei (Ngabo), "1959 nian '3 yue 10 ri shijian' de zhenxiang," in Zhang Xiaoming, *Jianzheng bainian Xizang,* 1:175–176.
33. Ji Youquan, *Xizang pingpan jishi,* 82.
34. See Chapter 4.
35. Tsering Shakya, *The Dragon in the Land of Snows,* 189.
36. Tarawa Tenzin Choenyi (Tara), *Introducing Myself.*
37. Author interview with Juchen Tubten, September 22, 2009.

8. THE MOST MOMENTOUS DAY IN TIBETAN HISTORY

Note: The phrase in the chapter title, "momentous day," comes from the Dalai Lama's *My Land and My People,* 139.

1. Author interview with the Dalai Lama, June 30, 2009.
2. Author interview with Ngari Rinpoché, July 18, 2009.
3. Tubten Khetsun's elder brother was a palace steward, and his uncle was a senior official with concomitant posts in the Tibetan government and the PCART.
4. Dialogue here and information in the following paragraph are based on Tubten Khetsun, *Memories of Life in Lhasa under Chinese Rule,* 24.
5. Author interview with Jampa Tenzin, October 12, 2009.
6. Sexin Luosangdunzhu (Seshing), "Yuan Zangjun jingweituan jingweiying de jianzhi ji youguan wo ren jingwei yingzhang shi fasheng panluan de qingkuang," 137. See also Phuntsok Tashi (Phuntsok), *A Life,* vol. 2.

7. Author interview with Jampa Tenzin, October 12, 2009.
8. The alert was lifted an hour later. Zong Zidu, "Niliu fangun de rizi—1959 nian 3 yue 10 ri caifang jianwen," 125–126.
9. The Dekyi Lingka housed the British Mission until 1947, after which it housed the Indian Consulate and its clinic.
10. Sonam also served in the PCART, and was the elder brother of reincarnate lama Phagpa Gelek Namgyal, who was the first vice-chairman of the Chamdo Liberation Committee from 1951 to 1956, and honorary chairman from December 1956 until its dissolution in April 1959.
11. Patt, "The Momo Gun," 143. Also, author interview with Tenpa Soepa, September 8, 2009.
12. Author interview with Thinley Phuntsok, April 19, 2009.
13. Hard numbers are difficult to compile for the Tibetan crowds around the Norbulingka on March 10, 1959. According to *Jiefang Xizangshi,* "[On the morning of March 10] at approximately eleven o'clock, a crowd of more than two thousand Tibetans converged on the Norbulingka, among them two or three hundred armed rebel elements." Tibetan estimates vary between ten and thirty thousand. The CCP Tibet Work Committee's March 10 cable to the Central Committee does not give a tally, but its March 11 cable asserts there was "a total of at least six or seven thousand rebel forces in Lhasa." See *Pingxi Xizang panluan,* 78. Tubten Khetsun, *Memories of Life in Lhasa under Chinese Rule* (25), estimates the crowd at ten thousand.
14. Diki Tsering, *Dalai Lama, My Son,* 169–170.
15. People had streamed into Lhasa from Kham and Amdo at the time, and Jampel Gyatso (Jiangbian Jiacuo), in his *Mao Zedong yu Dalai, Banchan,* calls them "members of the Chushi Gangdruk." This is not true of everyone who fled to Lhasa (or Lhokha) from these areas, however. All available historical sources indicate that the Chushi Gangdruk as an organization had no role in the March 10 Incident.
16. Dajie, *Guoluo jianwen yu huiyi,* 112–113. See also Jiangbian Jiacuo (Jampel Gyatso), *Shishi Banchan Lama zhuanji,* 98, and *Mao Zedong yu Dalai, Banchan,* 202.
17. For the former, see Chapter 3. The Third Arotsang Rinpoché was arrested as a "counterrevolutionary" in 1958 and died in prison on December 12 of that year. He was posthumously exonerated in June 1981. See *Xinghai xianzhi,* 471–472.
18. Cabinet Minister Sampo Tsewang Rigzin (1904–1973) was concurrently Tibetan Army commander-in-chief and vice-commander of the PLA Tibet Military Command.

19. "Xizang gaxia gongzuo riji" (translated excerpt), *Pingxi Xizang panluan,* 191; Apei Awangjinmei (Ngabo), "1959 nian '3 yue 10 ri shijian' de zhenxiang," in Zhang Xiaoming, *Jianzheng bainian Xizang,* 1:176.
20. Phuntsok Tashi (Phuntsok), *A Life,* vol. 2.
21. Su Zhuqing, "50 nian qian qinli Xizang minzhu gaige de diandi huiyi: maixiang xin qidian," *Xizang renquanwang,* at http://www.tibet328.cn/zxss/08/200903/t282351.htm.
22. *Lasa zai qianjin,* 7–14.
23. *Xizang de minzhu gaige,* 6.
24. Chen Jingbo, "Xizang tongyi zhanxian gongzuo de licheng," 120.
25. Author interview with Tenpa Soepa, September 9, 2009. Wearing a surgical face mask as a shield against dust and germs was a Chinese custom, which few Tibetans—mostly those closely associated with the Chinese—had adopted.
26. Author interview with Jampa Tenzin, October 12, 2009.
27. Author interview with Ngari Rinpoché, July 18, 2009.
28. There are conflicting accounts regarding Sonam's death. Phuntsok's memoir says that Sonam fired warning shots into the air when the crowd mobbed him, but Phuntsok was not an eyewitness; he got this information secondhand from a gate guard. According to Juchen Tubten, who witnessed the episode from a distance of about a dozen yards, Sonam did not fire his gun. Tenpa Soepa, who was guarding the gate at the time, heard gunfire but cannot confirm whether it came from Sonam. Several sources attest that Sonam was armed. According to Jiangbian Jiacuo (Jampel Gyatso), *Mao Zedong yu Dalai, Banchan* (201), Sonam carried a pistol in his robe.
29. Mahakala, one of the Dalai Lama's tutelary deities, is the wrathful aspect of Avalokiteshvara (Guanyin), the bodhisattva of compassion.
30. Phuntsok Tashi (Phuntsok), *A Life,* vol. 2.
31. Lhalu Tsewang Dorje had governed Kham from headquarters in Chamdo.
32. Author interviews with Thinley Phuntsok and Tenpa Soepa. See also Phuntsok Tashi (Phuntsok), *A Life,* vol. 2, and "Xizang gaxia gongzuo riji" (translated excerpt), in *Pingxi Xizang panluan* (a semiclassified source), 191.
33. Author interview with Juchen Tubten, September 22, 2009.
34. *Pingxi Xizang panluan,* 75.
35. Ibid.
36. Phuntsok Tashi (Phuntsok), *A Life,* vol. 2.
37. Ibid.
38. Ibid.
39. This Tibetan dignitary was the Seventh Gyatsoling Rinpoché of Gyatsoling Monastery in today's Palbar County, Chamdo Prefecture. He had coached

the Dalai Lama in scriptural debate, and was also deputy chairman of the Tibetan branch of the Chinese Buddhist Association, the organization through which the People's Republic of China supervises and regulates Buddhism. He was persecuted and died during the Cultural Revolution, and posthumously rehabilitated in 1979.

40. *Xizang gemingshi,* 122.
41. Author interview with Ngari Rinpoché, July 18, 2009.
42. *Pingxi Xizang panluan,* 76.
43. The term "people's representatives," which is used by both Chinese and Tibetan sources, refers to a shifting group during this chaotic, poorly documented period. At first, on March 10, 1959, they were people the demonstrators chose to enter the Norbulingka to plead their cause; they stayed and took part in the meetings there. For want of a better term, "people's representatives" is also used in this book to describe a bloc of approximately 860 people (exact number not completely verifiable) at the subsequent Shol meetings, although some of them may have been more casual attendees.
44. Gegyepa states that there were twenty-odd people's representatives, headed by some Tibetan government officials. Phuntsok and Tara say that there were thirty representatives chosen by the demonstrators outside of the Norbulingka. See Gejieba Danzengduoji (Gegyepa), "Fenlie zhuyi fenzi zai Lasa fadong wuzhuang panluan de qingkuang," 66–67; Phuntsok Tashi (Phuntsok), *A Life,* vol. 2; and Tarawa Tenzin Choenyi (Tara), *Introducing Myself.*
45. Gejieba Danzengduoji (Gegyepa), "Fenlie zhuyi fenzi zai Lasa fadong wuzhuang panluan de qingkuang," 67.
46. Tarawa Tenzin Choenyi (Tara), *Introducing Myself.*
47. Ibid.
48. Phuntsok Tashi (Phuntsok), *A Life,* vol. 2.
49. The Chinese recovered dozens of documents at the Norbulingka and at Kundeling Monastery after the Battle of Lhasa. The April and May 1959 issues of *Neibu cankao,* a classified journal from China's Xinhua News Agency, published Chinese translations of thirteen of these "reactionary bandit documents," and another six appeared in *Pingxi Xizang panluan,* which is semiclassified. Photocopies of four of the documents in the original Tibetan (with English captions) appear in *Concerning the Question of Tibet* (173).
50. According to this document, the fifty lamas from Sera and Drepung monasteries who were already present, along with some monk and lay officials, were assigned to guard the palace gates, directed by Tara, Shuguba, and some others; the palace security guards were also mobilized in appropriate numbers for duty. See "Yuan Xizang difang zhengfu gongzuo rizhi," *Neibu cankao,* May 27, 1959, 12–13. *Pingxi Xizang panluan* (191) also includes a "Daily

Proceedings of the Tibetan Cabinet," but these details are missing, probably removed by an editor.

51. "Zhebang, Sela, Gadan sandasi, sengsuguanyuan ji renmindaibiao yijianshu," *Pingxi Xizang panluan,* 185.
52. *Pingxi Xizang panluan,* 77. *Jiefang Xizangshi* (356–357), makes a similar claim.
53. Author interview with Jampa Tenzin, October 12, 2009. See also Tarawa Tenzin Choenyi (Tara), *Introducing Myself,* and Phuntsok Tashi (Phuntsok), *A Life,* vol. 2. Chinese sources corroborate that the people's representatives made this demand.
54. "Zai gongdeling jiaohuo yifen 'nangma kanqing kanqiong de yijianshu,'" *Neibu cankao,* April 25, 1959, 2–3.
55. Dalai Lama, *My Land and My People,* 186.
56. "Zai gongdeling jiaohuo yifen 'nangma kanqing kanqiong de yijianshu,'" *Neibu cankao,* April 25, 1959, 2–3.
57. Gejieba Danzengduoji (Gegyepa), "Fenlie zhuyi fenzi zai Lasa fadong wuzhuang panluan de qingkuang," 67–69. A semiclassified source published in 2006 indicates that Ngabo reported all of this information to the Chinese. See Zhang Xiangming, *Zhang Xiangming wushiwunian Xizang gongzuo shilu,* 83–85.
58. For a photo of an ID pass, see Lin Zhaozhen, *Lama sha ren,* 232.
59. Regiment 2 was known as the Drapchi Regiment; its barracks on the north side of town were converted into a notorious prison after 1959.
60. Upper and Lower Gyatso were areas immediately west of the Norbulingka.
61. The Chensel Phodrang was the Thirteenth Dalai Lama's palace at the Norbulingka.
62. Phuntsok Tashi (Phuntsok), *A Life,* vol. 2.
63. Author interview with Thinley Phuntsok, April 19, 2009.
64. "Jia Cuolin huofo tan ta jiang Tan Guansan jiangjun de xin songgei Dalai lama de jingli," *Pingxi Xizang panluan,* 196–198. According to Jiangbian Jiacuo (Jampel Gyatso), *Mao Zedong yu Dalai, Banchan,* Ngabo delivered this letter, but Ngabo did not go to the Norbulingka on March 10, 1959.

9. THE UNDERCOVER MEN OF KHAM

1. Athar Norbu, "The Life of Athar Norbu from Lithang," gives this date as the fifteenth day of the tenth month of the Tibetan calendar, which would probably correspond to December 5 or 6.
2. Taktser Rinpoché was the Dalai Lama's eldest brother.
3. East Pakistan is present-day Bangladesh.
4. Athar Norbu gives this date as the twentieth day of the tenth month of the Tibetan calendar, the last day of the full moon that month, probably corresponding to December 10 or 11.

5. Lhotse died in the mid-1960s in India without leaving any memoirs, and little is known of his biography. The main sources on the first batch of Tibetan CIA operatives are Athar's short memoir and the accounts published by Roger McCarthy, John Kenneth Knaus, Mikel Dunham, Kenneth J. Conboy, James Morrison, and Joe F. Leeker. These sources have been supplemented here with material derived from my personal interview with Athar's daughters, Tsering Dolma and Dolma Norbu on May 3, 2009.
6. In fact, only the first team was successfully reinfiltrated on this flight. The second team's drop into Kham, near the men's hometown of Lithang, was aborted because of weather and took place approximately a month later.
7. The Americans dropped this requirement later, after the establishment of the Chushi Gangdruk, and provided covert aid directly through the CIA's Far East Division.
8. Dunham, *Buddha's Warriors,* 215, 227, 228.
9. The plane flew over the Tsangpo River to the drop site, which was about half a mile from Samye Monastery, north of the Tsangpo and west of one of its unnamed tributaries.
10. Dunham, *Buddha's Warriors,* 223–224.
11. Ibid., 227.
12. Conboy and Morrison, *The CIA's Secret War in Tibet,* 42–43; author interview with Dolma Norbu, May 3, 2009.
13. Conboy and Morrison, *The CIA's Secret War in Tibet,* 22.
14. Derived from ibid., 43.
15. Taktser Rinpoché (Tubten Jigme Norbu) subsequently founded one of the first Tibetan studies programs in the United States, at Indiana University in Bloomington.
16. Author interview with Kelsang Gyadotsang, May 10, 2009.
17. The inventory of their supply bundle is based on the memoir of CIA operative Lhamo Tsering. A few items have been added here, such as the binoculars and teacups, based on Athar's memoir and my interview with Kelsang Gyadotsang. Lhamo Tsering says they had two light machine guns, but this may be an error. Athar's memoir states that they were submachine guns.
18. Dunham, *Buddha's Warriors,* 235.
19. Chinese: Pengbo.
20. Although Athar's memoir and Dunham's *Buddha's Warriors* (235) agree on the activities of Athar and Lhotse during this Lhasa visit, they conflict slightly about the sequence. I have followed Athar on this.
21. For more on the CIA airdrops, see Dawa Norbu, *China's Tibet Policy,* 268–271. For Athar, see Athar Norbu, "The Life of Athar Norbu from Lithang."
22. Dawa Norbu, *China's Tibet Policy,* 270.

10. PROTECT THE NORBULINGKA! PROTECT THE DALAI LAMA!

1. Sampo Tsewang Rigzin was still recovering from stones hurled by the crowd on March 10, 1959, the previous day.
2. A leading figure in the Chamdo Liberation Committee, Phagpa Gelek Namgyal was the brother of Sonam Gyatso (who was killed by the demonstrators on March 10).
3. The events described in this chapter were chaotic, and (not surprisingly) extant historical sources are scant and confusing. This account is based on the memoirs of Lalu Ciwangduoji (Lhalu), Jampa Phuntsok (Jampa), Sexin Luosangdunzhu (Seshing), and Tarawa Tenzin Choenyi (Tara), and interviews with Tenpa Soepa and Juchen Tubten.
4. Liao Li, *Zhongguo Zangjun*, 343.
5. Dalai Lama, *My Land and My People*, 188.
6. For the new formal term, see Sexin Luosangdunzhu (Seshing), "Yuan Zangjun jingweituan jingweiying de jianzhi ji youguan wo ren jingwei yingzhang shi fasheng panluan de qingkuang," 138. For the Tibetan National Assembly, see Shakabpa and Maher, *One Hundred Thousand Moons*, 1:81–83. Seshing's name for this body, as it appears in the Chinese translation of his memoir, includes the term "representatives," which is probably a reference to the "people's representatives" who were included in all of its sessions.
7. Sexin Luosangdunzhu (Seshing), "Yuan Zangjun jingweituan jingweiying de jianzhi ji youguan wo ren jingwei yingzhang shi fasheng panluan de qingkuang," 138–139.
8. The only extant primary sources describing the meeting in detail are Seshing's memoir (see the preceding note), Tarawa Tenzin Choenyi (Tara), *Introducing Myself*, and Lalu Ciwangduoji (Lhalu), "Youguan 1959 nian de panluan qingkuang." Tara and Lhalu, the only sources for names and numbers of active attendees, provide virtually identical lists. For the names of other attendees at this and the March 12 meeting, see Lhalu, 141–143.
9. Lalu Ciwangduoji (Lhalu), "Youguan 1959 nian de panluan qingkuang," 142.
10. Ibid.
11. *Neibu cankao*, April 25, 1959; see also "Nangma kanqinkangqiong yijianshu" and "Sandasi yijianshu," in *Pingxi Xizang panluan*, 205–207. For the cache in general, see Chapter 8.
12. Lhalu's memoir (Lalu Ciwangduoji, "Youguan 1959 nian de panluan qingkuang") refers to the members of this coordinating committee and the Norbulingka security committee as "army commanders" (*magchi*), a term that provided the Chinese with a pretext for dubbing them "Rebel Headquar-

ters (in such texts as Re Di, et al., comp. and ed., *Xizang geming huiyilu,* 4:3–4, or *Pingxi Xizang panluan,* 85). However, these groups did not, in fact, control the Tibetan Army. In a 2009 personal interview with me, Juchen Tubten shrugged the term off as merely a pompous, empty title.

13. Dalai Lama, *My Land and My People,* 189.
14. Phuntsok Tashi (Phuntsok), *A Life,* vol. 2. The Dalai Lama's autobiography does not give a date for this conversation with the people's representatives. Phuntsok's memoir places it on March 12, but by March 12, the meetings had already shifted out of the Norbulingka, so it seems more likely that it took place after the meeting had begun on March 11. Seshing corroborates that the Dalai Lama convened a meeting of officials at that time, after which Phala returned to the Assembly with the Dalai Lama's instructions "not to cause a disturbance at the Norbulingka." Sexin Luosangdunzhu (Seshing), "Yuan Zangjun jingweituan jingweiying de jianzhi ji youguan wo ren jingwei yingzhang shi fasheng panluan de qingkuang," 138.
15. Sexin Luosangdunzhu (Seshing), "Yuan Zangjun jingweituan jingweiying de jianzhi ji youguan wo ren jingwei yingzhang shi fasheng panluan de qingkuang," 138.
16. Tarawa Tenzin Choenyi (Tara), *Introducing Myself.* Lhadung's identity cannot be confirmed.
17. Xu Yan, *Taojin baizhan pingshuo gujin,* 286; information corroborated in author interview with Juchen Tubten, October 8, 2009.
18. Tarawa Tenzin Choenyi (Tara), *Introducing Myself.*
19. Tara's memoir mentions the existence of these arrangements. The details have been derived from personal interviews with Juchen Tubten.
20. Tarawa Tenzin Choenyi (Tara), *Introducing Myself.*
21. The Shol administration was responsible for public order in the Shol and eighteen manors on the outskirts of Lhasa.
22. Tarawa Tenzin Choenyi (Tara), *Introducing Myself.*
23. *Pingxi Xizang panluan,* 83.
24. Ibid.
25. Ibid.
26. Phuntsok Tashi (Phuntsok), *A Life,* vol. 2; Tarawa Tenzin Choenyi (Tara), *Introducing Myself;* Lalu Ciwangduoji (Lhalu), "Youguan 1959 nian de panluan qingkuang," 142–143; *Pingxi Xizang panluan,* 83–84.
27. A monk-secretary named Chopei Tubten proposed the security committee; it also included Khenchung Lobsang Tenzin, Thonpa Khenchung Jampa Khedrup, Phala Dorje Wangdu, and a fourth-rank official named Ngawang Gyaltsen.

28. See *Pingxi Xizang panluan* (83), for a typical Chinese misappellation of the session of the Tibetan National Assembly at the Shol Scriptural Printing House as the "People's Assembly of Independent Tibet." This misperception on the part of the Chinese is reflected in their actions in the aftermath of the Battle of Lhasa, when they rounded up all of the Shol attendees as "rebel elements" and seized the property of upper-echelon participants, even though some of the participants in the two earlier Norbulingka meetings went unpunished. Property was partially reimbursed for some under the policy of "paid confiscation." See Jiangbian Jiacuo (Jampel Gyatso), *Mao Zedong yu Dalai, Banchan,* 210.
29. *Pingxi Xizang panluan,* 84.
30. Sexin Luosangdunzhu (Seshing), "Yuan Zangjun jingweituan jingweiying de jianzhi ji youguan wo ren jingwei yingzhang shi fasheng panluan de qingkuang," 138–139.
31. The Dalai Lama's autobiography (*My Land and My People,* 185) makes the puzzling statement that the March 10 Norbulingka meeting "endorsed the declaration which had been made at the meetings in the city. They also made a declaration that Tibet no longer recognized Chinese authority." This statement seems at odds with the evidence, however.
32. "Xizang panfei fandui zhongyang de suowei 'shi da liyou,'" *Neibu cankao,* April 25, 1959, 4–6. Actually, there are only nine grievances, as the seventh item acknowledges that Chinese hospitals have brought benefit rather than harm.
33. See Chapter 1.
34. The Committee for Tibetan Social Welfare was an anti-Chinese political organization established in 1956 in Kalimpong by the Dalai Lama's elder brother Gyalo Dondrup, former Tibetan finance minister W. D. Shakabpa, and another Tibetan exile called Khenchung Lobsang Gyaltsen.
35. Chinese translations of both cables appear in *Neibu cankao* (April 25, 1959), 3–4. In this version, the March 16 cable is signed by Tubten Lekmon and an "Independent Assembly of Tibet," but when the same cable was reprinted in *Pingxi Xizang panluan* (189–190), his name was omitted, and the document was attributed to the "People's Assembly of Independent Tibet," a term that the Chinese applied indiscriminately—and inaccurately—to a number of organizations, including the Tibetan National Assembly. Since the Tibetan word *Gerlang* (in the name of the group that sent the first cable), rendered here as "Action," literally means "standing up," it could—with a stretch—be rendered as "independent," although it is still not clear whether that would refer to Tibet as an independent country or to the group's inde-

pendence from all other political forces (including the Tibetan ruling class). Thus, while "Independent Assembly of Tibet" may not be an extreme distortion of the Tibetan Bod Gerlang Tsokpa, the later Chinese insertion of the word *guo* (nation) into the group's name to arrive at "People's Assembly of Independent Tibet" is a distortion. Photocopies of both original cables in Tibetan are available in *Concerning the Question of Tibet,* 173. Many thanks to Matthew Akester for poring over the fuzzy photocopies of the original Tibetan cables and suggesting "Tibet People's Action Group" as a translation of Bod Gerlang Tsokpa.

36. "Wojun zai luobulinka jiaohuo yifen 'Xizang duli huiyi genbenfa,'" *Neibu cankao,* May 9, 1959, 2–8. Sources released later to the general public, such as *Jiefang Xizangshi,* do not mention this organization or this document, possibly because they suggest that anti-Chinese sentiment was pervasive at the grassroots level in Lhasa.
37. "Xizang fandidang zhangcheng," *Neibu cankao,* April 28, 1959, 7–11.
38. "Wojun zai luobulinka jiaohuo yifen 'Xizang duli huiyi genbenfa,'" *Neibu cankao,* May 9, 1959, 6.
39. "Xizang fandidang zhangcheng," *Neibu cankao,* April 28, 1959, 7–11.
40. See Chapter 16.
41. "Dalai Lama zai panluan fasheng hou de yici jianghua jilu," *Neibu cankao,* May 26, 1959, 13–14.
42. "Zhongyang zhuanfa Mao Zedong zhuxi guanyu Xizang shangceng panguo wenti de yixie yijian," *Pingxi Xizang panluan,* 81.
43. See Chapter 3.
44. See Chapter 11.
45. *Zhonggong Xizang dangshi dashiji, 1949–1994,* 92.
46. See Palden Gyatso, Tsering Shakya, and Liao Tianqi (trans.), *Xueshanxia de huoyan,* 89.
47. The Ganden Phodrang was the governmental system of Tibet as established by the Fifth Dalai Lama in 1642, named after his palace at Drepung Monastery, and voluntarily terminated by the present (Fourteenth) Dalai Lama in 2011.
48. This independent group was a precursor of today's Tibetan Women's Association, an active exile organization.
49. The description of Ngari Rinpoché's impressions in this section is based on my interview with him on July 18, 2009.
50. Huang Shaoyong, "Tieliu gungun, danxin yiyi—huiyi Lasa zhanyi zhong de qiche xingdong" (49), documents such transports.
51. Tarawa Tenzin Choenyi (Tara), *Introducing Myself.*

52. Zhang Xiangming, *Zhang Xiangming wushiwunian Xizang gongzuo shilu,* 85.
53. Lalu Ciwangduoji (Lhalu), "Youguan 1959 nian de panluan qingkuang," 140–148.
54. The Khampas accused Lhalu of abandoning his people when the PLA invaders were approaching Chamdo in 1950. Lhalu, who was the governor of Kham (with headquarters in Chamdo), had handed over the reins of government to Ngabo, his designated successor, and eventually returned to Lhasa.
55. Tarawa Tenzin Choenyi (Tara), *Introducing Myself.* Lhalu was released from prison in 1965.
56. See Chapter 2.

11. THE GATHERING CLOUDS OF WAR

1. Phala's memoir (Phala Tubten Wöden, *A Brief Life Story*) and my interviews with the Dalai Lama indicate that Phala started planning the Dalai Lama's exodus on March 11, 1959.
2. *Pingxi Xizang panluan,* 77. Dzasa Khemey was Khemey Sonam Wangdu, former commander-in-chief of the Tibetan Army. Lodoe Kalsang's rank as vice-commander of the Tibetan Army is not clear in Tibetan sources. No Tibetan memoirs, including those of Lhalu and Seshing (published in China), and those of Tara, Phuntsok, and Phala (published in Dharamsala) say that Chief of Staff Gadrang or any of the three cabinet ministers who were at the Norbulingka attended these meetings, nor do they mention the adoption of a resolution to launch a Tibetan independence movement. See Lalu Ciwangduoji (Lhalu), "Youguan 1959 nian de panluan qingkuang"; Sexin Luosangdunzhu (Seshing), "Yuan Zangjun jingweituan jingweiying de jianzhi ji youguan wo ren jingwei yingzhang shi fasheng panluan de qingkuang"; Tarawa Tenzin Choenyi (Tara), *Introducing Myself;* Phuntsok Tashi (Phuntsok), *A Life,* vol. 2; and Phala Tubten Wöden (Phala), *A Brief Life Story.*
3. *Pingxi Xizang panluan,* 78.
4. Chen Bing, "Panguo biwang," 18–31 (emphasis added).
5. *Jiefang Xizangshi,* 357 (emphasis added).
6. *Pingxi Xizang panluan,* 79–80. All quotes from the cable in this and the following paragraph are from this source.
7. Qi Xin, ed., "Dingzhi budui de Xizang pingpan zuozhan," 298; *Jiefang Xizangshi,* 369.
8. Xu Donghai, "Pingxi Lasa wuzhuang panluan muduji," 17.
9. See Chapter 2.
10. See Chapter 3.

11. See Chapter 6. *Zhongguo gongchandang Xizang zizhiqu zuzhishi ziliao, 1950–1987* (37–38) also states: "By the time of the pacification and reforms in 1959, 58 district level (analogous to today's county-level) Party branches had been formed (15 in Chamdo, 10 in Tengchen, 4 in Bomi, 3 in Lhasa, 6 in Gyantse, 7 in Shigatse, 4 in Ngari, 2 in Nagchu, and 7 in Lhokha)."
12. Xu Donghai, "Pingxi Lasa wuzhuang panluan muduji," 12.
13. Mao Zedong, "Zai Xizang junqu guanyu Bianba deng di panfei huodong de dianbao shang de piyu," *Jianguo yilai Mao Zedong wengao,* 8:12.
14. Mao Zedong, "Zai Xizang wuzhuang panluan qingkuang jianbao shang de piyu," ibid., 46.
15. Mao Zedong, "Dui zongcan zuozhanbu guanyu pingpan qingkuang baogao de piyu he xiugai," ibid., 47–48.
16. *Pingxi Xizang panluan,* 81–82. This semiclassified publication is, in turn, the source for the abridged text of the cable found in the open, official source, *Jiefang Xizangshi,* which quotes only the first half and omits the all-important second half.
17. For the Tibetan expulsion of the Chinese mission from Lhasa in July 1949, see Tsering Shakya, *The Dragon in the Land of Snows,* 7–8.
18. The complex issues of the Tibetan sociopolitical system are beyond the scope of this study. Interested readers may refer to Goldstein, *A History of Modern Tibet,* 2:9–13, or Carrasco Pizana, *Land and Polity in Tibet.*
19. *Pingxi Xizang panluan,* 85.
20. Ibid.
21. Ibid., 186–187 (emphasis added). It is difficult to determine this document's exact provenance, since Chinese sources such as the one in which it appears tend to attribute Tibetan documents indiscriminately to a misnamed "People's Assembly of Independent Tibet" (see Chapter 10), and this particular document seems to be mentioned nowhere else. If it is a draft proposal from one of the Norbulingka assemblies, it evidently came from the independence faction, which—although highly vocal—did not ultimately prevail there. (See Chapter 8.)
22. Dai Yisheng, "Gansa rexue xie chunqiu—huiyi wu, liushi niandai Xizang gong'an zhanxian de zhanyou," 55–60. Dai claims that the "heroic" Tibetan cadre who saved the day was a serf named Norbu Dorje who had escaped from the estate of the Dalai Lama's brother Gyalo Dondrup and joined the Chinese side because he hated "Tibetan feudalism." Dai adds, "Sad to say, he was hounded to death in the Cultural Revolution because of his connection to the Dalai Lama's family."
23. "Zhonggong Xizang gongwei guanyu zhixing zhongyang 3 yue 11 ri zhishi de yijian," *Pingxi Xizang panluan,* 86–87.

24. Qi Xin, "Dingzhi budui de Xizang pingpan zuozhan," 298.
25. In the 1950s, the Chinese army generally followed the Soviet system of "threes." Each army had three divisions, each division had three regiments, each regiment had three battalions, each battalion had three companies, each company had three platoons, and each platoon had three squads of ten soldiers each. In March 1959, all three regiments of Division 134 of the Fifty-Fourth Army were sent to Tibet, and Regiment 401 was the vanguard.
26. Lei Yinhai, "Jinzang pingpan jishi," 103–108.
27. *Jiefang Xizangshi*, 365.
28. The Jiangxi base area, otherwise known as the Jiangxi Soviet or the Chinese Soviet Republic, was founded in 1931 and headed by Mao Zedong within Guomindang-controlled China. It was the starting point of the Red Army's famed Long March, the Communist retreat from the Guomindang encirclement campaigns to Yan'an in 1934.
29. The Battle of Kumsong, the last battle of the Korean War, was a Chinese victory.
30. See http://baike.baidu.com/view/34448.htm.
31. Hu Liyan, *Zouguo xiaoyan: Huang Xinting zhuan*, 598. The People's Volunteer Army was Mao's designation for the PLA forces in Korea.
32. At the time, Xiadong Station (in Gansu, about 640 miles from Lanzhou) was the farthest the troops could travel by rail. They finished the long journey in a road convoy.
33. Lei Yinhai, "Jinzang pingpan jishi," 103.
34. Ibid.
35. Ji Youquan, *Xizang pingpan jishi*, 109.
36. The First and Fourth Field Armies are now subsumed into the newer system of regional military commands.
37. *Zhongguo renmin jiefangjun bubing dishiyi shi junzhanshi*, 219 ff.
38. As Regiment 401 had already been sent as a vanguard, this refers to the remaining two regiments in Division 134.
39. *Qinghai shengzhi*, 56:518.

12. A SECRET PLAN

1. Ji Youquan, *Xizang pingpan jishi*, 95; *Jiefang Xizangshi*, 370.
2. Both the temporal and spiritual roles are changing. In 2011, the Dalai Lama permanently transferred his temporal powers to an elected prime minister. He has also hinted recently that he might end his spiritual lineage and not reincarnate at all, which would stymie Chinese government plans to engineer a succession. See http://www.nytimes.com/2015/03/12/world/asia/chinas-tensions-with-dalai-lama-spill-into-the-afterlife.html?_r=0.

3. Author interview with the Dalai Lama, June 30, 2009.
4. Athar Norbu, "The Life of Athar Norbu from Lithang."
5. For the English versions of these missives, see *Concerning the Question of Tibet,* 26–35. For the Chinese versions, see *Pingxi Xizang panluan,* 128–133.
6. All the letters are quoted verbatim here from the official English version published in 1959 in Beijing for Chinese propaganda purposes. Quotations from this text preserve the spellings and terminology used in Beijing at the time.
7. The Dalai Lama wrote in Tibetan, and the correspondence was conducted through translation. He signed all of his letters "Ta bla," his own modest shorthand for "Ta la'i bla ma," although the Chinese translated it variously as "The Dalai" or "The Dalai Lama."
8. Dalai Lama, *Freedom in Exile,* 136.
9. See Chapter 11.
10. PLA convoys were probably a common sight in Lhasa in those days. Huang Shaoyong, political commissar of the PLA transport regiment, states that in January 1959, six hundred to seven hundred trucks were sent into Lhasa with construction supplies for Chinese installations to use to build fortifications. Huang Shaoyong, "Tieliu gungun, danxin yiyi—huiyi Lasa zhanyi zhong de qiche xingdong," 47–49.
11. *Pingxi Xizang panluan,* 81.
12. Tarawa Tenzin Choenyi (Tara), *Introducing Myself.*
13. Dalai Lama, *Freedom in Exile,* 135.
14. Kunga Samten's story in this section is based on Dewatshang Kunga Samten (Kunga Samten), *Flight at the Cuckoo's Behest,* 1–9.
15. Impressions and quotes attributed to Phala in this section are based on Phala Tubten Wöden (Phala), *A Brief Life Story.*
16. There were two sets of walls inside the Norbulingka complex, a white outer wall and a yellow inner one. The area within the yellow wall housed the Dalai Lama and a few of his essential chamberlains. The area between the inner yellow wall and the outer white wall contained a second "Yabshi House" for the Dalai Lama's family to use in the summer, his tutors' housing, the cabinet offices, stables, guard barracks, chamberlains' dormitories, storerooms, and other offices.
17. Author interview with the Dalai Lama, June 30, 2009.
18. Ibid.
19. Dalai Lama, *Freedom in Exile,* 135.
20. The word General Tan uses here implies being abducted or held hostage. This official 1959 translation into English has toned it down.

21. *Concerning the Question of Tibet,* 34.
22. *Jiefang Xizangshi,* 363. The Dalai Lama was very surprised when I informed him of the letter's authorship during a personal interview.
23. Mao Zedong, *Mao Zedong Xizang gongzuo wenxuan,* 165.
24. Dalai Lama, *My Land and My People,* 190–191.
25. *Concerning the Question of Tibet,* 35.
26. *Jiefang Xizangshi,* 365. This source also omits the information that Ngabo had first written to the Dalai Lama.
27. *Xizang gemingshi,* 127. This source was printed in an edition of only about seven thousand copies.
28. Wang Guozhen, "Tianjiang pili cheng xiongwan," 40. The location of Xishan, mentioned in Chinese sources of the time, is unknown today.
29. Ibid., 39.
30. Dalai Lama, *My Land and My People,* 192.
31. Chen Bing, "Panguo biwang,"19.
32. Phala Tubten Wöden (Phala), *A Brief Life Story.*

13. GO! GO! TONIGHT!

1. Yang Shangkun, *Yang Shangkun riji,* 366.
2. The officers Mao summoned included Zhang Jingwu and Zhang Guohua, as well as Huang Kecheng, PLA chief of staff and general secretary of the Chinese Central Military Commission.
3. Dalai Lama, *My Land and My People,* 137.
4. Ibid., 193–194.
5. Ngabo is using an honorific form of address for his fellow cabinet ministers.
6. Gejieba Danzengduoji (Gegyepa), "Fenlie zhuyi fenzi zai Lasa fadong wuzhuang panluan de qingkuang," 66–70. Extant sources are somewhat confused, and Gegyepa's dates seem incorrect. There were probably two messages to Ngabo, one delivered by Gegyepa on March 14 and the other by Minister Shasur's attendant on March 17.
7. Dalai Lama, *My Land and My People,* 194.
8. Yang Shangkun, *Yang Shangkun riji,* 366; Liu Chongwen and Chen Shaochou, eds., *Liu Shaoqi nianpu,* 2:453.
9. There are various reports of where the two shells landed. John F. Avedon's *In Exile from the Land of Snows,* which is based on refugee interviews, recounts that the first one landed in a marsh outside the northern palace wall, and that the second one landed in a pond near the Chensel Phodrang (54). Soon after the Dalai Lama reached India, he stated only that "the shells fell in a nearby pond" (*Concerning the Question of Tibet,* 78). His *Freedom in Exile* (136) says that the shells landed "in a marsh outside the northern gate." Chinese sources

such as *Xizang gemingshi* (124) state that the shells landed a few hundred yards outside the northern palace wall.

10. The description above is derived from the Dalai Lama's *My Land and My People,* 194–195, and my interview with the Dalai Lama on June 30, 2009.
11. Dalai Lama, *Freedom in Exile,* 136.
12. Author interview with the Dalai Lama, June 30, 2009.
13. Dalai Lama and A. A. Shiromany, *The Spirit of Tibet: Universal Heritage,* 6.
14. The Chinese rebuttal is quoted here verbatim from the official 1959 Chinese translation into English, in *Concerning the Question of Tibet,* 71–72. For the Chinese text, see "Ping suowei 'Dalai Lama de shengming,'" *Guanyu Xizang wenti,* 102.
15. *Xizang gemingshi,* 124.
16. The "economic policeman" was probably engaged in antismuggling operations.
17. Ji Youquan, *Xizang pingpan jishi,* 92. Ji seems to have slightly garbled the policeman's name, which is corrected here.
18. *Zhonggong Xizang dangshi dashiji, 1949–1994,* 92–93.
19. *Pingxi Xizang panluan,* 23.
20. *Jiefang Xizangshi,* 366.
21. This estimate was reported to me by Ngari Rinpoché on July 18, 2009. It is corroborated by an April 3 Indian newspaper report stating that "the total number of people who had come with the Dalai Lama and after him was 80" (Hutheesing, *A White Book,* 70). For the additional escorts, see Chapters 15 and 22.
22. Ji Youquan, *Xizang pingpan jishi,* 90.
23. *Pingxi Xizang panluan,* 25.
24. Author interview with Tenpa Soepa, October 9, 2009.
25. *Jiefang Xizangshi,* 363.
26. McCarthy, *Tears of the Lotus,* 183.
27. Phuntsok Tashi (Phuntsok), *A Life,* vol. 2.
28. Although these objects were of significant value, they were probably not sufficient to sustain the needs of the large party of escapees all the way into India; at the time of their departure, they had not yet planned that far ahead. There is some controversy about the date when the valuables were retrieved. Ji Youquan's *Xizang pingpan jishi* is unclear on the subject. *Jiefang Xizangshi* has March 16, but "Xizang gaxia gongzuo riji" (a translated excerpt in *Pingxi Xizang panluan*) has March 17. In "Fenlie zhuyi fenzi zai Lasa fadong wuzhuang panluan de qingkuang," Gegyepa (who went with Liushar) states that it was March 16, but later says that he saw Surkhang that night at 9:00, and the next morning he heard that the Dalai Lama had already left, which would suggest a date of March 17.

29. See Phuntsok Tashi (Phuntsok), *A Life,* vol. 2. He does not give the number of Tibetan guards.
30. Sexin Luosangdunzhu (Seshing), "Yuan Zangjun jingweituan jingweiying de jianzhi ji youguan wo ren jingwei yingzhang shi fasheng panluan de qingkuang," 138–139.
31. Ibid. "Rama Gang" is transliterated with the wrong Chinese characters in Seshing's account.
32. Phala Tubten Wöden (Phala), *A Brief Life Story.* According to Phala and my oral interview with Tenpa Soepa on October 9, 2009, Tenpa Soepa, who lived near the Indian Consulate, went with Tubten Tsepal.

14. THE NIGHT FERRY

Note: In addition to the sources cited below, in composing this chapter I have also consulted John F. Avedon, In *Exile from the Land of Snows,* chap. 2.

1. Quotes and impressions attributed to Ngari Rinpoché in this chapter are drawn from my interview with him on July 18, 2009.
2. This section is based on the Dalai Lama's *Freedom in Exile,* 137–139.
3. Palden Lhamo, one of the *dharmapalas* (wrathful deities who guard the Buddhist faith), is the consort of Mahakala (also a *dharmapala*) and a protector of Tibet and the Dalai Lama.
4. Phala Tubten Wöden (Phala), *A Brief Life Story.*
5. Phuntsok Tashi (Phuntsok), *A Life,* vol. 2.
6. Ibid.
7. Quotes and impressions attributed to Tenpa Soepa in this chapter are from my interview with him on September 8, 2009, and Patt, "The Momo Gun," 133–261.
8. Author interview with Thinley Phuntsok, April 19, 2009.
9. Tubten Khetsun, *Memories of Life in Lhasa Under Chinese Rule,* 32.
10. Dalai Lama interview with Cao Changqing. See http://caochangqing.com/gb/newsdisp.php?News_ID=568. He also described this moment in his *Freedom in Exile,* 139.

15. INTO THE HIMALAYAS

1. This section is based on Phuntsok Tashi (Phuntsok), *A Life,* vol. 2; it also draws from my interview with Ngari Rinpoché, July 18, 2009; Dewatshang Kunga Samten (Kunga Samten), *Flight at the Cuckoo's Behest,* 8–10; and the Dalai Lama, *My Land and My People,* 201–204. See Map 7 for the escape route.

2. Phuntsok Tashi (Phuntsok), *A Life*, vol. 2. Lumbala Pass, which is slightly to the east of Che Pass, is often considered to be part of Che Pass.
3. *Pingxi Xizang panluan*, 82. See Chapter 11.
4. Ji Youquan, *Baixue*, 494.
5. See Li Jue, "Li Jue jiangjun huiyi: Zhongguo diyike yuanzidan yanzhi de riri yeye," *Zhongguo xinwen wang*, March 8, 2006, at http://www.chinanews.com.cn/news/2006/2006-03-08/8/700285.shtml. Li Jue was vice-commander at the PLA Tibet Military Command from May 1955 to January 1958; he was Logistics department head from May 1955 until August 1957 (*Zhongguo gongchandang Xizang zizhiqu zuzhishi ziliao, 1950–1987*, 473). According to Jampel Gyatso (Jiangbian Jiacuo, *Li Jue zhuan*, 190–191), Li Jue was flown back specially to Lhasa for the 1958 purge at the CCP Tibet Work Committee, and probably returned to Beijing in June of that year.
6. This includes sources such as Li Jue's memoir, "Huiyi heping jiefang Xizang," or Jiangbian Jiacuo (Jampel Gyatso), *Li Jue zhuan*.
7. Ji Youquan, *Baixue*, 494.
8. Zhu Xiushan, "Lasa zhi zhan de huigu," 32–37.
9. Ji Youquan, *Baixue*, 494.
10. The March 19 date for Beijing's notification of the Dalai Lama's escape will be discussed below. See Yang Shangkun, *Yang Shangkun riji*, 367; Xu Donghai, "Pingxi Lasa wuzhuang panluan muduji," 17; *Pingxi Xizang panluan*, 27.
11. See Dalai Lama, *My Land and My People* and Phuntsok Tashi (Phuntsok), *A Life*, vol. 2. In personal interviews with me, Ngari Rinpoché, Juchen Tubten, and Tenpa Soepa have all confirmed that they remember it as a cloudy night.
12. The Dalai Lama's description of his decision-making process (*Freedom in Exile*, 136) indicates that he decided rather quickly, almost on the spot. After the Nechung Oracle urged him to go, he conducted a divination on his own, and then made up his mind. Once his decision was made, he has stated to me in an interview, he put his fears behind him and started to prepare for the journey.
13. Chen Bing, "Panguo biwang," 18–31.
14. Ji Youquan, *Xizang pingpan jishi*, 92.
15. See Chapter 13.
16. Zhang Xiangming, *Zhang Xiangming wushiwunian Xizang gongzuo shilu*, 85.
17. Yang Shangkun, *Yang Shangkun riji*, 367. The Dalai Lama left the Norbulingka shortly after 10:00 P.M. on March 17, Lhasa time, which would technically place his departure very early on March 18, Beijing time.
18. Xu Donghai, "Pingxi Lasa wuzhuang panluan muduji," 16.
19. *Pingxi Xizang panluan*, 79. See also Chapter 11.

20. Xu Donghai, "Pingxi Lasa wuzhuang panluan muduji," 17.
21. *Jiefang Xizangshi,* 366.
22. *Zhonggong Xizang dangshi dashiji, 1949–1994,* 93.
23. Yang Shangkun, *Yang Shangkun riji,* 367. Yang's diary is an open (unclassified) publication. Even as late as the battle-planning meeting on the morning of April 20, Tan Guansan was concerned that reports of the Dalai Lama's escape had not been completely verified. Ji Youquan, *Xizang pingpan jishi,* 111.
24. Xu Donghai, "Pingxi Lasa wuzhuang panluan muduji," 17.
25. *Pingxi Xizang panluan,* 27.
26. Xu Jiatun, *Xu Jiatun Xianggang huiyilu,* 327–328.
27. The Dalai Lama has stated in his autobiography (*My Land and My People,* 202) and in an interview with me that when he left the Norbulingka, he was not aware that he would be going into exile forever. His intention at first was to try to renegotiate with the Chinese from the safety of Lhokha. On March 22, 1959, when he finally learned of the Battle of Lhasa, he realized that he had no choice but to leave Tibet. (See Chapter 22.)
28. Phuntsok Tashi (Phuntsok), *A Life,* vol. 2. Dewatshang Kunga Samten's *Flight at the Cuckoo's Behest* also describes these nightly meetings.
29. Ji Youquan, *Xizang pingpan jishi,* 111–113.
30. See the end of Chapter 18.
31. Ji Youquan, *Xizang pingpan jishi,* 109–110.
32. See Tibetan memoirists Chogyam Trungpa (*Born in Tibet,* 70) and Jamyang Norbu (*Warriors of Tibet,* 115), both of whom mention that they heard the Dalai Lama had been "abducted to India" while they themselves were escaping across the Himalayas.
33. *Pingxi Xizang panluan,* 89.
34. *Jiefang Xizangshi,* 366.
35. This press release was issued at Tezpur, India, on April 18, 1959. Translation from *Concerning the Question of Tibet,* 78.
36. *Pingxi Xizang panluan,* 143–148; *Concerning the Question of Tibet,* 67–74.
37. Mao had nineteen thousand troops in all of Tibet at the time. See *Zhongguo gongchandang Xizang zizhiqu zuzhishi ziliao, 1950–1987,* 18.
38. There is an extant memoir by a Chinese pilot claiming to have seen the Dalai Lama and his entourage crossing the Tsangpo River, and refrained from shooting, but the incorrect details and dates in his account undermine its reliability.
39. The Sixteenth Gyalwa Karmapa, Rangjung Rigpe Dorje, left Tibet in March 1959, settled in Sikkim, and died during a speaking tour of the United States in 1981.

40. Author interview with Ngari Rinpoché, July 18, 2009.
41. Chonggye is the county seat of Chonggye County in today's Lhokha Prefecture, near the southern border of Tibet.
42. Phuntsok Tashi (Phuntsok), *A Life,* vol. 2; Phala Tubten Wöden (Phala), *A Brief Life Story;* and Dewatshang Kunga Samten, *Flight at the Cuckoo's Behest,* 10.
43. Tingri and Gyantse are located in today's Shigatse Prefecture.
44. Phuntsok Tashi (Phuntsok), *A Life,* vol. 2.
45. Ibid.
46. Ibid. The Ganden Phodrang was the ancient governmental system of Tibet. See Chapter 10.
47. *Pingxi Xizang panluan,* 88. It is not clear what the Panchen Lama meant by "armed rebellion." He sent this cable on March 19, but he was not formally notified of the Battle of Lhasa until noon on March 20. See Jiangbian Jiacuo (Jampel Gyatso), *Shishi Banchen Lama zhuanji,* 73.
48. *New York Times,* May 14, 1959, 30.
49. See *Zhongguo gongchandang Xizang zizhiqu zushishi ziliao, 1950–1987,* 69; *Tibetans in Exile, 1959–1969,* iii.
50. See Chogyam Trungpa, *Born in Tibet,* 185–195.
51. Extant memoirs provide many descriptions of fleeing nomads being strafed from the air by PLA bombers, although specific casualty tolls are not available. If they were kept at all by the Chinese, they have never been declassified. For a Tibetan description, see Jamyang Norbu, *Warriors of Tibet,* 140–141. For a Chinese one, see Hong Weiquan, "Xueyu jiaofei ji," 13–16.
52. In addition to the Dalai Lama and the Sixteenth Gyalwa Karmapa, the other two were the Second Dudjom Rinpoché Jigdral Yeshe Dorje (1904–1987), head of the Nyingma order, and the Sakya Trizin (b. 1945), head of the Sakya lineage.
53. Dalai Lama, *My Land and My People,* 209.
54. *New York Times,* March 21, 1959, 1.
55. Phuntsok Tashi (Phuntsok), *A Life,* vol. 2.
56. Athar's memoir does not give the date when he received Phala's letter. Chonggye (in Lhokha) was a major point on the route from Lhasa; it was therefore a likely spot for Athar to intercept the Dalai Lama. The weapons he and Lhotse were carrying had arrived in the CIA's second airdrop into Lhokha on February 22, 1959. See Dawa Norbu, *China's Tibet Policy,* 270.

16. BATTLE AT DAYBREAK

1. Patt, "The Momo Gun," 149–150; author interview with Tenpa Soepa, September 8, 2009.

2. The letter is published in Chinese translation in *Pingxi Xizang panluan*, 193–194.
3. See Chapter 10. Perhaps through an oversight, the Chinese translators and editors of *Pingxi Xizang panluan* retained the Dalai Lama's original reference to the "Expanded Tibetan National Assembly" within the text instead of substituting their customary misnomer, "People's Assembly of Independent Tibet."
4. Patt, "The Momo Gun," 149–150; author interview with Tenpa Soepa, September 8, 2009.
5. Tarawa Tenzin Choenyi (Tara), *Introducing Myself.* Tubten Khetsun also recalls that March 19 was ruled out as an inauspicious day. See Tubten Khetsun, *Memories of Life in Lhasa under Chinese Rule,* 33.
6. For Lobsang Tashi, see Chapter 1. Tarawa Tenzin Choenyi (Tara), *Introducing Myself.*
7. *Pingxi xizang panluan,* 193–194.
8. Author interview with Juchen Tubten, October 8, 2009.
9. Huang Shaoyong, "Tieliu gungun, danxin yiyi—huiyi Lasa zhanyi zhong de qiche xingdong," 51. The "August First Farm"—named to commemorate the 1927 Communist-led Nanchang uprising and the designated founding day of the PLA—was established in 1952 to produce food for the PLA in Lhasa. See Map 6 for the locations of the farm and the Artillery Regiment 308 camp.
10. Chen Bing, "Panguo biwang," 19–20.
11. Ibid.
12. Author interview with Thinley Phuntsok, April 19, 2009.
13. Huang Shaoyong, "Tieliu gungun, danxin yiyi—huiyi Lasa zhanyi zhong de qiche xingdong," 46–54.
14. Author interview with Juchen Tubten, September 22, 2009.
15. Qi Xin, ed., "Dingzhi budui de Xizang pingpan zuozhan," 298.
16. Tarawa Tenzin Choenyi (Tara), *Introducing Myself.*
17. Tsarong Dundul Namgyal and Trinlay Chödron, *In the Service of His Country,* 145.
18. Ji Youquan, *Xizang pingpan jishi,* 95. The Chinese called the place "Oxtail Hill," a name the Tibetans did not use.
19. Huang Shaoyong, "Tieliu gungun, danxin yiyi—huiyi Lasa zhanyi zhong de qiche xingdong," 51–52.
20. Patt, "The Momo Gun," 151.
21. Tarawa Tenzin Choenyi (Tara), *Introducing Myself.* See also Tubten Khetsun, *Memories of Life in Lhasa under Chinese Rule,* 34.
22. Yang Shangkun, *Yang Shangkun riji,* 366; Jiangbian Jiacuo (Jampel Gyatso), *Shishi Banchan Lama zhuanji,* 73.

23. See Chapter 11.
24. Sexin Luosangdunzhu (Seshing), "Yuan Zangjun jingweituan jingweiying de jianzhi ji youguan wo ren jingwei yingzhang shi fasheng panluan de qingkuang," 140.
25. Xu Donghai, "Pingxi Lasa wuzhuang panluan muduji," 17.
26. Wang Qixiu, "Qinli 1959 nian Xizang pingpan," at http://dangshi.people.com.cn/GB/8339083.html.
27. Zhu Xiushan, "Lasa zhi zhan de huigu," 32.
28. Ji Youquan, *Xizang pingpan jishi,* 96.
29. According to Ji Youquan (*Xizang pingpan jishi,* 87), the Soviet Union had set up satellite monitoring of Tibet on March 10, 1959.
30. See Chapter 11.
31. *Pingxi Xizang panluan,* 29. The overview was written by Chen Bing.
32. Ji Youquan, *Xizang pingpan jishi,* 95.
33. *Jiefang Xizangshi,* 37.
34. Xu Yan, *Taojin baizhan pingshuo gujin,* 287.
35. Ji Youquan, *Xizang pingpan jishi,* 113.
36. Xu Yan, *Taojin baizhan pingshuo gujin,* 287.
37. *Jiefang Xizangshi,* 363.
38. Chen Bing, "Zangjun shilüe," 85–99.
39. *Zhonggong Xizang dangshi dashiji, 1949–1994,* 83. See Chapter 4.
40. Wang Qixiu, "Qinli 1959 nian Xizang pingpan," at http://dangshi.people.com.cn/GB/8339083.html.
41. Xu Yan, *Taojin baizhan pingshuo gujin,* 286.
42. Chen Bing, "Zangjun shilüe," 85–99.
43. Chen Bing, "Panguo biwang," 20–21.
44. My account of Wu Chen's mission is based on Ji Youquan, *Xizang pingpan jishi,* 95–100. Zhang Xiangming quoted at the beginning of Chapter 17, also describes how the predawn "counterattack" was decided upon.
45. *Zhonggong Xizang dangshi dashiji, 1949–1994,* 95.
46. Ji Youquan, *Xizang pingpan jishi,* 109.
47. Some corroboration of this clash can be found in Tenpa Soepa's memoir (Patt, "The Momo Gun," 152), although the term "attack" hardly seems merited.
48. *Jiefang Xizangshi,* 370. See Chapter 19 for the Lhasa Construction Office conflict.
49. Ji Youquan, *Xizang pingpan jishi,* 101.
50. Zhu Xiushan, "Lasa zhi zhan de huigu," 33.
51. *Jiefang Xizangshi,* 372.
52. Ji Youquan, *Xizang pingpan jishi,* 117. Note that Chen Bing's "Panguo biwang" (22) puts the end of this battle with Tibetan Army Regiment 4 at around the

time of the fall of Chakpori Hill, approximately at noon on March 20, even though Zhu Xiushan (the commanding officer of the battle with Regiment 4) places it early that morning.

53. Xu Donghai, "Pingxi Lasa wuzhuang panluan muduji," 19.
54. *Zhonggong Xizang dangshi dashiji, 1949–1994,* 95.
55. *Jiefang Xizangshi,* 371.
56. *Guanyu Xizang wenti,* 12.
57. Author interview with Tenpa Soepa, September 8, 2009.
58. Tubten Khetsun, *Memories of Life in Lhasa under Chinese Rule,* 34.
59. Tarawa Tenzin Choenyi (Tara), *Introducing Myself.*
60. Author interview with Juchen Tubten, September 22, 2009.

17. THE DEATH OF THE MEDICINE BUDDHA

1. Zhang Xiangming (*Zhang Xiangming wushiwunian Xizang gongzuo shilu,* 86) says they had been there all night.
2. *Jiefang Xizangshi,* 371.
3. Zhang Xiangming, *Zhang Xiangming wushiwunian Xizang gongzuo shilu,* 86.
4. In fact, the Battle of Lhasa ultimately preempted any such announcement; although the Tibetans had planned to make one on March 20, they never had a chance to do so in the chaos of that day.
5. Ji Youquan, *Xizang pingpan jishi,* 110. "Kham" in this passage probably refers to the old province of Xikang.
6. Ibid., 22.
7. Huang Shaoyong, "Tieliu gungun, danxin yiyi—huiyi Lasa zhanyi zhong de qiche xingdong," 52. The PLA's July First Farm was named after the founding day of the Chinese Communist Party.
8. Ji Youquan, *Xizang pingpan jishi,* 110. Ji merely states that Huang's regiment was west of the Norbulingka at the time.
9. Lalu Ciwangduoji (Lhalu), "Youguan 1959 nian de panluan qingkuang," 146.
10. Author interview with Juchen Tubten, September 22, 2009.
11. Zhu Xiushan, "Lasa zhi zhan de huigu," 33.
12. Tudeng Ciren (a graduate of the Institute and later a chief faculty member), describes the holdings of the Institute and estimates the number of students at sixty-four (Tudeng Ciren, "Yaowangshan yixue lizhongyuan jianshi," 86–93). Many sources refer to the destruction of the Chakpori Hill campus by the Chinese, but available information about how many people may have been present on March 20, 1959, is scant. See, for example, Meyer, "The Golden Century of Tibetan Medicine," 117.

13. Wang Guozhen, "Tianjiang pili cheng xiongwan," 39.
14. Author interview with Juchen Tubten, September 22, 2009; Wang Guozhen, "Tianjiang pili cheng xiongwan," 40; Tudeng Ciren, "Yaowangshan yixue lizhongyuan jianshi," 86–93.
15. Wang Guozhen, "Tianjiang pili cheng xiongwan," 40–41.
16. Xu Yan, *Taojin baizhan pingshuo gujin,* 287.
17. Ji Youquan, *Xizang pingpan jishi,* 113.
18. Jamyang Norbu, "March Winds," at http://www.jamyangnorbu.com/blog/2009/03/06/march-winds/. For the presence of the Drapchi Regiment (Regiment 2) on Chakpori Hill, see Chapters 8 and 10.
19. *Xizang gongzuo wenxian xuanbian, 1949–2005,* 70.
20. Author interview with Juchen Tubten, September 22, 2009. In *Xizang pingpan jishi* (114), Ji Youquan says the shelling began at 8:00 A.M. He may have confused Beijing time and Lhasa time, but he does state that the shelling lasted for two hours and fifteen minutes. Major Chinese sources such as *Jiefang Xizangshi* (372) and *Xizang gemingshi* (130) say it began at 10:00 A.M. and lasted for approximately one hour.
21. Vice-Battalion Commander Zhang Fuchen and Political Instructor Cao Zhikai were members of Regiment 159's Battalion 2, Company 4.
22. Ji Youquan, *Xizang pingpan jishi,* 114.
23. Wang Guozhen, "Tianjiang pili cheng xiongwan," 41.
24. The *dungchen* is the Tibetan longhorn. This song is quoted from a Chinese translation of Tudeng Ciren's (originally Tibetan-language) study of Chakpori, "Yaowangshan yixue lizhongyuan jianshi" (90). The Chinese translation of the song has "*suona,*" which is a Chinese instrument comparable to the oboe. I have corrected it here to *dungchen* based on historical photographs of this Tibetan practice.
25. Ji Youquan, *Xizang pingpan jishi,* 116. See also Tarawa Tenzin Choenyi (Tara), *Introducing Myself.*
26. Chen Bing's "Panguo biwang" (22) and *Jiefang Xizangshi* (372) concur that the Chakpori shelling began around 10:00 A.M.; Ji Youquan's *Xizang pingpan jishi* (114), however, gives the time as 8:00 A.M., possibly in a confusion between Lhasa time and Beijing time. Sources tend to agree that the PLA had occupied the hill by around noon.
27. Wang Guozhen, "Tianjiang pili cheng xiongwan," 41–42.
28. Ji Youquan, *Xizang pingpan jishi,* 113–115.
29. Author interviews with Juchen Tubten, September 22 and October 8, 2009; Tarawa Tenzin Choenyi (Tara), *Introducing Myself;* Tubten Khetsun, *Memories of Life in Lhasa under Chinese Rule,* 35–36.

30. See the statement from Xu Yan's *Taojin baizhan pingshuo gujin* (287) quoted earlier in this chapter.
31. *Jiefang Xizangshi*, 372.
32. The photo and caption can be viewed at http://news.xinhuanet.com/english/2009-03/08/content_10967414.htm.

18. RIVER OF BLOOD

1. *Pingxi Xizang panluan*, 91. As Regiment 401 had already been sent as a vanguard, these orders for Division 134 apply to its remaining two regiments.
2. See Map 6. Regiment 308 was at the mouth of the Drip Valley, directly opposite the city, on the south bank of the river, to the east of the Rama Gang ferry. It is difficult to determine the precise location of the company from Regiment 159, although it was also on the south bank.
3. Patt, "The Momo Gun," 152–153.
4. Sexin Luosangdunzhu (Seshing), "Yuan Zangjun jingweituan jingweiying de jianzhi ji youguan wo ren jingwei yingzhang shi fasheng panluan de qingkuang," 140.
5. Gejieba Danzengduoji (Gegyepa), "Fenlie zhuyi fenzi zai Lasa fadong wuzhuang panluan de qingkuang," 70.
6. Ibid., 70.
7. *Neibu cankao*, May 7, 1959; reprinted in *Pingxi Xizang panluan*, 188.
8. See Chapter 10.
9. Tubten Khetsun, *Memories of Life in Lhasa under Chinese Rule*, 35–36.
10. Ibid. Tarawa Tenzin Choenyi (Tara), *Introducing Myself*, and my interviews with Juchen Tubten (September 22 and October 8, 2009) also indicate that the bombing intensified in the afternoon, reaching a peak at 3:00 to 4:00 P.M.
11. Tarawa Tenzin Choenyi (Tara), *Introducing Myself*; Patt, "The Momo Gun," 153.
12. *Jiefang Xizangshi*, 372.
13. Ji Youquan, *Xizang pingpan jishi*, 115.
14. Xu Yan, *Taojin baizhan pingshuo gujin*, 287–288.
15. Wang Guozhen, "Tianjiang pili cheng xiongwan," 42.
16. Ibid.
17. See Patt, "The Momo Gun," Tubten Khetsun, *Memories of Life in Lhasa under Chinese Rule*, and Tarawa Tenzin Choenyi (Tara), *Introducing Myself*.
18. Sexin Luosangdunzhu (Seshing), "Yuan Zangjun jingweituan jingweiying de jianzhi ji youguan wo ren jingwei yingzhang shi fasheng panluan de qingkuang," 141.
19. Tara's story in this section comes from Tarawa Tenzin Choenyi (Tara), *Introducing Myself*.

20. Tarawa Tenzin Choenyi (Tara), *Introducing Myself.* Tenpa Soepa's story in this section is based on Patt, "The Momo Gun," 153, and my interviews with him on September 8 and October 9, 2009; For Tubten Khetsun's, see his *Memories of Life in Lhasa under Chinese Rule,* 36.
21. Wang's Regiment 308 was on the south side of the river, but it had set up a lookout post on Chakpori Hill. He probably gave orders by telephone.
22. Wang Guozhen, "Tianjiang pili cheng xiongwan," 43.
23. Jiangbian Jiacuo (Jampel Gyatso), *Xueshan mingjiang Tan Guansan,* 190. Even though Tan was in Lhasa, he—like all the Chinese stationed there—set his watch by Beijing time.
24. *Zhonggong Xizang dangshi dashiji, 1949–1994,* 95.
25. Ji Youquan, *Xizang pingpan jishi,* 114.
26. Li Jue was pilloried for the "Five-Department Petition" that he had sent to Mao and the Chinese Central Military Commission on February 20, 1957, reporting problems faced by five PLA departments in Tibet with regard to issues including housing, pay, quality of life, officers' health, daily necessities, and cultural life. At the time of the purge he was flown back to Lhasa specially from Qinghai, where he had headed China's confidential Nuclear Weapons Bureau. See Jiangbian Jiacuo (Jampel Gyatso), *Li Jue zhuan,* 176–197.
27. *Zhonggong Xizang dangshi dashiji, 1949–1994,* 79.
28. The associates included United Front section chief Chen Jingbo and Propaganda section chief Bai Yunfeng. See Fan Ming and Hao Rui, *Xizang neibu zhi zheng,* 369–394, and *Zhonggong Xizang dangshi dashiji, 1949–1994,* 79.
29. Fan Ming's stance differed from Mao's on two important points: (1) he recommended immediate socialist reform in Tibet, whereas Mao espoused a more gradual approach; and (2) he advocated granting the Panchen Lama equal status with the Dalai Lama, whereas Zhang Jingwu and Zhang Guohua (and Mao) believed the Dalai Lama should rank above the Panchen Lama. See Fan Ming and Hao Rui, *Xizang neibu zhizheng,* 387–394.
30. Ji Youquan, *Xizang pingpan jishi,* 114–115.
31. Ibid., 115.
32. *Pingxi Xizang panluan,* 90. This source does not include a time stamp for the cable.
33. *Zhonggong Xizang dangshi dashiji, 1949–1994,* 95. This source gives a time of 6:00 P.M. Beijing time (4:00 P.M. Lhasa time), after the fall of Chakpori Hill and during the bombardment of the Norbulingka.
34. See Chapter 3.
35. Ji Youquan, *Xizang pingpan jishi,* 115.
36. This section is based on my interview with Juchen Tubten on September 22, 2009.

37. Wang Guozhen, "Tianjiang pili cheng xiongwan," 42–43.
38. Ji Youquan, *Xizang pingpan jishi,* 104.
39. Author interview with Juchen Tubten, September 22, 2009.
40. Wang Guozhen, "Tianjiang pili cheng xiongwan," 45.
41. Ibid., 43.
42. Tara's reference is to Lhasa time. Tarawa Tenzin Choenyi (Tara), *Introducing Myself.*
43. The Receiving Pavilion was a ceremonial building used during the Qing dynasty for installing and seeing off successive representatives of the Qing government in Tibet.
44. Wang Guozhen, "Tianjiang pili cheng xiongwan," 43. In this passage, the infantrymen were pleased because Wang's artillery had cleared the way for them.
45. Juchen Tubten's impressions in this section are from my interviews with him on September 22 and October 8, 2009.
46. Ji Youquan, *Xizang pingpan jishi,* 115–116.
47. This was Company 4 of Battalion 2, Regiment 155.
48. Tubten Khetsun, *Memories of Life in Lhasa under Chinese Rule,* 35–36.
49. Tarawa Tenzin Choenyi (Tara), *Introducing Myself.*
50. This tally is from Huang Shaoyong, "Tieliu gungun, danxin yiyi—huiyi Lasa zhanyi zhong de qiche xingdong," 53.

19. INFERNO

1. *Cankao ziliao,* March 18, 1959, afternoon edition. Nehru's speech is also quoted in the *New York Times* (March 21, 1959, 4), which emphasizes his "government's strenuous efforts in the past to play down the Khamba uprising." In this speech to Parliament, Nehru is probably referring to Tibetan strife in general, which had been reported in the Indian press. However, he may have heard about the trouble in Lhasa by March 17, as it seems likely that the Indian Consulate had cabled New Delhi about it by then. Lhasa had been in turmoil for a week, and the Indian Consulate had been involved from the outset on March 10. On that day, Tibetan Cabinet Minister Sampo was treated at the Indian Consulate clinic for wounds inflicted by stone-throwing demonstrators, and Tibetan demonstrators marched on the Consulate to demand that it cable the Indian government in support of their cause.
2. *Cankao ziliao,* March 31, 1959, afternoon edition, and April 10, 1959, morning edition.
3. Ji Youquan, *Xizang pingpan jishi,* 117.

4. Yulo Tulku Dawa Tsering (1926–2002) was arrested by the Chinese in the aftermath of the Battle at Ramoche Temple, and incarcerated for twenty years. He was released in 1979, and in 1982 he was appointed to the Lhasa People's Political Consultative Conference, the Tibet branch of the Chinese Buddhist Association, and the Lhasa Municipal Buddhist Association. He was arrested again in 1988 and released in 1994. His handwritten memoir, *A Pure Drop of Yulo's Sweat,* a main source for this chapter, was smuggled out to India and published in Dharamsala in 2006.
5. Yulo Tulku Dawa Tsering (Yulo), *A Pure Drop of Yulo's Sweat.*
6. Yulo's memoir describes the progress of the battle in detail, but specifies only one exact time point: that he spent the night before the battle (March 20) patrolling the temple. This places the battle on March 21. Additional details of the timing have been derived by corroborating Yulo's narration with Chinese sources such as *Jiefang Xizangshi,* although some confusion remains surrounding the exact hour of the attack on the Lhasa Construction Office.
7. This was the Ramoche Jowo statue, said to have been part of the dowry brought by the Nepali princess Bhrikuti when she came to Lhasa as a consort to King Songtsen Gampo in the seventh century.
8. *Zhonggong Xizang dangshi dashiji, 1949–1994,* 95.
9. Tibetan sources (such as Yulo, *A Pure Drop of Yulo's Sweat,* and my interview with Jampa Tenzin on October 12, 2009) indicate that a small contingent of Tibetan soldiers was sent to protect Ramoche Temple and the Jokhang. Some of them were involved in combat, although little is known about their role.
10. Ji Youquan's *Xizang pingpan jishi* says that Ramoche Temple was taken at 9:00 P.M. on March 20, 1959, but this seems incorrect.
11. This encounter evidently took place very near Ramoche Temple, although it is impossible to pinpoint the exact location.
12. Yulo Tulku Dawa Tsering (Yulo), *A Pure Drop of Yulo's Sweat.*
13. Chen Bing, "Panguo biwang," 23. Chen Bing and Yulo (*A Pure Drop of Yulo's Sweat*) concur in dating the battle of Ramoche Temple to March 21.
14. Yulo Tulku Dawa Tsering (Yulo), *A Pure Drop of Yulo's Sweat.* Tsemonling Temple, built in the 1820s, was the seat of successive regents.
15. Xu Donghai, "Pingxi Lasa wuzhuang panluan muduji," 8.
16. This and the following six paragraphs are based on Jampa Phuntsok, *A Life Undeterred.*
17. Wang Guozhen, "Tianjiang pili cheng xiongwan," 44.
18. Zhu Xiushan, "Lasa zhi zhan de huigu," 34.

19. McCarthy, *Tears of the Lotus*, 184.
20. Although it is difficult to track down the original directive, it is mentioned in several sources, such as *Jiefang Xizangshi*, 373, and Xu Yan, *Taojin baizhan pingshuo gujin*, 287.
21. Ji Youquan, *Xizang pingpan jishi*, 119–120.
22. Xu Yan, *Taojin baizhan pingshuo gujin*, 288.
23. Jampa Phuntsok, *A Life Undeterred*.
24. Ibid.
25. Wang Guozhen, "Tianjiang pili cheng xiongwan," 44.

20. SURRENDER, AND SAVE THE TEMPLE!

1. All quotes and impressions attributed to Jampa Tenzin in this chapter are based on my interview with him on October 12, 2009.
2. As Jampa Tenzin found out later, he had heard the shelling of Chakpori Hill, which—like the Potala—was to his west.
3. See the inside back cover of Noel Barber's *From the Land of Lost Content* for a diagram of the battle of the Jokhang Temple.
4. Xu Donghai, "Pingxi Lasa wuzhuang panluan muduji," 21.
5. Ibid.
6. *Jiefang Xizangshi*, 373; Yulo Tulku Dawa Tsering (Yulo), *A Pure Drop of Yulo's Sweat*.

21. THE AFTERMATH

1. Ji Youquan, *Xizang pingpan jishi*, 120; *Jiefang Xizangshi*, 373.
2. For the date of issuance of the PLA directive and the censored version of its text, see *Jiefang Xizangshi*, 375. For the full text, see the semiclassified volume, *Pingxi Xizang panluan*, 93–98.
3. *Jiefang Xizangshi*, 375.
4. *Pingxi Xizang panluan*, 97.
5. The Communist program in Tibet differed little from its antecedents in the Tibetan regions of China, except that collectivization (the next step after Land Reform) was implemented more gradually.
6. The term "local government of Tibet" mirrors the wording of the Seventeen-Point Agreement, and emphasizes China's claim over Tibet.
7. "Guanyu zai Xizang pingxi panluan zhong shixing minzhu gaigede ruogan zhengce wenti de zhishi," *Xizang de minzhu gaige*, 68.
8. Ibid.
9. *Zhonggong Xizang dangshi dashiji, 1949–1994*, 97.
10. Ibid.

11. "Fanyijia Jiangbian Jiacuo (Jampel Gyatso) huiyi 50 nianqian yi Xizang minzhu gaige ling," broadcast on CCTV, *Xinwen huiketing*, March 24, 2009, and at http://news.sina.com.cn/c/2009-03-24/231417473029.shtml. The "Order of the State Council" has been published in English in *Concerning the Question of Tibet*, 1–3.
12. Sources such as Ji Youquan, *Xizang pingpan jishi* (97); *Zhonggong Xizang dangshi dashiji, 1949–1994* (97); and *Jiefang Xizangshi* (376) conflict regarding the date(s) when Ding Sheng and Zhang Guohua arrived in Lhasa.
13. *Xizang de minzhu gaige*, 68.
14. *Concerning the Question of Tibet*, 1–3.
15. *Jiefang Xizangshi*, 376.
16. *Concerning the Question of Tibet*, 9.
17. Ibid.; see also "Xinhuashe guanyu Xizang panluan shijian de gongbao," *Guanyu Xizang wenti*, 7.
18. The communiqué's silence regarding casualities is echoed, for example, in Guo Ziwen, *Xizang dashiji, 1949–1959*, which was released to the Chinese public slightly over a month after the communiqué.
19. Ji Youquan, *Xizang pingpan jishi*, 121.
20. *Pingxi Xizang panluan*, 29.
21. *Zhonggong Xizang dangshi dashiji, 1949–1994*, 96.
22. *Jiefang Xizangshi*, 373.
23. See Chapter 11.
24. See Chapter 17. Ji Youquan's estimate comes from his *Xizang pingpan jishi*, 113.
25. Wang Guozhen, "Tianjiang pili cheng xiongwan," 41–43.
26. Ji Youquan, *Xizang pingpan jishi*, 115–116.
27. *Jiefang Xizangshi*, 372. Company 7 from Regiment 159, the unit led by Wu Chen that elicited "the first shot" on the hill near the Rama Gang ferry, was also assigned to mop up during the artillery barrage of the Norbulingka to ensure that no Tibetans succeeded in crossing the river.
28. Andrugtsang House was the home of Gonpo Tashi, founder of the Chushi Gangdruk.
29. See Chapter 18. Aside from the tallies presented by the Chinese, little information is available except, perhaps, a March 28 front-page *New York Times* article (discussed in Chapter 22), which hints at the numbers of Tibetan dead: "Chinese troops were on continuous duty for twelve hours burning the bodies of the fallen on the banks of the [Kyichu] River." This, of course, refers to only one day and one site; Tibetan eyewitness accounts (while failing to provide specific overall numbers) indicate that there may have been others like it.

30. *Xizang de minzhu gaige,* 71.
31. Some idea of their numbers can be gleaned from *Zhonggong Xizang dangshi dashiji, 1949–1994,* 213, 219.
32. *Jiefang Xizangshi,* 408.
33. *Xizang de minzhu gaige,* 251.
34. Ibid.
35. Ibid.
36. Author interview with Jampa Tenzin, October 12, 2009.
37. Author interview with Thinley Phuntsok, April 19, 2009.
38. Tubten Khetsun, *Memories of Life in Lhasa under Chinese Rule,* 57, 135.
39. Patt, "The Momo Gun," 162–163.
40. Author interview with Juchen Tubten, October 8, 2009.
41. Tarawa Tenzin Choenyi (Tara), *Introducing Myself.*

22. THE ETERNAL CROSSING

1. For the Dalai Lama's escape route, see Map 7. Riwo Dechen Monastery, located on the western slope of Mount Chingwa, approximately a hundred miles from Lhasa, was famed for its collection of treasures from past *dalai lamas.*
2. *Pingxi Xizang panluan,* 200.
3. Tsi-pon Namseling was the negotiator who had joined the Chushi Gangdruk resistance in 1958 instead of fulfilling his official assignment to persuade the guerrillas to lay down their arms. See Chapter 4.
4. "Management" of Tibet is Mao's term, used as early as 1950. See Mao Zedong, *Mao Zedong Xizang gongzuo wenxuan,* 9.
5. Athar Norbu, "The Life of Athar Norbu from Lithang." See also Knaus, *Orphans of the Cold War,* 168.
6. Although a very old Tibetan survivor named Lobsang—who served on the Dalai Lama's guard during the escape—claimed in a personal interview with me on October 13, 2008, to have fought off Chinese pursuers, his recollections may have been confused. No reliable confirmation of any encounters with—or even spottings of—the Dalai Lama en route can be found in Chinese sources.
7. Eh Chumdogyang is in today's Qusong County, TAR.
8. Athar Norbu, "The Life of Athar Norbu from Lithang." Athar's memoir is invaluable as a primary source, but his sequencing of events is unclear and benefits from corroboration with other sources when possible. In his memoir, *A Life* (311), Phuntsok Tashi (Phuntsok) recalls that Athar and Lhotse "brought out the airdropped weapons" at Eh Chumdogyang.
9. Author interview with Ngari Rinpoché, July 18, 2009.

10. Phuntsok Tashi (Phuntsok), *A Life,* vol. 2; *Pingxi Xizang panluan,* 201.
11. Andrugtsang Gonpo Tashi, *Four Rivers, Six Ranges,* 96.
12. Athar's story in this section comes from Athar Norbu, "The Life of Athar Norbu from Lithang." Although this memoir states that he cabled Phala's request immediately from Lhuntse Dzong on March 26, American sources indicate that it was received in the middle of the night on March 28. There may have been a delay due to CIA processing and translation or other factors.
13. Information derived from https://history.state.gov/historicaldocuments/frus1958-60v19/d367; see also Conboy and Morrison, *The CIA's Secret War in Tibet,* 92–93.
14. Teulhey is also spelled Dre'u Lhe.
15. This, and the information in the preceding three paragraphs, is based on Phuntsok Tashi (Phuntsok), *A Life,* vol. 2.
16. *New York Times,* March 28, 1959, 1.
17. Dalai Lama, *My Land and My People,* 214–215; Phuntsok Tashi (Phuntsok), *A Life,* vol. 2.
18. This, and the information in the preceding five paragraphs, is based on Phuntsok Tashi (Phuntsok), *A Life,* vol. 2.
19. Knaus, *Orphans of the Cold War,* 168.
20. Tawang, in today's Arunachal Pradesh, India, is a historically Tibetan area; also claimed by China, it has been the object of border disputes.
21. The Dalai Lama has estimated that his armed guard totaled approximately 350 men at this point. Phuntsok's estimate is 400, about half of whom were Tibetan Army soldiers from Regiments 1 and 2. The rest were Chushi Gangdruk guerrillas, who were probably under the command of the Tibetan Army officers. There were three contingents, one to guard each group of the escape party. See Phuntsok Tashi (Phuntsok), *A Life,* vol. 2, and Dalai Lama, *My Land and My People,* 204.
22. *Xizang wenshi ziliao xuanji,* 17:149. Although Surkhang drafted this initial press release for the Dalai Lama, this fact does not justify Chinese accusations that it was a forgery, released against his will by his "abductors."
23. This, and the information in the preceding four paragraphs, is based on Phuntsok Tashi (Phuntsok), *A Life,* vol. 2.
24. "XXXX" represents blacked-out names in this declassified CIA document, presumably those of Athar and Lhotse. The text of this message is quoted exactly as it appears in English at the CIA Freedom of Information Act Electronic Reading Room, at http://www.foia.cia.gov/document/untitled-re-dalai-lama-and-officials-arrived-safely-india.
25. Dalai Lama, *Freedom in Exile,* 143.

EPILOGUE

1. *Xizang de xingshi he renwu jiaoyu de jiben jiaocai (shiyongben)*, 6.
2. Andrugtsang Gonpo Tashi, *Four Rivers, Six Ranges*, 103–105.
3. *Zhongguo gongchandang Xizang zizhiqu zuzhishi ziliao, 1950–1987*, 480.
4. Dan Zeng, *Dangdai Xizang jianshi*, 269.
5. Jiangbian Jiacuo (Jampel Gyatso), *Shishi Banchan Lama zhuanji*, 166–180.
6. Dalai Lama, *Freedom in Exile*, 229–230; author interview with Juchen Tubten (member of the first fact-finding delegation), October 8, 2009.
7. Dalai Lama statement in his "Foreword" to the Tibetan constitution, which he promulgated in 1963. See http://www.tibetjustice.org/materials/tibet/tibet2.html.
8. For more information about the governance of the Central Tibetan Administration (as the Tibetan government-in-exile has been known since 2011), and a downloadable PDF of its constitution, see its official website at tibet.net.
9. These are the words of the Norwegian Nobel Committee, quoted in the *New York Times*, "Dalai Lama Wins the Nobel Peace Prize," October 6, 1989, A6.
10. See http://www.dalailama.com/messages/middle-way-approach.
11. Author interview with Tenpa Soepa, September 9, 2009.
12. Author interview with Jampa Tenzin, October 12, 2009.
13. Tarawa Tenzin Choenyi (Tara), *Introducing Myself.*
14. Author interview with Juchen Tubten, September 22, 2009; see also his obituary at http://tibet.net/2011/09/obituary-former-kalon-tripa-juchen-thupten-namgyal/.
15. Author interview with Dolma Norbu (Athar Norbu's daughter), May 3, 2009.
16. Author interview with Thinley Phuntsok, April 19, 2009.
17. Author interview with Ngari Rinpoché, July 18, 2009.
18. Tubten Khetsun, *Memories of Life in Lhasa under Chinese Rule.*
19. See http://baike.baidu.com/view/195297.htm.
20. https://en.wikipedia.org/wiki/Ngapoi_Ngawang_Jigme.
21. http://www.tibet.ca/en/library/wtn/archive/old?y=1999&m=7&p=9_2.
22. https://en.wikipedia.org/wiki/Tibet_Bureau_(Geneva).
23. Tan Xiaoying, "Huiyi bofu Tan Guansan," 56–57.
24. Marshal Peng Dehuai, defense minister of the People's Republic of China at the time of the Battle of Lhasa in 1959, was purged later that year as the leader of an "anti-Party clique," in punishment for speaking out against Mao's Great Leap Forward. See Wang Yan, comp. and ed., *Peng Dehuai nianpu*, 748, 750.

25. Fan Ming and Hao Rui, *Xizang neibu zhi zheng.*
26. Zhao Shenying, *Zhang Guohua jiangjun zai Xizang,* 155.
27. May Seventh Cadre Schools were Cultural Revolution labor camps for cadres and intellectuals. Zhang was sent to the Cadre School of the Ministry of Communications in the Weixu District of Beijing.
28. Zhao Shenying, *Zhongyang zhuzang daibiao Zhang Jingwu,* 171; for Zhang Jingwu's death, see Wang Xitang and Xie Xienong, "Zhongyang tongzhanbu fubuzhang Zhang Jingwu zhi si," 10–13, also at http://www.yhcqw.com/html/qsp/2008/412/08412183 67K709H998CB83DG3JD95CH69.html.
29. Dalai Lama, *Freedom in Exile,* 71.
30. *Hongqi,* no. 5 (1960): 29.

GLOSSARY OF NAMES

Note: While the concept of a family name is often not applicable to Tibetan names, for the sake of readability in English some of the principal figures in this book will be referred to throughout by an abbreviated form of their names, as indicated in parentheses below. When the words Tsi-pon, Khenchung, Dzasa, and Tsedrung appear along with a Tibetan name, these should be construed as lay or monastic official titles, not as part of the name.

Athar Norbu (Athar): monk from Lithang, Sichuan, one of the first Tibetan CIA (Central Intelligence Agency) operatives.

Barshi Ngawang Tenkyong (Barshi): Tibetan *tsedrung*.

Chen Bing: PLA (People's Liberation Army) officer.

Deng Shaodong: major general and vice-commander of the PLA Tibet Military Command.

Diki Tsering: the Dalai Lama's mother.

Dokharsey Sonam Dorje (Dokhar): Tibetan colonel (Regiment 4).

Fan Ming: PLA general; deputy secretary of the CCP (Chinese Communist Party) Tibet Work Committee until 1958 purge.

Gadrang Lobsang Rigzin (Gadrang): the Dalai Lama's chief of staff, third-rank monastic official.

Gegyepa Tenzin Dorje (Gegyepa): Tibetan government secretary.

[Andrugtsang] Gonpo Tashi (Gonpo Tashi): founder and commander-in-chief of the Tibetan guerrilla resistance forces known as the Chushi Gangdruk Defenders of the Faith.

Gyalo Dondrup: the Dalai Lama's second eldest brother.

Gyatsoling Rinpoché: the Dalai Lama's scriptural debate coach; deputy chairman of the Tibetan branch of the Chinese Buddhist Association.

Jampa Phuntsok (Jampa): monk at Namgyal Monastery at the Potala Palace; Potala battle eyewitness.

Jampa Tenzin (Jampa): PCART (Preparatory Committee for the Autonomous Region of Tibet) Business Office employee; seventh-rank Tibetan monastic official; Jokhang Temple battle eyewitness.

Ji Youquan: later chronicler of the events in this book; stationed in the PLA Tibet Military Command from 1974 to 1996; often provides a counterpoint to official historiography.

Jigme Taring: the Dalai Lama's photographer, member of the Sikkim royal family, settled in Lhasa after marrying into the aristocratic Tibetan Tsarong family.

Juchen Tubten: a Khampa from Mesho, Derge County, Sichuan. Guerrilla fighter in the Sichuan and Lhasa uprisings.

Junpa Dorje Tseten (Junpa): Tibetan colonel (Regiment 2).

Kundeling Dzasa Woeser Gyaltsen (Kundeling Dzasa): a monk-official, member of the coordinating group in the Norbulingka, escaped with the Dalai Lama to India.

[Dewatshang] Kunga Samten (Kunga Samten): Chushi Gangdruk guerrilla squad leader.

Le Yuhong: director of the Administrative Office of the CCP Tibet Work Committee, propaganda chief, and head of the Tibet branch office of Xinhua News Agency.

Lhalu Tsewang Dorje (Lhalu): former governor of Kham (from headquarters in Chamdo); active at the Norbulingka during the Lhasa Incident.

Lhotse: Athar's partner as one of the first Tibetan CIA agents.

Li Zuomin: United Front section chief at the PLA Tibet Military Command.

Ling Rinpoché: the Dalai Lama's Senior Tutor.

Liushar Tubten Tharpa (Liushar): Tibetan acting cabinet minister.

Lobsang Samten: the Dalai Lama's elder brother.

Lobsang Tashi: monastic official; anti-Chinese acting prime minister forced to resign in 1952; appointed to negotiate with the Chinese government after the Dalai Lama's escape.

Lukhangwa: lay official; anti-Chinese acting prime minister forced to resign in 1952; became an exile in Kalimpong in 1957.

Miao Zhongqin: chief of staff, Artillery Regiment 308.

Ngabo Ngawang Jigme (Ngabo): Tibetan cabinet minister, concurrently first vice-commander in the PLA Tibet Military Command. Stayed in Tibet after the battle and served two terms as chairman of the Tibet Autonomous Region.

Ngari Rinpoché (Tenzin Choegyal): the Dalai Lama's youngest brother.

Panchen Lama (Choekyi Gyaltsen): the Tenth Panchen Lama, installed at Shigatse as a puppet by the Chinese government.

Phala Tubten Wöden (Phala): the Dalai Lama's lord chamberlain, a monastic official.

Phuntsok Tashi (Phuntsok): the Dalai Lama's security chief (commander of the Dalai Lama's security guards, Tibetan Army Regiment 1); husband of the Dalai Lama's eldest sister, Tsering Dolma.

Sampo Tsewang Rigzin (Sampo): Tibetan cabinet minister; Tibetan Army commander-in-chief; PLA Tibet Military Command vice-commander; injured by stone-throwing demonstrators on March 10, 1959.

Seshing Lobsang Dondrup (Seshing): lieutenant colonel in the Dalai Lama's security guard regiment.

Shakabpa Losel Dondrup: member of the coordinating committee at the Norbulingka.

Shakabpa Wangchuk Deden (Shakabpa): a former finance minister of Tibet; went into exile in India in 1951; later became an organizer of the Kalimpong-based Committee for Tibetan Social Welfare.

Shuguba Jamyang Khedrup (Shuguba): member of the coordinating committee for the Lhasa Incident. His title was *tsi-pon,* sometimes translated as "finance minister."

Sonam Gyatso (Sonam): member of the Chamdo Liberation Committee and then the PCART; Tibetan monastic official with the title *khenchung;* killed in mob violence on March 10, 1959.

Sonam Tashi: lieutenant colonel in the Dalai Lama's security guard regiment.

Surkhang Wangchen Gelek (Surkhang): chief Tibetan cabinet minister.

Taktser Rinpoché: Tubten Jigme Norbu, the Dalai Lama's eldest brother.

Tan Guansan: PLA general; deputy secretary of the CCP Tibet Work Committee; PLA Tibet Military Command political commissar.

Tarawa Tenzin Choenyi (Tara): personal secretary to the Dalai Lama, with the title of *khenchung*. He was also known as Tara Do-nga Tharchin.

Tenpa Soepa: civil servant at the Dalai Lama's Reform Bureau.

Thinley Phuntsok (Thinley): Ling Rinpoché's servant and clerk.

Trijang Rinpoché: the Dalai Lama's Junior Tutor.

Tsering Dolma: the Dalai Lama's eldest sister, wife of Security Chief Phuntsok Tashi.

Tubten Khetsun (Tubten): seventh-rank Tibetan official at the Norbulingka; survivor of the bombardment of the Norbulingka.

Wang Guozhen: commander, Company 3 of PLA Artillery Regiment 308; an officer in charge of the shelling of Chakpori Hill, the Norbulingka, and the Potala.

Wu Chen: vice-commander of PLA Regiment 159.

Yeshi Lhundup (Yeshi): Tibetan *tsedrung*.

Yulo Dawa Tsering (Yulo Rinpoché, Yulo): monk from Gyuto Upper Tantric College; a defender of Ramoche Temple.

Zhang Guohua: PLA general; vice-secretary of the CCP Tibet Work Committee; commander, PLA Tibet Military Command; PLA Tibet Military Command party secretary.

Zhang Jingwu: PLA general; Chinese government representative in Tibet; secretary of the CCP Tibet Work Committee; director of the Chairman's Office of the People's Republic of China. Traveled back and forth between the latter job, which was in Beijing, and his posts in Tibet.

Zhu Xiushan: PLA Tibet Military Command guard battalion commander.

WYLIE TRANSLITERATION OF TIBETAN NAMES

Andrugtsang Gonpo Tashi	A 'brug tshang Mgon po bkra shis
Athar Norbu	A thar nor bu
Barshi Ngawang Tenkyong	Bar zhi Ngag dbang bstan skyong
Dewatshang Kunga Samten	Bde ba tshang Kun dga' bsam gtan
Diki Tsering	Bde skyid tshe ring
Dokharsey Sonam Dorje	mDo mkhar sras Bsod nams rdo rje
Gadrang Lobsang Rigzin	Dga' brang Blo bzang rig 'dzin
Gegyepa Tenzin Dorje	dGe rgyas pa Bstan 'dzin rdo rje
Gyalo Dondrup	Rgyal lo don grub
Gyatsoling Rinpoché	Rgya mtsho gling rin po che
Jampa Phuntsok	Byams pa phun tshogs
Jampa Tenzin	Byams pa bstan 'dzin
Jigme Taring	Phreng ring 'Jigs med
Juchen Tubten	'Ju chen Thub bstan
Junpa Dorje Tseten	Jun pa Rdo rje tshe brtan
Kundeling Dzasa	Kun bde gling dza sag
Lhalu Tsewang Dorje	Lha klu Tshe dbang rdo rje
Lhotse	Blo tshe
Ling Rinpoché	Gling rin po che
Liushar Tubten Tharpa	Sne'u shar Thub bstan thar pa
Lobsang Samten	Blo bzang bsam gtan
Lobsang Tashi	Blo bzang bkra shis
Lukhangwa	Klu khang ba Tshe dbang rab brtan
Ngabo Ngawang Jigme	Nga phod Ngag dbang 'jigs med
Ngari Rinpoché Tenzin Choegyal	Mnga' ris rin po che Bstan 'dzin chos rgyal
Panchen Lama Choekyi Gyaltsen	Pan chen Chos kyi rgyal mtshan
Phala Tubten Wöden	Pha lha Thub bstan 'od ldan
Phuntsok Tashi	Phun tshogs bkra shis
Sampo Tsewang Rigzin	Bsam pho tshe dbang rig 'dzin
Seshing Lobsang Dondrup	Sreg shing Blo bzang don grub
Shakabpa Losel Dondrup	Zhva sgab pa Blo gsal don grub
Shakabpa Wangchuk Deden	Zhva sgab pa Dbang phyug bde ldan

Shuguba Jamyang Khedrup	Shu khud pa 'Jam dbyangs mkhas grub
Sonam Gyatso	Mkhan chung Bsod nams rgya mtsho
Sonam Tashi	Bsod nams bkra shis
Surkhang Wangchen Gelek	Zur khang Dbang chen dge legs
Taktser Rinpoché Tubten Jigme Norbu	Stag 'tsher rin po che Thub bstan 'jigs med nor bu
Tarawa Tenzin Choenyi	Rta ra ba Bstan 'dzin chos nyid
Tenpa Soepa	Bstan 'dzin bzod pa
Thinley Phuntsok	Phrin las phun tshogs
Trijang Rinpoché	Khri byang rin po che
Tsering Dolma	Tshe ring sgrol ma
Tubten Khetsun	Thub bstan mkhas btsun
Yeshi Lhundup	Ye shes lhun grub
Yulo Dawa Tsering	G.yu lo Zla ba tshe ring

BIBLIOGRAPHY

Note: Books compiled by committees are alphabetized by title.

ENGLISH-LANGUAGE SOURCES

Adhe Tapontsang and Joy Blakeslee. *The Voice That Remembers: A Tibetan Woman's Inspiring Story of Survival.* Somerville, MA: Wisdom, 1997.

Andrugtsang Gonpo Tashi (Gonpo Tashi). *Four Rivers, Six Ranges: Reminiscences of the Resistance Movement in Tibet.* Dharamsala: Information and Publicity Office of the Dalai Lama, 1973.

Arjia Rinpoché. *Surviving the Dragon: A Tibetan Lama's Account of 40 Years under Chinese Rule.* New York: Rodale, 2010.

Arpi, Claude. "We Cleared the Route for the Dalai Lama." www.phayul.com/news/article.aspx?id=24364.

Athar Norbu. "Dalai Lama and Officials Arrived Safely in India." April 2, 1959. CIA Declassified Documents. http://www.foia.cia.gov/document/untitled-re-dalai-lama-and-officials-arrived-safely-india

Avedon, John F. *In Exile from the Land of Snows.* New York: Knopf, 1979.

Baba Phuntsok Wangyal, et al. *Witness to Tibet's History.* New Delhi: Paljor, 2007.

Barber, Noel. *The Flight of the Dalai Lama.* London: Hodder & Stoughton, 1960.

———. *From the Land of Lost Content: The Dalai Lama's Fight for Tibet.* Boston: Houghton Mifflin, 1970.

Bell, Charles A. *Tibet Past and Present.* Delhi: Motilal Banarsidass, 2000.

Carrasco Pizana, Pedro. *Land and Polity in Tibet.* Seattle: University of Washington Press, 1959.

Chhaya, Mayank. *Dalai Lama: Man, Monk, Mystic.* New York: Doubleday, 2007.

Chogyam Trungpa. *Born in Tibet.* Boston: Shambhala, 1995.

Conboy, Kenneth J., and James Morrison. *The CIA's Secret War in Tibet.* Lawrence: University Press of Kansas, 2002.

Concerning the Question of Tibet. Compiled and edited by Beijing Foreign Languages Press. Beijing: Foreign Languages Press, 1959.

Dalai Lama. *Freedom in Exile: The Autobiography of the Dalai Lama.* New York: Harper Perennial, 1991.

———. *My Land and My People: The Original Autobiography of His Holiness the Dalai Lama of Tibet.* New York: Potala Corp., 1983.

Dalai Lama and A. A. Shiromany. *The Spirit of Tibet: Universal Heritage.* New Delhi: Allied, 1995.

Dawa Norbu. *China's Tibet Policy.* Richmond, Surrey: Curzon, 2001.

———. *Red Star over Tibet.* New York: Envoy, 1987.

Dewatshang Kunga Samten (Kunga Samten). *Flight at the Cuckoo's Behest: The Life and Times of a Tibetan Freedom Fighter.* New Delhi: Paljor, 1997.

Diki Tsering. *Dalai Lama, My Son: A Mother's Story.* Khedroob Dondrup, ed. New York: Compass, 2001.

Dikötter, Frank. *Mao's Great Famine: The History of China's Most Devastating Catastrophe, 1958–1962.* New York: Walker, 2010.

———. *The Tragedy of Liberation: A History of the Chinese Revolution, 1945–1957.* New York: Bloomsbury, 2015.

Dunham, Mikel. *Buddha's Warriors: The Story of the CIA-Backed Tibetan Freedom Fighters, the Chinese Invasion, and the Ultimate Fall of Tibet.* New York: Jeremy P. Tarcher/Penguin, 2004.

Farjon, A. *A Monograph of Cupressaceae and Sciadopitys.* Kew, UK: Royal Botanic Gardens, 2005.

Goldstein, Melvyn C. *A History of Modern Tibet.* Vol. 1, *1913–1951: The Demise of the Lamaist State.* Berkeley: University of California Press, 1989.

———. *A History of Modern Tibet.* Vol. 2, *The Calm Before the Storm: 1951–1955.* Berkeley: University of California Press, 2007.

Goldstein, Melvyn C., Dawei Sherap, and William Siebenschuh. *A Tibetan Revolutionary: The Political Life and Times of Bapa Phüntso Wangye.* Berkeley: University of California Press, 2004.

Huang, Philip C. C. "Rural Class Struggle in the Chinese Revolution: Representational and Objective Realities from the Land Reform to the Cultural Revolution." *Modern China,* no. 21 (January 1995): 105–143.

Hutheesing, Raja, ed. *A White Book: Tibet Fights for Freedom: The Story of the March 1959 Uprising as Recorded in Documents, Despatches, Eye-witness Accounts and World-wide Reactions.* Bombay: Orient Longmans, 1960.

Jamyang Norbu. http://www/.jamyangnorbu.com/blog/2009/03/06/march-winds.

———. *Warriors of Tibet: The Story of Aten and the Khampas' Fight for the Freedom of Their Country.* London: Wisdom, 1986.

Knaus, John Kenneth. *Orphans of the Cold War: America and the Tibetan Struggle for Survival.* New York: Public Affairs, 1999.

Lamb, Alastair. *The McMahon Line: A Study in the Relations between India, China and Tibet, 1904 to 1914.* London: Routledge and Kegan Paul, 1966.

Larsen, Knud, and Amund Sinding-Larsen. *The Lhasa Atlas: Traditional Tibetan Architecture and Townscape.* Boston: Shambhala, 2001.

Leeker, Joe F. "Mission to Tibet." In *The History of Air America*. 2nd ed. August 24, 2015. e-book. http://www.utdallas.edu/library/specialcollections/hac/cataam/Leeker/history/Tibet.pdf.

Mao Tse-tung [Mao Zedong]. *Selected Works of Mao Tse-tung*. Vol. 1. Beijing: Foreign Languages Press, 1965.

———. *Selected Works of Mao Tsetung*. Vol. 5. Beijing: Foreign Languages Press, 1977.

Marcello, Patricia Cronin. *The Dalai Lama: A Biography*. Westport, CT: Greenwood Press, 2003.

McCarthy, Roger E. *Tears of the Lotus: Accounts of Tibetan Resistance to the Chinese Invasion, 1950–1962*. Jefferson, NC: McFarland, 1997.

McGranahan, Carole. *Arrested Histories: Tibet, the CIA, and Memories of a Forgotten War*. Durham, NC: Duke University Press, 2010.

Meyer, Fernand. "The Golden Century of Tibetan Medicine." In *Lhasa in the Seventeenth Century: Capital of the Dalai Lamas*, edited by Françoise Pommaret and translated by Howard Solverson. Boston: Brill, 2003.

Nehru, Jawaharlal. *Selected Works of Jawaharlal Nehru*. Second Series, vols. 35 and 36. New Delhi: Jawaharlal Nehru Memorial Fund, 2005.

———. *Selected Works of Jawaharlal Nehru*. Second Series, vol. 40. New Delhi: Jawaharlal Nehru Memorial Fund, 2009.

Palden Gyatso and Tsering Shakya. *The Autobiography of a Tibetan Monk*. New York: Grove, 1997.

Patt, David. "The Momo Gun: Tenpa Soepa's Story." In *A Strange Liberation: Tibetan Lives in Chinese Hands*, 133–261. Ithaca, NY: Snow Lion, 1992.

Patterson, George N. *Requiem for Tibet*. London: Aurum, 1990.

Richardson, Hugh. *Tibet and Its History*. 2nd ed. Boston: Shambhala, 1984.

Shakabpa, W. D., and Derek F. Maher. *One Hundred Thousand Moons: An Advanced Political History of Tibet*. Leiden: Brill, 2010.

Strong, Anna Louise. *When Serfs Stood Up in Tibet*. Marxists Internet Archive, 2008. http://www.marxists.org/reference/archive/strong-anna-louise/1959/tibet/index.htm. First published, Beijing: New World Press, 1960.

Taring Rinchen Dolma. *Daughter of Tibet*. London: Wisdom, 1986.

Tarthang Tulku and Jack Petranker. *From the Roof of the World: Refugees of Tibet*. Berkeley, CA: Dharma, 1992.

Thomas, Lowell. *The Silent War in Tibet*. New York: Doubleday, 1959.

Tibetans in Exile, 1959–1969: A Report on Ten Years of Rehabilitation in India. Compiled and edited by the Office of His Holiness the Dalai Lama. Dharamsala: Bureau of His Holiness the Dalai Lama, 1969.

Tsarong Dundul Namgyal and Trinlay Chödron. *In the Service of His Country: The Biography of Dasang Damdul Tsarong, Commander General of Tibet*. Ithaca, NY: Snow Lion, 2000.

Tsering Shakya. *The Dragon in the Land of Snows: A History of Modern Tibet since 1947*. New York: Columbia University Press, 1999.

Tsering Wangyal Shawa. *Tibet Township Map and Place Name Index* [*Bod kyi grong brtal dang grong tsho'i sa khra*]. Princeton, NJ: Princeton University Press, 2014.

Tubten Jigme Norbu. *Tibet Is My Home: The Autobiography of Tubten Jigme Norbu, Brother of the Dalai Lama as Told to Heinrich Harrer*. Translated by Edward Fitzgerald. New York: E. P. Dutton, 1961.

Tubten Khetsun. *Memories of Life in Lhasa under Chinese Rule*. Translated by Matthew Akester. New York: Columbia University Press, 2008.

Waddell, Laurence Austine. *Lhasa and Its Mysteries: With a Record of the Expedition of 1903–1904*. New York: E. P. Dutton, 1906.

Yang Jisheng. *Tombstone: The Great Chinese Famine, 1958–1962*. Translated by Stacy Mosher and Guo Jian. New York: Farrar, Strauss, and Giroux, 2012.

Yuthok Dorje Yudon. *House of the Turquoise Roof*. Ithaca, NY: Snow Lion, 1995.

CHINESE-LANGUAGE SOURCES

"1959: Xizang pingpan—shijie wuji shang de qiangsheng." *Jingu chuanqi—jishi ban*, no. 1 (2007). http://doc.qkzz.net/article/51e04039-c284-4045-bedc-37508a283880.htm.

Aba Zangzu Qiangzu zizhizhou junshizhi: gongyuanqian 316 nian-gongyuan 2005 nian. Compiled and edited by Sichuan sheng Aba junfenqu. Chengdu: Sichuan daxue chubanshe, 2007.

Aba Zangzu Qiangzu zizhizhou zhi. Compiled and edited by Sichuan sheng Aba Zangzu Qiangzu zizhizhou difangzhi bianzuan weiyuanhui. Chengdu: Minzu chubanshe, 1994.

Ajia Losangtudan (Arjia Lobsang Tubten Rinpoché). Foreword ("Xu") to *1959: Lhasa!*, by Li Jianglin, iii–iv. Taipei: Linking; Hong Kong: New Century Press, 2010.

Apei Awangjinmei (Ngabo). "1959 nian '3 yue 10 ri shijian' de zhenxiang." *Zhongguo Zangxue*, no. 2 (1988): 3–5. Republished in an expanded version in Zhang Xiaoming, ed. *Jianzheng bainian Xizang: Xizang lishi jianzhengren fangtanlu*. Vol. 1, 172–179. Beijing: Wuzhou chuanbo chubanshe, 2003.

Avedon, John F., and Yin Jianxin. *Xueyu jingwai liuwang ji*. Taipei: Huiju chubanshe, 1991.

Awang Jianzan. "Luobu lingka neiwai majiu shimo." In *Xizang wenshi ziliao xuanji*, compiled and edited by Xizang zizhiqu zhengxie wenshi ziliao yanjiu weiyuanhui, vol. 8, 179–186. [Semiclassified.] Lhasa, 1986.

Cao Yali. "Qinghai Ta'ersi qiangmu yuewu qianxi." *Qinghai minzu xueyuan xuebao* (shehui kexue ban), no. 1 (1999): 49–51.

Chen Bing. "Panguo biwang." In Re Di, et al., *Xizang geming huiyilu*, vol. 4, 18–31.

———. "Zangjun shilüe." In *Xizang wenshi ziliao xuanji,* compiled and edited by Xizang zizhiqu zhengxie wenshi ziliao yanjiu weiyuanhui, vol. 4, 85–99. [Semiclassified.] Lhasa, 1985.

Chen Guansheng and An Caidan. *Changjian Zangyu renming diming cidian.* Beijing: Waiwen chubanshe, 2004.

Chen Jingbo. "Xizang tongyi zhanxian gongzuo de licheng." In *Xizang wenshi ziliao xuanji: Jinian Xizang heping jiefang sishi zhounian zhuanji,* compiled and edited by Xizang zizhiqu zhengxie wenshi ziliao yanjiu weiyuanhui. [Semiclassified?]. Beijing: Minzu chubanshe, 1991, 116–130.

Chen Qingying. *Zhongguo Zangzu buluo.* Beijing: Zhongguo Zangxue chubanshe, 1991.

Cheng Yue, ed. *Zhongguo gongchandang Xizang Changdu diqu lishi dashiji, 1949–2009.* Beijing: Zhongguo Zangxue chubanshe, 2010.

Chizong Luosangtudeng. "Luobu lingka jianzhu he jiansai pozhang xiujian shimo." In *Xizang wenshi ziliao xuanji,* compiled and edited by Xizang zizhiqu zhengxie wenshi ziliao yanjiu weiyuanhui, vol. 21, 110–115. Beijing: Minzu chubanshe, 2004.

Ciren Dunzhu (Tsering Dondrup). *Chifeng huxiao.* Hong Kong: Tianyuan shuwu, 2012.

Dai Yisheng. "Gansa rexue xie chunqiu—huiyi wu, liushi niandai Xizang gong'an zhanxian de zhanyou." *Renmin gong'an,* no. 17 (2000): 56–60.

Dajie. *Guoluo jianwen yu huiyi.* [Semiclassified.] [Xining?], 2008.

Dan Zeng. *Dangdai Xizang jianshi.* Beijing: Dangdai Zhongguo chubanshe, 1996.

Dangdai Yunnan Zangzu jianshi. Compiled and edited by Dangdai Yunnan Zangzu jianshi bianji weiyuanhui. Kunming: Yunnan renmin chubanshe, 2009.

Dangdai Zhongguo minzu gongzuo dashiji, 1949–1988. Compiled and edited by "Dangdai Zhongguo de minzu gongzuo" bianjibu. Beijing: Minzu chubanshe, 1989.

Dangdai Zhongguo zhuangjia bing. Compiled and edited by Zongcanmoubu zhuangjiabingbu bianjibu. Beijing: Jiefangjun chubanshe, 1990.

Dawa Cairen (Dawa Tsering). *Xueji xueyu.* Taipei: Xueyu chubanshe, 2012.

Dege xianzhi. Compiled and edited by Sichuan sheng Dege xianzhi bianzuan weiyuanhui. Chengdu: Sichuan renmin chuban she, 1995.

Deqin xianzhi. Compiled and edited by Deqin xianzhi bianzuan weiyuanhui. Kunming: Yunnan minzu chubanshe, 1997.

Ding Sheng, Jin Guang, and Yu Ruxin. *Luonan yingxiong: Ding Sheng jiangjun huiyilu.* Hong Kong: Thinker Publishing, 2008.

Fan Ming and Hao Rui. *Xizang neibu zhi zheng.* Hong Kong: Mingjing chubanshe, 2009.

Feng Xianzhi and Jin Chongji. *Mao Zedong zhuan, 1949–1976.* Beijing: Zhongyang wenxian chubanshe, 2003.

Gama Quyang. "Dalai lama de shanshi jigou." In *Xizang wenshi ziliao xuanji,* compiled and edited by Xizang zizhiqu zhengxie wenshi ziliao yanjiu weiyuanhui, vol. 8, 94–127. [Semiclassified.] Lhasa, 1986.

Gangcha Xianzhi. Compiled and edited by Gangcha Xianzhi bianzuan weiyuanhui. Xi'an: Shaanxi renmin chubanshe, 1997.

Gannan Zangzu zizhizhou zhi. Compiled and edited by Gannan Zangzu zizhizhou difang shizhi bianzuan weiyuanhui. Beijing: Minzu chubanshe, 1999.

Ganzi Zangzu zizhizhou junshizhi. Compiled and edited by Sichuan sheng Ganzi junfenqu "junshi zhi" bianzuan weiyuanhui. [Semiclassified.] [Kangding?]: Sichuan sheng Ganzi junfenqu, 1999.

Ganzi Zangzu zizhizhou minzhu gaigeshi. Compiled and edited by Zhonggong Ganzi zhouwei. Chengdu: Sichuan minzu chubanshe, 2000.

Ganzi zhouzhi. Compiled and edited by Ganzi zhouzhi bianzuan weiyuanhui. Chengdu: Sichuan renmin chubanshe, 1997.

Gejieba Danzengduoji (Gegyepa). "Fenlie zhuyi fenzi zai Lasa fadong wuzhuang panluan de qingkuang." In *Xizang wenshi ziliao xuanji,* compiled and edited by Xizang zizhiqu zhengxie wenshi ziliao yanjiu weiyuanhui, vol. 12, 66–70. Beijng: Minzu chubanshe, 1990.

———. "Yuan Xizang difang zhengfu jigou." *Xizang yanjiu* 7, no. 2 (1989): 51–54.

Guanyu Xizang wenti: 1959 nian 3 yue–5 yue de wenjian, ziliao. Compiled and edited by Renmin chubanshe. Beijing: Renmin chubanshe, 1959.

Guo Ziwen. *Xizang dashiji, 1949–1959.* Beijing: Minzu chuban she, 1959.

Guoluo Zangzu zizhizhou zhi. Compiled and edited by Guoluo Zangzu zizhizhou difangzhi bianzuan weiyuanhui. Beijing: Minzu chubanshe, 2001.

Hainan Zangzu zizhizhou zhi. Compiled and edited by Hainan Zangzu zizhizhou difangzhi bianzuan weiyuanhui. Beijing: Minzu chubanshe, 1997.

Han Youren. *Yichang bei yinmoliaode guonei zhanzheng: ji 1958 nian Qinghai pingpan kuodahua ji qi jiuzheng shimo.* Hong Kong: Tianyuan shuwu, 2013.

Heping jiefang Xizang. Compiled and edited by Xizang zizhiqu dangshi ziliao zhengji weiyuanhui and Xizang junqu dangshi ziliao zhengji lingdao xiaozu. [Semiclassified.] [Lhasa]: Xizang renmin chubanshe, 1995.

Hong Weiquan. "Xueyu jiaofei ji: jiefangjun kongjun gaoyuan pingpan jishi." *Hangkong shi yanjiu,* no. 5 (2001): 13–16.

Hongqi. No. 5. Compiled by Zhongguo gongchandang zhongyang weiyuanhui. Beijing: Hongqi zazhishe, 1960.

Hu Liyan. *Zouguo xiaoyan: Huang Xinting zhuan.* Beijing: Zhongguo qingnian chubanshe, 1997.

Hu Yan. "Xizang wenti zhong de Sulian yinsu." *Xizang daxue xuebao,* no. 3 (2006). http://blog.ifeng.com/article/789267.html.

Huang Shaoyong. "Tieliu gungun, danxin yiyi—huiyi Lasa zhanyi zhong de qiche xingdong." In Re Di, et al. *Xizang geming huiyilu,* vol. 4, 46–54.

Huang Zongzhi. "Zhongguo geming zhong de nongcun jieji douzheng—cong tugai dao wenge shiqi de biaodaxing xianshi yu keguanxing xian shi." In *Zhongguo xiangcun yanjiu,* no. 2 (2003): 66–95. Beijing: Shangwu yinshuguan, 2003.

Huangnan Zangzu zizhizhou zhi. Compiled and edited by Huangnan Zangzu zizhizhou difangzhi bianzuan weiyuanhui. Lanzhou: Gansu renmin chubanshe, 1999.

Huangzhong xianzhi. Compiled and edited by Huangzhong xian difangzhi bianzuan weiyuanhui. Xining: Qinghai renmin chubanshe, 1990.

Ji Youquan. *Baixue: jiefang Xizang jishi.* Beijing: Zhongguo wuzhi chubanshe, 1993.

———. *Xizang pingpan jishi.* Lhasa: Xizang renmin chubanshe, 1993.

Jiang Dasan. "77 sui laofeixingrenyuan de boke." http://blog.sina.com.cn/jiangdasan.

Jiangbian Jiacuo (Jampel Gyatso). *Li Jue zhuan.* Beijing: Zhongguo Zangxue chubanshe, 2004.

———. *Mao Zedong yu Dalai, Banchan.* Hong Kong: Xin dalu chubanshe, 2008.

———. *Shishi Banchan Lama zhuanji.* Hong Kong: Kaifang chubanshe, 2008.

———. *Xueshan mingjiang Tan Guansan.* Beijing: Zhongguo Zangxue chubanshe, 1996.

Jiangre Awangcibai. "Dalai Lama chuxing yishi." In *Xizang wenshi ziliao xuanji,* compiled and edited by Xizang zizhiqu zhengxie wenshi ziliao yanjiu weiyuanhui, vol. 8, 1–9. [Semiclassified.] Lhasa, 1986.

Jianguo yilai zhongyao wenxian xuanbian. Compiled and edited by Zhonggong zhongyang wenxian yanjiushi. Beijing: Zhongyang wenxian chubanshe [Multivolume series, 1992–1998].

Jianzha xianzhi. Compiled and edited by Jianzha xian difangzhi bianzuan weiyuanhui. Lanzhou: Gansu renmin chubanshe, 2003.

Jiefang Xizangshi. Compiled and edited by "Jiefang Xizangshi" bianweihui. Beijing: Zhonggong dangshi chubanshe, 2008.

Lalu Ciwangduoji (Lhalu). "Youguan 1959 nian de panluan qingkuang." In *Xizang wenshi ziliao xuanji,* compiled and edited by Xizang zizhiqu zhengxie wenshi ziliao yanjiu weiyuanhui, vol. 16, *Lalu jiazu ji benren jingli,* 140–148. Beijing: Minzu chubanshe, 1995.

Lasa zai qianjin: jinian Lasa heping jiefang he jianli dang zuzhi sishi zhounian xuanji. Compiled and edited by Zhonggong Lasa shiwei dangshi ziliao zhengji lingdao xiaozu. [Semiclassified.] Lhasa: Lasa shiwei dangshi ziliao zhengji lingdao xiaozu, 1991.

Le'anwangdui. *Diqing Zangzu zizhizhou zhi.* Kunming: Yunnan minzu chubanshe, 2001.

Ledu xianzhi. Compiled and edited by Ledu xianzhi bianzhuan weiyuanhui. Xi'an: Shaanxi renmin chubanshe, 1992.

Lei Yinhai. "Jinzang pingpan jishi." In Re Di, et al., *Xizang geming huiyilu,* vol. 4, 103–108.

Li Jianglin. *Dangtieniao zai tiankong feixiang: 1956–1962 Qingzang gaoyuan shang de mimi zhanzheng.* Taibei: Lianjing, 2012.

Li Jue. "Huiyi heping jiefang Xizang." In *Shijie wuji fengyun lu,* vol. 1, 16–47. Beijing: Jiefangjun wenyi chubanshe, 1991.

Li Lifeng. "Tugai zhong de suku: yizhong minzhong dongyuan jishu de weiguan fenxi." *Nanjing daxue xuebao,* no. 5 (2007): 97–109.

Li Qiaoning. "Xinqu tugai zhong de 'dou dizhu.'" *Nanjing daxue xuebao,* no. 5 (2007): 97–109.

Liang Jingtai and Li Bixian. "Shisishi Dalai Lama chuzou ji." *Xianggang wenhui bao,* October 13–22, 1997.

Liao Dongfan. *Lasa zhanggu.* Beijing: Zhongguo Zangxue chubanshe, 2008.

Liao Li. *Zhongguo Zangjun.* Beijing: Zhongguo wenshi chubanshe, 2009.

Lin Zhaozhen. *Lama sha ren.* Taipei: Lianhe wenxue chubanshe, 1999.

Litang xianzhi. Compiled and edited by Sichuan sheng Litang xianzhi bianzuan weiyuanhui. Chengdu: Sichuan renmin chubanshe, 1996.

Liu Chongwen and Chen Shaochou, eds. *Liu Shaoqi nianpu, 1898–1969.* Beijing: Zhongyang wenxian chubanshe, 1996. http://www.gov.cn/test/2009-11/24/content_1471576.htm.

Liu Shaoqi. *Liu Shaoqi xuanji.* Vol. 2. Beijing: Renmin chubanshe, 1986.

Luo Liangxing. "Yichang tebie de yanchu." In Re Di, et al. *Xizang geming huiyilu,* vol. 4, 132–145.

Luosang Pengcuo. "Guanyu Zhebangsi tiebang lama de youlai jiqi zhiquan." In *Xizang wenshi ziliao xuanji,* compiled and edited by Xizang zizhiqu zhengxie wenshi ziliao yanjiu weiyuanhui, vol. 12, 53–62. Beijing: Minzu chubanshe, 1990.

Luozhu Quzeng. "Shisishi dalai lama xingong xiujian qingkuang." In *Xizang wenshi ziliao xuanji,* compiled and edited by Xizang zizhiqu zhengxie wenshi ziliao yanjiu weiyuanhui, vol. 4, 30–38. [Semiclassified.] [Lhasa?], 1985.

Luqu xianzhi. Compiled and edited by Luquxian difangzhi bianzuan weiyuanhui. Lanzhou: Gansu wenhua chubanshe, 2006.

Ma Hongchang. "Chicheng jiangchang 38 ge chunqiu—yingxiong de jiefangjun qibing diyishi." News of the Communist Party of China. http://cpc.people.com.cn/GB/64162/64172/85037/85038/6036998.html.

Ma Wanli, ed. *Jingjian: Qinghai minzu gongzuo ruogan zhongda lishi shijian huigu.* [Semiclassified.] [Xining?]: Qinghai renmin chubanshe, 2007.

Mao Zedong. *Jianguo yilai Mao Zedong wengao*. Vol. 6 (1992), Vol. 8 (1993). [Semiclassified.] Beijing: Zhongyang wenxian chubanshe.

———. *Mao Zedong wenji*. Vol. 7. Compiled by Zhongyang wenxian yanjiushi. Beijing: Renmin chubanshe, 1999.

———. *Mao Zedong Xizang gongzuo wenxuan*. Beijing: Zhongyang wenxian chubanshe, 2001.

Minzu zhengce de weida shengli—qingzhu Xizang zizhiqu choubei weiyuanhui chengli. Beijing: Minzu chubanshe, 1956.

Minzu zongjiao gongzuo wenjian huiji, 1949–1959. Compiled and edited by Zhonggong Qinghai shengwei tongzhanbu. [Semiclassified.] [Xining?], 1959.

Neibu cankao. Compiled and published by Xinhua tongxunshe. [Classified.]

"Nihelu zai renminyuan fabiao de guanyu Xizang wenti de tanhua." *Cankao ziliao*, March 17, 1959; March 18, 1959, A.M. edition.

"Nihelu zai renminyuan jiu Xizang jushi fabiao de shengming." *Cankao ziliao*, March 23, 1959; March 27, 1959, P.M. edition.

"Nihelu zai renminyuan jiu Xizang jushi suo ti de wenti shi fabiao de jianghua." *Cankao ziliao*, March 30, 1959; March 31, 1959, A.M. edition.

Palden Gyatso, Tsering Shakya, and Liao Tianqi, trans. *Xueshanxia de huoyan: yige Xizang fanren de zhengci*. Washington, DC: Laogai jijinhui, 2003.

Peng Xuetao and Zheng Ruifeng. "Zhong-E jiemi dangan—Mao Zedong sihui Heluxiaofu." *Wenshi jinghua*, no. 3 (2009): 4–7.

Pingcuo Wangjie (Phuntsok Wangyal). *Pingdeng tuanjie lu manman: dui woguo minzu guanxi de fansi*. Hong Kong: Xin shiji chubanshe, 2014.

Pingxi Xizang panluan. Compiled and edited by Xizang zizhiqu dangshi ziliao zhengji weiyuanhui and Xizang junqu dangshi ziliao zhengji lingdao xiaozu. [Semiclassified.] Lhasa: Xizang renmin chubanshe, 1995.

Qi Xin, ed. "Dingzhi budui de Xizang pingpan zuozhan." In Ding Sheng, et al., *Luonan yingxiong*, 298–314.

Qiaba Cidanpincuo. "Dazhaosi shishi shulüe." *Xizang yanjiu* 1, no. 1 (1981): 36–50.

Qin Heping. "Cong fandui tusi dao jieshou minzhu gaige—guanyu Xiakedaodeng de yanjiu." *Zhongguo Zangxue*, no. 1 (2014): 65–79.

———. *Sichuan minzu diqu minzhu gaige ziliaoji*. Beijing: Minzu chuban she, 2008.

Qin Heping and Ran Linwen. *Sichuan minzu diqu minzhu gaige dashiji*. Beijing: Minzu chubanshe, 2007.

Qinghai huabao. Nos. 5–6. [Xining?]: Qinghai huabaoshe, December 1958.

Qinghai shengzhi. Vol. 56, *Junshizhi*. Compiled and edited by Qinghaisheng difangzhi bianzuan weiyuanhui. Xining: Qinghai renmin chubanshe, 2001.

Qinghai shengzhi. Vol. 75, *Renkouzhi*. Compiled and edited by Qinghaisheng difangzhi bianzuan weiyuanhui. Xi'an: Xi'an chubanshe, 2000.

Qinghai shengzhi. Vol. 81, *Fulu*. Compiled and edited by Qinghaisheng difangzhi bianzuan weiyuanhui. Xining: Qinghai renmin chubanshe, 2003.

Qinghai Zangzu renkou. Compiled and edited by Qinghai Zangzu renkou pucha bangongshi. Beijing: Zhongguo tongji chubanshe, 1994.

Qinghaisheng Zangzu Mengguzu shehui lishi diaocha. Compiled and edited by Qinghaisheng bianjizu. Xining: Qinghai renmin chubanshe, 1985.

Re Di, et. al., comp. and ed. *Xizang geming huiyilu*. Vol. 4, *Jinian Xizang shixing minzhu gaige sanshi zhounian zhuanji*. Lhasa: Xizang renmin chubanshe, 1989.

Sanzhong quanhui yilai zhongyao wenxian huibian. Vol. 2. Compiled and edited by Zhonggong zhongyang wenxian yanjiushi. [Classified.] Beijing: Renmin chubanshe, 1982.

Sexin Luosangdunzhu (Seshing). "Wo suo zhidaode Zangjun qingkuang." In *Xizang wenshi ziliao xuanji*, compiled and edited by Xizang zizhiqu zhengxie wenshi ziliao yanjiu weiyuanhui, vol. 8, 21–32. [Semiclassified.] [Lhasa?], 1986.

———. "Yuan Zangjun jingweituan jingweiying de jianzhi ji youguan wo ren jingwei yingzhang shi fasheng panluan de qingkuang." In *Xizang wenshi ziliao xuanji*, compiled and edited by Xizang zizhiqu zhengxie wenshi ziliao yanjiu weiyuanhui, vol. 17, 132–142. Beijing: Minzu chubanshe, 1995.

Shi Zhe and Li Haiwen. *Zai lishi juren shenbian: Shi Zhe huiyilu*. Beijing: Zhongyang wenxian chubanshe, 1991.

Sichuan sheng Ganzi zhou Zangzu shehui lishi diaocha. Compiled and edited by Sichuan sheng bianjizu. Chengdu: Sichuan sheng shehui kexueyuan chubanshe, 1985.

Sichuan shengzhi junshizhi. Compiled and edited by Sichuan sheng bianzuan weiyuanhui. Chengdu: Sichuan renmin chubanshe, 1999.

Sichuan Zangzu renkou. Compiled and edited by Sichuan sheng renkou pucha bangongshi. Beijing: Zhongguo tongji chubanshe, 1994.

Song Yongyi. "Dayuejin shi ruhe tuidong de?—zhengzhi yundong zaojiude kongju he zaojia feng." Boxun wang. http://www.usc.cuhk.edu.hk/PaperCollection/Details.aspx?id=7038.

Song Yuehong, ed. *Zhongyang zhuzang daibiao Zhang Jingwu yu Xizang*. Beijing: Renmin chubanshe, 2007.

Sun Zihe. *Xizang shishi yu renwu*. Taipei: Taiwan shangwu yinshuguan, 1995.

Tan Xiaoying. "Huiyi bofu Tan Guansan." *Zhonghua ernü*, no. 11 (2007): 56–57.

Tianbao yu Xizang. Compiled and edited by Zhonggong Xizang zizhiqu weiyuanhui dangshi ziliao yanjiushi. Beijing: Zhonggong dangshi chubanshe, 2006.

Tie Mu'er. "Zai Kukunao'er yibei." *Xihu*, no. 6 (2007): 64–79.

Tongzhan zhengce wenjian huibian. Vol. 3. Compiled and published by Zhonggong zhongyang tongyi zhanxian gongzuobu. [Classified.] [Beijing: 1958.]

Tudeng Ciren. "Yaowangshan yixue lizhongyuan jianshi." *Zhongguo Zangxue*, no. 4 (2008): 86–93.

Wang Guozhen. "Tianjiang pili cheng xiongwan." In Re Di, et al., *Xizang geming huiyilu*, vol. 4, 38–45.

Wang Lixiong. *Tianzang: Xizang de mingyun*. Hong Kong: Mingjing chubanshe, 1998.

Wang Qixiu. "Qinli 1959 nian Xizang pingpan." *Bainian chao*, no. 10 (2008): 62–66; also http://dangshi.people.cn/GB/8339083.html.

Wang Xitang and Xie Xienong. "Zhongyang tongzhanbu fubuzhang Zhang Jingwu zhi si." *Yanhuang chunqiu*, no. 10 (2003): 10–13.

Wang Yan, comp. and ed. *Peng Dehuai nianpu*. Beijing: Renmin chubanshe, 1998.

Wang Zhongxing and Liu Liqin. *Guofang lishi*. Beijing: Junshi kexue chuban she, 2003.

Wen Feng. "Tan Guansan jiangjun zhihui Lasa pingpan shimo." *Wenshi jinghua*, no. 5 (2009): 4–12.

Wenbu qianjin zhong de Xizang. Beijing: Minzu chubanshe, 1958.

Wujing Duoji. "Heping jiefangqian de Lasa." In *Xizang wenshi ziliao xuanji*, compiled and edited by Xizang zizhiqu zhengxie wenshi ziliao yanjiu weiyuanhui, vol. 17, 103–113. Beijing: Minzu chubanshe, 1995.

Xie Youtian. *Xiangcun shehui de huimie*. Hong Kong: Mingjing chubanshe, 2010.

Xin Zhongguo guofang dashiji, 1955–1960. Compiled and edited by Shanghai guofang zhanlüe yanjiusuo. http://www.gf81.com.cn/secondlink/gfls/5.html.

Xinghai xianzhi. Compiled and edited by Xinghai xianzhi bianzuan weiyuanhui. Xi'an: San Qin chubanshe, 2000.

Xinlong xianzhi. Compiled and edited by Sichuan sheng Ganzi Zangzu zizhizhou Xinlong xianzhi bianzuan weiyuanhui. Chengdu: Sichuan renmin chubanshe, 1992.

Xinlongxian wenshi ziliao diyiji—jianguo wushinian Xinlong zhi bianhua zhuanji. Compiled and edited by Zhongguo renmin zhengzhi xieshang huiyi Xinlongxian weiyuanhui. [Xinlong?]: Zhongguo renmin zhengzhi xieshang huiyi Xinlongxian weiyuanhui, 1999.

Xizang dangshi tongxun. Vols. 1 and 2. Compiled, edited, and published by Zhonggong Xizang zizhiqu weiyuanhui dangshi ziliao zhengji weiyuanhui. Lhasa, 1986. [Semiclassified.]

Xizang de minzhu gaige. Compiled and edited by Xizang zizhiqu dangshi ziliao zhengji weiyuanhui. [Semiclassified.] Lhasa: Xizang renmin chubanshe, 1995.

Xizang de xingshi he renwu jiaoyu de jiben jiaocai (shiyong ben). Compiled and published by Zhongguo renmin jiefangjun Xizang junqu zhengzhibu. [Classified.] [Lhasa?], October 1, 1960.

Xizang gemingshi. Compiled and edited by Zhonggong Xizang zizhiqu weiyuanhui dangshi ziliao zhengji weiyuanhui. Lhasa: Xizang renmin chubanshe, 1991.

Xizang gongzuo wenxian xuanbian, 1949–2005. Compiled and edited by Zhonggong zhongyang wenxian yanjiushi and Zhonggong Xizang zizhiqu weiyuanhui. Beijing: Zhongyang wenxian chubanshe, 2005.

Xizang wenshi ziliao xuanji. Compiled and edited by Xizang zizhiqu zhengxie wenshi minzu zongjiao fazhi weiyuanhui. Beijing: Minzu chubanshe. Vol. 21 (2004); Vol. 24 (2008).

Xizang wenshi ziliao xuanji. Compiled and edited by Xizang zizhiqu zhengxie wenshi ziliao yanjiu weiyuanhui. Beijing: Minzu chubanshe. Vol. 4 (1985) [Semiclassified]; Vol. 8 (1986) [Semiclassified]; Vol. 9 (1986) [Semiclassified]; Vol. 12 (1990); Vol. 13 (1991); Vol. 16 (1995); Vol. 17 (1995).

Xizang wenshi ziliao xuanji: Jinian Xizang heping jiefang sishi zhounian zhuanji. Compiled and edited by Xizang zizhiqu zhengxie wenshi ziliao yanjiu weiyuanhui. [Semiclassified?] Beijing: Minzu chubanshe, 1991.

Xu Donghai. "Pingxi Lasa wuzhuang panluan muduji." *Xizang dangshi ziliao,* no. 2 (1999): 8–23. [Semiclassified.]

Xu Hongseng. "1958 nian qiba yuejian Zhang Jingwu tongzhi tong galunmen de jici tanhua jianlu." In *Xizang wenshi ziliao xuanji,* compiled and edited by Xizang zizhiqu zhengxie wenshi minzu zongjiao fazhi weiyuanhui, vol. 24, 196–207. Beijing: Minzu chubanshe, 2005.

Xu Jiatun. *Xu Jiatun Xianggang huiyilu.* Hong Kong: Xianggang lianhebao youxian gongsi, 1993.

Xu Yan. *Taojin baizhan pingshuo gujin.* Beijing: Changzheng chubanshe, 2013.

Xu Zhuoyun. *Wangu jianghe Zhongguo lishi wenhua de zhuanzhe yu kaizhan.* Shanghai: Shanghai wenyi chubanshe, 2006.

Yang Gongsu. *Cangsang jiushinian: yige waijiao teshi de huiyi.* Haikou: Hainan chubanshe, 1999.

Yang Kuisong. "Zhonggong tugai zhengce biandong de lishi kaocha." *Dongfang xuebao* 81 (2008): 258–191.

Yang Shangkun. *Yang Shangkun riji.* Vol. 1. Beijing: Zhongyang wenxian chubanshe, 2001.

Yin Shusheng. "Jinyin Tan zhitong." *Yanhuang chunqiu,* no. 3 (2012): 41–45.

Yixi Menglang and Jiedeng Banjue. "Lasa fasheng panluan shi wode zuowei." In *Xizang wenshi ziliao xuanji,* compiled and edited by Xizang zizhiqu zhengxie wenshi ziliao yanjiu weiyuanhui, vol. 17, 159–161. Beijing: Minzu chubanshe, 1995.

Yunnan shengzhi. Vol. 49, *Junshizhi.* Compiled and edited by Yunnan sheng difangzhi bianzuan weiyuanhui and Zhongguo renmin jiefangjun Yunnan junqu. Kunming: Yunnan renmin chubanshe, 1997.

Zaxi Ciren. "Wei shisishi Dalai Lama zhizuo xin baozuo de qingkuang jilüe." In *Xizang wenshi ziliao xuanji,* compiled and edited by Xizang zizhiqu zhengxie wenshi ziliao yanjiu weiyuanhui, vol. 17, 125–129. Beijing: Minzu chubanshe, 1995.

Zhang Guoxiang, as recorded by Lin Rusheng. "Zhongguo tu-4 chuanqi." *Bingqi zhishi,* no. 5 (2008): 32–35.

Zhang Lifan. "Xinan tugai fa zhengyan—xianfu Zhang Naiqi yu Liang Shuming yishi zhier." *Ershiyi shiji* 8 (2004): 113–116.

Zhang Lihe. "Chuan xibei gaoyuan de Zangchuan fojiao xianzhuang." *Zhongguo Xizang,* no. 1 (1998): 44–46.

Zhang Pingzhi. "Gaoyuan hongying." http://kong25.bokee.com/275102737.html.

Zhang Xiangming. *Zhang Xiangming wushiwunian Xizang gongzuo shilu.* [Semiclassified.] [City and publisher unknown, 2006.]

Zhang Xiaoming, ed. *Jianzheng bainian Xizang: Xizang lishi jianzhengren fangtanlu.* Vol. 1. Beijing: Wuzhou chuanbo chubanshe, 2003.

Zhao Shenying. *Zhang Guohua jiangjun zai Xizang.* Beijing: Zhongguo Zangxue chu ban she, 2001.

———. *Zhongyang zhuzang daibiao Zhang Jingwu.* Beijing: Zhongguo Zangxue chubanshe, 2001.

Zhonggong dui Zang zhengce yu celüe: dui Zhonggong qinzhan Xizang wushi nian de huigu. Dharamsala: Xizang liuwang zhengfu waijiao yu xinwen bu, 2004.

Zhonggong Lasa dangshi dashiji, 1951–1966. Compiled and edited by Zhonggong Lasa shiwei dangshi ziliao zhengji lingdao xiaozu. [Semiclassified.] Lhasa: Zhonggong Lasa shiwei dangshi ziliao zhengji lingdao xiaozu, 1991.

Zhonggong Xizang dangshi dashiji, 1949–1966. Compiled and edited by Zhonggong Xizang dangshi ziliao zhengji weiyuanhui. [Semiclassified.] Lhasa: Xizang renmin chubanshe, 1990.

Zhonggong Xizang dangshi dashiji, 1949–1994. Compiled and edited by Xizang zizhiqu dangshi ziliao zhengji weiyuanhui. Lhasa: Xizang renmin chubanshe, 1995. (For public circulation, a censored version of the 1990 semiclassified first edition covering 1949 to 1966, listed below.)

Zhongguo gongchandang Gannan lishi, 1921.7–2003.7. Compiled and edited by Zhonggong Gannan zhouwei. Lanzhou: Gansu minzu chubanshe, 2003.

Zhongguo gongchandang Sichuansheng Degexian zuzhishi ziliao, 1950–1993. Compiled and edited by Zhonggong Sichuansheng Degexianwei zuzhibu. Chengdu: Sichuan renmin chubanshe, 1996.

Zhongguo gongchandang Xizang zizhiqu zuzhishi ziliao, 1950–1987. Compiled and edited by Zhonggong Xizang zizhiqu weiyuanhui zuzhibu, Zhonggong

Xizang zizhiqu weiyuan hui dangshi ziliao zhengji weiyuanhui, and Xizang zizhiqu danganju. [Semiclassified.] Lhasa: Xizang renmin chubanshe, 1993.

Zhongguo renmin jiefangjun bubing dishiyi shi junzhanshi. Compiled and edited by Zhongguo renmin jiefangjun bubing dishiyi shi junzhanshi bianxiezu. [Semiclassified?] [Urumchi?]: Xinjiang renmin chubanshe, 1987.

Zhonghua Renmin Gongheguo guowuyuan guanyu Xizang gongzuo de jixiang jueding. Beijing: Minzu chubanshe, 1955.

Zhou Enlai. "Guanyu xibei diqu de minzu gongzuo." In *Zhou Enlai tongyi zhanxian wenxuan,* 191–195. Beijing: Renmin chubanshe, 1984.

Zhou Enlai yu Xizang. Compiled and edited by Xizang zizhiqu dangshi bangongshi. Beijing: Zhongguo Zangxue chubanshe, 1998.

Zhu Xiushan. "Lasa zhi zhan de huigu." In Re Di, et al., *Xizang geming huiyilu,* vol. 4, 32–37.

Zong Zidu. "Niliu fangun de rizi—1959 nian 3 yue 10 ri caifang jianwen." In Re Di, et al., *Xizang geming huiyilu,* vol. 4, 123–131.

TIBETAN-LANGUAGE SOURCES

Athar Norbu. "The Life of Athar Norbu from Lithang, Heroic Defender of the Faith." New Delhi: Phuntsok Choechen, 2004.

Jampa Phuntsok (Jampa). *A Life Undeterred* [Zhum pa med pa'i mi tshe]. Lives of Political Prisoners Series, no. 18. Dharmshala: Guchusum Ex-prisoners' Association, 2009.

Naktsang Nulo. *Joys and Sorrows of a Naktsang Kid* [Nags tshang zhi lu'i skyid sdug]. Qinghai: Privately published, 2007.

Phala Tubten Wöden (Phala). *A Brief Life Story* [sKu tshe'i lo rgyus hrag bsdus]. Library of Tibetan Works and Archives Oral History Series, no. 2. Dharamsala: LTWA, 1996.

Phuntsok Tashi (Phuntsok). *A Life.* Vol. 2. Dharamsala: Library of Tibetan Works and Archives, 1995.

Ratuk Ngawang. *The Fearless Defense of Lithang by Monastics and Civilians against Invasion (1936–1959)* [mDo khams spon'bor sgang gi sa'i char 'khod pa'i Li thang dgon yul gnyis kyis btsan 'dzul pa la zhum med ngo rgol gyis rang sa srung skyob byas pa'i skor]. Lithang Historical Records, vol. 2, edited by Tashi Tsering. Dharamsala: Amnye Machen Institute, 2006.

Tarawa Tenzin Choenyi (Tara). *Introducing Myself* [Rang nyid ngo sprod]. Library of Tibetan Works and Archives Oral History Series, no. 18. Dharamsala: LTWA, 2005.

Tibet Mirror [Yulchug Sosoi Sargyur Melong]. Vol. 23, no. 11 (October 12, 1956): 4.

Tsongkha Lhamo Tsering (Lhamo Tsering). Vol. 2, *Resistance* [bTsan rgol rgyal skyob], edited by Tashi Tsering. Dharamsala: Amnye Machen, 1998.

Yulo Tulku Dawa Tsering (Yulo). *A Pure Drop of Yulo's Sweat* [lHad med g.yu lo'i rngul thig], edited by Ganden Tashi and Tsering Sonam. Lives of Political Prisoners Series, no. 13. Dharmshala: Guchusum Ex-prisoners' Association, 2007.

INTERVIEWS

Note: Unless otherwise indicated, all interviews were conducted in person by the author.

Dhargye (late governor of the Golog Tibetan Autonomous Prefecture of Qinghai), August 8, August 22, and August 24, 2012. Xining.

Dolma Norbu (daughter of Athar Norbu), May 3, 2009. New York.

Dongyo Jargatsang (former CIA trainee), October 2, 2008. Tibetan refugee settlement at Bir, Himachal Pradesh, India.

Geshe Lobsang (monk from Lithang), November 21, 2009. Dharamsala, India.

His Holiness the Dalai Lama, June 27, June 28, and June 30, 2009. Dharamsala, India.

Jampa (former Chushi Gangdruk guerrilla), October 7, 2008. Kathmandu, Nepal.

Jampa Tenzin (participant in the battle for the Jokhang Temple), October 12, 2009. Dharamsala, India.

Juchen Tubten (participant in the Battle of Lhasa, 1959), September 22 and October 8, 2009. Dharamsala, India.

Kelsang Gyadotsang (nephew of Gonpo Tashi), May 10, 2009. New Jersey.

Lobsang (former Chushi Gangdruk guerrilla, member of the Dalai Lama's guard during the escape), October 13, 2008. Gangtok, Sikkim.

Lobsang Gonpo (former monk of Tajie Monastery, Garzê Tibetan Autonomous Prefecture), September 10, 2009. Dalhousie Tibetan Refugee Settlement, India.

Lobsang Tsagyal, November 21, 2009. Dharamsala, India.

Lobsang Yeshi (former monk, Ganden Monastery, Lhasa), September 11, 2009. Dalhousie Tibetan Refugee Settlement, India.

Lodi Gyari (son of Dorje Yudon), May 14, 2009. Washington, DC.

Ngari Rinpoché (the Dalai Lama's youngest brother), July 18, 2009. Dharamsala, India.

Ratuk Ngawang (former Chushi Gangdruk leader), October 3, 2009. Delhi, India.

Tenpa Soepa (former employee of the Tibetan Reform Bureau), September 8 and October 9, 2009. Dharamsala, India.

Thinley Phuntsok (clerk of Ling Rinpoché, the Dalai Lama's Senior Tutor), April 19, 2009. New Jersey.

Tsayang, October 7, 2008. Jawalakehl Tibetan Refugee Handicraft Center, Kathmandu, Nepal.

Tsering Dolma (daughter of Athar Norbu), May 3, 2009. New York.

Tsering Drolkar, April 19, 2009. New Jersey.

Yangling Dorje (distinguished Tibetan Communist), May 27, 2013. Chengdu, Sichuan. Interview recorded by Ding Yifu; transcript shared with the author.

ACKNOWLEDGMENTS

During the writing of this book, I have been the fortunate recipient of help and advice from many people. First, I would like to express my heartfelt gratitude to His Holiness the Dalai Lama, who kindly granted me his valuable time to clarify details in this narrative. Several other people also assisted tirelessly in the interview process: three of the Dalai Lama's secretaries, Chihmei Rigzin, Tsegyam, and Tenzin Taklha, who served as interpreters; and Tenpa Soepa, Lama Jampa Tenzin, and the Dalai Lama's youngest brother, Ngari Rinpoché, all of whom generously supplied a great deal of additional information in subsequent personal interviews. Juchen Tubten, former cabinet minister in the Tibetan government-in-exile, provided vivid eyewitness accounts of key events in this book and helped me verify many facts. The Dalai Lama's representative in Washington, DC, Lodi Gyari, also made time in his busy schedule to reply to a number of questions.

I am also indebted to many other people. Kelsang Gyaltsen and Phagpa Tsering supplied valuable materials. Sang Jey Kep accompanied me to refugee camps to interpret during my interviews with Tibetan exiles; afterward, he painstakingly translated the written transcripts and several other Tibetan documents for me. Dhargye, the late governor of the Golog Tibetan Autonomous Prefecture of Qinghai, allowed me to interview him in Xining in 2012, in time for this updated English edition. Geshe Lobsang, a monk originally from Lithang, told me the story of Yorupon the Bumyak headman found in the Prologue to this book. Athar Norbu's two daughters, Dolma Norbu and Tsering Dolma, shared their father's life story with me and provided photographs. A Tibetan monk in exile from Qinghai (who wishes to remain anonymous) helped with the transliteration of Tibetan names. Thanks are also due to Marvin Cao for his professional cartography, to Curtis Greene for his helpful suggestions, and to Robert Barnett for supplying antique maps.

I would like to express my deep appreciation to Susan Wilf, whose role in this book has risen above mere "translating"; to Matthew Akester for his thoughtful proofreading and input; to Perry Link for his advice and encouragement; to Peter Bernstein, my literary agent, for representing the book; to my daughter, Selina, for her understanding and support; to my editor at Harvard University Press, Kathleen McDermott, for her valuable suggestions and expert guidance; to Kate Brick at Harvard University Press and Debbie Masi at Westchester Publishing Services for shepherding the book through its final stages; and to Katrina Vassallo and everyone at Harvard University Press for bringing the book into print. Last but not least, I wish to thank the hundreds of exiled Tibetans who shared their wrenching life stories with me in oral interviews, some—but far from all—of whose names are listed in the Bibliography.

ILLUSTRATION CREDITS

1. Portrait of the Dalai Lama with his family at Yabshi House in the early 1950s. Courtesy of Mrs. Kesang Y. Takla.
2. The Chinese People's Liberation Army (PLA) entering Lhasa in 1951. Courtesy of the Department of Information and International Relations, Central Tibetan Administration.
3. Tibetan officials of the 1950s. Courtesy of the Office of Tibet, Washington, DC.
4. Tibetan and Chinese officials in Lhasa, 1951. Courtesy of the Department of Information and International Relations, Central Tibetan Administration.
5. Founding ceremony of the Patriotic Tibetan Women's League, March 8, 1954. Courtesy of the Department of Information and International Relations, Central Tibetan Administration.
6. Ling Rinpoché and Trijang Rinpoché with the Dalai Lama, India, 1956–1957. Courtesy of the Office of Tibet, Washington, DC.
7. The Dalai Lama and Jawaharlal Nehru in New Delhi, 1957. Courtesy of the Department of Information and International Relations, Central Tibetan Administration.
8. Security Chief Phuntsok. Courtesy of Mrs. Kesang Y. Takla.
9. Coracle boats crossing the Kyichu River near Lhasa. Courtesy of the Department of Information and International Relations, Central Tibetan Administration.
10. The Potala Palace. Courtesy of the Department of Information and International Relations, Central Tibetan Administration.
11. Drawing of the bombardment of Lithang Monastery (Jamchen Chokhor Ling), *Tibet Mirror* 23, no. 11 (Kalimpong: G. Tharchin, October 5, 1956), p. 4.
12. Gonpo Tashi. Courtesy of Tenzin Gawa (son of the late Ratuk Ngawang).
13. Chushi Gangdruk founding ceremony, June 1958. Courtesy of Tenzin Gawa (son of the late Ratuk Ngawang).

14. The *vajra* (Tibetan: *dorje*), a Buddhist ritual weapon. Courtesy of Curtis Greene.
15. Chushi Gangdruk guerrillas. Courtesy of Tenzin Gawa (son of the late Ratuk Ngawang).
16. The White Palace. Courtesy of Liu Zhi.
17. The Dalai Lama, February 1959. Courtesy of the Department of Information and International Relations, Central Tibetan Administration.
18. Athar Norbu, 1956 or 1957. Courtesy of Dolma Norbu.
19. The Gyadotsang brothers. Courtesy of Kelsang Gyadotsang.
20. Demonstrators in front of the Norbulingka on March 10, 1959. Courtesy of the Office of Tibet, Washington, DC.
21. Chakpori Hill, circa 1950. Courtesy of the Department of Information and International Relations, Central Tibetan Administration.
22. Chakpori Hill, 2016. Courtesy of an anonymous photographer in Lhasa.
23. The Dalai Lama and Ngari Rinpoché on the Himalayan crossing. Courtesy of the Office of Tibet, Washington, DC.
24. Establishment of the provisional government of Tibet at Lhuntse Dzong on March 26, 1959. Courtesy of the Office of Tibet, Washington, DC.
25. The Dalai Lama's entry into India on March 31, 1959. Courtesy of the Office of Tibet, Washington, DC.
26. Early Tibetan refugees in India. Courtesy of the Tibetan Refugee Self-Help Centre, Darjeeling.
27. Tenpa Soepa in recent years. Courtesy of the Tenpa Soepa family.
28. Jampa Tenzin in 2009. Photo © Jianglin Li.
29. Juchen Tubten in the 1960s. Courtesy of the Juchen Tubten family.
30. Thinley Phuntsok in the 1980s. Courtesy of Thinley Phuntsok.

INDEX

Note: Unless otherwise noted, all subheading references to the Dalai Lama refer to the Fourteenth Dalai Lama.